OXFORD STUDIES IN DEMOCRATIZATION

Series Editor: Laurence Whitehead

· · · · · · · · · · · · · · · · · ·

DEMOCRATIC ACCOUNTABILITY
IN LATIN AMERICA

OXFORD STUDIES IN DEMOCRATIZATION

Series Editor: Laurence Whitehead

· · · · · · · · · · · · · · · · ·

Oxford Studies in Democratization is a series for scholars and students of comparative politics and related disciplines. Volumes will concentrate on the comparative study of the democratization processes that accompanied the decline and termination of the cold war. The geographical focus of the series will primarily be Latin America, the Caribbean, Southern and Eastern Europe, and relevant experiences in Africa and Asia.

OTHER BOOKS IN THE SERIES

Democratization:
Theory and Experience
Laurence Whitehead

The New Politics of Inequality in Latin America:
Rethinking Participation and Representation
*Douglas A. Chalmers, Carlos M. Vilas, Katherine Roberts Hite,
Scott B. Martin, Kerianne Piester, and Monique Segarra*

Human Rights and Democratization in Latin America:
Uruguay and Chile
Alexandra Barahona de Brito

The Politics of Memory:
Transitional Justice in Democratizing Societies
Alexandra Barahona de Brito, Carmen González Enríquez, and Paloma Aguilar

Citizenship Rights and Social Movements:
A Comparative and Statistical Analysis
Joe Foweraker and Todd Landman

The Democratic Developmental State:
Politics and Institutional Design
Marc Robinson and Gordon White

The Legacy of Human Rights Violations in the Southern Cone:
Argentina, Chile, and Uruguay
Luis Roniger and Mario Sznajder

Democratic Consolidation in Eastern Europe:
Volume 1. Institutional Engineering
Jan Zielonka

Democratic Consolidation in Eastern Europe:
Volume 2. International and Transnational Factors
Jan Zielonka and Alex Pravda

The International Dimensions of Democratization:
Europe and the Americas
Laurence Whitehead

Institutions and Democratic Citizenship
Axel Hadenius

The European Union and the Promotion of Democracy:
Europe's Mediterranean and Asian Policies
Richard Youngs

The Architecture of Democracy:
Constitutional Design, Conflict Management, and Democracy
Andrew Reynolds

Gender Justice, Development, and Rights
Maxine Molyneux and Shahra Razavi

Democratic Accountability in Latin America

Edited by
SCOTT MAINWARING
and
CHRISTOPHER WELNA

OXFORD
UNIVERSITY PRESS

OXFORD

UNIVERSITY PRESS

Great Clarendon Street, Oxford OX2 6DP

Oxford University Press is a department of the University of Oxford.
It furthers the University's objective of excellence in research, scholarship,
and education by publishing worldwide in

Oxford New York

Auckland Bangkok Buenos Aires Cape Town Chennai
Dar es Salaam Delhi Hong Kong Istanbul Karachi Kolkata
Kuala Lumpur Madrid Melbourne Mexico City Mumbai Nairobi
São Paulo Shanghai Taipei Tokyo Toronto

Oxford is a registered trade mark of Oxford University Press
in the UK and in certain other countries

Published in the United States
by Oxford University Press Inc., New York

© the several contributors, 2003

The moral rights of the authors have been asserted
Database right Oxford University Press (maker)

First published 2003

British Library Cataloguing in Publication Data

Data available

Library of Congress Cataloging in Publication Data

Data available

ISBN 0–19–925637–3 (hbk.)
ISBN 0–19–925638–1 (pbk.)

1 3 5 7 9 10 8 6 4 2

Typeset in 10.5/12pt Newcentury
by Kolam Information Services Pvt. Ltd, Pondicherry, India
Printed in Great Britain on acid-free paper by
Biddles Ltd., Guildford and King's Lynn

Acknowledgements

The conference that gave rise to this volume was the sixth in a series sponsored by the Kellogg Institute for International Studies at the University of Notre Dame with generous support from The Coca-Cola Company. We are grateful to Donald Keough, Clyde Tuggle, Ingrid Saunders-Jones, and Pedro Pablo Díaz of The Coca-Cola Company for their support.

Many people beyond the contributors helped make this book possible. First and foremost, Guillermo O'Donnell's introduction of the concept 'horizontal accountability' effectively laid the foundation for the research presented here. We are grateful to all of the authors in this volume for their insightful work and careful revisions.

Other participants in the May 2000 conference enriched the discussion and the papers that now form the volume. They include Mariclaire Acosta, Adolfo Aguilar Zinser, Sergio Bitar, Michael Coppedge, Pedro Pablo Díaz, Pilar Domingo, Jonathan Fox, Frances Hagopian, Gretchen Helmke, Viviana Krsticevic, Steven Levitsky, Juan Méndez, Martha Merritt, Joy Moncrieffe, Lourdes Flores Nano, Luis Pásara, Jorge Santistevan de Noriega, David Samuels, Margaret Sarles, Susan Stokes, Marcos Pimental Tamassia, and Ignacio Walker.

Gabriela Mossi played a crucial role in organizing the conference that convened the authors. Christine Babick, Elizabeth Rankin and Pam Kistler-Osborn helped the editors to put the manuscript together. We thank them for their help.

Lastly, we wish to thank our editors at Oxford University Press, Gwen Booth, Dominic Byatt, Stuart Fowkes, and Jason Pearce for their support and careful recommendations, as well as the anonymous reviewers who provided valuable feedback to each of the authors.

Contents

List of Figures   ix
List of Tables   x
Notes on Contributors   xi

PART I. CONCEPTUAL AND THEORETICAL ISSUES   1

1. Introduction: Democratic Accountability in Latin America
   Scott Mainwaring   3

2. Horizontal Accountability: The Legal
   Institutionalization of Mistrust
   Guillermo O'Donnell   34

3. Horizontal Accountability: Concepts and Conflicts
   Charles D. Kenney   55

PART II. LEGISLATURES, EXECUTIVES, AND
           OVERSIGHT AGENCIES   77

4. The Accountability Deficit in Latin America
   Erika Moreno, Brian F. Crisp and
   Matthew Soberg Shugart   79

5. Legislative Oversight: Interests and Institutions
   in the United States and Argentina
   Scott Morgenstern and Luigi Manzetti   132

6. The Role of Congress as an Agency of Horizontal
   Accountability: Lessons from the Brazilian Experience
   Argelina Cheibub Figueiredo   170

PART III. THE JUDICIARY, THE PUBLIC
            PROSECUTION OFFICE, AND RULE OF LAW   199

   7. The New Brazilian Public Prosecution:
      An Agent of Accountability
      Maria Tereza Sadek and Rosângela Batista Cavalcanti   201

   8. Horizontal Accountability and the Rule
      of Law in Central America
      Michael Dodson and Donald W. Jackson   228

   9. Authoritarianism, Democracy and the Supreme Court:
      Horizontal Exchange and the Rule of Law in Mexico
      Beatriz Magaloni   266

PART IV. SOCIETAL ACCOUNTABILITY   307

  10. Societal and Horizontal Controls: Two Cases
      of a Fruitful Relationship
      Catalina Smulovitz and Enrique Peruzzotti   309

      Index   333

List of Figures

3.1. Horizontal and vertical accountability relationships   62

3.2. Three traditions intertwined in modern democracy   69

4.1. Relationships of delegation and accountability:
nested hierarchies in a parliamentary system.   87

4.2. Relationships of delegation and accountability
and horizontal exchange in a presidential system   88

4.3. Independence of high courts and superintendence
agencies in Latin America   105

5.1. Divided government in the United States, 1875–2000   141

9.1. The dual dimension of the Rule of Law   279

9.2. Crimes reported per 100,000 inhabitants   300

....
List of Tables
....

1.1. Conceptualizing political accountability 17
A 4.1. Constitutional provisions for separation of
origin and survival: Supreme Courts in Latin America 119
A 4.2. Constitutional provisions for separation of
origin and survival: Constitutional tribunals in
Latin America 121
A 4.3. Constitutional provisions for separation of origin
and survival: Attorneys General in Latin America 122
A 4.4. Constitutional provisions for separation of
origin and survival: Prosecutors General
in Latin America 123
A 4.5. Constitutional provisions for separation of
origin and survival: defenders for human
rights in Latin America 125
A 4.6. Constitutional provisions for separation of
origin and survival: Controllers General
in Latin America 126
6.1. CPIS by Government and Period—1946–64
and 1988–99 Democracies 178
6.2. Rates of Conclusion and Distribution of CPIS
Proposed and Concluded in the Lower House
According to the Proponent's Party Affiliation 181
6.3. Committee's Oversight Activities—1989–99 182
A 6.1. Presidents, coalitions, and parties' seats
in the Lower House 193
9.1. Constraints on the executive 274
9.2. Homicide rates per 100,000 inhabitants 277
9.3. Change of constitutional rules regarding size,
appointments, terms and dismissal of the
Supreme Court 284
9.4. Number of justices appointed by president 288
9.5. Turnover rates of Justices of the Supreme Court 289
9.6. Number of actions and controversies filed
at the Supreme Court 297
9.7. In your opinion, which is the principal
problem in Mexico City? 298

Notes on Contributors

Rosângela Batista Cavalcanti is a researcher at the Institute of Social, Economic and Political Studies (IDESP) in São Paulo. A Ph.D. candidate in Political Science at the Universidade de Campinas (UNICAMP), she is the author of the book *Cidadania e Acesso à Justiça* (Sumaré, 1999) as well as several articles in journals and collected volumes.

Brian F. Crisp received his Ph.D. in political science from the University of Michigan in 1992 and is currently Associate Professor and Director of Graduate Studies in the Department of Political Science at the University of Arizona. His work has appeared in the *American Journal of Political Science International Studies Quarterly, Legislative Studies Quarterly, Studies in Comparative International Development, Journal of Interamerican Studies and World Affairs*, and *Latin American Research Review*, as well as several edited volumes. His book *Democratic Institutional Design: The Powers and Incentives of Venezuelan Politicians and Interest Groups* was published by Stanford University Press (2000).

Michael Dodson is Professor of Political Science at Texas Christian University. He has held two National Endowment for the Humanities fellowships and was a Fulbright Senior Lecturer in Britain. His recent publications include: 'Re-inventing the Rule of Law: Human Rights in El Salvador', with Donald W. Jackson, *Democratization* 4, 1 (Winter 1997); 'Human Rights and the Salvadoran Judiciary: The Competing Values of Independence and Accountability', with Donald W. Jackson and Laura O'Shaughnessy, *The International Journal of Human Rights* 1, 4 (Winter 1997); and 'Protecting Human Rights: The Legitimacy of Judicial System Reforms in El Salvador', with Donald W. Jackson, *The Bulletin of Latin American Research* 18, 4 (Winter 1999).

Argelina Cheibub Figueiredo is *Professor Livre Docente* at the University of Campinas, Brazil, and senior researcher at the Centro Brasileiro de Analise e Planejamento (CEBRAP). She received her PhD from the University of Chicago in 1987. She is the author of

Democracia o reformas? Alternativas políticas a crise democrática
(Paz e Terra, 1993) and, with Fernando Limongi, *Executivo e legislativo na nova ordem constitucional* (FGV/FAPESP, 1999) and
'Presidential Power, Legislative Organization, and Party Behavior
in Brazil', *Comparative Politics* (2, 2000).

Donald Jackson has been a faculty member of the Texas Christian
University (TCU) since 1975 and is now the Herman Brown Professor of Political Science. Before joining TCU, he served as a Judicial
Fellow at the Supreme Court of the United States. His research has
been on various aspects of the intersection between law and politics. His book, *The United Kingdom Confronts the European Convention on Human Rights* (1997), represents his interest in
international human rights enforcement. Other publications include *Presidential Leadership and Civil Rights Policy* (1995), co-
edited with James Riddlesperger, Jr., and *Even the Children of
Strangers: Equality under the US Constitution* (1992). Professor
Jackson's current research on democratic transitions in Central
America, focusing especially on the rule of law, has led to a series of
articles co-written with Michael Dodson.

Charles D. Kenney received his Ph.D. from the University of Notre
Dame in 1998 and is an Assistant Professor of Comparative and
Latin American Politics at the University of Oklahoma. His primary areas of interest include democratization, constitutional
design, electoral and party systems, and Peruvian politics. He
lived in Peru from 1978–79 and 1984–91 and was a Fulbright
Fellow at the Pontificia Universidad Catolica del Peru from February to July 2000. He was an international electoral observer for
the 2000 and 2001 Peruvian elections and is the chair of the Peru
Section of the Latin American Studies Association. His book, 'Politics in Peru: Fujimori's Coup and the Dilemma of Democracy in
Latin America', will be published by the University of Notre Dame
Press.

Beatriz Magaloni is Assistant Professor of Political Science at
Stanford University. She is co-author, with Alberto Diaz-Cayeros,
of 'Party Dominance and the Logic of Electoral Design in the Mexican Transition to Democracy' (*Journal of Theoretical Politics* 13, 3,
2001). She won the Gabriel Almond Award for the best dissertation
in comparative politics (1998) and is co-winner, with Alberto Diaz-
Cayeros and Barry Weingast, of the 2001 prize for the best paper
in comparative politics presented at the 96th American Political

Science Association meeting. She is currently working on two books, one on the political economy of the Mexican democratization process, and the other on the Mexican Supreme Court.

Scott Mainwaring is Eugene Conley Professor of Political Science at the University of Notre Dame. Among his most recent books are *Rethinking Party Systems in the Third Wave of Democratization: The Case of Brazil* (Stanford University Press, 1999); *Presidentialism and Democracy in Latin America* (Cambridge University Press, 1997, co-edited); and *Building Democratic Institutions: Party Systems in Latin America* (Stanford University Press, 1995, co-edited).

Luigi Manzetti is an Associate Professor in the Political Science Department at Southern Methodist University. His scholarly work has dealt with regional integration in the Southern Cone, privatization and deregulation policies in Latin America, and corruption. He is the author of *Institutions, Parties and Coalitions in Argentine Politics* (Pittsburgh University Press, 1993) and *Privatization South American Style* (Oxford University Press, 1999) and the editor of *Regulatory Policy in Latin America: Post-Privatization Realities* (North-South Center Press at the University of Miami, 2000).

Erika Moreno received her Ph.D. in political science from the University of Arizona in 2001. She is an Assistant Professor of Political Science at the University of Iowa where she teaches and conducts research on democratic political institutions and party systems across Latin America.

Scott Morgenstern is Assistant Professor of Political Science at Duke University. He is the author of *Patterns of Legislative Politics: An Exploration of Roll Call Voting in the United States and Latin America* (forthcoming) and coeditor of and contributor to *Legislative Politics in Latin America* (Cambridge University Press, 2002). He has published articles on party politics and elections in *Party Politics, Comparative Politics, The Journal of Politics, Legislative Studies Quarterly*, and several Latin American journals.

Guillermo O'Donnell is former Academic Director of the Kellogg Institute and Helen Kellogg Professor of Government and International Studies at Notre Dame. He was the first Director of CEDES (Buenos Aires), a visiting professor at the Universities of

Michigan (Ann Arbor), California (Berkeley), and São Paulo, and a researcher of IUPERJ (Rio de Janeiro) and CEBRAP (São Paulo). He is a Fellow of the American Academy of Arts and Sciences. He has published extensively on comparative politics, authoritarianism, and democratization in several languages. Recent publications include *Counterpoints: Selected Essays on Authoritarianism and Democratization; The (Un)Rule of Law and the Underprivileged in Latin* America, coedited with Juan Méndez and Paulo Sérgio Pinheiro; and *Poverty and Inequality in Latin America*, coedited with Víctor Tokman (all in the Kellogg Institute series with the University of Notre Dame Press, 1999, 1999, and 1998).

Enrique Peruzzotti is a professor in the Department of Political Science and Government at the Torcuato Di Tella University in Buenos Aires. He has published articles on democratic theory and democratization in *Citizenship Studies, The Journal of Democracy, Constellations An International Journal of Critical and Democratic Theory, Thesis Eleven, Revista Mexicana de Sociología*, and the *Journal of Latin American Studies*. With Catalina Smulovitz he is conducting a research project funded by the Ford Foundation, 'The Emergence of a Politics of Societal Accountability in the New Latin American Democracies'. He co-edited (with Catalina Smulovitz) the volume *Contolando la Política. Ciudadanos y Medios en las Nuevas Democracias Latinoamericanas* (Temas, 2002). His current research analyses the emergence of a new form of politicization in Latin American civil societies organized around demands for accountable government.

Maria Tereza Sadek is a professor in the Political Science Department at the Universidade de São Paulo and a senior researcher at the Instituto de Estudos Econômicos, Sociais e Politicos de São Paulo (IDESP). She has published a number of books and contributed articles on the justice system to Brazilian and foreign journals and periodicals. Her books include *O Judiciário em Debate* (Sumaré, 1995), *O Ministério Público e a Justiça no Brasil* (Sumaré, 1997), *O Ministério Público Federal e a Administração da Justiça no Brasil* (co-authored, Sumaré, 1998), *Acesso à Justiça* (Konrad Adenauer, 2001), and *Reforma do Judiciário* (Konrad Adenauer, 2002).

Matthew Soberg Shugart is Professor at the Graduate School of International Relations and Pacific Studies, University of California, San Diego. He is a leading specialist on political institutions.

He has co-authored or co-edited five books on the topic: *Seats and Votes: The Effects and Determinants of Electoral Systems* (Yale, 1989), *Presidents and Assemblies: Constitutional Design and Electoral Dynamics* (Cambridge, 1992), *Presidentialism and Democracy in Latin America* (Cambridge, 1997), *Executive Decree Authority* (Cambridge, 1997), and *Mixed-Member Electoral Systems: The Best of Both Worlds?* (Oxford, 2001). He has also authored numerous articles on electoral systems, presidentialism, and Colombian politics in journals such as the *American Political Science Review*, *Comparative Political Studies*, *Constitutional Political Economy*, and *Electoral Studies*.

Catalina Smulovitz, an Argentine political scientist, is Professor at the Torcuato Di Tella University in Buenos Aires and a researcher at the Consejo Nacional de Investigaciones Científicas y Tecnológicas (CONICET). She is the author of *Oposición y gobierno: Los años de Frondizi* (Centro Editor de América Latina, 1988) and co-editor with Enrique Peruzzotti of volume *Contolando la Política. Ciudadanos y Medios en las Nuevas Democracias Latinoamericanas* (Temas, 2002). Her articles include 'Societal Accountability in Latin America' in *The Journal of Democracy* (Oct. 2000) with Enrique Peruzzotti; 'The Discovery of The Law: Political Consequences in the Argentine Experience', in Garth Brian and Yves Dezalay, eds., *Global Prescriptions* (University of Michigan Press, 2002); and 'Adjusting the Armed Forces to Democracy. Successes, Failures and Ambiguities of the Southern Cone Experiences', (co-authored with Carlos Acuña) in Elizabeth Jelin and Eric Hershberg, eds., *Constructing Democracy: Human Rights, Citizenship and Society in Latin America* (Westview, 1996).

Christopher Welna is Associate Director of the Kellogg Institute, Concurrent Assistant Professor in the Department of Political Science and Director of the Latin American Studies Program at the University of Notre Dame. He specializes in Latin American politics and public policy reform, especially in Mexico, Brazil, Colombia and Cuba. He has held fellowships from the Social Science Research Council and the Mellon and Thomas J. Watson Foundations. Before coming to Notre Dame, he taught at Duke University and worked for the Ford Foundation, the US Department of State, and the UN Institute for Training and Research. He holds a Ph.D. in political science from Duke University.

PART I

Conceptual and Theoretical Issues

Introduction: Democratic Accountability in Latin America*

Scott Mainwaring

This volume on democratic accountability addresses one of the burning issues on the agenda of policy-makers and citizens in contemporary Latin America. Collectively, we hope that the volume enhances understanding of three key issues. First, it enriches understanding of the state of non-electoral forms of democratic accountability in contemporary Latin America. What are some of the major shortcomings in democratic accountability? How can they be addressed? What are some of the major innovations in the efforts to enhance democratic accountability?

A second contribution of the volume is conceptual. Accountability is a key concept in the social sciences, yet its meaning varies widely from one author to the next. The authors in this volume, especially in the first four chapters, explicitly debate how best to define and delimit the concept. Although we cannot claim consensus in our understanding of this concept, we believe that the direct confrontation of ideas will advance the debate.

Finally, the volume also furthers understanding of the interaction between various mechanisms and institutions of accountability. Many of the authors address how electoral accountability (i.e., the accountability of elected officials to voters) interacts with other forms of accountability in which state agencies oversee and sanction public officials. The volume provides a fairly extensive treatment of this important but hitherto underexplored interaction.

Accountability has emerged as one of the key issues in the post-transition period of Latin American politics. In the 1980s, the

* I am grateful to Charles Kenney, Luigi Manzetti, Martha Merritt, Guillermo O'Donnell, Matthew Shugart, and Chris Welna for insightful suggestions and to David Altman for research assistance.

debate about democracy focused primarily on transitions to democracy and on ways of sustaining and consolidating democracy. Since then, Latin America has enjoyed its most democratic period ever. But in much of the region, disenchantment and indeed even cynicism have set in regarding the quality of these elected governments, raising the prospect of a new round of democratic erosion and breakdowns.

One of the important emerging challenges for improving the quality of democracy revolves around how to build more effective mechanisms of accountability. A widespread perception prevails in much of the region that government officials are not sufficiently subject to routinized controls by oversight agencies. Corruption, lack of oversight, impunity for state actors, and improper use of public resources continue to be major problems in most countries of the region. These problems have captured the attention of business, religious, and political leaders, as well as citizens and scholars. Dealing with these issues is paramount to restoring and deepening democratic legitimacy; public opinion surveys show that corruption has tarnished legitimacy. If these problems are not addressed, governmental instability may once again fester in the region, at a minimum through electoral upsets by anti-party outsiders and potentially through extra-institutional means (coup d'etats or popularly supported auto-golpes) as well.

The task facing Latin American democrats is not simply how to build more effective mechanisms of accountability. For while accountability is a desirable feature in political systems, so is governmental effectiveness,[1] which often is in tension with accountability. On the one hand, governments cannot deliver what citizens need if they are so hampered by mechanisms of oversight and sanctioning agencies that they cannot undertake new initiatives. Constitutional crises between powers or challenges to policy decisions by oversight bodies, ombudsmen or lawsuits can undermine government effectiveness. Governments that are immobilized by oversight mechanisms are sometimes perceived by voters or power groups as being indecisive, ineffective, or inept. Powerful mechanisms of accountability can impede governments from implementing policies that would benefit most citizens; they can give small minorities, even a few individuals in key institutions (e.g., the Supreme Court) veto power over policy changes. At a minimum, mechanisms of accountability impose modest transaction costs. On the other

---

[1] By governmental effectiveness, I mean simply the ability of governments to obtain good policy results.

hand, Latin Americans also have extensive experience with lack of governmental accountability. If public officials do not need to account for their actions, they may be unresponsive to citizen needs and to the public good.

Positing the existence of a potential tradeoff between accountability and government performance does not imply a zero sum conflict between these two desiderata. Unaccountable governments can produce terrible policy results, and accountable governments can produce excellent results. Powerful mechanisms of accountability make it easier to block governments from implementing disastrous policies.

The fundamental question in this volume is how democratic leaders in Latin America can improve accountability while simultaneously promoting governmental effectiveness. In this volume, the authors approach this question by focusing on democratic institutions, which are key to accountability. Institutions do not necessarily function as intended, especially in a region known for a gap between the law and political practice, but they are essential for establishing accountability. Without formal institutions designed for this purpose, effective accountability is impossible.

These concerns about combining the dual objectives of accountability and policy results have been at the forefront of the region's policy and scholarly agenda,[2] and they are the central concerns of this volume. These issues have acquired urgency in contemporary Latin America because of heightened public concern about corruption and improper governmental actions, on the one hand, and about the potential tradeoff between policy results and accountability, on the other.

Although accountability has become a salient concern in Latin America and other new democracies, only recently has a scholarly debate on non-electoral accountability started to emerge. Much of the bibliography on accountability deals with public administration (e.g., Day and Klein 1987), education, and other issues that fall outside the purview of this book. Przeworski, Stokes, and Manin's (1999) important book focuses on electoral accountability, and a substantial older literature has dealt with the closely related theme of retrospective voting, i.e., voting on the basis of elected officials' actions in office (Fiorina 1981; Key 1966). There is an abundant scholarly literature on some themes related to political accountability (legislatures, judiciaries, oversight agencies,

---

[2] For example, accountability was a prominent theme of the Quebec Summit of the Americas, signed by the presidents of the hemisphere. See http://www.summit-americas.org/List-Summit(new)-Eng.htm

corruption control), but little of this literature focuses specifically on accountability. Some books examine a specific slice of accountability; for example, Woodhouse (1994) studies the accountability of ministers to parliament.

Recently, O'Donnell (1994, 1999a, 1999b, this volume) has called attention to how important accountability is in understanding and conceptualizing differences among the post-1978 wave of democracies and differences between these democracies and the advanced industrial polyarchies. Even with O'Donnell's path-breaking contributions, the literature that deals explicitly with non-electoral democratic accountability is limited. Merritt (forthcoming) and Schedler, Diamond, and Plattner (1999) are among the few noteworthy contributions that conceptualize and analyze a broad range of institutions of accountability.

In this introduction, I take up three themes that run throughout the remainder of the volume. First, I discuss some controversies about defining accountability. These controversies run throughout this volume and more broadly throughout the literature on accountability. It is essential to tease out these different understandings of 'accountability' and to begin working toward greater conceptual clarity. Second, Moreno et al. (this volume) present an innovative but controversial argument about the relationship between electoral accountability and mechanisms of control and oversight of public agencies. This relationship requires more attention among scholars and democratic practitioners, so I highlight some of the key issues in the controversy. Finally, I present an overview of the debate about the shortcomings and advances in non-electoral forms of accountability in contemporary Latin America.

Defining and Delimiting Political Accountability

Accountability is a far-from-consensual concept. Indeed, the meaning of 'accountability' is about as muddled as concepts get in the social sciences. There are sharp differences in usage among authors in this volume and more broadly in the social sciences. One of the contributions that this volume offers is an explicit debate and disagreement especially in the four chapters of Part I regarding how to define and delimit 'accountability'. In this section, I present my own understanding of the concept. In the next, I survey the main sources of disagreement regarding the concept of accountability because a clear statement about where the disagreements lie can help illuminate the debate.

'Accountability' is used in many contexts, ranging from education to business firms, from public administration to politics. This volume is concerned specifically with political accountability, which—as all of the authors in this volume agree—refers to the answerability and responsibility of public officials.[3] I delimit the concept of political accountability to relationships that *formally* give some actor the authority of oversight and/or sanction relative to public officials. Political accountability is thus a formalized relationship of oversight and/or sanctions of public officials by other actors. In a relationship of political accountability, a public official gives a reckoning of the discharge of her public duties to actors that formally (via public law) have the capacity to demand such an accounting and/or to impose sanctions on the official. Thus, my understanding of political accountability hinges on whether an actor is formally ascribed the right to demand answerability of a public official or bureaucracy. When monitoring of public authorities takes place outside an institutionalized framework in which agents are formally charged with this responsibility, it falls outside the scope of my understanding of accountability.

Excluding non-legalized relationships from the concept of 'accountability' does not mean that relationships outside this boundary are less important than those that fall within it. The issue is one of conceptual demarcation, not political significance. As conceptualized here, 'accountability' implies not only answerability, but also the *legal obligation* to answer or the institutionalized right of an agent of accountability to impose sanctions on public officials. This focus on legalized authority to request answerability allows for a clearly delimited concept that still includes a range of relationships of answerability.

This definition excludes as agents of accountability the press and civil society organizations that investigate and denounce abuses and wrongdoings by public officials. Smulovitz and Peruzzotti call

---

[3] Even this point is not unanimous beyond the authors of this volume; some scholars prefer a less bounded concept. Moncrieffe (1998: 392) argued that '(T)he concept of accountability must focus not merely on the responsibilities to the governed of those who are elected to govern but also on the relations among groups or factions and their responsibilities to elected officials'. She avers that citizen willingness to participate in politics, the degree to which citizen rights are effectively enforced and institutionalized, and the extent to which legal mechanisms check the actions of factions and interest groups should be included in measuring accountability (394). She also argues that the notion of democratic accountability should extend beyond the accountability of public officials. I restrict 'political accountability' to the answerability of public officials and agencies to other actors.

such interactions 'societal accountability' in their chapter in this volume (see also Fox and Brown 1998). These exclusions may seem arbitrary in view of the undeniable fact that some social organizations and the press have a major impact, as Smulovitz and Peruzzotti argue, in exposing governmental wrongdoing and creating public oversight of government actions. Yet if we include all forms of public oversight or holding actors responsible, the concept becomes so elastic that it may not be useful.

Within this conception, two kinds of actors can provide political accountability. First, elected public officials are accountable to voters, at least in cases in which re-election is allowed. Second, many state agencies are formally charged with overseeing and/or sanctioning public officials and bureaucracies; I refer to these relationships as intrastate accountability. Examples include legislative committees that investigate possible wrongdoings of public officials, agencies that are created to monitor public officials and bureaucracies with an eye toward possible wrong doing, the legal system when it investigates the possible misdeeds of public officials and bureaucracies, the congress when it initiates a hearing against any public official, and the assembly in a parliamentary system when it makes a political judgment about whether to remove a minister or a cabinet. A third category analyzed by Smulovitz and Peruzzotti in this volume, societal oversight, falls outside the bounds of my definition of accountability, yet with important interactions with the formal network of institutions of accountability. Intrastate accountability and its interactions with electoral accountability and societal oversight are the primary focus of this book.

Democratic accountability refers to the accountability of two broad categories of public officials: elected and non-elected officials. Both of these broad categories should be accountable to different kinds of actors. Elected public officials are accountable first and foremost to the citizens whose votes put them into office. The ways in which elected politicians are accountable through the vote have been analysed at length by political scientists (Ferejohn 1999; Fiorina 1981; Key 1966; Maravall 1999; Powell Jr. 2000; Przeworski et al. 1999). Although this relationship between voters and representatives is not the primary subject of this volume, it is central to democratic politics.

In democracies, many non-elected officials are also presumably accountable to the executive or the legislature. These non-elected officials are in the first instance agents of the principals who appoint them. As with the relationship between voters and elected politicians, however, the relationship between non-elected officials and the principal who appointed them (and can in theory remove them) allows ample room for shirking. Agents can acquire considerable autonomy, and mechanisms for overseeing and controlling them are often tenuous.

Competing Conceptions of Accountability

Five areas of conceptual disagreement run throughout works on accountability in this volume (and beyond). All five involve the boundaries of the concept: how broad or narrow should it be?

The most fundamental question is whether all activities that involve holding public officials responsible for their discharge of duties should be included under the very broad rubric of accountability. Many scholars accept such a broad understanding (Day and Klein 1987; Diamond, Plattner, and Schedler 1999; Fox and Brown 1998: 12; Merritt forthcoming; Moncrieffe 1998; Paul 1992). For example, Paul (1992: 1047) states that 'Accountability means holding individuals and organizations responsible for their performance. Public accountability refers to the spectrum of approaches, mechanisms, and practices used by the stakeholders concerned with public services to ensure a desired level and type of performance.' Day and Klein (1987: 5) provide another broad definition: 'To account is to answer for the discharge of a duty or for conduct. It is to provide a reckoning. It is to give a satisfactory reason for or to explain. It is to acknowledge responsibility for one's actions.' D. Dunn (1999), Keohane (2002), and Oakerson (1989) stipulate that accountability also necessarily involves the capacity of actors to impose sanctions on public officials. Yet their definitions remain broad by virtue of including a wide range of non-institutionalized kinds of answerability and sanctions. For example, Keohane mentions reputational accountability, by which an actor can informally demand answerability and impose reputational costs on a public official.

The authors in this volume who explicitly take a position on this issue (O'Donnell, Kenney, and Moreno et al.) all advocate a concept that is more bounded than simply explaining one's public duties in response to such a request.[4] I agree that a more bounded concept is desirable and that it is important to specify what forms of

---

[4] However, they delimit the concept for different reasons and in different ways. O'Donnell and Kenney limit the notion of horizontal accountability to legal transgressions. Kenney and Moreno et al. limit 'accountability' to cases in which the agent of accountability has the capacity to impose sanctions. Moreno et al. limit 'accountability' to principal–agent relationships.

'answerability' constitute accountability. A broad conception of accountability as answerability or responsibility makes it difficult to understand where the boundaries of accountability are. While intuitively sensible and in step with quotidian understanding, this definition could be extended to a vast array of different arenas and actions, including some that many analysts would not consider relationships of accountability. For example, a wealthy campaign contributor's request that a politician pursue some action could be seen as a request for answerability with a corresponding potential for a sanction (withdrawing campaign support) in the event of non-compliance. If we considered such informal interactions a relationship of accountability, the concept would encompass an enormous and ill-defined range. Actions as different as a citizen's letter requesting that a public official explain her view on an issue, a court injunction that a public official must obey some regulation, elections, a citizen's law suit against a public official, social mobilization to get public officials to undertake some action, media denunciations of some public policy or actor, and the oversight that one state agency exercises over another could all be construed as demands for public answerability. Or if public opinion in some diffuse way seems to request a change of course on the government's part, this could be considered a request for answerability and hence a relationship of accountability.

It is difficult to impose meaningful boundaries on the concept if every action by which some actor requests or demands answerability of a public official is considered 'accountability'. Answerability combines many different agents and actions, and it makes the conceptual boundaries murky. My demarcation provides for much greater specificity and clarity than the excessively diffuse notions of answerability or holding actors responsible.

This first issue constitutes the biggest divide in conceptions of accountability. The remaining four sources of disagreement all revolve around how to delimit the quotidian use of 'accountability' as answerability.

A second source of disagreement is whether accountability should be restricted to cases of legal transgressions by state actors. Charles Kenney (this volume) and Guillermo O'Donnell (this volume) argue for such a restriction in cases of horizontal accountability. O'Donnell defined horizontal accountability as 'the existence of state agencies that are legally enabled and empowered, and factually willing and able, to take actions that span from routine oversight to criminal sanctions or impeachment in relation to actions or omissions by other agents or agencies of the state that may be qualified as unlawful.... (F)or this kind of accountability to be effective there must exist state agencies that are authorized and willing to oversee, control, redress, and/or sanction unlawful actions of other state agencies' (1999a: 38, 39). In this volume, O'Donnell writes that horizontal accountability 'deals *exclusively* with those (intrastate interactions) that...are undertaken with the explicit purpose of preventing, cancelling, redressing and/or punishing actions (or eventually non-actions) by another state agency *that are deemed unlawful, whether on grounds of encroachment or of corruption*' (emphasis added).

Whereas O'Donnell and Kenney limit the notion of horizontal accountability specifically to perceived legal transgressions, most of the literature suggests that accountability also involves oversight (or monitoring) and sanctions related to political disagreements that do not involve such transgressions (e.g., Magaloni, this volume; Moreno et al., this volume; Schedler 1999; Schmitter 1999; Woodhouse 1994). O'Donnell's focus on perceived legal violations excludes institutionalized relationships of answerability when one actor politically disagrees with and calls for an account from a public official.

In my view, the notion of accountability, including what O'Donnell calls horizontal accountability and I call intrastate accountability, should extend beyond issues where the legality of a state actor's behavior is at stake. Intrastate answerability and sanctioning are not limited to perceptions about the legality of a public official's or agency's actions. Public officials and agencies must provide political as well as juridical accountings of the discharge of their public duties. One of the classic forms of intrastate accountability is cabinet (Laver and Shepsle 1999; Strøm 2000) and ministerial accountability (Woodhouse 1994) to the legislature. These refer mainly to political answerability and the possibility of removal from office. In contrast to the situation with impeachment in presidential systems, when in a parliamentary democracy a cabinet or minister answers to the legislature, the sanction of the legislature usually does not rest upon a perceived juridical infraction. The idea that cabinets and ministers are answerable to (and can be removed by) the legislature was one of the earliest uses of 'accountability' in politics, and it remains an important one. Consistent with this traditional usage of 'accountability,' and in contrast to the boundaries created by O'Donnell's focus on legal transgressions, the political answerability of ministers and cabinets to the legislature is a fundamental aspect of intrastate accountability.

Kenney agrees that the relationship of cabinets to parliaments in parliamentary systems is one of accountability that rests on political judgements that are not limited to legal transgressions. He argues that in presidential systems, however, the notion of horizontal accountability should be limited to legal transgressions. This argument, however, raises a different difficulty: why should accountability in presidential systems be restricted to legal transgressions and encroachments when it is not so restricted in parliamentary systems?

As understood traditionally (Day and Klein 1987: 4–31; Woodhouse 1994: 3–39), the conception of accountability includes the answerability of public officials for the range of their public duties. By restricting the notion of horizontal accountability to perceived legal transgressions, Kenney and O'Donnell exclude political issues that in the dominant understanding of accountability should be included. Most chapters in this volume are predicated on this broader conception; they do not limit the analysis to cases of perceived legal transgressions.

This broader conception of accountability (including horizontal or intrastate accountability) is also more consistent with the common notion that elected political representatives are accountable to voters. Elected politicians are accountable to voters for their political actions regardless of whether they are perceived to have transgressed any constitutional norms. O'Donnell used the term 'vertical' accountability to refer to the oversight and sanctions that voters, the press, non-governmental organizations (NGOs), and other organizations of civil society exercise over public officials. For O'Donnell, vertical accountability includes political judgements as well as legal transgressions (most citizens vote on the basis of political judgements, not legal issues). It is not clear why one should restrict the concept of horizontal accountability to legal transgressions and encroachments while advocating a concept of electoral accountability and societal oversight that is more expansive and is principally based on political judgements. It seems preferable to have an isomorphic concept: if electoral accountability includes voters' judgements about political matters, so should accountability to state actors.

A third area of contention regarding the definition of accountability is whether the concept necessarily entails the capacity of sanctions on the part of the agent of accountability. D. Dunn (1999: 299), J. Dunn (1999: 337–8), Kenney (this volume), and Moreno et al. argue that a relationship of accountability exists only if the agent of accountability can impose sanctions on a transgressor. In contrast, Schedler (1999) (explicitly) and O'Donnell (implicitly)[5] argue that some mechanisms of accountability rely exclusively on answerability without necessarily having the capacity to impose sanctions. To disentangle this issue, I distinguish between *direct* legally ascribed sanctioning power and other sanctions. Accountability cannot exist with *no* sanctioning power; some capacity to redress wrongdoing by referring a case to other venues (especially the justice system) is critical to systems of accountability. As defined here, however, accountability does not require direct, legally ascribed sanctioning power. Agencies of oversight are expected to refer possible wrongdoings to actors that can impose sanctions; this indirect sanctioning power suffices to characterize a relationship of accountability.

Consider the institution of the ombudsman. The ombudsman is typically charged with investigating citizen complaints about improper state behaviour, ranging from state failure to protect constitutionally guaranteed rights to improper police conduct. The ombudsman fits within my definition of intrastate accountability in which one agent of accountability has a formalized authority of oversight over public officials even though the office cannot impose formal sanctions. Even without direct formal sanctioning power, the ombudsman generates a need for answerability of and accounting by public officials. The ombudsman in most countries is expected not merely to investigate abuses by public officials, but also to take some action to encourage redressing such wrongdoings. For example, the ombudsman may refer the case to the legal system. The failings of this institution (which has achieved important successes in some countries) have more to do with the shortcomings of the legal system in handling the cases referred to it than with the ombudsman's inability to directly prosecute cases. In a similar vein, the Public Prosecution in Brazil lacks direct sanctioning power but is expected to file law suits in cases of wrongdoings by public officials and agencies.

As Kenney and Moreno et al. imply, accountability is different if an agent of oversight also has formal sanctioning power. The difference, however, may be slim because agencies that oversee public officials can bring cases of wrongdoings to the legal system.

---

[5] O'Donnell (1999a: 30) includes as agents of horizontal accountability agencies such as the ombudsman, fiscalías, controllers, etc., that usually have no direct sanctioning authority. His chapter in this volume likewise does not restrict the notion of accountability to cases in which the agent of accountability can impose direct formal sanctions.

Conversely, many actors that can formally impose direct sanctions are de facto toothless. Thus, although sanctioning potential cannot be entirely absent in a relationship of accountability, it can be indirect (i.e., by referring the wrongdoing to the legal system) as well as direct. By delimiting the notion of accountability to formal institutional relationships, but not delimiting it to relationships that involve direct, legally ascribed sanctioning power, I am advocating a concept considerably narrower than that of answerability but broader than that proposed by Kenney, Moreno et al., and O'Donnell in this volume.

A fourth area of disagreement revolves around whether 'accountability' is limited to principal–agent relationships. In their chapter in this volume, Moreno, Crisp, and Shugart argue that 'accountability' should be restricted to such relationships, that is, relationships in which some principal commissions an agent to do something for him/her. In this conception, only if the principal can dismiss or decide against renewing the agent is there a relationship of accountability. To quote from their chapter, 'Accountability means that the principal has the right to withdraw the conditionally delegated authority altogether.' They argue that 'when institutions are formally independent of one another—as with the independent branches of presidential systems—they are not accountable to one another.'[6] Against this view, Kenney and O'Donnell in this volume argue that not all relationships of accountability involve a principal who can dismiss an agent. Most of the other chapters in this volume also understand relationships of accountability as extending beyond (though including) principal–agent relationships.

Restricting 'accountability' to principal–agent relationships calls attention to a substantive point: a relationship of power is different when a principal can dimiss or decide against renewing an agent compared to a context in which no such possibility exists. Under these circumstances, agents have an incentive to be responsible to a principal (though several contributions in Przeworski et al. (1999) question how compelling these incentives are in the voter–representative relationship). The advantages of limiting 'accountability' to principal–agent relationships, however, may be offset by other disadvantages—above all, the fact that this defin-

---

[6] Elster (1999), Fearon (1999), Laver and Shepsle (1999), and Strøm (2000) also analyse accountability in the context of principal–agent relationships, but they do not explicitly rule out the possibility that accountability could be extended to non-principal–agent relationships.

ition excessively narrows the concept and leaves out some formalized relationships of oversight and potential sanctioning. Whether or not a principal–agent relationship exists, a public official may formally need to answer for her action to some actor and may be subject to sanctions in the event of wrongdoing.

By my definition above, accountability relationships exist whenever a public agency or official is formally (i.e., by law or public decree) answerable to another actor. In this conception, agencies of oversight and the judiciary are parts of the web of accountability because they are formally charged with overseeing and/or sanctioning public officials for the discharge of their public duties. From this perspective, principal–agent relationships are a subset of accountability relationships. Hence, like Kenney and O'Donnell, I diverge from Moreno et al. on this point. The ombudsman and some other agencies in Latin American countries are not principals; they were not responsible for electing or appointing the president and the congress, and they cannot dismiss the president or members of congress. Indeed, the reverse may be true: in Argentina, Ecuador, Guatemala, and Peru, the congress can appoint and dismiss the ombudsman. But the president and legislators may be required to answer to (provide accounting to) the ombudsman, the *fiscalía*, the *controlador*, and other mechanisms of oversight. Kenney and Moreno et al. exclude such agents of oversight though on slightly different grounds—Kenney because they have no formal direct sanctioning power, and Moreno et al. for this reason and also more fundamentally because they are not principals in a principal–agent relationship.

In a similar vein, if a legislative committee investigates some putative wrongdoing of the president, that committee is formally charged with the responsibility to review the president's actions. Even though this is not a principal–agent relationship (the president did not 'hire' and cannot dismiss the committee as her agent, nor did the committee 'hire' the president), in my understanding, there is a relationship of accountability because the president must answer to the committee. For Moreno et al., the judiciary for the most part is not part of the network of accountability because it is neither a principal nor an agent but rather an independent branch of the state. In contrast, in my conception, as well as Kenney's and O'Donnell's, the judiciary is a key institution of accountability; public officials who are accused of a legal transgression need to answer to the courts.

One final doubt about the argument of Moreno et al. on this point: it is questionable whether the concept 'horizontal exchange', which they coin to refer to relationships of oversight and checks and balances that fall outside principal–agent relationships, serves us optimally. The notion of 'exchange' may not quite capture the interaction in a relationship of oversight. 'Accountability', 'checks and balances', 'superintendence', and 'oversight' are more specific and precise than 'exchange'.

A fifth area of disagreement involves which actors can serve as the mechanisms for providing accountability. The relatively unbounded definition of accountability as answerability and informal sanctions would allow almost any actor to be an agent of accountability. In contrast, with the exception of Smulovitz and Peruzzotti, the authors in this volume focus on a narrower range of actors that have formalized responsibilities to oversee public officials. Within this fundamental agreement about a bounded set of actors that can constitute agents of accountability, the authors in this volume nevertheless have some differences of opinion that stem directly from the previous disagreements. Because of their definition of accountability, Moreno et al. limit these actors to voters, to whom elected representatives are accountable; politicians, to whom some bureaucracies are accountable; parliaments, to which cabinets and ministers are responsible in parliamentary democracies; and other principals in principal–agent relationships. They explicitly exclude oversight agencies and institutions that are independent from each other. Kenney also excludes oversight agencies but includes actors that have sanctioning power (the primary example is the judiciary). O'Donnell includes not only principals in principal–agent relationships, but also oversight agencies and the judiciary as agents of horizontal accountability—although all three kinds of actors only when the actor being investigated or sanctioned has committed a legal infraction. I share his list of agents of accountability, but as noted above disagree that they are acting as agents of accountability only in cases of legal transgressions.

These arenas of agreement and disagreement about the concept of accountability are summarized in Table 1.1. In the final row, 'Agents of Accountability', the scholars who do not limit accountability to formal authority to oversee and/or sanction public officials have a much less restricted conception than the two possibilities shown in Table 1.1.

Kenney (this volume) raises one other important conceptual issue: the relationship between horizontal accountability and checks and balances. He properly argues that these two concepts should not be confounded or conflated; not all checks and balances

TABLE 1.1. *Conceptualizing political accountability*

	More restricted conception	Less restricted conception
Object of Political Accountability	State actors (all authors in this volume, but for Moreno et al., limited to agents in principal–agent relationships; Merritt forthcoming)	State actors and others (Moncrieffe 1998)
Is accountability limited to formal (legalized) authority to oversee and/or sanction	Yes (Kenny, this volume; Mainwaring; Moreno et al., this volume)	No (Day and Klein 1987; Fox and Brown 1998; Keohane 2002; Merritt forthcoming; Moncrieffe 1998)
Is direct formally ascribed sanctioning power a necessary component of accountability	Yes (Kenney, this volume; Moreno et al., this volume)	No (Mainwaring; O'Donnell, this volume; Schedler 1999; all authors named in the cell immediately above)
Are accountability relationships limited to principal–agent relationships?	Yes (Moreno et al., this volume, Elster 1999; Laver and Shepsle 1999)	No (Kenney, this volume; Mainwaring, Merritt forthcoming; O'Donnell, this volume)
Agents of accountability	Principals in principal–agent relationships (Moreno et al., this volume Elster 1999; Laver and Shepsle 1999)	All actors that formally oversee and/or sanction public officials (Kenney, this volume; Mainwaring, this volume; O'Donnell, this volume)

are a subset of accountability. Political disagreement per se between the legislature and the executive does not necessarily constitute a relationship of accountability. For example, if the legislature refuses to approve an executive-sponsored bill, this does not intrinsically constitute a relationship of accountability because it does not involve an element of answerability or sanctioning. The distinction between accountability and checks and balances, however, is sometimes a fine one; checks and balances can constitute mechanisms of accountability. The key issue according to the definition proposed here is whether an actor has the constitutional/legal capacity to request an accounting of a public official's (or agency's) discharge of duties or to impose sanctions on that official. If so, it is a relationship of accountability. When the legislature creates a commission to investigate executive actions, it is a form of oversight and creates a demand for answerability—hence constitutes a mechanism of accountability (see Figueiredo's chapter in this volume). In a similar vein, when the legislature charges a committee thereof to oversee an executive agency, a relationship of accountability exists.

A skeptic might wonder whether the concept of accountability can be rescued in light of the conceptual muddle that is reflected in Table 1.1. I believe that the answer is affirmative. Accountability is too substantively important a subject in the social sciences and in politics to abandon. Nonetheless, the vast differences that are synthesized in Table 1.1 indicate the need for more concerted theorizing about how to define and delimit the concept. Hopefully, this volume will advance thinking toward accomplishing this objective.

Distinguishing Among Types of Accountability

O'Donnell (1994, 1999a, 1999b, this volume) has been a pioneer in conceptualizing distinctions among different kinds of accountability. He developed a distinction between vertical and horizontal accountability. By vertical accountability, O'Donnell meant the accountability of state agents to citizens and to civil society. Elections are an important, indeed 'arguably the main facet of vertical accountability', but the notion of vertical accountability also includes actions by civil society and the media to expose 'apparently wrongful acts of the public authorities' (1999a: 30).

O'Donnell's distinction has set the agenda for contemporary debates about non-electoral forms of accountability, but it is questionable that his spatial metaphors provide the best way of differentiating among different kinds of accountability. His terminology has two problems. First, the physical metaphor conjured by the notion of vertical accountability is misleading except in principal–agent relationships. Vertical accountability expresses an image of asymmetry of power, that is, a hierarchical relationship. As Moreno et al. argue, the vertical metaphor can reasonably be extended to all principal–agent relationships, even to those in which the principal is in most respects vastly weaker than the agent. For example, they see voters as principals and elected officials as agents. The 'vertical' image, however, is inappropriate to describe relationships that do not have a hierarchical component.

O'Donnell (1999c) includes the monitoring by NGOs over public officials as an element of vertical accountability, but NGOs do not vertically control public officials in any way.

Second, O'Donnell's distinction conflates two different issues that should not be conflated: a physical metaphor that conveys images of independence (horizontality) and hierarchy (verticality), and the location of the agent of accountability (state versus societal actors, respectively). O'Donnell (1999c) stated that vertical accountability refers to voters and societal organizations while horizontal accountability refers to state and regime agencies. In his chapter in this volume, Kenney also views the distinction between horizontal and vertical accountability as resting on whether the agent of accountability is a state or societal actor. Yet the correspondence between horizontal and vertical relationships, on the one hand, and intrastate and electoral accountability (and societal oversight), on the other, is not perfect.

Principal–agent relationships can be seen as vertical: the principal commissions and can 'fire' the agent (see Moreno et al., this volume). The accountability of a cabinet to the assembly in a parliamentary system is clearly a case of what I call intrastate accountability, and it is also a principal–agent relationship. By suggesting that accountability is horizontal when state actors must answer to other state actors, Kenney and O'Donnell would consider this an example of horizontal accountability. Yet in constitutional terms, it is a vertical relationship; the cabinet serves at the disposition of the assembly. In a similar vein, relationships between the executive or the assembly and some bureaucracies are vertical in the sense that the executive or assembly creates the bureaucracy and formally has control over it, yet at the same time it is an intrastate relationship. In short, some intrastate relationships are vertical, at least in formal terms. For this reason, it is problematic to equate intrastate accountability with horizontal accountability, and more broadly it is problematic to combine, as Kenney and O'Donnell do, the vertical/horizontal distinction with a distinction based on the location (in society versus in the state) of the agent of accountability.

O'Donnell's categories of horizontal and vertical accountability largely (except in cases of legal transgressions) exclude one of the classic uses of 'accountability', namely, the accountability of cabinets and ministers to parliaments in parliamentary systems. According to his definition, only if the parliament removed a minister or cabinet because of legal transgressions would this be an instance of horizontal accountability. Because one state actor (the cabinet or minister) must answer to another state actor (the assembly), it is not a case of vertical accountability according to his definition.

Although O'Donnell's notions of horizontal and vertical accountability are problematic, it is useful to differentiate among different kinds of accountability. It is more fruitful to conceptualize these distinctions strictly according to the agent of accountability.[7] For the sake of parsimony, I propose a distinction between two main kinds of political accountability: electoral accountability or (synonymously) accountability to voters and intrastate accountability. This distinction parallels O'Donnell's but without the connotations of hierarchy and independence suggested by his metaphor, and without conflating the agent of accountability (state versus societal) with the nature of the relationship (horizontal versus vertical).

Intrastate accountability can be usefully subdivided into three different kinds of relationships. First, in principal–agent relationships, a principal commissions an agent to perform some function and has ultimate control over that agent. Bureaucracies created and ultimately controlled by the executive or legislature are prime examples. Moreno et al. restrict their understanding of 'accountability' to this first subcategory. Second, the legal system and on occasions some other state actor (example: a legislature that is trying a president on impeachment hearings) can impose sanctions on public officials accused of wrongdoing. These are not principal–agent relationships, but rather can be thought of as 'sanctioning actors'. The most common sanctioning actors are within the justice system. The congress becomes a sanctioning actor when it tries the president on impeachment charges. Kenney and O'Donnell include sanctioning actors as well as principal–agent relationships in their rubric of horizontal accountability. Finally, oversight actors have responsibility for monitoring the behavior of state officials and agencies. Kenney excludes oversight actors that do not have legally ascribed, direct sanctioning capacity, and O'Donnell includes them only when a legal transgression is at play.

---

[7] Moreno et al. also avoid distinguishing according to both the agent of accountability and the verticality or horizontality of the relationship, but they advocate the opposite way of resolving this tension. Rather than distinguishing between different types of accountability on the basis of the agent of accountability, they distinguish between vertical (principal–agent) relationships and relationships of horizontal exchange.

Interactions Between Electoral and Intrastate Accountability

A second key contribution of this volume is an effort, thanks above all to Moreno et al., to advance the debate about interactions among electoral accountability, intrastate accountability, and societal oversight. Rarely have these interactions been discussed in as detailed a manner as they are here—especially by Magaloni, Moreno et al., O'Donnell, and Smulovitz and Peruzzotti. On this point, too, we hope to advance the debate not through consensus but rather through explicit disagreement.

Moreno et al. argue that the linkage between voters and elected representations sets the tone for all other accountability relationships. In their argument, by getting electoral delegation and accountability right, politicians will address the most serious deficiencies in accountability. To quote from their chapter, 'The deficit of accountability lies in faulty vertical accountability—legislators who do not represent the values and preferences of the broad citizenry. If the accountability of elected officials were working as intended—such that voters could and would punish misdeeds—separate agencies of superintendence would be unnecessary.' Although none of the other authors take this argument as far, all agree that electoral accountability is important for intrastate accountability as well. But other contributors including O'Donnell argue that electoral and intrastate accountability have strong mutual effects. By this argument, electoral accountability and delegation do less to resolve the problems of intrastate accountability than Moreno et al. argue. Conversely, by this argument, it is possible to make greater gains in intrastate electoral accountability than Moreno et al. argue even without touching electoral rules. For example, Smulovitz and Peruzzotti argue that social mobilization, especially in conjunction with media coverage, can trigger improved intrastate accountability. Sadek and Cavalcanti document the impact of Brazil's Public Prosecution, which has enhanced intrastate accountability despite the lack of major electoral and party reform since 1988.

Although the contribution of Moreno et al. is an innovative and important work, intrastate and electoral accountability are more mutually interactive than they indicate. They overestimate the capacity to improve intrastate accountability by enhancing electoral accountability and understate the capacity to enhance intrastate accountability without changing electoral accountability.

It is questionable that the primary key to better intrastate accountability is balance in the continuum from a party centric to an individual centric electoral system for the national congress. They place great optimism in the capacity to effect change in the functioning of intrastate accountability through electoral reform.

The 'accountability deficiency' can be seen as a product of feeble sanctions. Whereas Moreno et al. locate the inefficacy of sanctions in electoral systems that set up inadequate mechanisms of accountability between voters and elected representatives, perhaps even more important are the failures of sanctions that should be imposed by the justice and penal systems for wrongdoings of public officials. The justice system works reasonably well at the upper echelon in some countries (see Magaloni, this volume), but in most of Latin America it is notoriously bad at the local level, where most cases are tried. In much of the region, at the local level, the 'justice' system ('injustice' system frequently more appropriately captures the reality) is still under the sway of powerful elites (Dodson and Jackson, this volume; Magaloni, this volume; Pásara 2002). In several countries, at the local level, drug barons with seemingly unlimited resources to buy off and intimidate the police, judges, and witnesses have captured the justice system. When public officials are confident that they can commit wrongdoings without facing penal and legal sanctions, electoral reform is not likely to fix the problem. Greatly compounding this problem is the inefficacy and frequent complicity of police forces in much of Latin America; they, too, are frequently captured and paid off by local elites from drug barons to landowners and traditional oligarchs.

With an important original argument and a wealth of new empirical information, Moreno et al. show that there is great variance in how independent one would expect oversight agencies to be on the basis of institutional arrangements (Figure 4.3 and the Appendix of their chapter). They argue that such agencies are likely to be more independent from political pressures, and hence more effective as mechanisms of oversight, if (a) they are not named directly and exclusively by the legislature and (b) they have long terms of office, such that they need not depend on the ongoing support of politicians for remaining in office. They conclude that many oversight agencies are insufficiently insulated from political pressures to be effective and that the only effective way to enhance accountability is the vertical (electoral) linkage between voters and representatives. But this argument overlooks the possibility of trying to boost the effectiveness of oversight agencies by making them more independent of political pressures. By the logic of their argument,[8] it should be possible to enhance the effectiveness of oversight agencies by changing the appointment procedures and lengthening the terms of office—a change that is in principle independent of changes in electoral accountability.

Moreno et al. are sanguine about the effects of electoral reform on intrastate accountability. Such optimism assumes that the connection between elected representatives and oversight and sanctioning agencies within the state is fairly tight: intrastate accountability (superintendence in the lexicon of Moreno et al.) will improve because elected politicians find it in their interest to make these institutions work better. This argument probably overstates the extent to which members of congresses would effect improvements in the justice system and oversight agencies even if stronger mechanisms of electoral accountability gave these politicians a bigger stake in national policy outcomes.

The argument also may be excessively sanguine about the effectiveness of electoral accountability between voters and members of national congresses in Latin America. Electoral accountability offers politicians enormous opportunities to shirk (Ferejohn 1999; Maravall 1999; Stokes 1999). Elections occur intermittently, usually every two to eight years, and nothing assures that elected representatives will behave as voters would prefer between elections. Tremendous information asymmetries between elected officials and the average voter give the former ample opportunities to behave with autonomy vis-à-vis the latter (Przeworski et al. 1999). As Schumpeter (1950: 256–64) and Downs (1957) argued long ago, the average voter cannot invest the considerable time needed to closely monitor representatives' actions. These information asymmetries are larger in Latin America, where most voters have limited education and little information about politics, than in the advanced industrial democracies.

Even if voters become disenchanted with a politician or a party in power, they may not believe that other options are better. The 'supply' of politicians or parties may appear to voters to be oligopolistic or quasi-monopolistic. This feeling that all politicians or parties are the same diminishes the extent to which elections serve as instruments of accountability: if voters do not believe that the competition is any better, they are less likely to punish

---

[8] In a region where many institutional reforms have produced less than their supporters hoped for (Pásara 2002), we cannot be sure that such reforms of institutional arrangements would really produce the desired effect of enhancing the independence of oversight agencies.

incumbents by voting them out of office. In sum, as Ferejohn (1999: 137) succinctly points out, 'Electoral punishment...is a fairly blunt instrument, and incumbent officials will be, at best, only moderately responsive to public wishes.' (See also J. Dunn 1999: 338–9; Fearon 1999; Manin et al. 1999; Maravall 1999.)

This book does not purport to resolve the important issues related to the interactions among electoral accountability, intrastate accountability, and societal oversight. It does, however, set out a new research agenda on this issue. The authors do not converge in their understanding of how electoral and intrastate accountability interact, but they advance the debate about this important subject.

Intrastate Accountability in Latin America

A third key debate in this book revolves around the quality of intrastate accountability in Latin America. In the past decade, accountability became salient in reflections about democracy among such organizations as the World Bank and the Interamerican Development Bank, as well as a host of NGOs.

One of O'Donnell's central claims is that mechanisms of horizontal accountability are weak in contemporary Latin America. Indeed, he sees the weakness of horizontal accountability as one of the most important differences between the old and wealthy democracies and the post-1978 democracies of Latin America (and elsewhere). His work over the last decade has addressed differences between these older democracies and Latin American regimes and called attention to deficiencies of elected governments in Latin America. In a seminal article (1994), he argued that weak horizontal accountability characterizes most of Latin America's elected governments—in particular, those that he labelled 'delegative democracies'. 'The horizontal accountability characteristic of representative democracy is extremely weak or non-existent in delegative democracies' (61). Subsequent articles (1999a, 1999b) furthered this argument.

Most scholars accept O'Donnell's viewpoint (e.g., Diamond et al. 1999: 1). While diverging from O'Donnell on other points, Moreno et al. (this volume) agree that there is an accountability deficit in the region. In a similar vein, Morgenstern and Manzetti note the deficiencies in mechanisms of oversight and corruption control in contemporary Argentina compared to the United States, Dodson and Jackson underscore the severe deficiencies of the judiciary in contemporary El Salvador and Guatemala (see also Pásara 2002). These deficiencies make it difficult for these judiciaries to serve either of the two functions central to O'Donnell's notion of horizontal accountability: preventing corruption and preventing improper state encroachments.

Other authors in this volume, however, point to innovations in intrastate accountability in the region. The authors who focus on innovations show that in some countries, there is potential to redress the accountability deficit. Smulovitz and Peruzzotti note promising innovations in what they call 'societal accountability', and I call societal oversight. Civil society has organized to oversee public officials and agencies. Civil society organizations denounce, mobilize, and forge alliances with the independent media to call attention to problems in the discharge of public officials.

Sadek and Cavalcanti (this volume) analyze an old but transformed Brazilian institution whose mandate in the 1988 constitution is broad: the Public Prosecutor's Office (Ministério Público). This institution is charged with undertaking criminal prosecution, defending collective rights and public goods, and defending minority rights. The 1988 constitution devised multiple means to ensure the autonomy of the Public Prosecutor's Office vis-à-vis politicians. Its oversight of and eventually prosecution of state actors (including individuals in the executive, legislative, and judicial branches) falls within the broad domain of accountability. Their chapter underscores the innovative and transformative potential that this institution has manifested. Their portrait of the judiciary and the Public Prosecutor's Office differs sharply from the one that Dodson and Jackson draw of the Salvadorean and Guatemalan judiciaries. It suggests that some mechanisms of accountability in the region are innovative, vibrant, and somewhat powerful. Morgenstern and Manzetti, while underscoring the limitations of mechanisms of oversight in Argentina, also note some promising developments in recent years.

Figueiredo presents a mixed assessment of intrastate accountability in contemporary Brazil. She argues that several potentially important mechanisms of oversight—parliamentary investigative commissions, the Federal Accounting Tribunal (Tribunal de Contas da União), the Joint Congressional Budgetary Committee (Comissão Mista de Orçamento), and a wide range of other tools at the hands of the legislature—have been relatively toothless in practice. As mechanisms of intrastate accountability, they have not been as effective as their legal mandates allow. On the other hand, she argues that they generate information and stimulate debate, both of which might be important in triggering mechanisms of electoral accountability.

I *generally* agree with Moreno et al. and O'Donnell that mechanisms of intrastate accountability tend to be weak in contemporary Latin America. Yet I would qualify this generalization in two ways. First, the quality of intrastate accountability in contemporary Latin America is more promising than many critics suggest, not because a critical assessment is usually wrong but rather because it understates variance. An earlier article of O'Donnell's (1993) properly emphasized gross within country differences in the enforcement of the rule of law (see also Magaloni, this volume). Some Latin American countries (e.g., Brazil) have among the starkest intracountry socioeconomic and political differences in the world. O'Donnell's 1993 article suggested that one key actor of intrastate accountability, the judiciary, is less effective and more patrimonial in the poor 'brown' areas of Latin America than in the developed areas ('the green areas'). By implication, analysts need to be attentive to both the serious deficiencies of accountability with some institutions and in the poor regions and to innovations and promising developments in other institutions, especially in the more developed regions.

Collectively, the essays in the volume strike such a balance, and some chapters, especially Magaloni's, simultaneously call attention to the glaring deficiencies of accountability at some levels and the striking advances at others. Magaloni's argument about intrastate accountability and the courts is two-sided. On the one hand, she notes that the Supreme Court has become more independent vis-à-vis the president and has become a more significant actor in preventing and sanctioning infractions of public officials. This strengthening of the Supreme Court better enables it to exercise the functions associated with intrastate accountability. On the other hand, Magaloni emphasizes the ongoing subordination of local judges and courts to state governors and impunity at the local level. Law-enforcement institutions such as the police and local courts have remained authoritarian enclaves, and they are ineffectual as mechanisms of accountability. The weakness of local courts and law-enforcement agencies means effective impunity for state actors who violate the law—a key aspect of O'Donnell's argument about the weakness of horizontal accountability.

In many countries, Latin American legislatures are important sources of oversight of presidential action. The portrait of delegative democracy that O'Donnell drew in 1994, in which presidents dominated the political systems and mechanisms of horizontal accountability were very weak, is exaggerated in many countries. The judiciaries are undertrained and ineffective in most of the region (see Dodson and Jackson, this volume; Pásara 2002), but even seemingly compliant judiciaries sometimes rear their heads and declare presidential initiatives unconstitutional (Helmke 2000, 2002). As Sadek and Cavalcanti (this volume) argue in their chapter on the Ministério Público in Brazil, in some countries, important innovations are surfacing within the judiciary and related institutions. Indeed, it seems likely that some Latin American countries today have stronger mechanisms of intrastate accountability than the United States did in the 19th century. This is striking because most analysts see the Latin American judiciary as woefully inadequate.

Some nontraditional mechanisms of oversight have become visible and effective institutions. For example, under the leadership of Jorge Santiestevan, the Ombudsman (Defensor del Pueblo) in Peru acquired notable autonomy and efficacy even as President Alberto Fujimori crushed most of the rest of Peru's network of accountability institutions. As Kenney notes, Santiestevan's impact was limited by his need to rely on sanctioning agents—the courts, whose independence was undermined by Fujimori. Nonetheless, even under the highly inauspicious conditions of Fujimori's regime, new mechanisms of accountability could work.

In his analysis of horizontal accountability (though not in some of his other work), O'Donnell generalized too much across countries. His 1994 article on delegative democracy carefully distinguished between Chile and Uruguay, on the one hand, and Peru, Argentina, and Brazil, on the other. He noted that Chile and Uruguay have a more solid network of democratic institutions, hence do not fit the category of delegative democracies. But it tended to lump together Argentina, Brazil, and Peru. Peru under Fujimori fits O'Donnell's description of feeble mechanisms of intrastate accountability. Fujimori emasculated the judiciary, the legislature, and other institutions of intrastate accountability.

In the 1990s, mechanisms of intrastate accountability were less emasculated in Argentina than in Fujimori's Peru. Menem's temporary concentration of power in the early 1990s was a reflection more of Peronista majorities in both chambers of congress and of the extraordinary economic crisis of the late 1980s and early 1990s (hyperinflation and steep economic decline) than of the normal functioning of Argentine democracy. After 1993, the judiciary dealt Menem some key setbacks (Helmke 2000, 2002) notwithstanding its failure to address notorious corruption within his administration.

Mechanisms of corruption control were feeble, but some mechanisms for overseeing the president politically were important.

Brazil also has mechanisms of intrastate accountability more robust than O'Donnell's characterization of delegative democracies suggested. The judiciary has many shortcomings, but it is becoming an activist judiciary that is not readily dominated by the president or by other executive authority, except at the local level (as Magaloni argues occurs in Mexico), especially in the poor regions. Sadek and Cavalcanti (this volume) note the activist nature of the Public Prosecutor's Office in Brazil. The impeachment of President Fernando Collor de Melo in 1992 showed a willingness and capability of the legislature to exercise a dramatic form of accountability. It was followed by presidential impeachments in Venezuela in 1992 and Paraguay in 1999. Pérez-Liñán (2001) has aptly termed these impeachments cases of spasmodic and politicized horizontal accountability.

Second, the contrast that O'Donnell draws between the older democracies, in which mechanisms of horizontal accountability are generally effective, and Latin America's elected regimes, in which they are purportedly much weaker, is too stark if the comparison is intended to illuminate different points in the development of democracy (Schmitter 1999). Latin America's elected regimes have weaker mechanisms of intrastate accountability than the older contemporary wealthy democracies. But it is questionable whether that is the best temporal comparison. If instead we compare today's elected regimes of Latin America with the (now) older democracies during their younger years, then it is less certain whether there is a stark contrast in the efficacy of horizontal accountability. As the chapter by Morgenstern and Manzetti shows, most mechanisms of intrastate accountability were woefully weak in the 19th century United States. The spoils system was pervasive and powerful, and it was predicated on the idea that public agencies would not check executive power. The executive branch generally appointed and could easily remove those who served in public agencies.

These disagreements with O'Donnell's arguments do not take away from their importance. He galvanized a rich discussion on a vital and previously understudied subject. Moreover, if Latin American governments are not able to meet citizen needs, especially in the areas of material well-being and citizen security, there is a grave risk of growing dissatisfaction with democracy. This dissatisfaction could generate support for populists such as Fujimori and Venezuelan President Hugo Chávez (1998–present). These two

presidents severely damaged mechanisms of democratic accountability, and it is no accident that they came to power in response to
particularly severe (Peru) or protracted (Venezuela) economic
demise (and a serious terrorist threat as well in Peru). If citizens
believe that their physical security and livelihood are at stake, they
are more apt to turn an ear to politicians who promise government
efficiency even at the expense of greatly diminished accountability.
Thus, although several chapters in this volume analyze promising
innovations in intrastate accountability and societal oversight, the
dismal performance of many Latin American democracies in providing material well-being and citizen security may open the doors
to regressions. Such regressions would mean a growing approxima-
tion to O'Donnell's portrait of extremely weak intrastate accountability.

The different portraits drawn by those who emphasize innovations in intrastate accountability and those who emphasize ongoing failures suggests the need for a clearer empirical comparative
mapping of Latin America, by country, region, and specific agent of
accountability. The negative overall portrait is surely largely correct, but it is far from uniform.

The Book

However contestable the boundaries of the concept are, and however difficult it is to assess and measure, 'accountability' has for at
least a century been a key part of the lexicon of democratic politics.
Democracy cannot exist without accountability. The concept is complex and difficult to measure, but turning our backs on what has
become a key issue in Latin America and many new democracies
elsewhere is ill-advised. Moreover, because of O'Donnell's contributions, the concept has recently taken center stage in theoretical
thinking about new democracies. Both because the theme has assumed visibility in Latin America and other new democracies
around the world, and because of its growing theoretical importance in understanding the dynamics and deficiencies of democracy,
organizing a book around the theme of accountability seemed potentially fruitful.

This volume advances thinking about the web of institutions that
together form the mechanisms of accountability, and about the
interaction among these institutions and the interaction between
electoral accountability, intrastate accountability, and societal
oversight. The advantage of cutting across a variety of institutions

and focusing on accountability, as this volume does, is that institutions interact to form a web of mechanisms of accountability.

The volume deliberately brings together authors from different theoretical perspectives working on the same theme. Moreno et al. work from a political economy approach whereas Kenney and O'Donnell are working from more eclectic approaches. These theoretical differences are reflected in the diverging definitions of accountability. This diversity of meta-theoretical frameworks enriches the volume by allowing for the kind of direct clashes that can advance thinking in the social sciences. It also enhances the volume because both conceptions of accountability and both theoretical frameworks illuminate important dimensions of the problem.

Two mainly conceptual and theoretical chapters about accountability follow. These chapters lay the groundwork for chapters that, although theoretically driven, also have an empirical focus. Part II has three chapters on legislatures, executives, and oversight agencies. Part III has three chapters on the judiciary and related mechanisms of accountability. Finally, Part IV discusses the important innovations in oversight of public officials made possible by organizations in civil society.

References

Day, Patricia, and Rudolf Klein. 1987. *Accountabilities: Five Public Services*. London and New York: Tavistock.

Diamond, Larry, Marc F. Plattner, and Andreas Schedler. 1999. 'Introduction'. In Andreas Schedler, Larry Diamond, and Marc F. Plattner, eds., *The Self-Restraining State: Power and Accountability in New Democracies*, pp. 1–10. Boulder, CO: Lynne Rienner.

Downs, Anthony. 1957. *An Economic Theory of Democracy*. New York, NY: Harper & Row.

Dunn, Delmer D. 1999. 'Mixing Elected and Nonelected Officials in Democratic Policy Making: Fundamentals of Accountability and Responsibility'. In Adam Przeworski, Susan C. Stokes, and Bernard Manin, eds., *Democracy, Accountability, and Representation*, pp. 297–325. Cambridge: Cambridge University Press.

Dunn, John. 1999. 'Situating Political Accountability'. In Adam Przeworski, Susan C. Stokes, and Bernard Manin, eds., *Democracy, Accountability, and Representation*, pp. 329–44. Cambridge: Cambridge University Press.

Elster, Jon. 1999. 'Accountability in Athenian Politics'. In Adam Przeworski, Susan C. Stokes, and Bernard Manin, eds., *Democracy, Ac-*

countability, and Representation, pp. 253–78. Cambridge: Cambridge University Press.

Fearon, James D. 1999. 'Electoral Accuntability and the Control of Politicians: Selecting Good Types versus Sanctioning Poor Performance'. In Adam Przeworski, Susan C. Stokes, and Bernard Manin, eds., *Democracy, Accountability, and Representation*, pp. 55–97. Cambridge: Cambridge University Press.

Ferejohn, John. 1999. 'Accountability and Authority: Toward a Theory of Political Accountability'. In Adam Przeworski, Susan C. Stokes, and Bernard Manin, eds., *Democracy, Accountability, and Representation*, pp. 131–153. Cambridge: Cambridge University Press.

Fiorina, Morris P. 1981. *Retrospective Voting in American National Elections*. New Haven, CT: Yale University Press.

Fox, Jonathan A., and L. David Brown. 1998. 'Introduction'. In Jonathan A. Fox and L. David Brown, eds., *The Struggle for Accountability: The World Bank, NGOs, and Grassroots Movements*, pp. 1–47. Cambridge, MA: The MIT Press.

Helmke, Gretchen. 2000. *Ruling Against the Rulers: Court-Executive Relations in Argentina Under Dictatorship and Democracy*. Ph.D. dissertation, University of Chicago.

——. 2002. 'The Logic of Strategic Defection: Court–Executive Relations in Argentina Under Dictatorship and Democracy'. *American Political Science Review* 96, 2 (June): 291–303.

Keohane, Robert O. 2002. 'Global Governance and Democratic Accountability'. Unpublished paper.

Key, Vernon O. 1966. *The Responsible Electorate*. New York: Vintage Books.

Laver, Michael and Kenneth A. Shepsle. 1999. 'Government Accountability in Parliamentary Democracies'. In Adam Przeworski, Susan C. Stokes, and Bernard Manin, eds., *Democracy, Accountability, and Representation*, pp. 279–96. Cambridge: Cambridge University Press.

Manin, Bernard, Adam Przeworski, and Susan C. Stokes. 1999. 'Elections and Representation'. In Adam Przeworski, Susan C. Stokes, and Bernard Manin, eds., *Democracy, Accountability, and Representation*, pp. 29–54. Cambridge: Cambridge University Press.

Maravall, José María. 1999. 'Accountability and Manipulation'. In Adam Przeworski, Susan C. Stokes, and Bernard Manin, eds., *Democracy, Accountability, and Representation*, pp. 154–96. Cambridge: Cambridge University Press.

Merritt, Martha. Forthcoming. *Accountability in Russian Politics*.

Moncrieffe, Joy Marie. 1998. 'Reconceptualizing Political Accountability'. *International Political Science Review* 19, 4 (October): 387–406.

Oakerson, Ronald J. 1989. 'Governance Structures for Enhancing Accountability and Responsiveness'. In James L. Perry, ed., *Handbook of Public Administration*, pp. 114–30. San Francisco, CA: Jossey-Bass Publishers.

O'Donnell, Guillermo. 1993. 'On the State, Democratization, and Some Conceptual Problems: A Latin American View with Glances at Some Postcommunist Countries'. *World Development* 21, 8: 1355–69.

——. 1994. 'Delegative Democracy'. *The Journal of Democracy* 5, 1 (January): 55–69.

——. 1999a. 'Horizontal Accountability in New Democracies'. In Andreas Schedler, Larry Diamond, and Marc F. Plattner, eds., *The Self-Restraining State: Power and Accountability in New Democracies*, pp. 29–51. Boulder, CO: Lynne Rienner.

——. 1999b. 'Polyarchies and the (Un)Rule of Law in Latin America: A Partial Conclusion'. In Juan Méndez, Guillermo O'Donnell, and Paulo Sérgio Pinheiro, eds., *The (Un)Rule of Law and the Underprivileged in Latin America*, pp. 303–37. Notre Dame, IN: University of Notre Dame Press.

——. 1999c. 'A Response to My Commentators'. In Andreas Schedler, Larry Diamond, and Marc F. Plattner, eds., *The Self-Restraining State: Power and Accountability in New Democracies*, pp. 68–71. Boulder, CO: Lynne Rienner.

Pásara, Luis. 2002. 'Justicia y ciudadanía realmente existentes'. *Política y gobierno* IX, 2 (Second semester): 361–402.

Paul, Samuel. 1992. 'Accountability in Public Services: Exit, Voice, and Control'. *World Development* 29, 7 (July): 1047–60.

Pérez-Liñán, Aníbal. 2001. 'Crisis without Breakdown: Presidential Impeachment in Latin America'. Ph.D. dissertation, University of Notre Dame.

Powell Jr., G. Bingham. 2000. *Elections as Instruments of Democracy: Majoritarian and Proportional Visions*. New Haven, CT: Yale University Press.

Przeworski, Adam, Susan C. Stokes, and Bernard Manin, eds. 1999. *Democracy, Accountability, and Representation*. Cambridge: Cambridge University Press.

Schedler, Andreas. 1999. 'Conceptualizing Accountability'. In Andreas Schedler, Larry Diamond, and Marc F. Plattner, eds., *The Self-Restraining State: Power and Accountability in New Democracies*, pp. 13–28. Boulder, CO: Lynne Rienner.

Schedler, Andreas, Larry Diamond, and Marc F. Plattner, eds. 1999. *The Self-Restraining State: Power and Accountability in New Democracies*. Boulder, CO: Lynne Rienner.

Schmitter, Philippe C. 1999. 'The Limits of Horizontal Accountability'. In Andreas Schedler, Larry Diamond, and Marc F. Plattner, eds., *The Self-Restraining State: Power and Accountability in New Democracies*, pp. 59–62. Boulder, CO: Lynne Rienner.

Schumpeter, Joseph. 1950. *Capitalism, Socialism, and Democracy*, 3rd edn. New York, NY: Harper & Row.

Smulovitz, Catalina, and Enrique Peruzzotti. 2000. 'Societal Accountability in Latin America'. *The Journal of Democracy* 11, 4 (October): 147–58.

Stokes, Susan C. 1999. 'What Do Policy Switches Tell Us about Democracy?' In Adam Przeworski, Susan C. Stokes, and Bernard Manin, eds., *Democracy, Accountability, and Representation*, pp. 98–130. Cambridge: Cambridge University Press.

Strøm, Kaare. 2000. 'Delegation and Accountability in Parliamentary Democracies'. *European Journal of Political Research* 37, 3: 261–89.

Woodhouse, Diana. 1994. *Ministers and Parliament: Accountability in Theory and Practice*. Oxford: Clarendon Press.

2

Horizontal Accountability: The Legal Institutionalization of Mistrust

Guillermo O'Donnell*

Introduction

For good reasons, contemporary social science has been paying close attention to trust and its interplay with institutions. The present chapter, however, deals with *mis*trust and its institutionalized expressions in the political sphere. The topic I discuss here is horizontal accountability (from now on HA) (proposed in O'Donnell 1999a). I am pleased that this concept has elicited quite a lot of attention, both positive and critical, of which the present volume is an expression. Not to abuse the patience of the reader, in the present chapter I do not repeat my arguments in this text. I need, however, to transcribe the definition that I offered of HA:

The existence of state agencies that are legally enabled and empowered, and factually willing and able, to take actions that span from routine oversight to criminal sanctions or impeachment in relation to actions or omissions by other agents or agencies of the state that may be qualified as unlawful. (O'Donnell 1999a: 38)

In the same text I distinguish 'two main directions' in which HA may come into play:

One consists of the unlawful *encroachment* by one state agency upon the proper authority of another; the other [*corruption*] consists of unlawful advantages that public officials obtain for themselves and/or their associates. (O'Donnell 1999a: 41, italics added)

---

* Once more, I dedicate this text to Gabriela, my always beloved agency of horizontal accountability.

I appreciate the comments received from the editors of this volume, as well as from Michael Coppedge, Frances Hagopian, and Gabriela Ippolito-O'Donnell.

There is a point that may seem obvious from these citations but that I want to highlight. State agencies and individual agent(s)[1] interact in many ways; often they make and do not make decisions because de facto or *de jure* they take into account the jurisdiction, the decisions, and the preferences of other agencies, public and otherwise. In this sense, the interacting agencies are in a relation of mutual control and/or, as Moreno et al. (this volume) put it, of exchange. This is a broad category that covers many kinds of intrastate interactions. This category is *not* what, according to my definition, HA is. HA refers to a subset of these interactions. It deals exclusively with those that share a common characteristic: they are undertaken by a state agency with the explicit purpose of preventing, cancelling, redressing and/or punishing actions (or eventually non-actions) by another state agency that are deemed unlawful, whether on grounds of encroachment or of corruption. This concept delimits a particular kind of interaction among state agencies, narrower than the whole set of controls and exchanges among these agencies. In all cases of HA, a given state agency, directly or by means of mobilizing another agency (often a court) addresses another state agency (or agencies), on the basis of legally-grounded arguments about presumably unlawful actions or inactions of the latter. We may want or not to label this kind of situation 'horizontal accountability;' the only real issue is if the concept, as defined, conveniently designates an important or interesting kind of interaction among some state agencies.[2]

Another point of clarification is that, as I mention at the beginning, I became interested in HA because of its absence or severe weakness in many new and some not-so-new democracies, in Latin America and elsewhere. Whether we want to call these regimes 'delegative' or not, the concrete fact is that in many of these

---

[1] From now on, when I speak of 'agencies' I mean both institutions and individual agent(s) performing roles in such organizations.

[2] Moreno et al. in this volume assert that accountability can only refer to vertical, not horizontal relationships. Humpty Dumpty knew that essentialist definitions are bad logic because we can freely decide what our words mean. I am surprised that sophisticated scholars such as Moreno, Crisp and Shugart seem to ignore this point, as witnessed, among others, by the following expressions: 'accountability as an *inherently* vertical relationship' and 'That [delegation of authority] may be withdrawn is the *very essence* of accountability' (Moreno et al., this volume, italics added). Since, however, among state agencies there exist a series of important interactions, some of which fall under the definition of HA, these authors propose the term *horizontal exchange*. The terminological change would be irrelevant, except that these authors vaguely include under 'exchange' all sorts of interactions in addition to the legally-grounded ones I have specified.

democracies the executive does its very best to eliminate or render ineffective all sorts of agencies of HA. I believe, and will substantiate, that the absence or weakness of HA is a serious flaw. Yet this does not mean that I regard as unimportant the kind of vertical accountability furnished by reasonably fair elections[3]—so much so that if this kind of election were lacking, the respective case simply would not be a democratic regime and we would not be worrying about its flaws in terms of HA.

A Contradiction

Every complex organization, polities included, is subject to a contradiction, an inherent tension that admits no final, fully consensual, or stable solution. On one hand, the members of the organization normally expect the provision of some public goods and the solution of some collective action problems. This expectation entails making decisions which are both effective (i.e., they usually produce such provisions and solutions) and collectively binding (i.e., the decisions are made on behalf of the members of the organization and apply to all of them, in principle irrespective of their opinions about such decisions). In a firm or a university or a union I may opt for exit (Hirschman 1970). As a member of a state, I normally want the provision of some public goods and the solution of some collective action problems. Yet I may disagree with some public policies and/or with the procedures through which they are made; I may even find these policies offensive to deeply valued aspects of my identity or interests.

The other pole of the contradiction results from the widely shared belief that it is dangerous to endow individuals with too much power. This danger seems to increase geometrically when these individuals have the authority to make collectively binding decisions which are backed with the supremacy in the control of the means of coercion in an organization from which it is difficult or costly to exit. Even if a given power holder may be trusted not to abuse her position, there is no guarantee that this will not happen in the future. The rational conclusion is that somehow power has to be controlled. Yet the same conclusion holds for whatever solution may be adopted: since none of us can be safely presumed to be angelic altruists, the motivations of those who control the powerful, and the powers that

---

[3] For a discussion of the concept of fair (and decisive) elections see O'Donnell (2001).

must be attached to the former if they will be effective controllers, are also suspect. The old formula *Quis custodiet ipsos custodes?* summarizes this puzzle. In a world in which not everyone is a knave but where not many may be presumed to be truly altruistic and, especially, where no one can be presumed immune to the temptations of power, how can effective controls be established?

This is, obviously, a contradiction: it exists, on one hand, between my desire to live, out of a Hobbesian state of nature, under political arrangements that furnish some basic public goods and collective solutions, and, on the other, my fear of the dangers that lurk behind the great power that must be constituted if such goods and solutions are to be furnished. This is an unsolvable tension between two equally rational desires: one, that those who make decisions which are binding on me do it effectively (i.e., with sufficient decisiveness so as to normally achieve the desired ends) and, another, that there exist sufficient controls on those decision-makers to protect me from outcomes that I may find severely harming to my interests or identity. The joint desire for decisiveness and control is both rational and contradictory.

In respect of this contradiction, there is not—and there never will be—a clear-cut, or stable, or definitive, or fully consensual solution to it. Tyrannies grossly tilt the balance in one direction, while deadlocked regimes tilt it in the other. Many other regimes are placed somewhere between these extremes. Yet none of them has ever achieved a durable equilibrium; rather, these regimes perpetually oscillate between periods when highly decisive leadership and policies are demanded, and periods in which strong barriers against governmental intrusiveness are claimed.[4]

Of course, contemporary democracies have not solved this contradiction, but their institutional design is the most complex and, by and large, the most successful attempt to ameliorate it. In my work quoted at the beginning, I argue that contemporary democracies (or polyarchies) are the complex distillation of three great historical currents, which have combined in various degrees across countries and historical periods. Here I mention quite schematically what these currents mean in terms of the contradiction I am highlighting here.

[4] John Dunn, who phrases this issue as a 'conundrum', puts in different but converging terms: 'Democracy... seeks to provide, if with necessarily imperfect success, at least some degree of remedy for [the hazards derived from political power], short of simply abandoning the practice of public action. Unlike anarchism, it cleaves to the practice of public action because it views the state of nature... as generically far more dangerous than vertical subjection to such authority.' (1999: 229, 331)

1. Democracy At its origins in Athens, the basic idea of democracy is monistic. It does not postulate a sharp division between the public and the private spheres or, at any event, it does not recognize proper entity to the latter, except as endowing some individuals, the (male) citizens, with the time and means for devoting themselves to public life. Democracy is also strongly majoritarian; ultimately what is decided by the majority is effected without impediment from individual or prepolitical rights. This, of course, is dangerous, as the memory of Socrates has attested since then. On the other hand, the very short terms of incumbency (many of them for just a day), the *post-facto* audit of the conduct of many of these incumbents, ostracism, and the ever-present possibility of suffering severe sanctions under the accusation of having proposed decisions contrary to the basic laws of Athens, established some controls against the, in this city-state, highly mistrusted incumbents of positions of public power.[5]

2. Republicanism It establishes a sharp distinction between the private and public spheres, asserting that it is in the latter that the proper flourishing of the human being (once again, male citizens) may be achieved. Virtue is dedicating oneself unselfishly to the public good, without allowing private or factional interests to interfere with this pursuit.[6] As with democracy, republicanism may be dangerous, because it easily leads to elitism and oligarchy: why should those who claim to be virtuous represent, or even listen to, those who are submerged in the pettiness of private pursuits? The tyranny of Savonarola and the cruelty of Robespierre are reminders of this danger. On the other hand, republicanism's insistence on virtuous dedication to the public good and, consequently, the jealous controls of incumbents that it established where this current was stronger, the Italian medieval republics,[7] placed some barriers to the pursuit of private or factional interests from the public sphere.

[5] Elster (1999) discusses these controls; for details see Hansen (1991).

[6] Wood (1992: 104) puts it well: 'According to the republican tradition, man was by nature a political being, a citizen who achieved his greatest moral fulfillment by participating in a self-governing republic.... Liberty was realized when the citizens were virtuous—that is, willing to sacrifice their private interests for the sake of the community.... Public virtue was the sacrifice of private desires and interests for the public interest.'

[7] See Waley (1988) for details, including the fascinating figure of the *Podestá*, arguably the ultimate expression of mistrust toward political power holders.

3. Liberalism Liberalism is the only one of these great currents that is, to a large but not exclusive extent, a direct manifestation of mistrust of political power. Liberalism, like republicanism, postulates a distinction between the public and the private spheres, but it inverts their valence. It is in the manifold activities of the private sphere—beginning, historically, with the freedom of contract and of religious belief—that the best potentialities of the human being may be achieved. The resulting 'private' freedoms (which I will call civil) are seen, as the consequence of some kind of contract, or consensus, or natural law, as previous and/or superior to the public sphere, which is deemed to exist basically for protecting, and eventually nurturing, these rights.

In synthesis, both democracy and republicanism tend toward the pole of high decisiveness. Yet, because those who implanted the historically original versions of these currents profoundly mistrusted those who they endowed with potentially invasive powers, democracy and republicanism established institutional mechanisms —some of them later on adopted by modern democratic constitutions—intended to ameliorate this risk. Most of these mechanisms were horizontal ones, consisting of agencies in the public sphere aimed at controlling or overseeing other agencies or individuals located in the same sphere. This location was consistent with democracy's denial of substantive entity to the private sphere and with republicanism's assertion of the public sphere as the privileged one.

Instead, liberalism tends to the pole of high protection, centered in the private sphere. However, the effective protection of the freedoms cherished by liberalism entails the construction of a strong political power that, among other things, commands important economic resources and establishes a complex system of courts and auxiliary institutions for the adjudication of conflicts over these rights, both between 'private' citizens and the state, and among the former.[8] As a result, one of the distinctive marks of liberalism is its more ambivalent position than democracy and republicanism with respect to the contradiction I am discussing: in order to obtain effective protection of its rights, liberalism, in fact if not in purpose, cannot but endow the state with great, and consequently always threatening, powers.[9]

---

[8] For pertinent argument about the 'cost of rights' and their ultimate dependence on the political process, see Holmes and Sunstein (1999).

[9] The ambiguities of John Locke on this matter are emblematic; see especially Scott (2000) and Zuckert (1996).

Constitution Making

This contradiction and the convenience of achieving some kind of balance was evident to the individuals that faced the historically unique challenge of creating, practically *ex novo*, a political unit that, to further complicate matters, was supposed to be based on the assent of its members. This was the challenge faced by the framers of the Constitution of the United States. Nobody recognized more clearly the contradiction I identified above, and proposed more influential partial solutions, than James Madison in *The Federalist Papers*. In this great collection of writings, one can see the contradiction operating. Madison, at the same time that he was trying to create a functioning political unit, was worried by the fact that '[P]ower is of an encroaching nature and that it ought to be effectually restrained from passing the limits assigned to it' (*The Federalist* No. 48). Instead, Hamilton,[10] albeit also warning against the dangers of encroachment, emphasized that the creation of an effective political unit required a more 'affirmative government' than Madison envisaged. In part because of this tension operating at the core of the thinking of its more influential framers and advocates, the Constitution of the United States is a complex and in some senses contradictory mix of elements of control and of decisiveness. This mix gives the politics of constitutional interpretation its unending vitality and conflictivity. This is also true of all other democratic constitutions, although some of them (such as the unwritten British one, the present French Constitution, and many of the Latin American presidentialisms) tend more than the United States toward the pole of decisiveness, while others (broadly identifiable under Lijphart's category of consensual or consociational democracies (Lijphart 1984)) tend toward the pole of control. However, none of these constitutions has been able to dissolve the underlying contradiction; their continued tilting along time toward one or the other pole is an inherent component of political life. Furthermore, even though at times these matters are debated in highly aggregated terms (e.g., as in recent times, the state vs. the market), normally individual policy preferences vary across issue areas, each of which may move toward the poles of decisiveness or of control quite independently from the others. The impossibility of collectively aggregating preferences across these issue areas is another reason for the unsolvability of this contradiction.

[10] As Hamilton, *The Federalist* No. 70, put it, 'Energy in the executive is a leading character in the definition of good government.'

Institutional Logics

The mistrust of power, especially of power that can muster overwhelming coercion on its behalf, is as old as human society. We saw that already at its origins democracy and republicanism shared this mistrust, and invented several institutional controls. These controls are based on the idea of dividing and, as far as possible, balancing various agencies located at the apex of that 'something' (whether it is called kingdom, empire, republic, or state) that can issue collectively binding decisions and back them with the supremacy of coercion. The idea that division and balance may produce mutual controls among the feared powers is as old as Aristotle and Polybius, but nobody put it better than Madison:

Ambition must be made to counteract ambition. . . . It may be a reflection on human nature that such devices should be necessary to control the abuses of government. But what is government itself but the greatest of all reflections on human nature? . . . In framing a government which is to be administered by men over men, the great difficulty lies in this: you must first enable the government to control the governed; and in the next place oblige it to control itself. . . . This policy of supplying, by opposite and rival interests, the defect of better motives might be traced through the whole system of human affairs, private as well as public. . . . (*The Federalist* No. 51)

Furthermore, by means of a brilliant innovation than run counter to the views of 'the oracle' (*The Federalist* No. 47) Montesquieu and the common sense of the times, Madison devised further 'auxiliary precautions' (*The Federalist* No. 51): since he was persuaded that a sheer separation of powers was not enough guarantee, he advocated that these powers would better control each other if each of them had some jurisdiction over important decisions of the others. Consequently, what this constitution created was not separation of powers but the partial interpenetration of relatively autonomous and balanced powers.[11]

In some of his tracts Madison expresses, rather inconsistently with the assumptions that inspired his institutional design, the hope that anyhow virtuous republicans would govern. But this

[11] On this matter, see Manin (1994); of course, federalism and a bicameral national legislature were other important 'auxiliary precautions' adopted in this constitution. On the important differences between institutional models of mixed government, of separation of powers, and of checks and balances, see the classic book of M. J. C. Vile (1967).

clearly was not the guiding trust of his arguments: it was that it would be extremely unwise to design political institutions ignoring that human beings are likely to abuse the power these institutions confer upon them. But none of these institutional controls prevents a collusion among the relevant powers from running roughshod over their subjects. It is here that liberalism erects other barriers: it asserts there are some rights that no political power may ignore or void, because these rights are superior to and/or precede that power. Truly, political and moral philosophers have offered many ways to justify this claim, and no less often it has been challenged. In spite of these disagreements, constitutionalism, declarations of rights, and judicial or constitutional review embody the purpose of protecting some civil rights from majorities and other collusive or abusive constellations of power. Yet, as the history of Latin America illustrates, however much enshrined in constitutions these protections may be no more than 'parchment barriers' (*The Federalist* No. 48) if courts, and eventually other agencies, would not uphold those rights. History and comparative politics teach us that, even with the barriers that liberalism erected in modern times, there is no ultimate guarantee against the abuse of political power.

Grounding

The Athenians came out with an idea that in their time was completely counterintuitive: political power is not only *for* its subjects but also, and more importantly, *from* them. After the long process of democratization and universalistic assignment of various kinds of rights that I have recounted in another work (O'Donnell 2000) the basic idea of contemporary political democracy is that political power (more precisely, the authority to exercise political power) comes from the citizens, that is, the vast majority of adult individuals that inhabit the territory delimited by a state. Citizens are individuals with rights. These include the right to participate in the processes that lead to incumbency in governmental roles, and at least a minimum set of civil rights (especially of expression, association, access to information, and movement) without which such participation would be at best vicarious. The reasonable effectiveness of these rights is a necessary condition for the existence of democratic political power and of its authority to rule. Consequently, the exercise of this power should be guided—negatively—

by the constraint of not infringing on these rights, and—positively[12]—of fostering their diffusion and enjoyment.

We should note that upholding these rights requires more than legal rules to enact them. It requires the effectiveness of a legal system, a network of legal rules and of legally enabled institutions that, at least in terms of the rights I have mentioned, apply them consistently in the territory of a state. In a democratic *Rechsstaat*, or *Estado Democrático de Derecho* or, more or less equivalently, under a democratic rule of law, nobody is *de legibus solutus*.[13] In plain language, under this kind of situation nobody is above or beyond submitting to the obligations established by the legal system (the constitution of course included).[14] Notice that this is a corollary of the protection of participatory and civil rights; otherwise, there would subsist the serious risk that those in power may void these rights—exactly what those who mistrust power holders hope to prevent.

Balance and Mandated Agencies

The preceding overview entails the construction of successive institutional trenches which were first erected, by democracy and republicanism, within the public sphere and which, under liberalism, were also built, as it were, in some of the most private sites of society—the civil rights I mention above. Due to the partially diverging character of these three currents, and the conflicts and uncertainties that surround the construction of the barriers in each specific case, there is no way their content and consequences may be fully consistent among themselves, even within a single period of a single country. In spite of the resulting ambiguities, a democratic legal system establishes that not only private individuals but also the most powerful, and threatening, powers of the state are

[12] This positive side is disputed by influential authors, prominently Rawls (1993). I include it, however, because even though I cannot substantiate my position here, I am persuaded that these 'neutralist' positions are wrong.

[13] For elaboration see O'Donnell (1999b and 2001), where I argue that the prohibition of *de legibus solutus* is one of the distinctive characteristics of political democracy in relation to all sorts of authoritarian rule.

[14] As Preuss (1996: 24) puts it: 'The quality of constitutions as laws, i.e., as generating the *legal* obligations of the governors, is essential. Only if the bond between governors and the ruled obligates the ruler... and if it cannot be revoked unilaterally by the ruler, is it possible to form a reliable institutional structure of government in which the governed are recognized as the ultimate source of political authority.'

subject to its rules. Contemporary[15] democratic constitutions, following the example of the United States, make these powers relatively autonomous by means of their division and partial inter-penetration, and assign to them jurisdictions that are carefully spe-cified by legal, including constitutional, rules. As noted above, many of the resulting relationships may be conceived as instances, depending on the case, of mutual control or of exchange. These relationships are based on the idea that the jurisdiction of state agencies has lawfully defined limits that they are forbidden to transgress. This idea holds even for the carefully specified in-stances in which, as Madison designed them, the jurisdiction of a given power penetrates the jurisdiction of another one (see also Manin 1994). From these rules results a legally delimited map of the jurisdiction of state institutions, including the three pre-eminent ones, executive, legislative, and judiciary. This is not only a system of mutual controls. It organizes the flow of power and authority in the government and the state, thus normally produc-ing a division of labor among the relevant public institutions, which are therefore enabled to discharge their respective responsi-bilities.[16]

Some of these relationships, however, originate in the view by a given agency that another one has unlawfully transgressed its own jurisdiction, and encroached on the jurisdiction of the former (or a third agency, in some cases). When a situation of this kind is acti-vated, we face a case of *horizontal balance accountability*. I adopt this nomenclature because this kind of horizontal accountability is enacted by some of the powers (executive, legislative, or judiciary) that contemporary democratic constitutions attempt to keep roughly in balance.[17] Originally, in the United States and elsewhere

---

[15] I say 'contemporary' because only after the Second World War continental European constitutions, basically by means of the enactment of various kinds of judicial or constitutional review, cancelled the formal supremacy of the legislature. This way the differences that *in this respect* exist between presidentialist and parliamentary regimes have been significantly mitigated; see Guarnieri and Ped-erzoli (1996), Pasquino (1998), Stone Sweet (1992 and 2000), and Vanberg (1998). After Communism, the Central/Eastern European countries have also adopted various kinds of judicial or constitutional review (see Magalhães 1999 and Schwartz 1993); this is also true of new democracies elsewhere (see Maddex 1995 and Tate and Valloder 1995).

[16] On this positive, enabling aspect of the legally-delimited jurisdiction of state agencies see Holmes (1995) and Waldron (1999).

[17] As noted, with the arguable exception of the United Kingdom, this is gener-ally true of both presidentialist and parliamentary regimes, after the adoption by most of the latter of some form of judicial or constitutional review.

the main fear was of excessive supremacy of the legislature; however, along time, with the growth of the state apparatus it turned out that often the more serious threat consisted of encroachments and corruption by the executive and by non-elected state bureaucrats. In view of these threats, balance HA suffers several limitations. One is that the balance institutions (executive, legislature, and judiciary) tend to act reactively and, consequently, intermittently in front of presumed transgressions by other state institutions. A second limitation is that the actions toward horizontal accountability of balance institutions tend to be very dramatic. These actions may create highly visible and costly conflicts between the supreme state institutions. These conflicts further sharpen when, as in presidentialist regimes, they may involve powers—the executive and legislative—that share electoral legitimacy. Thirdly, the actors in these conflicts are often perceived as mainly motivated by partisan reasons, thus adding to the sharpening and the difficulties of solving the given conflict. Finally, because of their own main functions and consequently of the foci of attention of their leaders, the balance institutions are too blunt an instrument of control for the growing complexity of state agencies and their policies.

The realization of these limitations for the effectiveness of HA led practically everywhere, albeit with varying timing and characteristics, to the addition of agencies of *mandated horizontal accountability*. These are the various agencies (ombudsmen, accounting offices, controllers, *conseils d'Etat, fiscalías, contralorías*, and the like) that are legally assigned to oversee, prevent, discourage, promote the sanctioning, or sanction presumably unlawful actions or omissions of other state agencies, national or subnational. These agencies, unlike the older ones, were invented not so much having in mind overall balances of power but rather specific, but still quite general, risks of encroachment and/or corruption. In principle, the mandated agencies have several advantages over the balance ones. One is that they can be proactive and continuous in their activity. Another is that, by the same token, they can be effective in preventing or deterring unlawful actions by the agencies they oversee. Still another advantage is that they can invoke for their actions criteria that are professional rather than partisan or 'political'. Finally, these agencies can develop capabilities that allow them to examine complex issues of policy. Having said this, I hasten to add that, ideally, mandated agencies should not be conceived as substitutes for the balance institutions—a reasonably working democracy finds in the former a useful complement and reinforcement of the latter. We shall see, on the other hand, that in less than smoothly working democracies, mandated agencies can be important in facilitating and even promoting various kinds of *vertical* accountability.

Before discussing other topics, here I want to emphasize two points. One, the enactment of horizontal accountability by whatever institutional mechanism is entailed by the prohibition of *de legibus solutus*. Two, this prohibition is in turn entailed by a conception of democracy that includes the protection of some basic participatory and civil rights.

A Map

Let me propose an image. It is a space marked by a series of boundaries, or limits, the biggest of which lies between a public and private sphere, as postulated (albeit, as we saw, with different valences) by republicanism and liberalism. Empirically this is a rather fuzzy limit, especially after new patterns of state and social activity have created numerous mixed public–private zones. But in spite of its imprecision this is still an important boundary, as it separates those who can mobilize the collectively binding and ultimately coercive powers of the state from those who hold rights that these powers are prohibited to void. In another part of the map, at the level of the state, we see a series of institutions, including those that concern themselves, whether in a reactive and intermittent or a proactive and continuous way, with issues of HA. Precisely because, as we saw, the balance institutions are designed so as to partially interpenetrate, the idea of legally defined limits is extremely important. Encroaching occurs when a state institution oversteps the limits of its own legally mandated jurisdiction, and invades those of another; redressing encroachment is to restore those limits and eventually punish the transgressors. In still another part of our map, the level of society, there exist the manifold boundaries entailed by the rights of individuals and various kinds of associations. Some of these boundaries are solid, as they consist of rights that are widely respected and, if necessary, upheld by courts. Other boundaries may be weak, because the respective rights are legally or politically problematic or because, as I have argued is the case in some new democracies (O'Donnell 1999b), rights are selectively upheld across various regions and categories of citizens. The strength and actual functioning of all these boundaries, across cases and time, is a major issue that needs research.

Now I come back to an argument that needs emphasizing. For HA to effectively function it is not only necessary that for a given issue a given state agency is legally empowered and willing to act. It is also necessary that there exists a whole network of state agencies, culminating in high courts, committed to preserving and eventually enforcing horizontal accountability, if necessary against the highest powers of the state. Otherwise, the investigations of *auditorías, fiscalías* and the like may feed an angry public opinion but do not reach legally appropriate resolution.[18] As noted, in a democracy a legal system is supposed to be such a *system*, one that 'closes,' in the sense that nobody is exempt from it. This system consists not only of legal rules but also of institutions committed to upholding these rules. Surely the acid test of the existence of this kind of system is if it applies or not in terms of the horizontal accountability of the highest powers of the state.

(Vertical) Societal Accountability

Recently Catalina Smulovitz and Enrique Peruzzotti, have proposed a concept that I find very useful, a type of vertical but non-electoral accountability that they call 'societal'. They define it as follows:

Societal accountability is a non-electoral, yet vertical, mechanism of control of political authorities that rests on the actions of a multiple array of citizens' associations and movements and on the media, action that aim at exposing governmental wrongdoing, bringing new issues to the public agenda, or activating the operation of horizontal agencies. It employs both institutional and non-institutional tools. The activation of legal actions or claims before oversight agencies are examples of institutional resources; social mobilizations and *exposés* illustrates some of the non-institutional ones, [the effectiveness of which] is based on symbolic sanctions. (2000: 8. See also this volume.)

These authors argue persuasively that it would be wrong to limit the concept of vertical accountability to elections. There exist manifold actions, individual and collective, that take place in society at any time between elections. A good part of these actions is aimed at redressing, stopping and/or sanctioning actions, and sometimes omissions, of elected (national or subnational) individuals, as well as non-elected state officers, also national or subnational. Especially

---

[18] See, for example, the impotence of the Ombudsman in Fujimori's Peru, discussed by Kenney (this volume).

in countries where, as in Latin America, *electoral vertical account-ability* functions quite deficiently,[19] the *societal* version of vertical accountability becomes extremely important for the workings and, eventually, even for the survival of a democratic regime.[20]

This concept advances over and usefully elaborates my original remarks (O'Donnell 1999a) about the importance of the linkages between the horizontal and vertical dimensions of accountability. On one hand, an alert and reasonably well-organized society, and a media that does not shy away from reporting cases of encroach-ment and corruption, provide crucial information, support, and political incentives for the often uphill battles that agencies of horizontal accountability may wage against powerful transgres-sors. On the other hand, the perceived availability of this kind of horizontal agency may encourage undertaking actions of vertical societal accountability. These effects, respectively of *stimulation* of horizontal and of *inducement* of vertical societal accountability, are extremely important for understanding the dynamics of demo-cratic politics, especially in countries where, as noted, vertical electoral accountability works quite deficiently. Furthermore, actions of societal accountability—particularly if they are vigorous, sustained, and gain widespread public attention—may send strong signals to politicians wishing to be elected or re-elected.

These various vertical/horizontal interactions are another im-portant frontier for future research. This frontier would remain closed if, as Moreno et al. demonstrate, the vertical dimension of accountability is restricted to the electoral one and if, in addition, horizontal accountability is conceived as a mere 'adjunct' of the electoral. Furthermore, these authors are unduly optimistic about what, even under ideal circumstances, electoral accountability can accomplish. See, for example, '[I]f the accountability of elected offi-cials were working as intended—such that voters could and would punish misdeeds—separate branches of [horizontal, O'D] superin-tendence would be unnecessary' (Moreno et al., this volume). This assertion contradicts the findings of a large and solid literature on

---

[19] For a series of reasons closely related to the party systems as well as to the electoral and party legislation. These reasons are well spelled out, among others, in Mainwaring (1999) and Moreno et al. (this volume).

[20] This importance is worn out by Smulovitz and Peruzzotti (2000 and this volume), as well as by the analyses and the case studies contained in their edited volume (2002). Incidentally, the sections on the United States of Morgenstern and Manzetti in this volume provide interesting evidence on the impact of societal accountability in the history of the United States.

voting, elections, and the aggregation of preferences, including the conclusions reached by Bernard Manin, Adam Przeworski, and Susan Stokes in a recent careful study of these matters:

[T]he conclusion of this analysis must be that citizen's control over politicians is at best highly imperfect in most democracies. Elections are not a sufficient mechanism to insure that governments will do everything they can to maximize citizen's welfare....Yet even if responsibilities are clearly assigned, bad governments can be punished and good ones chosen, voters are well informed about the relations between politicians and special interests, and the rent-seeking behavior of politicians is well scrutinized, elections are just not a sufficient instrument of control over politicians. Governments make thousands of decisions that affect individual welfare; citizens have only one instrument to control these decisions: the vote. One cannot control a thousand targets with one instrument (1999: 50).

It is, precisely, the experience of the deficiencies of electoral accountability that has encouraged the development of both vertical and horizontal accountability.

Linkages and Interactions

It follows from the preceding discussion that all types of accountability are important for the workings of a democratic regime. Among these types, vertical *electoral* accountability has logical priority due to the sheer fact, already noted, that without fair elections and, with them, the possibility of unseating the incumbents in the next round, simply there would not exist, by definition, a democratic regime. But it is mistaken to equate logical priority with pre-eminent factual importance. In the present stage of our knowledge, the only point that I believe may be confidently made is that the more important effects, and the more intriguing ones as a frontier for research, are the ones to be found at the *interactions* among various kinds of accountability.[21]

Of course, too much of a good thing can be bad. For example, excessive horizontal accountability moves the situation toward the pole of deadlock and, consequently, very low decisiveness. But we are in a terrain that may invite simplistic conclusions. Consider what I have called 'delegative democracy' (O'Donnell 1994).

[21] For evidence on the importance of these interactions see Manin, Przewroski and Stokes (1999). For these interactions in relation to the office of the public prosecution in Brazil, see Sadek and Cavalcanti (this volume).

Without entering into the discussions that this concept has generated, I note that a delegative conception and practice of political power is centrally based in the denial of the appropriateness of boundaries among state institutions. For a delegative view, balance and mandated institutions are a tremendous nuisance, impediments placed by the 'formalities' of the legal system to the high decisiveness that delegative rulers claim it is their right and duty to exercise. In turn, authoritarian rulers are more radical than delegative ones: intrinsically hostile to all kinds of accountability, they void the legal rules that promote it and, in addition, they make the effectiveness of civil rights contingent on their *de legibus solutus* expediency. Yet none of this, I want to emphasize, make authoritarian rulers, and even less so delegative ones, omnipotent. Often these rulers find constraints in their power relations with other segments of their regimes and powerful social actors. Yet, in contrast with horizontal accountability, these constraints do not result from the effectiveness of legally enacted rules. The constraints are the result of naked power relationships which may, as in fact they have in not a few cases, lead to severe deadlocks.[22]

In addition to the mutual relationships of stimulus and inducement already noted, another aspect of horizontal accountability provides an important link with its vertical side. As conceived in Athens, if the citizens are the source of the authority of the political power exercised over them, then they have the right to be informed of the decisions of this power. It follows that the decisions of democratic authorities must be public, in the double sense that the rationale and content of these decisions must be 'made public', and that the procedures[23] that lead to these decisions are specified in legal rules that are also publicly available.[24] Truly, no democracy has ever fully complied with this requirement, and even among highly established ones there are important variations in this matter. But the contrast remains with the secrecy with which authoritarian regimes surround many decisions.[25] HA is an important generator of information that becomes publicly available. The relationships among balance institutions generate large flows of

[22] I insist on this observation because, even though I took care to make it explicit in O'Donnell (1994), some readers have interpreted that there I assert that delegative rulers are in all circumstances close to omnipotent.

[23] And, in Athens, the deliberations themselves.

[24] Bobbio (1989) and Garzón Valdés (1993) usefully analyze these and other aspects of the publicness of democracy.

[25] To the point of the absurdity of the 'secret laws' enacted by Stalinist and some military rulers.

this kind of information, because it is legally required and undue secrecy would generate horizontal accountability actions. On their part, some mandated agencies dig into what at times are arcane ambits of the agencies they oversee. Usually this adds a lot of free-floating public information. This information can be utilized by those who are exercising vertical accountability, not only voting but also societal accountability. Little of this information would exist were it not for the functioning of HA. Actually, this availability is a by-product of the functioning of balance and mandated institutions (in general, they are not designed with the purpose of generating this kind of information), but they do provide links that at least potentially invigorate electoral and societal vertical accountability. This increases the 'availability of alternative sources of information' that Robert Dahl correctly lists as one of the central characteristics of polyarchy or political democracy (1989: 120).

A final comment on HA pushes us away from its interactions and into the mysterious but relevant world of non-events. Presumably (but, I take it, very plausibly) no small part of the importance of HA, insofar as it is effective and perceived to be so, lies in the transgressions it prevents or deters. We do not have hard data on this matter, but it stands to reason that the decision function of a would-be transgressor will be heavily influenced by her assessment of the probability of being caught and sanctioned. It may well be that the effectiveness of HA, both balance and mandated, is curvilinear. It works well when very little happens in this matter, because there are few and not serious transgressions; yet it also works well when some agencies bring to the top of the public agenda, and sanction, serious transgressions perpetrated by high state powers.

Some Conclusions

HA is a legally grounded and legally activated interaction between state agencies in view of presumed unlawful actions or omissions (encroachment or corruption). Horizontal accountability, thus, is a small subset of the manifold interactions that state agencies undertake among themselves. Its importance lies not only in the actions it triggers but also in the transgressions it prevents or deters. Conversely, if responsibilities of horizontal accountability exist in the letter of the law but the respective agencies are rendered ineffective by superior powers, the consequence will be not only facilitating transgressions of these powers but also the discrediting of those agencies.

HA does not extend only to national elected officials; its scope includes sub-national elected officials and non-elected members of the state bureaucracies, national and sub-national. Not neglecting the sub-national level of HA seems to me particularly important in countries where the legal system operates rather effectively in some regions but not in others. At all these levels HA is an important component of a democratic regime, per se and because of its linkages, actual and potential, with both electoral and societal vertical accountability. These linkages need much research, among other reasons because they may identify strategic opportunities for improving the presently poor functioning of many democracies. On the other hand, I agree that 'fundamental party and electoral reform is a necessary condition for improving the quality of democracy in the region' (Moreno et al., this volume). But the necessary efforts in this direction should be complemented by no less persistent efforts to solve the serious deficits in HA existing in many new, and some not so new, democratic regimes. Any view that unilaterally asserts the pre-eminence of a single dimension of accountability is not likely to be helpful for the achievement of the goals of democracy-enhancement that the contributors to this volume share.

References

Bobbio, Norberto. 1989. *Democracy and Dictatorship: The Nature and Limits of State Power*. Minneapolis, MN: University of Minnesota Press.

Dahl, Robert. 1989. *Democracy and Its Critics*. New Haven, CT: Yale University Press.

Dunn, John. 1999. 'Situating Democratic Political Accountability'. In Bernard Manin, Adam Przeworski and Susan Stokes, eds., *Democracy, Accountability, and Representation*, pp. 329–51. New York, NY: Cambridge University Press.

Elster, Jon. 1999. 'Accountability in Athenian Politics'. In Bernard Manin, Adam Przeworski and Susan Stokes, eds., *Democracy, Accountability, and Representation*, pp. 253–78. New York, NY: Cambridge University Press.

The Federalist. 1961. *The Federalist Papers: A Collection of Essays Written in Support of the Constitution of the United States, from the Original Text of Alexander Hamilton, James Madison, John Jay*. Roy P. Fairfield, ed. Garden City, NY: Anchor Books.

Garzón Valdes, Ernesto. 1993. 'Acerca de los Conceptos de Publicidad, Opinion Pública, Opinión de la Mayoría y sus Relaciones Recíprocas'. *Doxa* 14: 77–95.

Guarnieri, Carlo and Patrizia Pederzoli. 1996. *La Puissance de Juger. Pouvoir Judiciare et Démocratie*. Paris: Michalon.

Hansen, M. H. 1991. *The Athenian Democracy in the Age of Demosthenes*. Oxford: Oxford University Press.

Hirschman, Albert. 1970. *Exit, Voice, and Loyalty: Responses to Decline in Firms, Organizations, and States*. Cambridge, MA: Harvard University Press.

Holmes, Stephen. 1995. 'Constitutionalism'. In Seymour Martin Lipset, ed., *The Encyclopedia of Democracy*, pp. 299–306. London: Routledge.

Holmes, Stephen and Cass R. Sunstein. 1999. *The Cost of Rights: Why Liberty Depends on Taxes*. New York, NY: W.W. Norton.

Lijphart, Arend. 1984. *Democracies: Patterns of Majoritarian and Consensus Government in Twenty-One Countries*. New Haven, CT: Yale University Press.

Maddex, Robert. 1995. *Constitutions of the World*. Washington DC: Congressional Quarterly Inc.

Magalhães, Pedro. 1999. 'The Politics of Judicial Reform in Eastern Europe'. *Comparative Politics* 32, 1: 43–62.

Mainwaring, Scott. 1999. *Rethinking Party Systems in the Third Wave: The Case of Brazil*. Stanford, CA: Stanford University Press.

Manin, Bernard. 1994. 'Checks, Balances and Boundaries: The Separation of Powers in the Constitutional Debate of 1787'. In Biancamaria Fontana, ed., *The Invention of the Modern Republic*, pp. 27–62. Cambridge, UK: Cambridge University Press.

Manin, Bernard, Adam Przeworski and Susan Stokes 1999. 'Elections and Representation'. In Bernard Manin, Adam Przeworski and Susan Stokes, eds., *Democracy, Accountability, and Representation*, pp. 29–54. New York, NY: Cambridge University Press.

O'Donnell, Guillermo. 1994. 'Delegative Democracy'. *Journal of Democracy* 5, 1: 55–69. First published as Kellogg Institute Working Paper No. 172, 1992.

——. 1999a. 'Horizontal Accountability and New Polyarchies'. In Andreas Schedler, Larry Diamond, and Marc F. Plattner, eds., *The Self-Restraining State: Power and Accountability in New Democracies*, pp. 29–52. Boulder, CO and London: Lynne Rienner. First published as Kellogg Institute Working Paper No. 254, May 1998.

——. 1999b. 'Polyarchies and the (Un)Rule of Law in Latin America'. In Juan Méndez, Guillermo O'Donnell, and Paulo Sérgio Pinheiro, eds., *The (Un)Rule of Law and the Underprivileged in Latin America*, pp. 303–37. Notre Dame, IN: University of Notre Dame Press.

——. 2001. 'Law, Democracy, and Comparative Politics'. *Studies in Comparative International Development* 36, 1 (Spring). Previously published as Kellogg Institute Working Paper No. 274 (April).

O'Donnell, Guillermo. 2002. 'Acerca de varias accountabilities y sus interrelaciones'. In Catalina Smulovitz and Enrique Peruzzotti, eds., *Controlando la Politica. Ciudadanos y Medios en las Nuevas Democracias Latinoamericanas*, pp. 87–102. Buenos Aires: Temas.

Pasquino, Pasquale. 1998. 'Constitutional Adjudication and Democracy. Comparative Perspectives: USA, France, Italy'. *Ratio Juris* 11, 1: 38–50.

Preuss, Ulrich. 1996. 'The Political Meaning of Constitutionalism'. In Richard Bellamy, ed., *Constitutionalism, Democracy, and Sovereignty: American and European Perspectives*, pp. 11–27. Aldershot: Avebury.

Rawls, John. 1993. *Political Liberalism*. New York, NY: Columbia University Press.

Schwartz, Herman. 1993. 'The New East European Constitutional Courts'. In A.E. Dick Howard, ed., *Constitution Making in Eastern Europe*, pp. 163–207. Baltimore, MD: The Johns Hopkins University Press.

Scott, John T. 2000. 'The Sovereignless State and Locke's Language of Obligation'. *American Political Science Review* 94, 3: 547–61.

Smulovitz, Catalina and Enrique Peruzzotti. 2000. 'Societal Accountability in Latin America'. *Journal of Democracy* 11, 4: 147–58.

Stone Sweet, Alec. 1992. *The Birth of Judicial Politics in France: The Constitutional Council in Comparative Perspective*. New York, NY: Oxford University Press.

——. Governing with Judges. 2000. Constitutional Politics in Europe. London: Oxford University Press.

Tate, C. Neal and Torbjorn Valloder, eds. 1995. *The Global Expansion of Judicial Power*. New York, NY: New York University Press.

Vanberg, Georg. 1998. 'Abstract Judicial Review, Legislative Bargaining, and Policy Compromise'. *Journal of Theoretical Politics* 10, 3: 299–326.

Vile, M. J. C. 1967. *Constitutionalism and the Separation of Powers*. Oxford: Clarendon Press.

Waldron, Jeremy. 1999. *Law and Disagreement*. Oxford: Clarendon Press.

Waley, Daniel. 1988. *The Italian City Republics*. London: Longman.

Wood, Gordon S. 1992. 'Democracy and the American Revolution'. In John Dunn, ed., *Democracy: The Unfinished Journey, 508 BC to AD 1993*, pp. 91–106. Oxford: Oxford University Press.

Zuckert, Michael. 1996. *The Natural Rights Republic: Studies on the Foundation of the American Political Tradition*. Notre Dame, IN: University of Notre Dame Press.

Horizontal Accountability:
Concepts and Conflicts

Charles D. Kenney*

Introduction

One of the important contributions Guillermo O'Donnell has made
to recent debates about democracy is the conceptual framework of
vertical and horizontal accountability.[1] According to O'Donnell's initial presentation of this framework, accountability was said to run

not only vertically, making elected officials answerable to the ballot
box, but also horizontally, across a network of relatively autonomous
powers (i.e., other institutions) that can call into question, and eventually

* The original version of this chapter was written for the conference on Insti-
tutions, Accountability, and Democratic Governance in Latin America held at the
Kellogg Institute for International Studies at the University of Notre Dame in
May 2000. An earlier version was presented at the Latin American Studies Associ-
ation meeting in March 2000. David Close, Michael Coppedge, Jonathan Hartlyn,
Scott Mainwaring, Philip Mauceri, Guillermo O'Donnell, Andreas Schedler, and
Chris Welna offered thoughtful comments that enabled me to improve this chap-
ter, although a number of their concerns have not received proper attention here.

[1] I refer here to O'Donnell's writings on delegative democracy, first published in
Spanish in 1991 and then in English in 1992 as a Working Paper of the Kellogg
Institute for International Studies and in 1994 in the *Journal of Democracy*, and
to his article on horizontal accountability published in 1998 in the *Journal of
Democracy*. For further explorations of the theme of horizontal accountability, see
Schedler, Diamond, and Plattner (1999); for studies on the topic of vertical accountability, see Przeworski, Stokes, and Manin (1999). As Robert Pastor (1999)
and Andreas Schedler (1999: 25) point out, there is an important third dimension
of accountability not theorized here, that exercised by the international community. Much of what passes for international relations falls more in the category of
'naked power relationships' than those of accountability relationships governed by
some sort of rule of law. Increasingly, however, governments find themselves engaged in agreements and treaties that form a body of international law within
which accountability relationships may develop.

punish, improper ways of discharging the responsibilities of a given office. (1999a: 165)

Democratization, O'Donnell argued, required not only the strengthening of vertical accountability—which at the time was making great strides in Latin America—but also the building of an institutional network to provide horizontal accountability—something which was famously lacking in Latin America.

Since O'Donnell's initial work, a fruitful debate on the concept of horizontal accountability itself has emerged. In the first part of this chapter, I will take up this debate and attempt to clarify what horizontal accountability is and is not. The main issues I discuss are whether horizontal accountability is best conceived in terms of principal–agent relationships, whether horizontal accountability is the same as checks and balances, whether it requires sanctions, and whether it extends to actions not considered unlawful. The second part of this chapter explores a puzzle related to democratic legitimacy. In recent years, many observers have been surprised and often dismayed by the ability of undemocratic leaders like Fujimori in Peru and Chávez in Venezuela to win critical battles for domestic democratic legitimacy. Why did democratic legitimacy sometimes accrue to these apparently undemocratic leaders? The key to understanding this puzzle, I argue below, lies in recognizing the ways in which vertical and horizontal accountability may come into conflict in modern democracies.

What Horizontal Accountability Is and Is Not

The Concept of Horizontal Accountability

The concept of accountability has long been present in political discourse, but it has generally been used to refer to what O'Donnell calls vertical accountability (citizens holding officials accountable) and less often to what he calls horizontal accountability (officials holding one another accountable). Madison and Hamilton used the terms 'accountable' and 'unaccountable' in the sense of vertical accountability in *The Federalist* Nos. 55 and 70. According to the *Oxford English Dictionary*, the term 'accountability' was first used by Samuel Williams in 1794 when describing the government of the Native Americans living in Vermont. According to Williams, this government had 'no written constitution, or bill of rights; no mutual checks, and balances, accountability and responsibility...' (1794: 140). 'Responsibility' and 'accountability' appear to be roughly synonymous in Williams' usage, and today one may say—as Jon Elster does—that 'accountability', 'responsibility', and 'answerability' are 'near synonymous terms' (1999: 255).

If this is the nature of accountability, what precisely is horizontal accountability? According to O'Donnell,

horizontal accountability...is the existence of state agencies that are legally enabled and empowered, and factually willing and able, to take actions that span from routine oversight to criminal sanctions or impeachment in relation to actions or omissions by other agents or agencies of the state that may be qualified as unlawful. (1999b: 38)

Four aspects of horizontal accountability are specified in O'Donnell's definition:

1. As is the case with vertical accountability, the objects of horizontal accountability are state agents.
2. Unlike vertical accountability, the subjects of horizontal accountability are also state agents.
3. The means of horizontal accountability include oversight, sanctions, and impeachment.
4. The scope of horizontal accountability is limited to actions or omissions qualified as unlawful (including violations of a country's highest law, its constitution).

That horizontal accountability is about controlling the actions of state agents is commonly accepted. The subjects, means, and scope of horizontal accountability are, in contrast, disputed. Before entering into these disputes, I would like to take up two prior questions, namely how horizontal accountability may be understood as a relationship between principals and agents, and how horizontal accountability relates to other forms of governmental self-control, such as legislative checks and balances.

Elster holds that accountability has a 'formal triadic structure: an agent A is accountable *to* a principal B *for* an action X' (1999: 255). This is a useful observation, but one that also may prove misleading, because the relationships at the heart of horizontal accountability often do not align simply with relationships between principals and their agents. When a popularly elected legislature impeaches and removes from office a popularly elected president, both the legislature and the executive may be said to act as agents of the electorate, their principal. In this case, the impeached president can be considered an agent of the legislature only in a tautological sense: if one *defines* accountability relationships as principals holding agents accountable, as Elster does, then the president would perforce be the agent of the legislature when it removes him or her from office. In a more meaningful sense, however, in this case the object of horizontal accountability is the president, the subject of horizontal accountability is the legislature, and neither is an agent of the other. The fact that the president can be held accountable for unlawful acts by the legislature does not change the more basic fact that both the president and the legislature are primarily agents of the electorate. To take another example, if an ombudsman is appointed by an extraordinary majority in congress, which also has the power to remove the ombudsman from office, it might be said that congress is the principal and the ombudsman its agent. When the ombudsman accuses a member of congress of wrongdoing, however, or when that office attempts to hold the military or other government agencies accountable for unlawful behavior, it would be misleading to say that the member of congress or the military have become agents of the ombudsman. Although one could stipulate that all accountability involves principals holding agents accountable, it makes little sense to think of an ombudsman's exercise of horizontal accountability with respect to the military or members of congress in this way. Horizontal accountability, as defined by O'Donnell, is often exercised along lines that do not coincide neatly with those of principal–agent relationships.

A confusion of this kind appears in the contribution to this volume by Moreno, Crisp and Shugart. They agree that the executive and legislature are 'agents of the voters, not one another', but they conclude from this that the two branches are 'therefore not institutionally accountable to one another' (Moreno et al., this volume). Since accountability relationships can only exist between principals and their agents, they reason, and since legislatures and presidents are not agents of one another, the relationship between legislatures and presidents cannot be one of accountability. But surely, as argued in the previous paragraph, legislatures can and do hold presidents accountable, as the impeachment of Presidents Collor (Brazil 1992), Pérez (Venezuela 1993), Samper (Colombia 1996), Bucarám (Ecuador 1997), Clinton (United States 1998), and Cubas (Paraguay 1999), exemplify.[2]

Likewise, Moreno, Crisp, and Shugart's contention that 'the very idea of *horizontal* accountability [is] an oxymoron' (Moreno et al.,

---

[2] Of these six, Bucarám, Collor, Cubas, and Pérez were removed from or resigned the presidency, while Clinton and Samper survived in office. Technically, Bucarám was not impeached, but declared to have vacated the presidency due to mental incapacity, in accordance with Article 100 of the 1996 Ecuadorian Constitution.

this volume) is based on a faulty syllogism. According to their reasoning, all relationships in which one party has the authority to impose sanctions on another are vertical relationships. Accountability relationships, they argue, involve the authority to impose sanctions; therefore accountability relationships are vertical. The problem lies with the major premise: it is not true that relationships involving sanctions are necessarily vertical, for two reasons. First, if 'horizontal' refers to intrastate relations and 'vertical' refers to state–society relations, as in O'Donnell's conceptualization of horizontal accountability, it is evident that relationships involving the authority to impose sanctions may exist between agencies of the state, and are therefore horizontal. Second, it is also not true that all intrastate relations involving the authority to sanction are vertical even in the sense argued by Moreno, Crisp, and Shugart. Despite the authors' contention that 'the legislative majority in a prototypical presidential democracy cannot dismiss the president' (Moreno et al., this volume), in most presidential regimes congress can remove the president from office with either a simple or qualified majority, alone or in conjunction with other institutions, such as the Supreme Court. Although these authors consider the legislature and the president to be on the same level, and therefore insist that the relations between them are those of 'horizontal exchange' and not accountability—except for 'the carrying out of discrete tasks' (Moreno et al., this volume)—the legislature's removal of the president is clearly an accountability relationship involving sanctions. It is not a vertical relationship, either in O'Donnell's sense of state–society relations, or in their own sense of principal–agent relations, because the legislature is not withdrawing a conditional authority that it had delegated when it removes a president from office (see Moreno et al., this volume). Relationships involving sanctions are not necessarily vertical.

This brings up a second source of confusion: the conflation of horizontal accountability with checks and balances. The quest to oblige government to control itself takes many forms, three of which are central to the present discussion.[3] To what Hamilton describes in *The Federalist* No. 9 as 'the regular distribution of

[3] The classic text is Madison's, from *The Federalist* No. 51: 'You must first enable the government to control the governed; and in the next place, oblige it to control itself. A dependence on the people is no doubt the primary control on the government; but experience has taught mankind the necessity of auxiliary precautions.' The goal, then, is for government to control the governed, for the governed to control government, and for the government to control itself. The present discussion concerns itself with the last of these goals.

power into distinct departments' and 'the introduction of legislative balances and checks', we can add what in *The Federalist* Nos.
69, 77, and 79 is discussed mainly in terms of impeachment and
what O'Donnell calls horizontal accountability. The first of these
forms of governmental self-control is a condition for the other two:
without branches and agencies sufficiently distinct from one another with respect to their origin, operation, and survival, there
would be little point in discussing checks and balances or horizontal accountability. As Madison put it, following Jefferson's lead,
'the accumulation of all powers legislative, executive and judiciary
in the same hands... may justly be pronounced the very definition
of tyranny' (*The Federalist* No. 47). Likewise, legislative checks
and balances and horizontal accountability are a condition for the
effective separation of powers: without such mechanisms, the diverse agencies of government would be unable to defend their
autonomy against encroachment, as Madison explains in *The
Federalist* No. 51. The second form of governmental self-control,
checks and balances, involves power-sharing by the distinct agencies of government. Legislative checks and balances refer to the
means by which different parts of government are constrained in
setting and enacting policy by being forced to share authority over
legislation and appointment to offices with other parts of government. Horizontal accountability entails a third dimension of governmental self-control, in which some members of a government's
distinct branches and agencies are liable to being sanctioned by
other state actors. Horizontal accountability is thus distinct from
checks and balances, which, though crucially important controls
on power, are not exercises of accountability at all. When a president vetoes legislation or a congress refuses to confirm an appointment, no agents or agencies are being held accountable for any act.
Horizontal accountability, therefore, is best understood as part of a
broader category of controls government places on itself, and
should not be confused with the separation of powers or legislative
checks and balances.[4]

Accountability between Agencies of the State

We can now take up the discussion of the subjects, means, and
scope of horizontal accountability. If we are agreed that the objects

[4] In an earlier work (Kenney 1998) and in an earlier draft of this chapter I did
not clearly distinguish horizontal accountability from the concept of checks and
balances. O'Donnell's definition is itself clear enough, but often his readers—
myself included—are insufficiently attentive to the parameters he sets out.

of horizontal accountability are state agents, is it necessary that subjects of horizontal accountability be limited to state agents as well? Philip Schmitter has argued that 'non-state actors—media organizations, party secretariats, trade union confederations, business peak associations, lawyers' guilds, mass social movements, even large capitalist firms' should be included among those capable of exercising horizontal accountability (Schmitter 1999: 60).[5] O'Donnell's response to Schmitter clarifies the issue: the horizontal and vertical planes in his conceptualization of accountability correspond to the distinction between state and society (O'Donnell 1999c: 68). Vertical accountability is exercised by societal actors with respect to state actors, and horizontal accountability is exercised within the state by different state agencies. The accountability exercised by non-state actors described by Schmitter—and more recently by Catalina Smulovitz and Enrique Peruzzotti (2000)—is consequently conceived of in O'Donnell's scheme as a form of vertical, not horizontal, accountability (see Figure 3.1).

Furthermore, if political and legal sanctions are central to the concept of horizontal accountability—as I will argue below—it becomes clearer why only agencies of the state may exercise horizontal accountability. Schmitter suggests that non-state actors could 'not only denounce the infractions of officials but even bring appropriate sanctions to bear on them' (Schmitter 1999: 60). Sanctions, however, whether of the legal variety or those involving removal from office, are the exclusive prerogative of state agencies—unless we move outside the province of institutional relationships and into the realm of raw power confrontations. Criminal and civil punishments are the province of the courts, and the removal of an office-holder from office prior to the expiration of the office-holder's term can be effected only by other office-holders. The only exception to this is the recall election, and then removal from office becomes a form of vertical accountability, not horizontal. Non-state actors cannot exercise that horizontal accountability in which sanctions play a necessary role.

A final clarification is in order concerning state agencies as the subjects and objects of horizontal accountability. In most organizations, leaders may sanction and dismiss subordinates for reasons that have nothing to do with unlawful behavior or political differences. This is also true of agencies within the state. These

---

[5] In addition to the points discussed here, see also the comments offered by Richard Sklar (1999) and Marc Plattner (1999), as well as the response by O'Donnell (1999c).

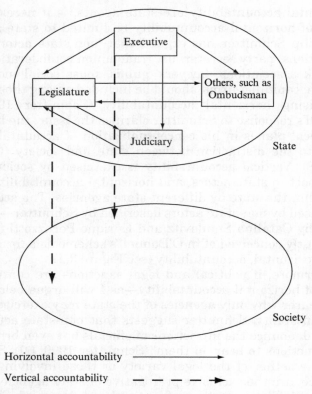

FIG. 3.1. *Horizontal and vertical accountability relationships*

relations might be mistaken for examples of horizontal accountability under O'Donnell's definition since they take place within the state, not between society and the state. However, horizontal accountability focuses primarily on accountability relationships between agencies, not within them, and according to O'Donnell's definition such intra-agency relationships do not fall under the concept of horizontal accountability.

Horizontal Accountability and Sanctions

Does horizontal accountability require the capacity to sanction? This is a second disputed aspect of O'Donnell's definition of horizontal accountability. Andreas Schedler (1999) has raised questions about the centrality of sanctions in the concept of horizontal accountability, and in the concept of accountability more generally.

Schedler argues that the concept of accountability contains two irreducible dimensions, those of enforcement and answerability (Schedler 1999: 14). Noting that accountability is defined by some in terms of answerability, he holds that answerability implies the requirement that agents both inform about and explain their actions, and that accountability implies something more than just information and explanation: it connotes the ability to punish unsatisfactory behavior. This would seem to place the capacity to sanction at the heart of horizontal accountability. Schedler goes on to argue, however, that in some cases 'accountability may be divorced from sanctions... without necessarily creating "diminished subtypes" as a result' (18).

In contrast to Schedler, I would argue that the capacity for sanction is essential to the concept of accountability, and that accountability without sanctions is indeed a diminished form of accountability. Schedler distinguishes between enforcement and answerability, presenting the latter as if it were limited to information and explanations. I think this distinction is inaccurate. Answerability is not just a matter of information and explanation, but itself connotes the capacity to punish. If I am answerable to someone, that person has some power with respect to me that can be exercised in the form of sanction under certain circumstances.[6] Answerability and accountability are near synonyms: to be accountable/answerable means that someone else has the power to sanction you. Even if answerability were conceived as simply the obligation to provide information and explanations, this too would require the capacity for sanction. The obligation of A to provide information and explanations to B may be distinguished analytically from the capacity of B to sanction A, but the fact is that the former depends on the latter—without sanctions, there is no obligation.

So understood, the capacity to sanction is an essential dimension of accountability, without which accountability exists only in a limited, truncated form. Schedler is ambivalent on this point. He

[6] According to the *Oxford English Dictionary* the primary meaning of 'answerable', one that dates from the sixteenth century, is 'liable to answer to a charge' and 'liable to be called to account; under legal or moral obligation; responsible, accountable'. The original sense of 'answer' is 'to make a statement in reply to a legal charge; to meet a charge of any kind; to be liable to do so, or to suffer the consequences, to atone, pay the penalty'. The word 'answerability' is not found in the *Oxford English Dictionary*, but it seems clear from the above that answerability should be understood as directly tied to enforcement, rather than as a separate matter of information and explanation.

recognizes that 'academic writers are often quite emphatic in stating that the capacity to punish forms an integral part of political accountability' (Schedler 1999: 16), but he argues that accountability without sanctions—such as can be found in central banks and in the experiences of truth commissions in Chile and South Africa—is not a 'diminished subtype' (17–18). Yet these are clearly instances of limited, diminished forms of accountability. Chile's truth commission was limited to describing what happened to the victims of the Pinochet regime, without identifying or punishing those responsible, while in South Africa those responsible for human rights violations were identified and their actions publicized, but they were not otherwise punished for actions they confessed. (This is not an argument about the political and moral character of these commissions, but about the degree of accountability exercised.) That these are limited, diminished forms of accountability seems apparent from what Schedler himself writes: 'exercises of accountability that expose misdeeds but do not impose material consequences will usually appear as weak, toothless, "diminished" forms of accountability' (15–16). In this sense, I think that he is closest to the mark when he writes 'unless there is some punishment for demonstrated abuses of authority, there is no rule of law and no accountability' (17).

For O'Donnell, the sanctions inherent in horizontal accountability include the capacity to remove someone from office and to apply civil and criminal penalties. Publicity can contribute powerfully to accountability, especially where information about misdeeds has been concealed, but accountability itself requires penalties beyond publicity—at the very least the capacity to remove an office-holder from office. Without political or legal sanctions, publicity can remain at the level of mere allegations that the powerful often find ways to manage.

A case in point is that of Vladimiro Montesinos, Fujimori's powerful de facto intelligence chief for the last decade in Peru. Many of Montesinos' alleged misdeeds were widely publicized during the 1990s, but while he remained in control of the agencies that were designed to provide horizontal accountability, his impunity was guaranteed and his power was scarcely affected. Even after apparently irrefutable evidence of corruption emerged with the airing of a video in September 2000 that showed him bribing a congressman-elect, the attorney general's office found that no crime had been committed. According to the prosecutor, since Montesinos was using his own money, no misuse of *public* funds had taken place, and since the congressman had not yet taken office at the time of the bribe, no bribery of a *public* official had occurred. Case dismissed. Subsequent events undermined Montesinos' impunity, but the point is clear: publicity cannot substitute for sanctions.

The question about the role of sanctions also points to the importance of O'Donnell's (1999a: 165) insistence on the need for a 'network of relatively autonomous powers' within the state for the exercise of horizontal accountability:

An important but seldom noticed point is that if these agencies are to be effective, they very rarely can operate in isolation. They can shake public opinion with their proceedings, but normally their ultimate effectiveness depends on decisions by courts (or eventually by legislatures willing to consider impeachment), especially in cases that are salient and/or involve highly placed officials. Effective horizontal accountability is not the product of isolated agencies but of networks of agencies that include at their top—because that is where a constitutional legal system 'closes' by means of ultimate decisions—courts (including the highest ones) committed to such accountability. (O'Donnell 1999b: 39)

Horizontal accountability depends on a network of state agencies, but this does not mean that all such agencies must be located along a vertical chain of command. When children play 'rock, scissors, paper', with each element beating the next in an intransitive chain of relationships, what is essential is not hierarchy but a network of accountability relationships that leaves no agency unaccountable. Agencies that lack the power to apply sanctions directly may yet play key roles in providing horizontal accountability within such a network. When the network breaks down, however, these agencies will be able to exercise only limited, diminished forms of horizontal accountability.

This point is well illustrated by the experience of Peru's ombudsman's office (Defensoría del Pueblo) during President Fujimori's second term in office. Created by the 1993 Constitution, the ombudsman's office began to function only in 1996 and quickly became almost the only source of horizontal accountability within the Peruvian State. This was true because the executive controlled all of the other institutions that should have provided horizontal accountability within the State. By means of its legislative majority, the executive came to control the judiciary, the constitutional tribunal, the attorney general, and the comptroller. The ombudsman's office escaped executive control via the legislature largely because a super-majority of two-thirds of congress was required both to name and to remove the ombudsman from office. In addition to its relative immunity from executive control, the ombudsman's willingness and ability to exercise a degree of horizontal accountability was due both to the quality of its leadership and to the support—both in terms of material resources and public backing—given by a number of foreign governments, including the United States. The ombudsman's office became a vigorous and widely respected defender of citizens' rights and a thorn in the side of the Fujimori administration. At the same time, Peru's ombudsman's office constituted but an island in a truncated network of horizontal accountability, and—without underestimating the political significance of its actions—the accountability it exercised was limited. The ombudsman could investigate and publicize alleged violations of citizen's rights, but it was the attorney general's office and the judiciary that were in the end responsible for further investigating and acting on the allegations presented by the ombudsman. In other words, the accountability exercised by the ombudsman's office was a diminished, limited form of horizontal accountability, because the other powers on which accountability depended often failed to act.

Horizontal Accountability and Unlawfulness

A third disputed aspect of O'Donnell's definition is the scope of horizontal accountability. Schmitter argues that horizontal accountability should be construed so as to 'hold rulers accountable for the political and not just legal consequences of their behavior in office' (1999: 60). Under what circumstances might state agencies exercise horizontal accountability for actions that are not unlawful, but only impolitic? Certainly, legal sanctions would be inappropriate in such cases. Although it is often difficult to disentangle personal and political motives from arguments over the lawfulness of acts and omissions, the imposition of legal sanctions without evidence of illegality would itself be illegal.

The question of political sanctions is less clear. O'Donnell's unlawfulness requirement works well within the framework of presidential regimes, in which the survival of office-holders in each branch of government is politically independent of the other branches, and impeachment requires allegations of unlawful behavior. When we consider parliamentary regimes, however, or regimes such as Peru's in which ministers can be constitutionally censured and removed from office by the legislature for purely political reasons, we are left with a conceptual gap.[7] In these cases, agents of the state are empowered to politically sanction other agents of the state for actions or omissions that are not qualified as unlawful. Clearly, these are accountability relationships and not power-sharing checks and balances. Clearly too, they are horizontal relationships within the state, not vertical relationships between society and state. In other words, they meet all the requirements for O'Donnell's definition of horizontal accountability, save one—they need not be responses to allegedly unlawful acts and omissions.

We are faced, then, with a choice: either we broaden O'Donnell's definition of horizontal accountability to include some relationships in which one state agent holds another state agent accountable for acts that are not alleged to be unlawful, or we hold on to O'Donnell's unlawfulness requirement and are left with a set of accountability relationships that fall outside both the categories of vertical and of horizontal accountability. Given the importance of lawfulness in O'Donnell's theoretical work on democracy and the rule of law, the stipulation that horizontal accountability be always a response to improper and unlawful behavior cannot be set aside lightly. In parliamentary regimes, however, it makes sense to relax this requirement and include parliaments holding ministers politically accountable within the concept of horizontal accountability. This move allows us to restate the unlawfulness requirement in terms of lawfulness: horizontal accountability involves state actors or agencies willing and able to sanction other state actors and agencies for their acts and omissions, in accordance with the law and the constitution. For presidential regimes, this definition denotes the same set of cases as O'Donnell's definition, since allegations of unlawfulness are usually required in such regimes for the application of sanctions. For parliamentary regimes, however, this definition would also denote cases in which state agents are held accountable for actions that are politically objectionable, but not illegal, as long as the authority to apply sanctions in such cases is recognized as conforming to the law and the constitution.

---

[7] This problem also arises where legislatures can remove presidents from office for mental, moral, or physical incapacity, without alleging unlawful actions. As noted above, the Ecuadorian Legislature used such a measure to remove President Bucarám from office in 1997, and similar provisions exist in a number of Latin American constitutions.

To summarize, then, horizontal accountability shares with other forms of accountability—such as vertical accountability—the idea that some actors may sanction other actors for their acts and omissions. Horizontal accountability shares with other kinds of governmental self-controls—such as legislative checks and balances—the idea that these are intrastate and interagency relationships designed to constrain the exercise of power. For O'Donnell, horizontal accountability's specific difference is that it takes place only with respect to behavior regarded as unlawful, but I argue that this need apply only to purely presidential regimes. In regimes that legally empower some state agents to sanction other state agents for actions that are not unlawful, such sanctions would also form part of the exercise of horizontal accountability.

Accountability, Democracy's Multiple Origins, and the Battle for Democratic Legitimacy

Three Traditions: Democratic, Republican, and Liberal

O'Donnell's (1999b) discussion of horizontal accountability is cast within a broader theoretical construct that emphasizes the importance of distinguishing and recognizing the tension between the democratic, republican and liberal traditions that intertwine in modern representative democracy.[8] The core of the democratic tradition is rule by the people. In the city-states of Ancient Greece, democracy entailed the idea that citizens participate directly in ruling and in being ruled in turn, with the majority of citizens gathered in assembly directly making some of the most important decisions affecting the whole. As O'Donnell points out in his contribution to this volume, this democratic tradition is both monistic and strongly majoritarian. Transformed from direct popular rule to rule through representatives, the democratic tradition now emphasizes the idea that 'citizens can exercise their participatory right to choose who is going to rule them for some time, and they can freely express their opinions and demands' (O'Donnell 1999b: 30–1). (See Figure 3.2.)

The core of the republican tradition is the idea of rule in the public interest. As O'Donnell puts it, the republican tradition

---

[8] For another view of democracy as the confluence of democratic, republican, and liberal traditions, see Lakoff (1996).

	Democratic	Republican	Liberal
Nature of rule	Rule by the people —in practice, the majority —today, through representatives	Rule in the public interest —emphasizes the difference between public and private interests —institutional design and moral education used to control corruption of power	Rule limited by rights —some rights are seen as inalienable —the purpose of government is to protect rights.
Role of vertical accountability	Vertical accountability of officals to the citizens is essential	Vertical accountability is not strictly speaking necessary	Vertical accountability is not strictly speaking necessary
Role of horizontal accountability	Horizontal accountability is less centrally important, except to prevent undermining of vertical accountability	Horizontal accountability is central to controlling power and its corruption	Horizontal accountability is central to protecting rights

Fig. 3.2. *Three traditions intertwined in modern democracy*

focuses on 'the idea that the discharge of public duties is an ennobling activity that demands careful subjection to the law and devoted service to the public interest, even at the expense of sacrificing the private interests of the officials (1999b: 31). Corruption, understood as public rule for private interests, is a central problem to be fought with careful institutional design and moral education of citizens. Finally, the liberal tradition's central theme is that rule must be limited by rights, the most important of which are inalienable. In O'Donnell's words, the liberal tradition brings to modern representative democracy 'the idea that there are some rights that should not be encroached upon by any power, including the state' (31).

As O'Donnell explains, these traditions are in many ways compatible, but an attention to vertical and horizontal accountability helps illustrate the ways in which they may conflict with one another. Vertical accountability—the idea that those who govern are chosen by and can be removed from office by those who are governed—is essential to the democratic tradition, for example, but is not strictly necessary in the republican and liberal traditions.[9] Horizontal accountability, on the other hand, tends to be supported by the republican and liberal traditions due to their distrust of political power, while the democratic principle can be hostile to horizontal accountability when this appears to wrest authority from the sovereign decisions of the people. At one level, the republican tradition might also be thought to be hostile to horizontal accountability. As O'Donnell puts it, 'why should those who are better, or more virtuous than the rest, be prevented from governing for the sake of the common good?' (1999b: 33) On the whole, however, the republican tradition is much more embracing of horizontal accountability than it is hostile, because its central concern with civic virtue entails a view of citizens and leaders as easily corruptible.

The Consequences of Conflict

Understanding the ways in which these traditions can conflict in modern democracies can help us understand more fully the tasks and challenges of democratization today. Take, for example, O'Donnell's analysis of what he calls delegative democracy. He coined the term 'delegative democracy' to denote a type of polyarchy in which vertical accountability is present, but in which horizontal accountability is extremely weak or absent. Representative democracy, in contrast, is said to be a polyarchy in which both vertical and horizontal accountability are present (1999a).[10]

[9] To what extent vertical accountability is actually exercised is a separate question. On this point, see Przeworski, Stokes, and Manin (1999).

[10] One might amend O'Donnell's description of delegative democracy to specify that such regimes lack not only horizontal accountability, but they are also lacking other forms of governmental self-control. In O'Donnell's view, delegative democracy is characterized not only by certain institutional relationships, but also by a style of leadership linked to those relationships. In his words, 'Delegative democracies rest on the premise that whoever wins election to the presidency is thereby entitled to govern as he or she sees fit, constrained only by the hard facts of existing power relations and by a constitutionally limited term of office. The presi-

Highlighting the potential of conflict between modern democracy's constitutive traditions, O'Donnell holds that delegative democracy 'is more democratic, but less liberal [and, as he makes clear in a subsequent passage, less republican], than representative democracy' (1999a: 164). This statement is easily misunderstood. Delegative democracies are by definition polyarchies—regimes in which inclusive and competitive elections for the most important offices are held under conditions of broad respect for freedom of association, expression and access to information (Dahl 1989). If a regime does not qualify as a polyarchy, it is not a delegative democracy. This marks an important difference between O'Donnell's concept of delegative democracy and Fareed Zakaria's discussion of 'illiberal democracy' (1997). Zakaria focuses on regimes with competitive elections, but which do not necessarily qualify as polyarchies due to their lack of respect for fundamental liberties of expression, association and information, while O'Donnell's delegative democracies must by definition be polyarchies.

In what sense might delegative democracy be 'more democratic' than representative democracy? As noted above, the core principle of democracy is rule by the people. O'Donnell emphasizes the idea that delegative democracy is strongly majoritarian (1999a: 164), and it is in this narrow and original sense that delegative democracy may be said to be more democratic than representative democracy. In regimes where both vertical and horizontal accountability are strongly effective, democracy's majoritarian impulse is constrained by horizontal accountability, and, one might add, by other forms of governmental self-control.

Democratic Caudillos?

The conflict between the democratic, republican, and liberal traditions is also important in understanding why leaders such as

dent is taken to be the embodiment of the nation and the main custodian and definer of its interests. The policies of his government need bear no resemblance to the promises of his campaign—has not the president been authorized to govern as he (or she) thinks best? In this view, other institutions—courts and legislatures, for instance—are nuisances ... a mere impediment to the full authority that the president has been delegated to exercise' (O'Donnell 1999a: 164). There remains the empirical question of just which regimes qualify as delegative, a question that hinges in large part on the operationalization of the concept of horizontal accountability. It should be recalled that the concept of delegative democracy does not entail the existence of an all-powerful executive, but of an executive that experiences relatively little constraint from the agencies of horizontal accountability and constitutionally prescribed checks and balances.

Fujimori in Peru and Chávez in Venezuela have not only been applauded as caudillos, but have also been able to present themselves—and be perceived by many—as more democratic than their predecessors. For those who see these leaders as the antithesis of democracy—as elected dictators dedicated to subverting the institutional basis for democracy—it may be difficult to understand why many citizens have perceived them as democratizing leaders whose first order of business was the dismantling of corrupt populist or partyarchic oligarchies.

The high level of democratic legitimacy accorded these leaders by their citizens is critical to understanding their success. Undoubtedly, this democratic legitimacy mixes in complex ways with more authoritarian–charismatic sources of legitimacy. But what interests me here is that in the very act of subverting those institutions—legislature, judiciary, constitution—that some see as the *sine qua non* of democracy, these leaders are often seen as more democratic than the institutions they have undermined. One way of understanding this is to see that leaders like Fujimori and Chávez are claiming legitimacy as democrats in the narrow, majoritarian, sense with less concern for democracy's republican and liberal dimensions. They can frequently demonstrate that their anti-institutional actions have the support of a large majority of the population, and argue that this makes their actions democratic in the primary sense of 'rule by the many'. It is as if the legitimacy derived from vertical accountability—with its roots deep in the democratic tradition—were at war with institutions of horizontal accountability whose roots are more republican and liberal than democratic. One dimension of democracy overcomes another, all in the name of democracy. This is one reason why those who defend institutions of horizontal accountability often have such difficulty. The institutions they hold to be essential for modern representative democracy are overwhelmed by an executive armed with a discourse that is more democratic, in the majoritarian sense of the word, than the republican and liberal arguments on which these institutions rest. These leaders call to mind Giovanni Sartori's observation that 'democracy still has foes; but it is now best evaded in its own name and by means of its own name' (1987: 4).

The Republican Argument

The new caudillos' majoritarian support constitutes their strongest card in the battle for democratic legitimacy, but it is not the only one. Another reason for the success of such leaders is that, surprisingly, their actions are also presented and perceived by many as consistent with the republican and liberal dimensions of democracy. The minority's cry that the new caudillo is a threat to the institutions of democracy is overwhelmed in the public forum by the caudillos' argument that the primary threat to democracy comes from the fact that its public institutions have fallen under the control of private interests. These private interests vary, but in the case of the legislature they include the interests of politicians who pursue ends of a purely private nature (corruption) and ends that favour the political 'class' generally, and their own party specifically. In some cases, the only interests politicians appear to serve beyond their own are the private interests of business elites, both national and foreign. Judges and other judicial personnel are widely perceived to serve a combination of their own private interests (corruption), the private interests of those who corrupt them (usually the economically powerful), and in some cases the particular interests of those political parties with whom they are aligned or that guarantee them impunity. Despite much rhetoric to the contrary, what is absent in each case is the public's perception that these institutions serve the public interest in any meaningful way. This perception is especially strong in highly unequal societies in which the immense majority of citizens feel that their interests are rarely, if ever, represented or defended. Where private interests are perceived to have hijacked these public institutions, democracy is fatally undermined, and the way is open for leaders such as Fujimori and Chávez to 'save' democracy by radically reforming its institutions.

The new caudillos—who resist any exercise of horizontal accountability tending to limit their freedom of action—nonetheless present themselves as agents of accountability confronting the corruption of unaccountable legislative and judicial institutions and political parties. In addition, these presidents present the attempts of the legislatures and judiciaries to hold them accountable as nothing more than the actions of private, often party, interests attempting to resist those who act to defend public interests. In doing so they claim not only the moral higher ground, but also the democratic legitimacy accruing to those who both enjoy majority support and who promise to rescue the institutions of modern representative democracy from private interests and return them to the service of the public interest.

The democratic legitimacy thus gained by these caudillos may not endure, but it is critical to their initial success in overwhelming the institutions of accountability. For the defenders of horizontal accountability to win the battle for democratic legitimacy, it is first necessary that they recognize the sources of their illegitimacy in the eyes of many citizens, so that they might act to gain the legitimacy necessary to sustain themselves in a conflict with the executive. One critical aspect (that calls us back to the conceptual discussion earlier in this chapter) is the distinction between politically objectionable actions and those that are unlawful. To the extent that agents of horizontal accountability attempt to check lawful actions by presenting them as illicit or unconstitutional, they end up undermining the legitimacy that flows from the proper exercise of their duties. In presidential regimes, at least, the more the exercise of horizontal accountability appears to be nothing but a reflection of personal or partisan interests, the less legitimate it will appear.

Finally, democratic legitimacy accrues to caudillos like Fujimori and Chávez to the extent that they are able to avoid the appearance of being unambiguously repressive of liberal rights to property, free expression, and assembly. Never paragons of liberal rights, they nonetheless must avoid the wholesale repression common to most dictatorships if they are not to forfeit an important piece of this valuable democratic legitimacy. If these freedoms do become significantly restricted and if this becomes widely known, this source of democratic legitimacy will be eroded and eventually lost.

Conclusions

I have made two points in these reflections on horizontal accountability in Latin America. I first argued for the appropriateness of a definition of horizontal accountability in which the agents of accountability are limited to those within the state (and not actors outside the state), in which the means of accountability include the application of sanctions (and not just publicity), and in which the scope of accountability is generally limited to actions or omissions that are unlawful, but which in some systems may include actions that are not unlawful.

I then explored the ways in which an attention to the democratic, republican, and liberal dimensions of modern representative democracy helps us understand the initial success of leaders like Fujimori in Peru and Chávez in Venezuela. These contemporary caudillos often win the battle for democratic legitimacy at critical moments because their evidently massive public support constitutes a democratic trump of their more republican opposition and because those who raise the republican banner of horizontal accountability have themselves often lost even the republican bases for legitimacy.

References

Dahl, R. A. 1989. *Democracy and its Critics*. New Haven, CT: Yale University Press.

Elster, J. 1999. 'Accountability in Athenian Politics'. In A. Przeworski, S. Stokes and B. Manin, eds., *Democracy, Accountability, and Representation*, pp. 253–78. Cambridge: Cambridge University Press.

The Federalist. 1990. *The Federalist: A Collection of Essays Written in Favor of the New Constitution As Agreed Upon By the Federal Convention, September 17, 1787, by Alexander Hamilton, John Jay, James Madison*. George W. Carey and James McClellan, eds. Dubuque, IA: Kendall/Hunt Publishing Company.

Kenney, C. D. 1998. 'Institutionalized Instability? Questions for Democracy from Peru, 1980–1992'. Ph.D. dissertation, University of Notre Dame.

Lakoff, S. 1996. *Democracy: History, Theory, Practice*. Boulder, CO: Westview Press.

O'Donnell, G. 1999a. 'Delegative Democracy'. In *Counterpoints: Selected Essays on Authoritarianism and Democratization*, pp. 159–74. Notre Dame: University of Notre Dame Press.

——. 1999b. 'Horizontal Accountability in New Democracies'. In A. Schedler, L. Diamond and M. F. Plattner, eds., *The Self-Restraining State: Power and Accountability in New Democracies*, pp. 29–51. Boulder, CO: Lynne Rienner Publishers.

——. 1999c. 'A Response to my Commentators'. In A. Schedler, L. Diamond and M. F. Plattner, eds., *The Self-Restraining State: Power and Accountability in New Democracies*, pp. 68–71. Boulder, CO: Lynne Rienner Publishers.

Pastor, R. A. 1999. 'The Third Dimension of Accountability: The International Community in National Elections'. In A. Schedler, L. Diamond and M. F. Plattner, eds., *The Self-Restraining State: Power and Accountability in New Democracies*, pp. 123–42. Boulder, CO: Lynne Rienner Publishers.

Plattner, M. 1999. 'Traditions of Accountability'. In A. Schedler, L. Diamond and M. F. Plattner, eds., *The Self-Restraining State: Power and Accountability in New Democracies*, pp. 63–7. Boulder, CO: Lynne Rienner Publishers.

Przeworski, A., S. Stokes, and B. Manin, eds. 1999. *Democracy, Accountability, and Representation*. Cambridge: Cambridge University Press.

Sartori, G. 1987. *The Theory of Democracy Revisited*. Chatham: Chatham House Publishers.

Schedler, A. 1999. 'Conceptualizing Accountability'. In A. Schedler, L. Diamond and M. F. Plattner, eds., *The Self-Restraining State: Power and Accountability in New Democracies*, pp. 13–28. Boulder, CO: Lynne Rienner Publishers.

Schedler, A., L. Diamond and M. F. Plattner, eds. 1999. *The Self-Restraining State: Power and Accountability in New Democracies*. Boulder, CO: Lynne Rienner Publishers.

Schmitter, P. 1999. 'The Limits of Horizontal Accountability'. In A. Schedler, L. Diamond and M. F. Plattner, eds., *The Self-Restraining State: Power and Accountability in New Democracies*, pp. 59–62. Boulder, CO: Lynne Rienner Publishers.

Sklar, R. 1999. 'Democracy and Constitutionalism'. In A. Schedler, L. Diamond and M. F. Plattner, eds., *The Self-Restraining State: Power and Accountability in New Democracies*, pp. 53–8. Boulder, CO: Lynne Rienner Publishers.

Smulovitz, C. and E. Peruzzotti. 2000. 'Societal Accountability in Latin America'. *Journal of Democracy* 11, 4: 147–58.

Williams, S. 1794. *The Natural and Civil History of Vermont*. Walpole, Newhampshire: Isaiah Thomas and David Carlisle.

Zakaria, F. 1997. 'The Rise of Illiberal Democracy'. *Foreign Affairs* 76, 6: 22–43.

PART II

Legislatures, Executives, and Oversight Agencies

4

The Accountability Deficit
in Latin America

Erika Moreno
Brian F. Crisp
Matthew Soberg Shugart

As a result of much human sacrifice, democracy made a comeback in Latin America in the 1980s and 1990s, and scholars turned their attention to the explanations for these transitions from authoritarianism. More than a decade has passed since most of the transitions and now the primary focus of most research on Latin American democracy is on the illusive concept of its 'quality'. Even casual observation was sufficient to recognize that the re-establishment of elections guaranteed neither decision-makers responsive to popular will nor unfettered political rights and civil liberties. Unpopular economic policies, striking levels of corruption, recurring constitutional crises, ongoing civil unrest (often violent), and popular sympathy for coup attempts highlighted the level of disjunction between politicians and their citizenry.

Guillermo O'Donnell (1994) characterized these less than satisfying regimes as 'delegative democracies'—as opposed to more liberal 'representative democracies'. While evocative and intuitive, the term proved complex, defying parsimonious definition or systematic operationalization. In an effort to clarify the exact nature of the shortcomings, more recently O'Donnell (1999) has argued that liberal, representative relationships fail (or delegative democracy results) because there is a lack of 'horizontal accountability', defined as:

the existence of state agencies that are legally enabled and empowered and factually willing and able to take actions that span from routine oversight to minimal sanctions or impeachment in relation to actions or omissions by other agents or agencies of the state that may be qualified as unlawful (38).

The concept of 'horizontal accountability' has spawned a considerable commentary, redefinition, and criticism—some of which is on display in the various chapters of this volume. We shall argue below that accountability is best understood as a concept that refers not only to 'answerability' for one's actions (see Mainwaring, this volume; Dunn 1999), but also to sanctions. In other words, holding someone accountable means not only learning what someone has done, but punishing him for it if what he has done is in some sense 'wrong'. In this sense, our understanding of accountability differs from that of O'Donnell and Kenney in their chapters in this volume. In light of this understanding of what accountability is, then, we consider the very idea of *horizontal* accountability to be an oxymoron. The term, 'horizontal', when applied to a political system implies two or more actors or institutions at the same level, but if one considers accountability to involve the possibility of sanctions, then the ability of one actor to sanction another implies that the one who may mete out sanctions has authority over the other. In other words, accountability implies that the actors in a political relationship are not at the same level.

In an effort to have as concise a concept as possible, we limit the term, accountability, to the sanctioning rights that are inherent in hierarchical relationships, which by their very nature exist when actors are in a vertical relationship with one another—one is higher in the chain of authority than another and thus can sanction the other.[1] Horizontal relationships, on the other hand, imply the checks and balances that exist between separate agencies that are sheltered from sanctioning by one another in order to maintain their (relative) independence. We argue that, in presidential democracies, the separate origin and survival of the executive and legislature makes them agents of the voters, not one another, and therefore not institutionally accountable to one another (Shugart and Carey 1992). We call relations between them horizontal *exchange*, in the sense that they are co-equal branches (hence in a horizontal relationship to one another) that must trade (i.e., exchange) with one another to produce policy. In the theory of separation of powers, first advanced by James Madison, these exchanges prevent a tyranny from developing, thereby protecting the rights of citizens.

---

[1] Thus, accountability in this sense is not restricted to sanctions imposed for legal violations, but applies to (potential) sanctions for any failure of subordinates to carry out a task in a manner desired by their superiors.

However, actual practice of democratic systems, especially in Latin America, frequently departs from this Madisonian theoretical expectation. Recognizing the limits of horizontal exchanges between (supposedly) independent legislative, executive, and judicial[2] branches, designers of presidential constitutions have increasingly turned to new horizontal relationships within the state. Examples include public prosecutors, ombudsmen, and controllers-general that are endowed with some institutional independence—meaning they cannot be dismissed by the president or a simple legislative majority. We call these forms of horizontal relationships *superintendence*. This term captures their role as watchdogs and providers of information—a role that suggests they may fulfil the answerability component of accountability. However, if accountability is understood as sanctioning authority, few of these entities meet the standard for being agencies of accountability—'horizontal' or otherwise. Thus, for example, we do not consider the ombudsman's provision of information regarding human rights abuses committed by officials of the executive branch (including the police or armed forces) to be a relationship of accountability, for there may be no consequences of the revelation of the information. If there are consequences, it is because perhaps the president fires the subordinate employees who perpetrated the abuses, or the legislature, using its power of the purse, reduces or revokes funding for the office in question, or the voters refuse to re-elect a president deemed to be complicit in rights violations. Only with sanctioning has the actor been held accountable, but if the actor who reveals the information does not impose the sanctions, then that actor is not holding the abusers accountable. It is, however, providing crucial information for others to hold the abusers accountable. Such is the essence of the horizontal relationships that we define as superintendence in this chapter.

Decades of reform across Latin America have produced a bewildering array of non-elected agencies responsible for superintendence functions over the branches of government. The core of our argument is that these agencies have emerged as antidotes to the

---

[2] It is worth recalling that judicial review—the authority of the courts to declare laws unconstitutional—is not mentioned in the United States constitution. It was an authority asserted by the Supreme Court in *Marbury vs. Madison*. More recent presidential (and some parliamentary) constitutions often make such judicial authority explicit, thereby increasing the range of independent actors with which politicians must exchange.

perceived shortcomings of democratic accountability in Latin America, but that the roots of those shortcomings are not to be found in the horizontal dimension of the state. That is, the deficit of accountability lies in faulty *vertical* accountability—legislators who do not represent the values and preferences of the broad citizenry. That is, if the accountability of elected officials were working as intended—such that voters could and would punish misdeeds—separate agencies of superintendence would be unnecessary, at least from the theoretical tradition inspired by Madison and on which the very structure of presidential democracy is based. The proliferation of entities of superintendence in Latin America, then, must be seen as largely a product of discontent with the functioning of accountability and it represents an effort to find a way around the problem without tackling the roots of the accountability deficit. Accordingly, we shall review the deficit of vertical accountability, and suggest remedies that, we believe, would be more helpful in the long run to solving the accountability deficit.

The structure of our argument is as follows. First we elaborate on the notion of accountability as an inherently vertical relationship. Next we show how the constitutional design of accountability varies between parliamentary and presidential systems. We then elaborate on the difficult interplay between vertical accountability, horizontal exchange, and superintendence in presidential systems. Next we provide a descriptive overview of the institutions of the justice system in Latin America, assessing the degrees to which they are independent of the elected branches. Then we elaborate on how to strengthen vertical accountability through candidate selection procedures and electoral rules. Finally, we conclude by reiterating that relations among the agents of the state are a function of their connections to the ultimate principal—the citizenry—and note that the proliferation of superintendence agencies is likely to raise expectations that cannot be met without an overhaul of the institutions of vertical accountability in Latin America.

Accountability in Presidential Systems

We tackle the concept of accountability from the perspective of a principal–agent approach. The reason for doing so is that we are persuaded by the arguments of those scholars who see the modern principal–agent approach, as applied to politics, as most consistent with the theory of government advanced by James Madison

(Grofman 1987, 1989; Kiewiet and McCubbins 1991; see also Palmer 1995; Elster 1999; Laver and Shepsle 1999, Strøm 2000). *The Federalist Papers* explained Madison's theory, justifying the design of the original presidential system, that enshrined in the American constitution of 1789. From this perspective, decision-making in large entities, such as democratic states, implies *delegation* of authority. In agency relationships, the right to make a decision is assigned by a 'principal' to an 'agent', but this assignment, i.e. delegation, is conditional. That is, it continues only at the pleasure of the principal. That it may be withdrawn is the very essence of *accountability*. Only when the right to make a decision is subject to withdrawal can we understand a relationship founded on accountability to be in place. Thus delegation occurs within hierarchies when one person or entity, as agent, receives conditional authority from another person or entity, as principal. Relations of delegation run in one direction—from principal to agent—while relations of accountability run in the opposite direction—from agent to principal.

Accountability means that the principal has the right to withdraw the conditionally delegated authority altogether. This usually means dismissing (firing) the agent. However, especially in politics, often it means something short of immediate dismissal. It may mean refusing to renew a delegation relationship that has a fixed endpoint or it may mean simply downgrading the agent's authority, but allowing the agent to retain her office. For instance, voters as principals can exercise accountability over their legislator-agents only at election time. As elections may occur only at intervals of anywhere from two to six years,[3] there are obviously ample opportunities for the agent to 'shirk' at the expense of the principal. This is one of the reasons that delegation relationships are more imperfect in democratic politics than in, for example, the firm.[4] Holding an agent accountable may also imply—instead of removing the agent—withdrawing some portion of the delegated

---

[3] We are ignoring here the possibility of recall elections, a prospect that exists in some states of the United States and in the 2000 Venezuelan constitution.

[4] There are other reasons, which include agents exercising effective authority in politics (Moe 1984) and the principal (i.e., the citizenry) as a large group, facing serious problems of collective action. On the problems of effective monitoring by collective principals and other principal–agent problems more generally, see Kiewiet and McCubbins (1991, Chapter 2). On the problems of collective action, see Olson (1965) and Cox and McCubbins (1993, Chapter 4). Cox and McCubbins specifically focus on the role of political parties in (partially) overcoming the collective action problems of the citizens and legislators.

authority. This form of accountability is especially common in presidential systems. For example, a legislature can rescind or allow to expire delegated decree authority or it can reinstate constitutional guarantees, the suspension of which gave the executive 'emergency' powers.

One of our key points is that when institutions are formally independent of one another—as in presidential systems—they are *not* accountable to one another. Independence and accountability are two contradictory features of institutional design. The legislative majority in a prototypical presidential democracy cannot dismiss the president and only the voters (or not even the voters) can decide whether or not to renew the president's right to exercise the executive authority for a new term.[5] While one branch may be answerable to another, this answerability takes place within the broader context of the ultimate accountability of all politicians to citizen-principals. That is why the way in which delegation and accountability relationships between citizens and politicians are structured is so crucial to the overall functioning of accountability—a theme we return to at length in a later section of this chapter.

While the executive branch is not an agent of the legislature in a presidential system in the sense of deriving its authority from the legislature, the executive can be the legislature's agent in the carrying out of discrete tasks. For instance, Congress may delegate by statute the right to negotiate trade agreements to the president, as under the United States 'fast track' trade negotiating authority, which existed until the Congress let it expire in 1995. In delegating such authority, it establishes a 'contract' that states the terms under which the president may bargain with foreign governments and the terms under which an agreement may be brought before the Congress for ratification. In this sense, the president is the Congress's agent for the purposes of forging trade agreements and is accountable to the Congress for the conduct of his trade policy and for the ultimate enactment of any trade agreement he

[5] Wherever presidents are barred from immediate re-election—as in most Latin American countries—the accountability relationship is severely weakened. See Shugart and Carey (1992: 87–91). Accountability of presidents is most effectively exercised when the president is subject to personal accountability as an incumbent running for re-election. However, where parties are important channels of presidential recruitment they may become agents of accountability if the president himself is term-limited. More amorphously, presidents' desire to protect their legacy or to remain active in politics as 'elder statesmen' or in lower elected office, may prevent their accountability from being totally severed even where they are ineligible for re-election.

negotiates. If the Congress is unsatisfied with the president's actions in the area of trade, it can withdraw the delegated authority, either by passing legislation rescinding the right to negotiate future trade agreements or by failing to renew that right when it comes up for 'sunset' review. Note that in this example, the principal is not denying the agent his position (through dismissal). The president remains president, but with somewhat diminished authority.

In the various examples just cited, the agency relationship is vertical in the sense that the principal is holding accountable an agent who is, by definition, inferior to the principal in a hierarchy. The electorate is superior to the legislator in the hierarchy of democracy, and can hold the legislator accountable by not renewing her authority to exercise delegated rights as the voters' representative. In trade policy—at least in the American example—the Congress is superior to the president, because only it can enact trade agreements into law, and it can hold the president accountable by withdrawing his conditional authority to engage in trade negotiations. This is a ubiquitous fact of delegation and accountability relationships: they are *vertical relations between subordinate agents and superior principals*.

Accountability in Hierarchical vs. Horizontal Relationships

Government, in theory, is an agent of the citizenry in democracies. If this is not the case, then, simply put, the government is not democratic. Of course, under representative democracy, the citizens do not exercise direct authority, rather they delegate it. Alternative forms of constitutional design establish different relations of delegation and accountability as means to further the interests and rights of citizens. There are two basic ways in which constitutions attempt to ensure that the basic rights and interests of citizens as the ultimate principal are not harmed. One is through nested hierarchies, which are typical of parliamentary design. The other is through horizontal exchange, common in presidential systems.[6]

Nested Hierarchies Parliamentary systems in their purest form consist of a single chain of nested principal–agent relationships. As depicted in stylized form in Figure 4.1, parliamentary democracy entails each entity as a single agent of its immediately

---

[6] We are speaking here of pure types, for the sake of illustration. Both forms of accountability relationships are employed to some degree in all democracies.

superior principal.[7] Voters make only one voting choice: they select
a candidate (or list of candidates) to represent them in parliament.[8] Parties serve as a screening mechanism for voters, enabling
them to select legislators who will in turn select cabinet ministers
who share their policy preferences. Voters hold legislators accountable through the shadow of future elections and with the assistance of 'fire alarms', i.e. third-party provision of information that
assists voter-principals in monitoring their politician-agents
(McCubbins and Schwartz 1984). Opposition parties and the
media provide these fire alarms for voters by publicizing alleged
misdeeds by politicians.

The executive enjoys no constitutional independence from the
legislature and no direct connection to the electorate. It is instead
a pure agent of the parliament, and accountable to that majority
in the most simple and direct way: subject to being ousted at any
time by a vote-of-no-confidence. The cabinet is also accountable
through oversight committees in parliament or through other institutions such as the 'question period' used in the British House
of Commons. The bureaucracy is an agent of the cabinet in that,
even if individual bureaucrats enjoy civil service protection, they
must carry out the legislation and ministerial orders by which
their political principals delegate tasks to them. The cabinet can
sanction bureaucrats through its control over budgets or, ultimately, the structure of the agencies and the civil service system
itself (Moe and Caldwell 1994). In the sense described here, a
parliamentary system is a nested hierarchy in that each link in
the chain is uniquely accountable to its principal.[9]

Horizontal Exchange In contrast to the single chain of nested
hierarchies found in pure parliamentary systems, presidential

[7] In Figures 4.1 and 4.2, the 'superior' principal (the electorate) is shown at
the bottom in keeping with common parlance of authority stemming in a democracy 'from below'. Nonetheless, in principal–agent terms, those below are in
fact superior in the sense of assigning conditional authority to their delegated
agents.

[8] The example assumes unicameralism as an essential feature of the pure type
of parliamentarism. In fact, many parliamentary systems are bicameral, and even
weak upper houses may exercise important powers (Tsebelis and Money 1997).
However, nearly all parliamentary systems make the cabinet an agent only of the
lower house (i.e., the upper house has no right to cast no-confidence votes). Italy is
one of the few exceptions to this rule. On the other hand, most presidential democracies have co-equal upper houses.

[9] As Strøm (2000) has noted, there are informal senses in which the cabinet is
directly accountable to the electorate, but there is no formal link between them.

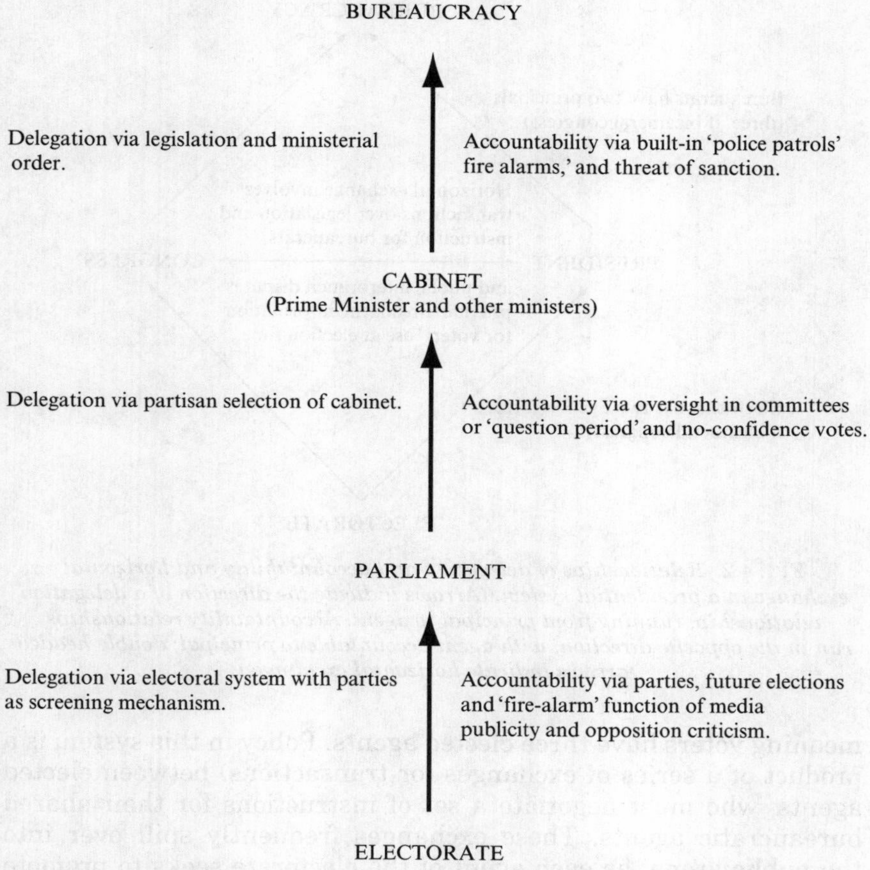

BUREAUCRACY

Delegation via legislation and ministerial order.

Accountability via built-in 'police patrols' fire alarms,' and threat of sanction.

CABINET
(Prime Minister and other ministers)

Delegation via partisan selection of cabinet.

Accountability via oversight in committees or 'question period' and no-confidence votes.

PARLIAMENT

Delegation via electoral system with parties as screening mechanism.

Accountability via parties, future elections and 'fire-alarm' function of media publicity and opposition criticism.

ELECTORATE

FIG. 4.1. *Relationships of delegation and accountability: nested hierarchies in a parliamentary system. (Arrows indicate the direction of a delegation relationship, running from principal to agent. Accountability relationships run in the opposite direction, with agent accountable to principal.)*

systems establish the executive and legislature as separate and independent agents of the electorate. The president and legislature then transact with one another in a series of exchanges to produce policy and, in theory at least, prevent a 'tyranny of the majority' from developing. Instead of being accountable to the legislative majority through votes of no confidence, the executive has a fixed term and serves as a check on the ambitions of the legislative majority. For simplicity, Figure 4.2 depicts a unicameral congress, but in fact most presidential systems are bicameral,

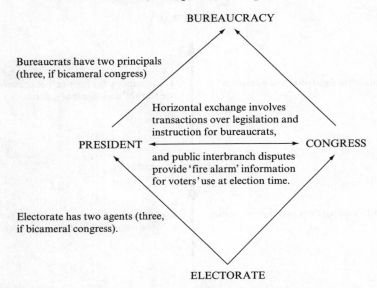

BUREAUCRACY

Bureaucrats have two principals
(three, if bicameral congress)

Horizontal exchange involves
transactions over legislation and
instruction for bureaucrats,

PRESIDENT ←————————→ CONGRESS

and public interbranch disputes
provide 'fire alarm' information
for voters' use at election time.

Electorate has two agents (three,
if bicameral congress).

ELECTORATE

FIG. 4.2. *Relationships of delegation and accountability and horizontal
exchange in a presidential system. (Arrows indicate the direction of a delegation
relationship, running from principal to agent. Accountability relationships
run in the opposite direction, with agent accountable to principal; double-headed
arrows indicate horizontal exchange.)*

meaning voters have three elected agents. Policy in this system is a
product of a series of exchanges (or transactions) between elected
agents, who must negotiate a set of instructions for their shared
bureaucratic agents. These exchanges frequently spill over into
the public arena, as each agent of the electorate seeks to promote
its own preferred policy outcomes and blame the other for the failure to enact its own conception of popular preferences. This spill-
over of disagreements arising out of horizontal exchange serves a
fire-alarm function in the sense of providing information for voters
to use in assessing the performance of their agents, and voters can
use this information in subsequent elections. Because of the separation between executive and legislature, each has an incentive to
point out misdeeds by the other, which in theory at least, helps
reveal information about scandals or other breaches of faith. In all
presidential constitutions, the Congress has the authority to demand information and hold hearings into alleged executive-branch
wrongdoing. The information produced by public interbranch disputes thus augments that provided by opposition parties and the
media and implies that presidential systems potentially provide

more information for voter-principals to use in monitoring their agents than do parliamentary systems.[10]

Bureaucrats in presidential systems, then, are accountable to two principals (three in a bicameral system). They are accountable in that their political principals define through a 'contract' the process by which decisions are to be reached and what interests are to be represented in an agency's decision-making process. Administrative procedures ensure that affected interests have a right to participate in rule-making (McCubbins, Noll, and Weingast 1987, 1989). Moreover, legislators build into the enabling legislation of each bureaucratic agency fire alarms whereby the constituents that they seek to have represented in the decision-making process can inform legislators of bureaucratic transgressions. We know less about how this form of decentralized monitoring and accountability of agents works in Latin America than we do about the United States, but growing evidence suggests that the basic logic holds.[11]

Courts in Hierarchical vs. Transactional Systems

In a pure hierarchical political system, the courts are essentially another part of the bureaucracy (Ramseyer and Rosenbluth 1993), responsible for applying the laws enacted by parliament on behalf of the citizenry, and not empowered to overturn laws. By contrast, in transactional presidential systems, where there is no notion of parliamentary sovereignty, courts typically have authority that overlaps with the elected bodies and may even overturn acts of the elected bodies on constitutional grounds. Increasingly, even in parliamentary systems, constitutional courts or other bodies are being endowed with sufficient independence to serve as checks on the parliamentary majority (Lijphart 1999; Stone 1992), though the origin of constitutional arbiters almost always is based in appointment for relatively short terms by elected agents of the electorate. That is, they typically undercut the sovereignty (or tyranny, if one

[10] The quality and usefulness of that information is a separate matter, and depends to a large degree on the mechanisms of accountability of legislators and presidents to voters. We take up the issue of legislative accountability in detail below. For a parallel argument about the information content of accountability relations in presidential and parliamentary democracies, see Strøm (2000).

[11] See the various chapters in Haggard and McCubbins (2000) and Levy and Spiller (1993).

prefers) of the legislative *majority*, but do not enjoy much separation of origin and survival from legislative politicians.

Much of the action of courts in democracies concerns applying and enforcing the law. Even without a right to declare laws themselves unconstitutional, courts would be expected to be more active in presidential systems than in parliamentary, because bureaucrats serve multiple principals (Moe and Caldwell 1994; McCubbins, Noll and Weingast 1987, 1989). Because of the transactional nature of law-making in presidential systems, there is more potential for conflicting interpretations of legislative intent. There are also the built-in fire-alarm procedures referred to above, which often explicitly allow affected parties to sue agencies for alleged failure to conform properly to procedures or to allow necessary evidence into their decision-making process. Courts can be a tool for ensuring the vertical accountability of bureaucracies to their political principals, especially legislators.[12] This may even be the most fundamental function of courts in modern democracies. This is why—as we shall develop below—it is so important that legislators be real partners with the executive branch in policy-making, for if they are not, they are far less likely to have an interest in independent courts as a check on the executive and its bureaucracy.

In presidential systems—and increasingly in parliamentary systems, too—judicial bodies are taking on more and more the role of a check on the legislative process itself, in addition to ensuring the proper application of laws duly enacted by legislators. Courts that have the authority to veto legislative acts are thus another actor in the process of horizontal exchange. Courts are independent to the extent that they are *not* accountable to the political bodies. They are engaged in horizontal exchange to the extent that they share powers in some areas with the political bodies—or with other independent agencies.

Superintendence Agencies

O'Donnell's definition of horizontal accountability appears to be directed less at the legislative branch or the judiciary and more at the assemblage of so-called autonomous agencies of government

---

[12] Because of the single-line hierarchy, agencies in parliamentary systems are more directly accountable to the executive. Thus the opportunities for third-party intervention through recourse to the courts are diminished. As a result, recourse to the courts in parliamentary systems is more likely to take the form of ensuring compliance with an agency decision than overturning it, let alone overturning a law.

established in numerous constitutions in Latin America. These include the various components, aside from the judiciary, of the justice system: the *Contraloría*, *Fiscalía*, *Defensoría*, and other entities charged with watching over the actions of the executive (and sometimes legislative) branch. Sometimes these entities have sanctioning authority, but often their primary function is to pull a 'fire alarm' when they witness misdeeds. For instance, they may publicize misdeeds and perhaps refer them to the courts or to a congressional committee charged with opening an impeachment inquiry. That is, they substitute for the reticence of regular institutions of horizontal exchange and legislative oversight to detect and punish official wrongdoing, for various reasons that are often rooted in a breakdown of vertical accountability institutions between legislators and citizens. In the following section, we explore the complex relationship between vertical accountability, horizontal exchange and superintendence, especially as it pertains to superintendence agencies in presidential systems.

Vertical Accountability, Horizontal Exchange, and Superintendence

Presidential systems entail a mixture of vertical accountability and horizontal exchange. Additionally, Latin American systems are creating more and more superintendence agencies. These oversight entities are part of the horizontal structure of the state to the extent that they have constitutional status alongside the executive, legislative, and judicial branches, but one of their most important functions is to assist vertical accountability by providing information that elected politicians and citizens can use in holding their agents accountable. Some of the oversight agencies also have prosecutorial functions, bringing cases of alleged legal violations before the judiciary or imposing their own sanctions.

The Madisonian principles of constitutional design that modern presidentialism rests upon rely on horizontal exchange between agents with different vertical accountability ties to the citizenry. In Madison's famous phrase, ambition must be pitted against ambition. The notion is that of countervailing incentives, such that legislators and the executive do not collude with one another to the detriment of the principal (citizens). Countervailing incentives between legislators and the executive arise when each represents a different manifestation of the electorate, through the different electoral systems or drawing of constituencies. The ambitions of legislators are to a significant degree set by the institutions of vertical accountability between them and their constituents. In this section, we discuss the interplay between vertical accountability and horizontal exchange. We argue that the nature of the vertical accountability relationship between voters and legislators is crucial to the functioning of a system of horizontal exchange. We argue further that when vertical accountability breaks down, such that legislators fail to be good agents of the citizenry, there is a tendency for constitutional reformers to see superintendence agencies as a solution. However, these entities are a poor substitute for a well functioning interplay of vertical accountability and horizontal exchange.

Vertical Accountability vs. Horizontal Exchange Legislators in presidential systems are vertically accountable to citizens just as in parliamentary systems, so it follows that the electoral system that defines the nature of the hierarchy between voter-principals and legislator-agents is a crucial aspect of the design of a presidential system. The fundamental difference between presidential and parliamentary democracies is that the hierarchical connection between voter-principals and the executive authority is not mediated through the legislative majority in a presidential system as it is in a parliamentary system. That is, whereas parliamentary democracies are based principally on nested hierarchies of vertical accountability, presidential systems are built on the interaction of horizontal exchange and vertical accountability. This fundamental distinction has serious consequences for legislative incentives in presidential systems (Shugart and Haggard 2000), and, in turn, for how well horizontal exchange functions to align the incentives of actors in the various branches with the interests of the ultimate principal, the citizenry.

It has been argued in the literature on the United States presidential system that legislators are single-minded in their pursuit of re-election and that they have designed the institutions of the United States Congress in order to facilitate that goal (Mayhew 1974). A large literature has developed that traces the organization of Congress—especially the House of Representatives—as a series of institutions that enable legislators to 'claim credit' for particularistic services to their constituents (e.g., Weingast 1984; Shepsle 1986, Weingast and Marshall 1988). It is not that legislators in parliamentary systems are not as interested in furthering their own political careers; rather what distinguishes parliamentary legislators is that the parliamentary majority is *collectively responsible* for governing. As a result, the pursuit of individual political careers takes place within a framework of much stronger parties than we find in the United States, because such parties are needed to bind the nested hierarchies of parliamentarism to one another. The absence of (or reduced role for) collective responsibility in presidential systems means that it is harder to achieve vertical accountability of the entire policy-making apparatus to the broad preferences of the citizens. Hence mechanisms of oversight and sanctions are handed off to non-elected agencies in an effort to rein in the citizens' agents and reduce shirking.[13]

In a parliamentary system, one of the principal commitments legislative candidates have to offer their voters is their engagement with a collective entity, a party, that seeks to claim executive authority, or a share of it (Epstein 1967; Cox 1987; Shugart and Carey 1992; Palmer 1995; Moe and Caldwell 1994; Strøm 2000). This collective commitment does not exist in presidential systems because the electoral connection between voters and the executive does not run through legislators, but is direct, via presidential elections. Because legislators are bypassed in the connection between voters and the executive, voters tend to demand different things from legislative candidates than they demand from the executive. This phenomenon has been noted in the United States literature (Jacobson 1990; Moe 1990; Moe and Caldwell 1994). Presidents are held accountable for overall management of the economy—and, given the United States' status as a great power, for foreign affairs. Legislators, on the other hand, are held accountable to a large degree for distributive policies, and are also expected to deliver pork-barrel favours to their districts.

If this distinction between what legislative candidates and presidential candidates offer their voter-principals is significant in the United States, it is even more so in other presidential systems. Latin American electoral systems tend to one or the other extreme, compared to the participatory nomination procedures and single-seat districts of the United States (Shugart 2001). They tend either to emphasize party even less than in the United States, as a

---

[13] It should be noted that in those parliamentary systems in which fragmentation and factionalism lead to an obscuring of collective accountability, superintendence organs often take on an important role as they do in Latin America. An example would be Italy, where the pervasive corruption was finally brought to official light, and sanctions were imposed, through the work of independent magistrates.

result of intraparty competition—as in Brazil, Colombia, and Peru—or to centralize party control at the expense of individual legislators, as a result of closed party-list systems—as in Argentina, Mexico, and Venezuela. Thus at the 'weak-party' extreme, legislators have even less incentive to offer voters a commitment to a party and its national-policy priorities than in the United States, while at the 'strong-party' extreme, legislators are not individually accountable to their constituents at all.

If legislators in presidential systems lack a balance between collective accountability to parties and individual accountability to constituents, a crucial link in the interplay between vertical accountability and horizontal exchange is lacking. If legislators are either uninterested in national policy (excessively weak parties) or unaccountable to voters (excessively strong parties) they have little interest in exercising oversight and 'political control' over the executive. That is, they are neither partners in the crafting of national policy, nor engaged in ongoing monitoring of the executive branch's policy-making process. Instead, much of the policy relationship between legislator-principals and the executive as an agent to carry out legislation will look more like abdication than delegation, and the dominant feature of interbranch transactions will not be exchanges over broad policy but exchanges of votes for patronage. It is in this context, then, that the attention of 'good-government' reformers turns to the creation of more and more 'independent' superintendence agencies to augment or replace the oversight and sanctioning power that should be provided by legislators, through horizontal exchange, and by voters, through vertical accountability of law-makers.

Horizontal exchange involves the existence of independent agencies that check one another. As we have argued, horizontal exchange is not a form of accountability because the very notion of independent branches is that they are not accountable to one another. Indeed, their independence and lack of mutual accountability, along with the overlap of functions, is what allows them to function as checks and balances. No branch can effectively serve as a check on the other if its authority is derived from serving as the agent of the branch to be overseen. The only senses in which relationships between separate branches are ones of accountability, are first, in the assignment of discrete tasks (such as the trade-negotiation process referred to earlier), and, second, impeachment. When one branch initiates impeachment over another, the officials subject to possible impeachment are accountable to another branch—always the legislature, though the legislative authority of impeachment may be shared with other agencies in some systems. The evocation of impeachment proceedings, then, is the conversion of a constitutionally horizontal relationship between branches into a legal relationship of accountability in which, typically, legislators intercede between the impeached official and the ultimate principal, the voters. Thus relations between branches are horizontal, and they are not relations of accountability. Impeachment is a relationship of accountability, but in being so, it ceases to be horizontal. Having discussed the distinction between horizontal exchange and vertical accountability in greater depth, we now seek to further define the distinction between horizontal exchange and superintendence.

Horizontal Exchange vs. Superintendence   A necessary condition for effective horizontal exchange is overlapping functions between branches. In order for horizontal exchange to take place, each branch that is party to the exchange must have something to offer the other in a transaction. For instance, in the standard legislative process of a presidential system, the Congress has the authority to pass—or not pass—legislation desired by the president. The president, in turn, typically has the authority to veto legislation passed by the Congress, and also has some discretion over the enforcement of enacted legislation. Thus each of these two branches has something the other side wants. The president wants votes in Congress, and the Congress wants the president's assent to legislation and his commitment to enforce it vigorously. Such is the essence of exchange: while the branches are independent in the sense that they have separate bases of authority, they are not fully separate in terms of their functions. They need to cooperate with one another in order to accomplish their tasks. Their functions, in short, overlap.

Overlapping functions also may occur with respect to the non-elected agencies. For instance, where there is a constitutional tribunal empowered to exercise review of the constitutionality of laws, legislators and the executive must engage in exchange with the tribunal in order to enact their preferred legislation. This is especially true in those systems in which a court or tribunal may exercise 'abstract review', whereby a law that is challenged on constitutional grounds cannot be promulgated until it is approved by the branch that exercises constitutional control; in such cases, entire laws may be effectively rewritten by the tribunal and legislators often incorporate the tribunal's text to ensure promulgation can proceed the second time around (Stone 1992).

Another example of non-elected agencies taking part in horizontal exchange may be found in the judiciary-dominant model of impeachment (Kada n.d.). Under this impeachment process, the legislature is not the only branch that determines whether a case against the president (or other official) may go forward. In such cases the Supreme Court or an independent attorney general or public prosecutor must also give assent, and thus functions overlap between elected and non-elected entities, with each holding some authority that the other needs to pursue its preferences.

An agency may be independent (in the sense of having a reasonably high degree of separation of origin and survival), yet not be equipped to engage in horizontal exchange if its functions do not overlap in some respects with those of other branches and, in particular, of the elected branches. Absent overlap of functions, whereby one agency needs the cooperation of another to perform certain tasks, no horizontal exchange—let alone accountability—exists. For instance, the ombudsman's office in Peru is a constitutionally defined office with some degree of separation of origin, in the form of an extraordinary congressional majority for appointment. Yet the authority delegated to it by the constitution is quite limited. According to Kenney (this volume), the ombudsman can do little more than investigate and publicize violations of rights; even this function is severely limited by the military's legal right to withhold information for 'security' reasons. The ombudsman is not engaged in exchanges with any other branches that need the ombudsman's cooperation in order to perform their own tasks.

If the ombudsman is not institutionally equipped to engage in horizontal exchange, this does not mean it is irrelevant. Indeed, in publicizing misdeeds, a credible ombudsman or other independent oversight agency may play a vital role as a fire alarm in *vertical* accountability. Recall that fire alarms are third-party opportunities to reveal an agent's misdeeds to the agent's principal. If shedding light on abuses of human rights by agents within the executive branch provides information that legislators can use to sanction the executive, or that voters can use in the next election, then the ombudsman has played a role in enhancing vertical accountability. For another example of actions by an independent agency that is not horizontal exchange, suppose a *Fiscal* exists who can blow the whistle on corruption. If the *Fiscal* has sufficient independence (from his origin and survival) to reveal the corruption of a legislator, that information may be useful to the legislator's principals, the voters. The extent to which this information leads to punishment of the legislator, then, depends on the extent to which the electoral process facilitates the accountability of legislators, as well as the preferences of the voters for non-corrupt legislators. The extent to which credible information about official misdeeds will lead to the ultimate principal—voters—holding the official accountable therefore depends on institutions of vertical accountability. We return to this theme below.

Countervailing Ambitions   A condition for horizontal exchange or superintendence to work is countervailing ambitions. Madison's pitting of ambitions against one another assumes that agents have incentives to do different things. For instance, firms often require large expenditures to be approved concurrently by both the CEO and the controller. The CEO is rewarded for increasing profits, but the controller is rewarded for holding down costs. Both are agents of the firm's board (and, through the board, of the stockholders), but they have countervailing ambitions in the sense that each has a different incentive. In political systems founded on a horizontal separation of powers, similarly, separate institutions must have different incentives.

In presidential systems, countervailing ambitions are implied by separate electoral origin of the president and executive. Presidents are elected in a nationwide race for a single office, while legislators are typically elected at least partially in regional districts. Even in those rare cases of single nationwide legislative districts (e.g., Peru and the Colombian senate), the use of a non-majoritarian electoral system implies that the congressional majority is accountable to a different manifestation of the electorate than is the president.[14]

The greatest threat to the existence of countervailing ambitions is the presence of informal hierarchical relations between formally independent branches. If a hierarchy exists between separately elected agents of the electorate, then separation is replaced by accountability to a single principal. An example occurs under what might be called majoritarian presidentialism. For instance, if the president is the head of the majority party in the sense of nominating the party's legislative candidates and offering them post-legislative 'pensions' in the form of government patronage, then the president becomes a principal over legislators. In this scenario—which approximates to that seen in Mexico until recent years

---

[14] Related to this point, the much lower threshold for obtaining a seat, relative to the presidency, means that a Congress member's constituency can be geographically compact, notwithstanding the nationwide district.

(Weldon 1997)—legislators and president continue to have formally separate origin and survival in the electoral process, but cease to have countervailing ambitions.[15] While full-blown majoritarian presidentialism is rare, approximations to it may be found at various times in many Latin American countries, undercutting both the vertical accountability of politicians to voters and the horizontal exchange that is supposed to keep the elected branches in competition with one another for public support. In such situation, demands for the creation of superintendence institutions are likely to arise.

Even without a majority party headed by the president, the countervailing ambitions on which horizontal exchange depends can be overridden by relations of de facto accountability that make the legislators dependent on the president. Where legislators win office primarily on patronage rather than on policy-based campaigning, they are in a dependent position vis-à-vis the president, whose position at the head of the executive branch gives him vast patronage resources with which to 'buy' votes in congress. Although not a formal relationship of accountability, this sort of interbranch bargaining of votes for patronage undermines the countervailing ambitions of the branches by inducing legislators to abdicate the autonomy of their branch and hence its ability to serve as a forum for the reconciliation of policy disagreements. In such situations, which are probably very common in Latin America, corruption is likely to be rife (because legislators' demand for patronage induces them to look the other way, or even be party to, bureaucratic misappropriation of funds, for example). Again, demands for the creation of independent institutions of superintendence are likely to arise.

It follows from this discussion that either situation—the president as the head of a majority party or parties so weak that patronage pervades legislators' election campaigns—undermines countervailing ambitions. Both situations place the executive in a de facto superior position and short-circuit horizontal exchange. It follows further, then, that situations of moderately strong parties, none of which is subordinate to the president, are the most prom-

---

[15] It should be noted that this model of majoritarian presidentialism is quite different from the model of majoritarian parliamentarism. In the latter, the executive is the agent of the legislative majority, accountable to it. In majoritarian presidentialism, accountability relations run in the opposite direction—from the chief executive (in his capacity as party leader) to legislators—implying a much greater concentration of authority in the executive branch.

ising means of ensuring countervailing ambitions. Parties are the
principal means of ensuring collective accountability of policy-
makers to voters, so their virtual absence as coordinators of the
legislative process makes legislators highly dependent upon executive patronage. Parties and legislators must retain sufficient
independence from the president that they can represent the preferences of their voter-principals.

In courts and superintendence agencies, the same fundamental
limitations on countervailing ambitions apply. For example, when
the same unified party controls both elected branches, justices are
unlikely to be appointed who are independent of politicians even if
both branches must participate in their appointment (see Magaloni, this volume). If the overwhelming majority of legislators is
primarily interested in patronage, they will have little incentive to
select officials for the non-elected agencies who will exercise effective control over the source of patronage, the executive, even if the
selection process requires a supermajority. Thus the independence
of the non-elected agencies is largely dependent upon the incentives of legislators who play a part in staffing them. If the vertical
delegation from voters to legislators is not designed properly to
reflect the collective wishes of the electorate, then oversight is
unlikely to work and politicians may be able to collude to oppress
citizens. We take up the issue of independence across several non-
elected superintendence agencies in the following section.

Degrees of Independence of Non-elected
Agencies in Latin America

We posit that the proliferation of superintendence agencies across
the region is indicative of a breakdown in the interplay of the
vertical and horizontal dimensions of the state that we have identified up to now. A crucial question remains as to whether agencies
of superintendence are endowed with genuine independence vis-
à-vis the elected branches so that they can compensate for the
malfunctioning of countervailing ambitions between the elected
branches. As we shall see, the picture is mixed, but a great many
are dependent on elected branches for their origin and survival. In
the following pages, we briefly review the provisions for separate
origin and survival as well as some of the key overlapping functions in Latin America's non-elected agencies charged with oversight or control of politicians. We will consider the following

classes of non-elected agencies: supreme courts, constitutional tribunals, attorneys general (state legal counsel), prosecutors general
(public ministries), public defenders (human rights ombudsmen),
and controllers general. Rather than explore the entire gamut of
non-elected agencies, we have chosen to focus on the agencies of
the 'justice system' that are found in many constitutions of Latin
America because they are part of the ongoing process of maintaining accountability and ensuring compliance with the constitution
and law.[16]

Functions of Non-elected Agencies   Justice systems across the
region have grown increasingly complex, with distinct agencies
performing myriad functions. For instance, supreme courts or constitutional tribunals are engaged in horizontal exchange to the
extent that they are empowered to overturn legislation that they
find unconstitutional. This role most closely conforms to our definition of horizontal exchange when it is exercised in the abstract,
that is, before a bill may be promulgated.[17] Of course, the most
basic function of the Supreme Court or constitutional tribunal is to
uphold the rule of law. Many of the oversight and exchange functions of other non-elected agencies depend on the willingness of
the high courts to sanction violators of constitutional rights. Thus
if the highest courts are not geniunely independent, it is likely
that other non-elected agencies will fail to perform their duties.

Attorneys and prosecutors general are charged with ensuring
obedience of the law. The precise terms used vary from one constitution to another, and often posts with different functions go by
the same name (e.g., *Procurador General* or *Fiscal General*) in
different countries. For present purposes we have made a distinction between those bodies whose primary role is to oversee the
enforcement of criminal law and/or to represent the government in
judicial proceedings (which we call the attorney general), and those
whose role extends to ensuring public officials' compliance with the
law and investigating corruption (which we call the prosecutor
general). Typically, these two functions are performed by separate
entities.[18] The attorney general or state legal counsel is sometimes

---

[16] This list is not exhaustive. For example, some constitutions provide for independent entities charged with controlling corruption, while others place this function in the offices of the prosecutor general and/or controller general.

[17] Abstract review is usually performed by constitutional tribunals, but less
often by supreme courts, which usually perform judicial review only in concrete
cases (i.e., in controversies that arise after promulgation), if at all.

[18] In some cases, these two functions are unified under one attorney general.

a direct executive appointee (especially where the official's role is to serve as the government's legal advocate), while the prosecutor general typically enjoys greater independence from the president and the legislative majority. Prosecutors general typically serve the role of the citizenry's advocate against official wrongdoing, making them clearly agents of superintendence. The powers of this organ are sometimes quite sweeping, as in Brazil (see Sadek and Cavalcanti, this volume). Powers can even extend to the suspension of officials from office for reasons of corruption, as occurred in Colombia in April 2000, when the *Procurador General*, for the first time in the nation's history, suspended two sitting members of the Congress for alleged misappropriation of funds. In this sense, they are adjuncts to vertical accountability, and their presence—and, often, considerable independence—can be seen as a product of the relative difficulty of holding officials accountable in presidential systems through ordinary electoral and legislative institutions, due to fixed terms, separated powers, and faulty electoral laws. Ideally, the accountability functions of legislative hearings (oversight of the executive and internal policing of the legislature's own members) and elections would be sufficient to deter or punish official malfeasance. However, where standard processes of vertical accountability break down, constitution-makers seek recourse in independent agencies to carry out these functions.[19]

Public defenders for human rights—sometimes called human rights ombudsmen—play an important role in providing fire-alarm oversight. Not all Latin American constitutions make provisions for human rights defenders. Those that do often place the defender within the public ministry (under the prosecutor general), but nonetheless establish a separate organ, sometimes called the *Defensoría*, charged with investigating human rights abuses. Most

[19] In the United States, the creation of the Office of Independent Counsel (OIC) is a similar response to the difficulty of detecting and prosecuting scandals in the separation-of-powers system. Not surprisingly, given that the OIC was created by legislation and not by constitutional amendment, the reach of the OIC did not extend to the legislative branch, as does the reach of some public ministries in Latin America. Wrongdoing by legislators in the United States is handled by Ethics Committees within the Congress itself. The OIC's reputation for being out of control as a result of Kenneth Starr's pursuit of President Bill Clinton led Congress to allow the statute to expire. As a result, the United States, at least for now, is relying on the Department of Justice (headed by an executive cabinet secretary), Congress's own judiciary committees, and the electoral process to keep executive misdeeds in check.

human rights defenders lack enforcement or sanctioning powers. Their duties are mainly confined to publicizing abuses, thereby serving a fire-alarm function, and to referring abuses to the prosecutor for possible judicial action.

Finally, controllers general are authorized to audit officials and governmental agencies and participate in the formulation and execution of the national budget. Therefore, they have a series of tools at their disposal that may facilitate holding other officials, primarily in the executive branch, accountable in the sense of ensuring compliance with budgets and other laws passed by the Congress. Controllers engage not in fire-alarm oversight, but in the more active and direct form of oversight dubbed 'police-patrol'.

Assessing the Independence of Agencies of the Justice System   Now we turn our attention to the degrees of formal independence enjoyed by the agencies of the justice system. We assess independence in two dimensions, the appointment process, and tenure in office. The appointment process is considered to offer minimal independence if it is dominated by legislators, although appointment by an extraordinary majority of legislators affords somewhat greater separation than selection by a mere majority. Mixed appointment processes offer somewhat greater independence—less so if appointment involves two elected branches (president and Congress) than if it involves politicians and non-elected actors (courts or councils of civic groups). Some constitutions employ mixed procedures involving both judicial councils and politicians. For example, the Venezuelan constitution establishes a council called the *Poder Ciudadano*[20] that nominates candidates to the very same positions that comprise the council, and the nominees are confirmed by the Congress. Also in the mixed category are some judicial councils that actually contain a majority of politicians among their membership (as in the Dominican Republic) or leave it entirely to the Congress to decide how the council shall be constituted (as in Ecuador). Because of the opportunity for direct political influence in these councils, there is somewhat less separation of origin than at first meets the eye.

Considerably greater independence results from a judicial-dominant process, leaving politicians out of the selection of justices or superintendents. For instance, in Colombia and Ecuador the Supreme Court itself sits as a judicial council for the purposes of

---

[20] The council is composed of several officials, including the Human Rights Defender and Prosecutor General.

filling vacancies in the court. Chile uses a form of this procedure, in which politicians have a veto over nominees originating from within the Supreme Court itself. Judicial-dominant procedures establish a self-perpetuating court that is likely to be quite independent of politicians. In fact, one could argue that it goes too far, tending to create a court that is very homogeneous and potentially cut off from the citizenry it ultimately is supposed to serve (Correa Sutil 1993).

The greatest independence is afforded by the still-rare civil-society-dominant process. When civil society dominates the appointment process, politicians are left formally out of the selection entirely, and the process is controlled by groups such as bar associations or a commission of academics. Of course, if these civil society groups themselves are entwined with politicians through patron-client ties, there may be less real independence than meets the eye; nonetheless, this mode of appointment offers the greatest potential for making courts and superintendence agencies true agents of civil society rather than of politicians. Peru is the only Latin American country that currently uses this process (for appointing supreme court justices).[21]

The second dimension of independence is the tenure in office of the officials that head a non-elected agency. We assess this dimension by means of a 'term ratio', which is the ratio of the official's term to the term of the elected branch that is involved in appointing. Life terms are coded as 20 years (thereby producing a high score for term ratio). Where there are two elected branches (or two legislative chambers) involved in appointment, the one with the shorter term is used.[22] Thus, for example, the United States Supreme Court's term ratio would be $20/4 = 5$, because justices are appointed for life terms by a president who has a four-year term. The Senate, which must confirm appointments, has a longer term, at six years, and hence is not included in the calculation (though its involvement shows up on the vertical axis). In cases where politically insulated councils alone appoint officials to life terms (including where Supreme Court justices select their own new colleagues), the term ratio is shown as 5.00, equivalent to the

[21] However, as we shall see, the potential independence that this procedure brings to the Supreme Court is vitiated in Peru by the ease with which a congressional majority may impeach justices.

[22] The elected branch with the shorter term is used because the more frequently elected branches turn over relative to non-elected, the more independent the latter will tend to be vis-à-vis the elected officeholders of the day.

maximum found in Latin America. These calculations of term ratios are based on an assumption of *fixed terms* that can be shortened only through extraordinary impeachment procedures. However, in some cases, nominally long terms can be shortened relatively easily, thereby vitiating the supposedly fixed term. Thus, in instances in which appointed officials can be dismissed by a legislative majority, the term is considered effectively zero, regardless of the ratio that would be obtained by considering only the appointment side of the process.[23]

Term ratios of 1.00 or less imply essentially no independence, because each legislature (or president) has an opportunity to replace the official. Term ratios from 1.01 to 1.49 provide only slightly more independence, because every other legislature (or president) is likely to have a chance to replace or reconfirm the official. Longer fixed terms increase the opportunities for independence by an official of a non-elected agency by enhancing the attractiveness of the post as a career option and by making more remote the prospect of punishment by elected officials.

Figure 4.3 shows the degree of independence of non-elected agencies charged with checking or overseeing the elected branches. Basic data on the appointment and dismissal processes and term lengths of these entities are given in Tables A4.1 to A4.6 of the appendix. The upper-right region of the figure shows where the criteria for 'independence' are met, as opposed to high dependence on the elected branches; movement from any point in the two-dimensional space either upward or to the right indicates an increase in independence. From the abbreviation for each country, dashed lines extend to all of that country's high courts and superintendence agencies, so that one can see at a glance how the overall structure of the justice system in that country affords independence or not.

As can be seen, there is a wide variation in the degree of independence of courts and agencies of superintendence in Latin

---

[23] The Ecuadorian case is the most difficult to code. No specific term for Supreme Court magistrates is mentioned in the constitution; in fact Art. 202 states that magistrates do not have a fixed term. However, unlike other officials of the Ecuadorian justice system, Supreme Court magistrates are not subject to a 'political trial' by the congressional majority. However, apparently they can be disciplined by a National Judicial Council, whose structure and functions are determined by law. Because this provision appears to leave ample room for political influence, we have considered the term of office of Ecuadorian Supreme Court magistrates to be effectively zero.

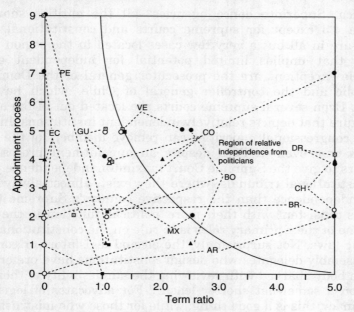

FIG. 4.3. *Independence of high courts and superintendence agencies in Latin America*
(*Source*: Appendix Tables.)

Key to scale on appointment process:

Legislative-dominant: appointment by:

0. Legislative majority only
1. Legislators, with opposition participation

Mixed: appointment by:

2. Legislators and elected president
3. State entity other than legislature or elected
   president (e.g. weak upper house or head of state)
4. Judges and politicians
5. Civic groups and politicians

Judicial-dominant: appointment by:

6. Supreme court or council of judges with participation
   by state entity other than legislature or elected
   president
7. Supreme court or council of judges

Civil-society-dominant: appointment by:

8. Commission of lawyers, academics, etc., with
   participation by state entity other than legislature or
   elected president
9. Commission of lawyers, academics, etc.

Key to country abbreviations

AR	Argentina
BO	Bolivia
BR	Brazil
CH	Chile
CO	Colombia
CR	Costa Rica
DR	Dominican Republic
EC	Ecuador
GU	Guatemala
MX	Mexico
PE	Peru
VE	Venezuela

Key to symbols

● Supreme Court
▲ Constitutional Tribunal
△ Attorney General
▣ Prosecutor General
■ Ombudsman or Defender of human rights
○ Controller General or audit court

America. Superintendence agencies—all the entities shown in Figure 4.3 except for supreme courts and constitutional tribunals—are in all but a very few cases located in the region of the figure that implies limited potential for independent action. Notable exceptions are the prosecutor general of the Dominican Republic and the controller general of Chile, which have life terms. Even several supreme courts are located out of the area of the figure that depicts relatively independent institutions. In a few cases, congressional majorities can remove members of the court; this is true even in Peru despite an appointment process that appears to give the Supreme Court maximum independence.[24]

Constitutional tribunals, where they exist, almost always have less independence than the respective country's Supreme Court. This is consistent with their more 'political' function in the sense that one of their primary roles is to rule on the constitutionality of specific laws. Not surprisingly, the elected legislators or constituent assembly delegates who design constitutions have preferred to keep a body charged with reviewing the admissibility of their own laws on a somewhat shorter leash.[25] For advocates of legislative supremacy, this is a good thing, while for those who mistrust legislative bodies, this would be a bad thing. The perils of too little independence were demonstrated clearly in the Peruvian case. When President Alberto Fujimori sought to overturn a ruling of the Tribunal concerning his eligibility to run for a third term, he was able, through the atomized legislative majority that was dependent on his patronage, to have the Tribunal magistrates impeached on trumped-up charges. Figure 4.3 shows why this was possible within the parameters of Peru's constitution: a simple majority of Peru's unicameral congress is sufficient to impeach and remove a judge from office, meaning effectively the Peruvian Supreme Court and constitutional tribunal magistrates do not have fixed terms at all.

Prosecutors general vary greatly in the independence they are accorded. Only the Dominican Republic provides its public prosecutor with a very high degree of independence—appointment by a judicial council for a life term—although politicians comprise a

---

[24] As noted by Flores Nano (2000), the executive's compliant congressional majority passed legislation that circumvented the formally independent appointment process.

[25] In Ecuador, there is a mix of different entities—some political and some not—charged with nominating magistrates for confirmation by Congress (see Table A4.2). We have coded this as roughly equivalent to nomination of the entire body by a politicized council (4 on the vertical dimension of Figure 4.3).

majority of the council. Also quite independent (formally) is the prosecutor general of Venezuela. On the other hand, those of Ecuador, Guatemala, and Peru, have very independent appointment processes, but lack the security of a fixed term. Strikingly, one of the least independent in formal terms is that of Brazil, where the public prosecutor is appointed by the president, with consent of the senate, for a term of only two years. Thus the considerable behavioral independence identified by Sadek (this volume) does not rest on constitutional provisions for separate origin and survival. The constitution does mandate that the officers within the public prosecution, and the public prosecutor who heads the entity, come from an internal career path, thereby ensuring a high degree of professionalism. Further, the way in which the federal public prosecution is integrated with the decentralized prosecutorial bodies of the states in Brazil's federal system reduces the potential for political influence at the federal level (see Sadek and Cavalcanti, this volume). Nonetheless, the appointment process and exceedingly short term work against the independence of the institution, and thus the relative freedom of the public prosecution from political influence could vary with the commitment to prosecutorial independence of specific federal administrations.

Public defenders or ombudsmen for human rights are generally quite dependent upon Congress for both appointment and survival in office. Among the very few exceptions to this generalization are those of Guatemala and Venezuela, though even in these cases the ombudsman has a short term. In most other cases, Congress is solely charged with the election and dismissal of individuals to this office, although interbranch consent is required for appointment in Colombia.

There are many examples of legislative dominance in the selection process of the controller general, though only in Mexico is the controller a simple agent of the legislative majority. In fact, most of these entities are located in the lower-left area of the figure where independence is at its lowest. There are some exceptions, however. The most notable is Chile, where the controller, although appointed by the consent of the president and senate, is granted a life term. In Argentina, the controller is dependent on politicians, but not those in the majority; the largest opposition party selects the controller. In Costa Rica, Colombia, and Guatemala the controllers also enjoy considerable formal independence, although through different means: selection from a slate prepared by the high courts in Colombia; the involvement of an apolitical screening committee in Guatemala; a term twice that of the legislature's in Costa Rica.

Thus the record with respect to independent agencies set up to monitor or check the activities of elected branches (and their subordinates in their respective bureaucracies) is mixed. Some non-elected agencies in Latin America enjoy substantial independence. New or amended constitutions in Argentina, the Dominican Republic, and Mexico have greatly enhanced the independence of their supreme courts (on Mexico, see Magaloni, this volume). On the other hand, the lower-left area of Figure 4.3, where independence is at its lowest, shows the greatest cluster of non-elected justice-system agencies in Latin America. This region includes mainly human rights defenders (who are relatively powerless anyway) and controllers (whose typical relative dependence on the legislature is consistent with the notion of congress as having the power of the purse[26]). Where superintendence is left to entities that are dependent on political branches for their origin and survival, then creating more and more of them can be only a poor substitute for establishing legislative accountability to the citizenry. That is, if legislators do not care about (and perhaps even benefit from) executive corruption or are not motivated by their own accountability to the voters to rein in human rights abuses, then it is probably too much to ask of officials that are accountable to them to do so. Thus, for the remainder of this paper, we return to the prospects for electoral reforms that would increase the chances that legislators see their role as representing the values and preferences of the broad national citizenry.

Improving Vertical Accountability: Candidate Selection and Electoral Rules

Thus far, we have shown that presidential systems rely on horizontal exchange between elected branches to prevent oppression of citizens and to reveal information about wrongdoing in one branch or the other. We have noted that horizontal exchange between elected branches often fails, and that the separation of powers

---

[26] Of course, as we have argued above, if the legislature itself has little incentive to see that the executive correctly uses funds—perhaps because misappropriated funds provide patronage or personal-enrichment opportunities for legislators—then a controller's office that is an agent of the legislature is doomed to fail. For this reason, Colombia and Guatemala have increased their controller's autonomy, as shown in Figure 4.3. It is also clear from Figure 4.3 why the controller general in Chile is seen as such an important institution in that country.

itself undercuts vertical accountability, because the assigning of blame and meting out of electoral punishment is more difficult than in the nested hierarchy of a parliamentary system. Both vertical accountability and horizontal exchange are prone to break down, because executives and legislators might collude with one another, as when legislators seek patronage and thus have reduced incentive to be vigilant with respect to the executive branch. In this context, reformers in presidential systems often turn to 'independent' agencies of superintendence in an effort to generate oversight and compliance that is lacking in the electoral and legislative institutions. However, as we have seen, only some of the superintendence institutions are in fact really independent, thus completing a vicious circle: superintendence agencies are created because politicians may fail in their collective duty to provide good government, but politicians usually appoint or confirm (and sometimes may dismiss) their own overseers.

In this section, we briefly review some of the critical problems of vertical accountability in Latin America, and suggest solutions to them. We argue that much of the problem of legislators' shirking their duties to provide collective oversight of the executive is rooted in party and electoral systems that fail to connect legislators to the interests of the broad citizenry. This failure comes in two stages of the process of choosing legislators, the nomination process and the electoral rules. We review each stage of the process in turn, but first we briefly consider what would be the ideal system of vertical accountability, keeping in mind its limitations under a system of separated powers.

Effective Vertical Accountability   As we introduced the concept of accountability above, we noted that achieving both effective legislative oversight of the executive and effective non-elected agencies requires what we might call 'getting vertical accountability right'. The apparent dearth of what O'Donnell and others call 'horizontal accountability' is largely a malfunctioning of vertical accountability. We do not claim that strengthening vertical accountability is a sufficient condition for redressing the accountability deficit, but we do claim that it is a necessary one. As we have already mentioned, the checks and balances required to enhance accountability only emerge through purposive action by elected officials. With respect to the creation or maintenance of superintendence agencies, it is evident that their very existence and capacity to check the powers of elected officials are dependent upon the roles/resources assigned to them by elected officials.

As we noted above, the design of presidential systems requires the elected executive and legislative branches to work together to produce policy outputs. It further assumes that exchanges between the executive, legislative, and judicial branches will prevent oppression of citizens, because the checks and balances among the several branches will prevent the tyranny of concentrated authority. Put simply, horizontal exchanges (among separate branches) promote vertical accountability (of the entire governance system to the citizenry). However, this interplay is prone to failure if the crucial link between voters and their elected legislators is not functioning well. If parties are excessively top-heavy, dominated by national leaders, then legislators will have little incentive to articulate the interests of the voters whom they supposedly represent, and hence are unlikely to organize the legislature in such a way as to serve as an independent actor in the policy-making process. On the other hand, if parties are excessively weak, lacking discipline over individual members, then the legislature will be unable to engage in the collective action needed to serve as a counterweight to the executive. Again, in this situation, legislators are unlikely to invest in making the legislature an independent policy-making actor. While superintendence institutions added onto the horizontal dimension of the democratic state may assist in holding the overall governance structure accountable, as we saw in the last section, legislators are usually deeply involved in selecting those very same superintendents. If legislators lack the incentive to exchange with the executive over policies preferred by their constituents, and are instead motivated primarily by patronage, then superintendence institutions may fail to perform their roles. Thus, a prominent task for political reform in Latin America must be to redesign incentive structures that maximize the potential for effective vertical accountability, so that legislators advance the broad interests of their citizen-principals. We do not argue that such redesign SO would be a panacea, or that the various superintendence agencies could then be abolished, but we do argue that fundamental party and electoral reform is a necessary condition for improving the quality of democracy in the region. We now take up candidate selection (an internal party process) and electoral rules, in turn.

Nomination Processes The candidate selection process is chronologically the first opportunity to establish the relations of vertical accountability. It precedes the general election and, if poorly designed, can prevent what might otherwise be appropriate electoral arrangements from establishing a link of accountability between the electorate and legislators. For vertical accountability to work legislators must feel both the need to serve a particular district/ constituency but to do so as members of a partisan delegation. Candidate selection processes that are overly decentralized, allowing a group of partisans who constitute only a small subset of the partisans in the district to choose nominees, will err in the direction of emphasizing district over party (constituency service of narrow interests). Processes that are highly centralized, allowing a group outside of the district to choose nominees (including leaving candidate selection in the hands of the party elite), will err in the direction of emphasizing party over district.

A common shortcoming of candidate selection processes in Latin America is excessive centralization—leading to legislators who are responsive to party elites rather than voters. A prominent example was the Venezuelan system from 1958 till at least the 1990s, in which the central party leadership could replace and reorder candidates submitted by state-level parties. Internally undemocratic parties where national leaders hand-pick legislative candidates eliminate any sense of connection legislators might feel to a particular electoral district. Highly centralized candidate-selection processes increase the prospects that a nominee with no personal history in a district or special knowledge of its characteristics will be imposed upon the district from the outside.

At the other extreme, it is possible to imagine very small portions of the selectorate placing candidates on the ballot who would then be beholden to those very narrow interests rather than the interests of the party as a whole. This, of course, would only lead to a breakdown in the programmatic aspect of vertical accountability if the electoral system did not somehow compensate for these particularistic incentives by assuring that narrowly selected candidates could not be elected without a broader base of support. Electoral systems with very high district magnitudes and highly proportional seat allocation formulas, for example, would not compensate for decentralizing tendencies in the candidate selection process. Candidates would have every incentive to cater to the very defined needs of a particular selectorate (and electorate) rather than thinking of the district as a whole, not to mention the party platform.

In other systems there is virtually no formalized candidate-selection process at all. In such systems the prospects for vertical accountability are determined by the electoral rules alone. Where the electoral rules encourage particularistic, pork-barrel forms of representation, the candidate-selection process cannot counteract them. Perhaps the best example is Colombia where party leaders do not exercise any effective control over candidates' use of the party label. These legislators then have incentives to deliver patronage or 'pork' to a small subset of their parties' following. Similarly in Brazil, the *candidato nato* clause, which guarantees incumbents the right to renomination by the same party (Mainwaring 1991), in essence eliminates partisan selection of candidates. Incumbents running for office do not have to cater to broader party interests in order to assure themselves a viable place on the ballot.

Electoral Rules   The electoral rules are a critical link in any process of strengthening the accountability of the policy-making process to voter-principals. As we have stressed, the fact that the connection between voters and the executive does not run through legislators in presidential systems (as it does in parliamentary systems) means that legislators have little incentive to take into account the consequences of their actions for the executive's national policy program. Thus, if legislators' exchanges with the executive branch are to take place in a context of bargaining over policy, rather than an exchange of executive-offered patronage for legislators' votes, the electoral system must encourage legislators to emphasize voters' policy preferences. In this section we discuss features of electoral systems that help encourage legislators to be collectively accountable to their constituents over policy.

Electoral rules vary greatly in the degree to which they encourage candidates to cultivate a 'personal' or a 'party' vote (Carey and Shugart 1995). When the incentive to cultivate a personal vote is very high, as a result of competition for votes within parties, candidates tend not to campaign on broad policy issues. The reason is that in systems of intraparty competition, candidates need to emphasize the areas in which they *differ* from other candidates of the same party. Emphasizing issues, on the other hand, implies focusing on characteristics that they *share* with co-partisans.

When the incentive to cultivate a party vote is very high, candidates can run as partisan teams, and the potential to articulate shared themes outlined in a party platform is high. However, there is no guarantee that the partisan team will emphasize policy, because of an incentive-incompatibility problem brought on by institutions that create a high party-vote incentive. Such institutions are those that block intraparty competition by requiring voters to give only a party vote. The election of specific candidates in such *closed-list* systems is a product exclusively of the nomination and ranking of candidates on the ballot by the party. Thus the candidate-selection process is crucial within closed lists. If that selection process is decentralized and democratic, it may encourage candidates to remain close to the interests and policy preferences of rank-and-file party activists and voters, while then allowing them to campaign as policy-motivated teams in the general election. However, if the selection process is highly centralized and not subject to democratic procedures, then candidates will cater not to their supposed constituents, but instead to party leaders. In such highly centralized parties, it is sometimes said, accurately, that there is no accountability of legislators to voters.

Because of the dearth of accountability within parties when the nomination process is centralized and the electoral system is closed list, reformers often turn to various systems of preference voting within lists. In such systems, voters reorder the list, encouraging candidates to be responsive to voters instead of just to party leaders. However, having a preference vote means that candidates of the same party are in competition with one another, and as we noted above, such systems generate a personal vote and encourage attention to ways in which co-partisans differ. The surest way in which they differ is in the blocs of voters to whom they deliver pork-barrel and patronage favours.

Thus there is a very delicate balance in the design of electoral rules. Overemphasis on the incentive to cultivate a personal vote risks undermining parties and making legislators conduits of patronage demands rather than of policy preferences. Overemphasis on the incentive to cultivate a party vote risks cutting legislators off from the preferences of voters and makes them dependent on party leaders, especially if the nomination process itself is centralized. It happens that Latin America is home to electoral systems that are very extreme on the incentive to cultivate a personal or party vote. For instance, Colombia elects its senate in a single nationwide district of 100 seats under a formula employing personal lists. Most of these lists elect only one candidate, and no votes are pooled from one list to others of the same party. Brazil uses an open list with an average district magnitude (number of seats per district) of about nineteen. Uruguay and Peru likewise use systems of intraparty competition in large districts. As noted by Carey and Shugart (1995), the premium placed on cultivating a personal vote increases with magnitude in systems in which voters are casting votes below the party level (for one or more candidates or for one of several lists presented by a given party). On the other hand, there are also some very high-magnitude districts in Latin America in countries that use closed lists. Many of the closed-list systems, including those of Costa Rica, the Dominican Republic, and El Salvador, have at least one district with over 20 seats. Under a closed list the incentive for members to cultivate a personal vote decreases as magnitude increases, because the longer the list, the more legislators there are in electorally unassailable list positions. The important decisions concerning members' careers are made at the nomination stage, when their list positions are determined, not at the election.

Given the tendency of many Latin American countries to have systems that generate either a very high or very low incentive to cultivate a personal vote, electoral reforms should centre on making these incentives more moderate. With less extreme incentives, candidates' responsiveness to a national party, on the one hand, and to their own constituents, on the other hand, would be balanced.[27] One way of achieving a balance between local and party interests is the increasingly popular 'mixed-member' system. In such a system some members are elected in single-seat districts (SSDs) and some from party lists, and voters are generally given both a list vote and a vote for a candidate in their SSD (Shugart and Wattenberg 2001). Mixed-member systems generate countervailing ambitions within the party, in that to do well in the overall system, at least the major parties must present both candidates who are attractive to local constituencies and a party label that can attract list votes. Studies of mixed-member systems have shown that even members elected from lists tend to be responsive to localities, probably because their parties recognize the importance of maintaining a profile in SSDs that they may not have won in the last election, but may hope to win in the future (Barker et al. 2001; Klingemann and Wessels 2001). However, we would caution that the hopes of reformers who advocate mixed-member systems could be dashed if the nomination process is not opened up. This is especially crucial for the list portion of the mixed-member system, as often some of the list-tier districts have very high magnitudes.

---

[27] In parliamentary systems this is not such a delicate balance because the executive itself is collectively accountable to the parliament and therefore legislators themselves are collectively accountable for their position for or against the government and its policies. In presidential systems, the separation of executive and legislative powers implies greater opportunity for legislators to go their own way and duck governing responsibility, if they have electoral incentives to do so.

Moderate forms of intraparty competition in general elections may also provide a balance of incentives. The key is not to allow the share of the party's vote—or the total vote—needed for election to be so small that simply providing pork or clientelistic services to a very narrow constituency is sufficient to win a seat. For example, the Chilean system is obviously compatible with meaningful party labels despite its provision for candidate preference voting. No doubt the strength of Chilean parties derives in part from their significant connections to social groups (Valenzuela 1978; Scully 1995), but even a party with a strong social identity must develop a strategy for coping with intraparty competition when the electoral system requires it, as it did in Chile. Since the return to democracy in 1989, there is not actual intra-*party* competition, because the two-seat districts have encouraged alliances that nominate only one (at most) candidate of any one component party in each district. However, from 1958 through 1969, interparty alliances were not common and the district magnitude was greater than two, yet the preference voting did not undermine party labels. The larger the magnitude, the more co-partisans one candidate must face, and thus the smaller is the average number of votes per candidate. Thus the low magnitudes in pre-Pinochet Chile (average five, largest eighteen) imply larger personal-vote constituencies than the very high magnitudes in Brazil (average about nineteen, largest seventy)[28] or formerly Peru (single national district of 120 in 1995 and 2000). Systems of intraparty competition can be consistent with the countervailing ambitions of both local personal-vote-seeking and allegiance to a party where the district magnitude is relatively low because it is not possible to win with extremely narrow personal-vote constituencies—party incentives can counter the personal-vote incentives.

No electoral system single-handedly can transform a personalistic system into one where legislators begin campaigning on party labels and policy. Nor can electoral reform assure that a hyper-centralized system is replaced by one in which individual candidates cater to voter policy preferences rather than primarily to party leaders. However, electoral reform can shift the calculus of candidates in the desired direction, by eliminating or reducing incentives to cultivate a personal vote in personalistic systems or adding a constituency feature of decentralized nominations in

---

[28] In Brazil, the share of votes needed to win is made even smaller by a provision that permits parties to nominate one-and-a-half times as many candidates as there are seats in the district.

hyper-centralized systems. Where an electoral system provides for countervailing personal-vote and party-vote incentives, the odds are increased that candidates will be both responsive to local interests and articulators of national policy, because such mixed strategies are more likely to pay off electorally.

The Importance of Balance in Achieving Vertical Accountability
The key to improving vertical accountability of legislators to the citizenry is to find moderation or balance between extremes that will eliminate the tension between representing a particular constituency and representing a programmatic party. Legislators subject to incentive structures at either extreme will not have the countervailing ambitions necessary to check and balance presidents. Those facing excessively decentralized candidate-selection processes will be easily bought out by presidents as legislators pursue resources to distribute to their districts. Regarding the case of Peru, Lourdes Flores Nano notes how vulnerable individualistic legislators lacking any party or ideological commitments are to succumbing to executive-branch pressures.[29] On the other hand, legislators from excessively centralized parties will abdicate vigilant participation in the policy-making process in favour of slavish loyalty to the party line, as noted for the case of Mexico by Adolfo Aguilar Zinser.[30] Under either extreme, then, legislatures become empty shells devoid of interest to those who want to shape policy outcomes. Organized interests turn their attention to the executive and/or national party offices, neither of which is interested in district-level concerns, and thus the collective accountability of legislators for policy concerns—on which effective horizontal exchange depends—is short-circuited.

Candidate-selection processes and electoral rules are stages of the same process, and, as a result, their combination greatly affects the prospects for getting vertical accountability 'right'. There is as

[29] Comments prepared by Lourdes Flores Nano (2000), a prominent Peruvian legislator and later a presidential candidate, at the conference on which this volume is based.

[30] Comments prepared by Adolfo Aguilar Zinser, an independent senator, at the conference on which this volume is based. Aguilar Zinser further noted that the situation in Mexico is not only one of absolute party control over nominations, but also of a ban on consecutive reelection. With no prospect for congressional careers, legislators have no incentive to invest in the institutional integrity of the legislature, as after three or six years (depending on the chamber) they will move on to another job—typically a patronage position provided by their party or the executive.

yet little research on the combination of these stages, but we can make some preliminary assessments. It would seem that excessive centralization in the candidate-selection stage is likely to swamp decentralizing incentives at the electoral stage. Thus, for example, the adoption of single-seat districts for about half the seats in Venezuela in 1993 showed little effect on the tendencies of legislators to represent district interests, because the nomination process remained as centralized as ever in the then-dominant AD (Kulisheck and Crisp 2001). On the other hand, an overly open nomination process may vitiate the party-centred institutions at the electoral stage. For example, in Ecuador before 1996, most parties required practically no commitment of prospective candidates to a party organization (let alone a policy platform) to get on the party list, so parties were weak, undisciplined, and personalistic in spite of a closed-list system (Conaghan 1995). If getting vertical accountability 'right' in the principal–agent relation between voters and politicians means encouraging candidates to represent the collective preferences of their constituents with respect to policy issues, as we have argued, both the candidate-selection and electoral stages of that relationship must be designed well. Thus reformers need to consider both stages carefully.

Relations Among Agents Are a Function of Their Connections to the Principal

Agents cannot hold other agents accountable, only their principals can. Horizontal exchange based on the policy preferences of the electorate, the ultimate principal in a democratic system, will occur only where the vertical connections between the electorate and its multiple agents encourage those elected officials to act upon countervailing ambitions. Presidential systems provide for separate origin and survival and overlapping functions; candidate-selection and electoral processes (are supposed to) assure that incentives for countervailing ambitions over programmatic policy outcomes lead to horizontal exchange among agents. Where horizontal exchange over policy preferences is lacking it is because the vertical links between voters and elected officials are malfunctioning. In this context, there is a tendency to see the superintendence agencies as a panacea, enforcing 'accountability' where legislators fail to check the executive and uncover wrongdoing and where voters are incapable of sanctioning their elected agents.

The solution to the accountability deficit in Latin America is not the rapid proliferation of new non-elected agencies of superintendence. These agencies may be helpful in deterring or punishing official transgressions against the ultimate principal (the citizenry), but only as an adjunct to vertical accountability. They are unlikely to function well in a context of especially poor accountability of legislators to citizens, especially when legislators are de facto accountable to the executive instead. Assuring that the vertical links between legislators and voters encourage effective horizontal exchange is thus a necessary first step. Once this is accomplished, the creation of new actors may not be necessary, but, if it is, the prospects that they will fulfil the roles for which they are intended increase dramatically when the legislators who participate in their appointment are vertically accountable to citizen interests. In fact, creating additional agencies without repairing the vertical accountability of legislators will raise expectations that have little hope of being fulfilled. Creating a new agency with much fanfare but then failing to endow it with the necessary faculties to fulfil its role only heightens the public's sense of disillusionment, and undermines the integrity and legitimacy of the very democracy-strengthening project to which the authors of new or reformed constitutions have committed so much effort.

TABLE A4.1. *Constitutional provisions for separation of origin and survival: Supreme Courts in Latin America*

Country	Nominate	Confirm/Appoint	Term (years)	Accuse/initiate dismissal	Dismiss
Argentina	President	Senate—2/3	Lifetime	Chamber of Deputies (authorizes trial —2/3 vote)	Senate
Bolivia	Council of Judicature[a]	Congress—2/3	10	Chamber of Deputies	Senate—2/3
Brazil	President	Senate	Lifetime, after 2 yrs	(Not identified)	Senate—2/3
Chile	Supreme Ct.—slate of 3	President	Lifetime	Chamber of Deputies	Senate—2/3
Colombia	Council of Judicature[b]	Supreme Court	8	Chamber of Deputies	Senate—2/3
Costa Rica	Congress	Congress—2/3 vote	8		Supreme Court—2/3 vote
Dominican Republic	National Council of Magistrates[c]	National Council of Magistrates	Lifetime		Supreme Court
Ecuador	Supreme Court	Supreme Court	Not specified		National Council of the Judicature
El Salvador	Congress—2/3	Congress—2/3	5		Congress—2/3
Guatemala	Postulation Committee—slate of 26 by 2/3 vote[d]	Congress	5		Congress—2/3
Honduras	Congress	Congress	4	Congress	Supreme Court
Mexico	President	Senate—2/3	15	Chamber of Deputies	Senate—2/3 vote
Nicaragua	President or Congress (w/consultation from civic gps.)	Congress—3/5	7	Congress—2/3 vote (removes immunity)	Tried criminally

TABLE A4.1. (*cont'd*)

Country	Nominate	Confirm/Elect	Term (years)	Accuse/initiate dismissal	Dismissal
Panama	President (with VP & ministers)	Congress	10 (every 2 yrs)		Supreme Court
Paraguay	President from list submitted by Council of Magistrates[e]	Senate	5	Chamber of Deputies	Senate—2/3 vote
Peru	National Council of Magistrates[f]	National Council of Magistrates	Life	Congressional Permanent Committee	Congress
Uruguay	Congress	Congress—2/3 vote	10	Chamber of Deputies	Senate—2/3 vote
Venezuela	Postulation Committee and *Poder Ciudadano*[g]	Congress	12	*Poder Ciudadano*	Congress—2/3 vote

[a] Elected by Congress by two-thirds vote from among experienced lawyers.

[b] Seven experienced lawyers elected by Congress, six members elected by high courts.

[c] Composed of the President, Public Prosecutor, President of Senate, a senate member, President of Chamber of Deputies, one deputy, President of Supreme Court, and one Supreme Court justice.

[d] Selection body includes President (or Vice-President), President of Senate, President of chamber, President of Supreme Court, one Supreme Court justice.

[e] Consists of one Supreme Court justice chosen by the Court, one member appointed by President, one by the Senate, one by the Chamber of Deputies, two lawyers chosen by law associations, and two law professors chosen by their colleagues.

[f] Selection body includes officials from other branches (Supreme Court justices) and members of civil society (lawyers, university deans).

[g] The Committee on Judicial Postulations is composed of representatives of societal groups connected with the judiciary; the Poder Ciudadano is composed of the National Public Defender of Human Rights, the Controller General, the Public Minister, and the Public Prosecutor.

Source: Constitutions available from the Political Database of the Americas at http://www.georgetown.edu/pdba/

TABLE A4.2. *Constitutional provisions for separation of origin and survival: Constitutional tribunals in Latin America*

Country	Nominate	Confirm/Appoint	Term (years)	Accuse/initiate dismissal	Dismiss
Bolivia		Congress—2/3	10	Chamber of Deputies	Senate—2/3
Chile		3 by Sup. Ct., 1 by Pres., 2 by Nat. Sec. Council, 1 by Sen.	8	Chamber of Deputies	Senate—2/3
Colombia	Slate by Pres., Sup. Ct., Council of State.	Senate	8	Chamber of Deputies	Senate—2/3
Ecuador	2 by Pres, 2 by Sup. Ct., 2 by Cong, 1 by local officials, 2 from civil society organizations	Congress	4		Congress
Peru		Congress—2/3	5	Congressional Permanent Committee	Congress

Note: For countries not listed, constitutional review is typically a function of the Supreme Court.

Source: Constitutions available from the Political Database of the Americas at http://www.georgetown.edu/pdba/

TABLE A4.3. *Constitutional provisions for separation of origin and survival: Attorneys General in Latin America*

Country	Nominate	Confirm/Elect	Term (years)	Accuse/initiate dismissal	Dismiss
Colombia (*Fiscal General*)	President	Supreme Court	4	Chamber of Deputies	Senate (charges of common crimes referred to Supreme Court)
Ecuador	President—slate of 3	Congress	4	Congress	Congress
El Salvador	Congress	Congress	3		Congress—2/3
Honduras	Congress	Congress	4	Congress	Supreme Court trial
Mexico	President	Senate	Not fixed		President may dismiss at will
Panama	President	Congress	10	(Not identified)	Supreme Court trial
Paraguay	President from list submitted by Council of Magistrates	Senate	Not fixed		President
Venezuela	President	Congress	Not specified		President

Source: Constitutions available from the Political Database of the Americas at http://www.georgetown.edu/pdba/

TABLE A4.4. *Constitutional provisions for separation of origin and survival: Prosecutors General in Latin America*

Country	Appoint	Confirm/Elect	Term (years)	Accuse/initiate dismissal	Dismiss
Bolivia	President	President	Not specified	Chamber of Deputies	Senate
Brazil (*Procurador-General*)	President	Senate	2	President	Senate
Colombia (*Procurador General*)	President, Supreme Court, and Council of State—slate of 3	Senate	4		Determined by law
Dominican Republic	National Council of Magistrates (see Table A4.1)	National Council of Magistrates	Life		Supreme Court
Ecuador	National Council of Judicature—slate of 3[a]	Congress	4	Congress	Congress; National Judicature may also dismiss members.
El Salvador	Congress	Congress	3		Congress—2/3
Guatemala	Postulation Committee—slate of 6 by 2/3 vote[b]	President	4		President removes for 'just cause'
Honduras (*Director General de Probidad*)	Congress	Congress	5	Congress	Supreme Court trial
Nicaragua	President or Congress	Congress—3/5	Not specified		Determined by law

TABLE A4.4. (cont'd)

Country	Appoint	Confirm/Elect	Term (years)	Accuse/initiate dismissal	Dismiss
Panama	President	Congress	5		Supreme Court
Paraguay	President (Council of magistrates submits slate)	Senate	5	Chamber of Deputies	Senate—2/3 vote
Peru	National Committee of Attorneys General	National Committee of Attorneys General	3	Congressional Permanent Committee	Congress
Venezuela	Postulation Committee submits slate^c	Congress—2/3	7	Supreme Court	Congress

[a] Composition determined by law.

[b] Composed of representatives for the deans of universities throughout the country, deans of law departments, deans of law/social science departments of each university in the country and an equivalent number of representatives from the National Assembly of Lawyers and Notaries.

[c] Originates in the *Poder Ciudadano* branch of government (see note g to Table A4.1).

Source: Constitutions available from the Political Database of the Americas at http://www.georgetown.edu/pdba/

TABLE A4.5. *Constitutional provisions for separation of origin and survival: defenders for human rights in Latin America*

Country	Nominate	Confirm/Elect	Term (years)	Accuse/initiate dismissal	Dismiss
Argentina	Congress	Congress—2/3 vote	5		Congress—2/3 vote
Bolivia	Congress	Congress—2/3 vote	5	Attorney General requests trial	Supreme Court
Colombia	President—slate of 3	Chamber of Deputies	4		Determined by law
Ecuador	Congress (w/hearing from human rights organizations)[a]	Congress	5	Congress	Congress; National Judicature may also dismiss members
El Salvador	Congress	Congress—2/3 vote	3		Congress—2/3
Guatemala	Committee of Congress[b]	Congress	5		Congress—2/3
Nicaragua	Congress	Congress	Determined by law	Congress—2/3 vote	Tried criminally
Paraguay	Senate—slate of 3	Chamber of Deputies	5[c]	Chamber of Deputies	Senate—2/3 vote
Peru	Congress	Congress—2/3 vote	5	Congressional Permanent Committee	Congress—2/3 vote
Venezuela	Postulation Committee[d]	Congress—2/3	7	Supreme Court	Congress

[a] Selection process includes a hearing in which non-governmental actors may participate but do not vote.
[b] A nominating committee composed of representatives from all represented parties presents 3 nominees. Congress makes a final selection.
[c] Concurrent with legislative term.
[d] Originates in the *Poder Ciudadano* branch of government (see note g to Table A4.1).

Source: Constitutions available from the Political Database of the Americas at http://www.georgetown.edu/pdba/

TABLE A4.6. *Constitutional provisions for separation of origin and survival: Controllers General in Latin America*

Country	Nominate	Confirm/Elect	Term (years)	Accuse/initiate dismissal	Dismissal
Argentina		Opposition party with most seats in congress	Not specified	Not specified	Not specified
Bolivia (*Tribunal de Cuentas*)	Senate—slate of 3	President	4	Chamber of Deputies	Senate—2/3
Brazil		1/3 chosen by President; 2/3 chosen by congress	Not specified		Determined by law (criminal)
Chile	President	Senate	Life	Chamber of Deputies	Senate—2/3
Colombia	Constitutional court, Sup. Ct, and Council of State—slate of 3	Congress	4		Determined by law
Costa Rica	Congress	Congress	8, 2 yrs after pres term		Chamber dismisses with 2/3 vote
Dominican Republic	President—slate of 3	Senate	4	Chamber of Deputies—3/4	Senate—3/4
Ecuador	Congress—slate of 3	President	4	Congress	Congress
El Salvador (*Corte de Cuentas*)	Congress	Congress	3	Congress	Congress—2/3
Guatemala	Postulation Committee (2/3 vote)[a]	Congress—2/3 vote	4		Congress (mental incapacity, crime, negligence)

Honduras	Congress	Congress	5	Congress	Supreme Court trial
Mexico	Congress	Congress	Determined by law	Congress	Chamber supervises performance. No specific dismissal procedures.
Nicaragua	Congress—3/5	President or Congress (w/consultation of civic groups)	6	Congress—2/3 vote	Tried criminally
Panama	Congress	Congress	6	Congress	Supreme Court
Paraguay	Chamber of Deputies—2/3 vote	Senate—slate of 3	5	Chamber of Deputies	Senate—2/3 vote
Peru	Congress	Congress	7	Congressional Permanent Committee	Congress; National Council of Magistrates also oversees/ratifies members every 7 yrs
Uruguay (*Tribunal de Cuentas*)	Congress—2/3 vote	Congress	5	Congress—2/3 vote	Congress—2/3 vote
Venezuela	Congress—2/3	Committee of Postulation[b]	7	Supreme Court	Congress

[a] Composed of representatives of university deans of accounting and auditing departments throughout the country and an equal number of representatives chosen by the National Assembly of Economists, Accountants, Auditors, and Business Administrators.

[b] Originates in the 'Poder Ciudadano' branch of government (see note g to Table A4.1).

Source: Constitutions available from the Political Database of the Americas at http://www.georgetown.edu/pdba/

References

Barker, F., J. Boston, S. Levine, E. McLeay, and S. Roberts. 2001. 'An Initial Assessment of the Consequences of MMP in New Zealand'. In Matthew Soberg Shugart and Martin Wattenberg, eds., *Mixed-Member Electoral Systems: The Best of Both Worlds?* Oxford: Oxford University Press.

Carey, John, and Matthew S. Shugart. 1995. 'Incentives to Cultivate a Personal Vote: A Rank Ordering of Electoral Formulas'. *Electoral Studies* 14, 4: 417–39.

Conaghan, Catherine M. 1995. 'Politicians Against Parties: Discord and Disconnection in Ecuador's Party System'. In Scott Mainwaring and Timothy Scully, eds., *Building Democratic Institutions: Party Systems in Latin America*. Stanford, CA: Stanford University Press.

Correa Sutil, Jorge. 1993. 'The Judiciary and the Political System in Chile: The Dilemmas of Judicial Independence During the Transition to Democracy'. In Irwin P. Stotzky, ed., *Transition to Democracy in Latin America: The Role of the Judiciary*. Boulder, CO: Westview Press.

Cox, Gary. 1987. *The Efficient Secret: The Cabinet and the Development of Political Parties in Victorian England*. New York, NY: Cambridge University Press.

Cox, Gary, and Matthew McCubbins. 1993. *Legislative Leviathan: Party Government in the House*. Berkeley, CA: University of California Press.

Dunn, John. 1999. 'Situating Democratic Political Accountability'. In Bernard Manin, Adam Przeworski and Susan Stokes, eds., *Democracy, Accountability, and Representation*, pp. 329–51. New York, NY: Cambridge University Press.

Elster, J. 1999. 'Accountability in Athenian Politics'. In A. Przeworski, S. Stokes and B. Manin, eds., *Democracy, Accountability, and Representation*, pp. 253–78. Cambridge: Cambridge University Press.

Epstein, Leon D. 1967. *Political Parties in Western Democracies*. New York, NY: Praeger.

Flores Nano, Lourdes. 2000. 'El Caso Peruano'. Paper presented at the conference Institutions, Accountability and Democratic Governance in Latin America, Kellogg Institute for International Studies, University of Notre Dame, May 8–9.

Grofman, Bernard N. 1987. 'Will the New Real Institutionalism Please Stand Up and Take a Bow?' Unpublished paper.

——. 1989. 'The Federalist Papers and the New Institutionalism: An Overview'. In Bernard Grofman and Donald Wittman, eds., *The Federalist Papers and the New Institutionalism*. New York, NY: Agathon Press.

Haggard, Stephan, and Mathew D. McCubbins, eds. 2000. *Structure and Policy in Presidential Democracies*. New York, NY: Cambridge University Press.

Jacobson, Gary. 1990. *The Electoral Origins of Divided Government: Competition in U.S. House Elections, 1946–1988*. Boulder, CO: Westview Press.

Kada, Naoko. n.d. 'The Politics of Impeachment'. Ph.D. dissertation. University of California, San Diego.

Kiewet, D. Roderick, and Mathew D. McCubbins. 1991. *The Logic of Delegation: Congressional Parties and the Appropriations Process*. Chicago, IL: University of Chicago Press.

Klingemann, H., and Wessels, B. 2001. 'The Political Consequences of Germany's Mixed-Member System: Personalization at the Grass Roots?' In Matthew Soberg Shugart and Martin Wattenberg, eds., *Mixed-Member Electoral Systems: The Best of Both Worlds?* Oxford: Oxford University Press.

Kulisheck, Michael, and Brian F. Crisp. 2001. 'The Legislative Consequences of MMP Electoral Rules in Venezuela'. In Matthew Soberg Shugart and Martin Wattenberg, eds., *Mixed-Member Electoral Systems: The Best of Both Worlds?* Oxford: Oxford University Press.

Laver, Michael and Kenneth Shepsle. 1999. 'Government Accountability in Parliamentary Democracy'. In Adam Przeworski, Susan Stokes, and Bernard Manin, eds., *Democracy, Accountability and Representation*. Cambridge: Cambridge University Press.

Levy, Brian, and Pablo Spiller. 1993. The Institutional Foundations of Regulatory Commitment, Cambridge: Cambridge University Press.

Lijphart, Arend. 1999. *Patterns of Democracy: Government Forms and Performance in Thirty-six Countries*. New Haven, CT: Yale University Press.

Mainwaring, Scott. 1991. 'Politicians, Parties, and Electoral Systems: Brazil in Comparative Perspective'. *Comparative Politics* 24, 1 (October): 21–43.

Mayhew, David. 1974. *Congress: The Electoral Connection*. New Haven, CT: Yale University Press.

McCubbins, Mathew, Roger G. Noll, and Barry R. Weingast. 1987. 'Administrative Procedures as Instruments of Political Control'. *Journal of Law, Economics, and Organizations* 3: 243–77.

——. 1989. 'Structure and Process, Politics and Policy: Administrative Arrangements and the Political Control of Agencies'. *Virginia Law Review* 75: 431–82.

McCubbins, Mathew D., and Thomas Schwartz. 1984. 'Congressional Oversight Overlooked: Police Patrols vs. Fire Alarms'. *American Journal of Political Science* 28: 165–79.

Moe, Terry. 1984. 'The New Economics of Organization'. *American Journal of Political Science* 28, 4: 739–77.

——. 1990. 'Political Institutions: The Neglected Side of the Story'. *Journal of Law, Economics, and Organization*, Special issue.

Moe, Terry and Michael Caldwell. 1994. 'The Institutional Foundations of Democratic Government: A Comparison of Presidential and Parliamentary Systems'. *Journal of Institutional and Theoretical Economics* 150, 1: 171–95.

O'Donnell, Guillermo. 1994. 'Delegative Democracy'. *Journal of Democracy* 5, 1: 55–70.

——. 1999. 'Horizontal Accountability in New Democracies'. In Andreas Schedler, Larry Diamond, and Marc F. Plattner, eds., *The Self Restraining State: Power and Accountability in New Democracies*. Boulder, CO: Lynne Rienner Publishers.

Olson, Mancur. 1965. *The Logic of Collective Action: Public Goods and the Theory of Groups*. Cambridge, MA: Harvard University Press.

Palmer, Matthew. 1995. 'Toward an Economics of Comparative Political Organization: Examining Ministerial Responsibility'. *Journal of Law, Economics and Organization* 11, 1:164–88

Ramseyer, J. Mark and Frances McCall Rosenbluth. 1993. *Japan's Political Marketplace*. Cambridge, MA: Harvard University Press.

Scully, Timothy. 1995. 'Reconstituting Party Politics in Chile'. In Scott Mainwaring and Timothy Scully, eds., *Building Democratic Institutions: Party Systems in Latin America*. Stanford, CA: Stanford University Press.

Shepsle, Kenneth A. 1986. 'Institutional Equilibrium and Equilibrium Institutions'. In Herbert F. Weisberg, ed., *Political Science: The Science of Politics*. New York, NY: Agathon Press.

Shugart, Matthew Soberg. 2001. 'Extreme Electoral Systems and the Appeal of the Mixed-Member Alternative'. In Matthew Soberg Shugart and Martin Wattenberg, eds., *Mixed-Member Electoral Systems: The Best of Both Worlds?* Oxford: Oxford University Press.

Shugart, Matthew Soberg and John Carey. 1992. *Presidents and Assemblies: Constitutional Design and Electoral Dynamics*. Cambridge: Cambridge University Press.

Shugart, Matthew Soberg and Stephan Haggard. 2000. 'Institutions and Public Policy in Presidential Systems'. In Stephan Haggard and Mathew D. McCubbins, eds., *Structure and Policy in Presidential Democracies*. New York, NY: Cambridge University Press.

Shugart, Matthew Soberg and Martin Wattenberg, eds. 2001. *Mixed-Member Electoral Systems: The Best of Both Worlds?* Oxford: Oxford University Press.

Stone, Alec. 1992. *The Birth of Judicial Politics in France: The Constitutional Council in Comparative Perspective*. New York, NY: Oxford University Press.

Strøm, Kaare. 2000. 'Delegation and Accountability in Parliamentary Democracies'. *European Journal of Political Research* 37, 3 (May): 261–89.

Tsebelis, George and Jeannette Money. 1997. *Bicameralism*. Cambridge: Cambridge University Press.

Valenzuela, Arturo. 1978. *The Breakdown of Democratic Regimes*. Baltimore, MD: The Johns Hopkins University Press.

Weingast, Barry R. 1984. 'The Congressional-Bureaucratic System: A Principal–Agent Perspective'. *Public Choice* 44: 147–92.

Weingast, Barry R. and William Marshall. 1988. 'The Industrial Organization of Congress'. *Journal of Political Economy* 96: 132–63.

Weldon, Jeffrey. 1997. 'Political Sources of *Presidencialismo* in Mexico'. In Scott Mainwaring and Matthew S. Shugart, eds., *Presidentialism and Democracy in Latin America*. Cambridge: Cambridge University Press.

Legislative Oversight: Interests and Institutions in the United States and Argentina

Scott Morgenstern
Luigi Manzetti

'The prevalence of charges of corruption and of actual corruption in American politics is not of itself proof of our inferiority in political morality to the other great nations of the world.' (Brooks 1909: 21)

'The age of Walpole was marked by corruption greater and apparently more irremediable than any which we have yet known in American political life. Who could have predicted that...the administrative side of British government, instead of becoming hopelessly incapable under the increasing strain, would have become the purest and most nearly perfect mechanism thus far known in political history?' (Howard 1899: 240)

Introduction

The concept of oversight is based upon the notion that while government is necessary for democracy to prosper in an orderly fashion, its institutions and the people who staff them must be accountable for their actions. Doing otherwise invites people in official positions to abuse their discretionary power in order to pursue particular interests rather than the public good. The United States was the first democracy to espouse this concept by creating checks and balances among the executive, legislative, and judicial branches of government to keep public officials in line. Yet, an effective oversight system did not develop overnight just because the United States Constitution called for it. Such systems have still failed to fully develop in most Latin American countries, in spite of their adoption of United States-style presidential governments.

Our goal in this chapter is to explain how similar institutions in the 19th century ended up producing widely different results in terms of oversight enforcement by the end of the 20th century. Drawing from North (1990: 101), our research question is 'What happens when a common set of rules is imposed on two different societies?' Thus, our study is one in institutional development.

We take as our case studies the United States and Argentina. At the turn of the 20th century these two nations shared three notable features. They had similar constitutional arrangements, were among the fastest growing economies in the developing world, and their polities were very corrupt. While we do not claim a direct link between corruption and development, during the 20th century the two countries diverged both economically and in terms of government accountability. To this day Argentina and many other Latin American countries are still plagued with corruption and are troubled by a pernicious form of democracy in which presidents are seldom held to constitutional limits on their power. In the United States, on the contrary, people have come to expect public officials to act honestly and government institutions to prosecute and punish those who engage in unlawful behavior.

However, it was not always so in the United States. Indeed, the situation must have seemed as hopeless to the United States citizens of the late 1800s, or the British at the time of Walpole, as it does to Latin Americans today. The United States society at the end of the 19th century was riddled with corruption, political fraud, and business collusion. Big business trampled on workers as local and federal governments, far from able to control the problem, were implicated themselves. The spoils system had become a source of inefficiency and corruption and had led to the assassination of President Garfield; emerging giant corporations were seen as eating away at democracy, in part by buying politicians; anti-democratic and fraud-plagued machine governments took hold of our biggest cities; and elections, the very base of democracy, were plagued with fraud.

As the quotations above remind us, there were large doubts about whether remedy was possible, given beliefs in the cultural roots of the problem. Beginning around the turn of the 20th century, however, change did occur. In this chapter we focus on three important changes. First, the adoption of the secret (Australian) ballot and direct primaries had great impacts in limiting electoral fraud and winning the legislators' independence from machines and parties. Second, civil service reforms helped end the rotten spoils system and professionalize the bureaucracy. Third, the legislature's own professionalization led members of Congress to create and control a budget and accounting office to monitor and verify the workings of government services.

We argue in this chapter that these specific changes and the overall move to a more transparent government, came about over time, as a result of the conjunction of several factors. First, the United States citizens began screaming from the ballot boxes for social and economic change. The Populist and Progressive movements were expressions of the discontent of multiple societal groups regarding the corrupt political machines and corporations that had purportedly stolen our economic liberalism and political democracy (Hofstadter 1955: 5). As a result, third parties gained new heights and traditional parties moved to adapt the movements' reformist platforms. Further, the legislature gained greater independence from the executive as a result of Johnson's impeachment and the frequent occurrence of divided government. The political competition led to a number of significant institutional changes—upheld by the courts—which collectively helped set the course for transparent, and thus clean, government. In addition, we follow Mayhew (1974) and Fiorina (1977, 1989) in arguing that legislators' independence from their parties (which partly result from the single-member districts combined with primaries) motivated them to professionalize their workplace. Among other changes, this instigated their interest in creating a budget and accounting office controlled by the legislature.

Unfortunately, the democratic process has hardly shone through in Latin America. As a result, even well-intentioned reforms have been hindered or sullied. For example, during the 1990s, the wave of market reforms that rolled across Latin America succeeded in addressing unprecedented economic crises, but democracy and the economic gains were often undercut by blatant violations of the legal process and corruption, even at the highest level of government. With a focus on Argentina, we argue that the lack of reform has resulted from the lack of independence among the three branches of government, as well as the continual interruptions of the democratic process. Further, the short legislative careers and strong party system worked against the professionalization of the legislature.

Still, the successful reform process in the United States leads us to conclude that reform is also possible in Latin American societies. In light of the dramatic investigative popular-press books about corruption in Argentina (Verbitsky 1991, 1993), Chile (Matus 1999), and Mexico (Gómez 1996) concomitant with impeachment or resignations of presidents in Brazil, Venezuela, Ecuador, and Peru on corruption charges, we may well be witnessing the inauguration of their 'age of reform'.[1]

The chapter is organized in the following manner. In the second section we define oversight and present our theoretical argument. We focus on the degree to which the legislative branch has developed the technocratic institutions necessary for ensuring the financial and administrative accountability of the presidency and executive-controlled bureaucratic agencies. Our analysis will include, but will not be limited to, corrupt practices of the executive. In the analysis we will also discuss the judiciary, which can play a crucial role in limiting or allowing corruption or reining in executive abuses.

The third section explores the development of oversight institutions in the United States. Keeping in mind the strong public demand for reform to which the assassination of President Garfield and the muckraking press were important contributors, we first discuss the motivations that have led the United States legislators to develop the institutions that have aided their oversight role. There we look into United States history to explore the electoral changes and frequent experiences of divided government that helped establish the legislators' independence from party bosses and the legislature's independence from the executive branch. We then argue that the conjunction of these and some contextual factors aided the development of the civil service reforms and the Congressional Budget Office, two of the many innovations that have played important roles in ending widespread political corruption in the United States.

In the fourth section turn to the Argentine experience. Our focus there is on the failed attempts to develop oversight of the budget process and an explanation of why the Argentine Congress has been much less effective than its United States counterpart. Our argument is based on the infrequent control of the Congress by the opposition, the economic crises that have reinforced presidential control, and the frequent military governments that suspended any attempts by the legislators to professionalize their institution and develop effective oversight mechanisms. In

---

[1] This term comes from Hofstadter (1955). We discuss the resignation of Argentine President de la Rúa below.

the concluding section, however, we note that aided by the long retreat of the militaries to their barracks, the legislatures in Argentina and other Latin American countries have begun to take much more active political roles than in times past. In Argentina this has led to what appears on paper as an impressive set of oversight institutions. If given enough time, these institutions could prove to be the first important steps on their road to reform.

Oversight and a Theory of Reform

This chapter was not spurred by an interest in corruption per se, but by the issue of 'delegative democracy' described by O'Donnell (1994). In that well-known paper, O'Donnell argues that Latin American presidents operate with general impunity, seldom slowed by the constitutional stipulations of legislative procedures. While others argue that the legislatures are not supine, it is clear that the Latin American legislatures frequently fail to curtail executive excesses (Cox and Morgenstern 2001).

Oversight is the monitoring and control of one person or institution (generally termed the agent) by another (the principal), so that the agent acts in the principal's interest. Agency slack implies the ability of the agent to pursue his or her own interests. This slack may or may not be illegal. Only when it crosses a clear legal line is the agency slack termed corruption. Oversight, therefore, encompasses, but is not limited to, corruption. As such, effective oversight implies the principal's ability to both verify actions and sanction wrongdoers or correct an agent's objectionable decisions. As noted earlier, in an effort to understand the feasibility of effective oversight in Latin America, we focus primarily (but not exclusively) on legislative control of the executive branch in the United States and Argentina.

The road to reform began in the United States in the latter half of the 19th century with public demands for restraining executive abuse. These demands were (eventually) met by legislators who had personal interests in responding to constituents as opposed to the executive. The United States legislators have also had a long period of uninterrupted democracy to develop and adapt institutions, such as the Civil Service, the Government Accounting Office and the Congressional Budget Office. Laws such as the Freedom of Information Act have also allowed legislators to get a handle on the monstrous and changing federal government. In contrast,

Argentine legislators have had relatively short periods of democracy in which to work and have had limited levels of expertise as a result of their short congressional careers. This, combined with ties to the president or party leaders that are generally stronger than to constituents, has limited the legislators' interests in developing effective oversight institutions.

Thus, our thesis in this chapter is that the particular conjunction of factors that led the United States legislators to develop their own capacity to fulfil their oversight role has not yet come together in Argentina, and as a result, oversight has been rather undeveloped and ineffective in that country. Specifically, we argue that the development of legislative oversight of the executive requires legislators who are motivated by

a. a public outcry for reform (which generally implies the existence of a free and independent press) and
b. career or other interests in confronting, rather than supporting the executive.

Oversight may also be advanced, as we explain below, by legislators who are relatively independent of their party leaders.

In order to pursue their interests, the legislators require means, which are a function of:

a. a high level of professionalization of the legislature,
b. a long-lived democracy to continue developing the institutions for vigilance among which an independent judiciary is paramount, and
c. sufficient constitutional authority to pursue their interests.

Admittedly, this is an inductive theory based on the United States' relatively successful experience in creating a functioning system of checks and balances. However, since our interest concentrates on presidential models of oversight as found in the United States and throughout Latin America, we think that our comparison is meaningful and can shed light on the divergence of institutional development of other countries sharing similar features.

The means and motive are not independent of one another—in particular, if the legislators have a strong interest in conducting oversight, they are likely to develop (or at least attempt to develop) the tools necessary to undertake the task. Our primary argument, then, is that while the majority of Argentine legislators have generally been beholden to their president and lacked the other incentives that could have led them to create effective oversight mechanisms, the majority of the United States legislators have often been opponents of the president and have seen benefits for promoting reform (or anti-executive) policies.

Leaving aside public demands for vigilance (which, as we mentioned above, have been present in both countries), interests in oversight first require that the legislature takes an opposition stance. The earliest institutionalist, James Madison, saw the necessity of having competing branches of government to prevent the corruption of power. He therefore proposed strong motivations for each side to keep watch over their rivals. To this end, the constitution that Madison and the other United States founders created provided for legislative houses with members elected[2] from different constituencies and at different times, and theoretically, the executive was to be relatively uninvolved in legislative elections. Partisan politics, however, can threaten the barrier between the houses and branches. Following this logic, effective oversight is more likely to develop where the legislative majority opposes the president.

Aside from the inter-branch issues, there seems a reasonable case for the proposition that legislators will be more collectively interested in oversight when they are relatively independent of their party leaders.[3] Where rank-and-file legislators are sycophants, the burden for pursing policy initiatives, and hence oversight, falls to the party leaders. A leader-led model is plausible theoretically and would probably be effective in exposing some crimes or abuses. Still, for several reasons it seems less likely to lead to a comprehensive and institutionalized oversight system. First, though opposition leaders can certainly gain from exposing government excesses, they may wish to avoid institutionalized mechanisms of oversight that could hinder their own future government. As a result, oversight processes might be more political than technocratic.

Second, party leaders may oppose creating technocratic oversight institutions in order to retain control. If oversight is conducted by technocratic institutions, by definition the party leaders must cede power to the technocrats. Many strong leaders will surely oppose such a dispersion of their powers. Thus, while strong party leaders can use oversight to gain advantage over current

---

[2] Senators were originally elected indirectly, through the state legislatures.

[3] Collective action problems could come into play, but the potential payoffs to the political entrepreneur who wrote the legislation or organized the legislators should override these concerns.

governors, they might resist implementing an impartial and comprehensive system.

For similar reasons leaders of strong parties may also resist developing the legislature into a professionalized organization, preferring to use the party that they control to undertake their political operations. But where legislators are interested in re-election and are relatively independent of the executive and their party leaders, Mayhew's and Fiorina's analyses suggest that legislators will be motivated to professionalize their organization. Professionalization implies a level of specialization and expertise that by itself should aid the legislature in understanding, reviewing, and investigating the executive branch. If there were also a demand from constituents that the legislators rein in executive abuses, the re-election–seekers should direct this professionalization process towards institutions of oversight.

The other aspects of the legislature's capacity to develop effective oversight are based on the constitution and time. While all Latin American constitutions are modeled on the United States system, many grant their presidents powers—such as the line item veto, decree and urgency powers, and limitations on the legislature's ability to modify the budget—that upset the balance prescribed by the founders of the United States democracy. While the Latin American constitutions do not proscribe oversight per se, centralizing power in the executive can circumscribe legislative attempts to increase vigilance.

Finally, a long period of uninterrupted democracy is unquestionably crucial to oversight. Time aids the development of a free press, which is necessary to help generate and maintain public demands for clean and responsive government. A significant period of time is also needed to develop the complex accounting and information-sifting institutions. These control mechanisms then require constant tinkering to close different loopholes and deal with new government issues and agencies. To do so requires a professionalized legislature, the development of which is also a slow process. Lastly, it takes time to beat back the entrenched interests that resist oversight of their actions and instill a culture in which politicians act as if their abuses will be exposed.

The next section discusses how this conjunction of factors has aided the United States in developing its oversight institutions. This is contrasted, in the subsequent section, with the Argentine experience.

Developing Oversight in the United States

The theory that we presented suggests that in addition to a long uninterrupted democracy, developing legislative oversight of the executive and limiting government corruption has required properly motivated legislators who are relatively independent of both their parties and the president, along with public pressures for reforms. The public pressures, as mentioned above, grew to a crescendo after Garfield's assassination. Citing a 1904 article, Heidenheimer (1997) explains that political virtue became a great value for political challengers. Further, 'the half million of individually elected local and state politicians... can... enhance both their personal reputation and the public interest by calling for or expanding investigations (576).'

The legislators' independence from the party bosses, as well as increased separation of the legislature from the executive, were the result of two institutional factors and one landmark event. The event was the impeachment of President Johnson in 1868, which was caused by what legislators saw as an attempt by the President to usurp power. Though Johnson narrowly escaped conviction, the attempt returned the Congress to 'political supremacy' (Van Riper 1958: 67). Illustrative of this new position, Van Riper notes that the Congress did not see it necessary to repeal the law that was the center of the impeachment quagmire, the Tenure of Office Act,[4] until 1887.

Though the impeachment helped establish the legislature's potential, institutional oversight mechanisms required that legislators gain independence from their bosses and the executive. These breaks were assured due to frequent divided government and electoral reforms, both of which were inaugurated at the end of the 19th century.

Until 1875, the United States federal government (as well as many big city governments) were frequently under the control of single parties.[5] Not only were a majority of legislators and the president of the same party, the legislators were under the direct control of the bosses and leaders that controlled the nominations. This helped generate machine politics, irresponsible government,

---

[4] The law forbade the president from removing appointees without congressional approval.

[5] From 1800 to 1834 a single party generally held the presidency and dominated the legislature. Divided government was then common until 1860, until the Republicans gained and held unified power for 14 years.

and corruption. Writing of his own times, Cleveland rants against political bosses who controlled elections and avoided responsibility for their actions. He scowls that after elections, voters':

slumbers have been disturbed by the odor of stink-bombs and the coarse gossip of scandal-mongers, the insidious methods of a hungry and disappointed clientele of the 'organization' through which bosses work to weaken the confidence of the people in the man who has had the courage to take a stand against the bosses. (Cleveland 1919: 249)

Others concur about the pernicious effect of unified party control. Discussing the United States state and city governments, Benson (1978: 169) argues that 'most electoral fraud occurs in areas of one party dominance'. These pernicious effects have been countered in the post-civil war period by the frequent divided government (Figure 5.1).

In spite of the evident pressures and motivations, the changes have taken many years to implement, and new loopholes are continually dealt with. While the secret ballot was introduced in the 1880s, the GAO was not founded until 1921, and other important reforms took effect much after the 'age of reform'. The Administrative Reform Act in 1946 forced agencies to announce their consideration of issues with enough advance warning to allow the legislature and other interested parties to respond, and the Freedom of Information Act (first passed in 1966) has allowed the public, the prosecutors, and the Congress to access information on government dealings. Further, the office of the independent counsel, created in 1973, gave teeth to the investigations. Still today we

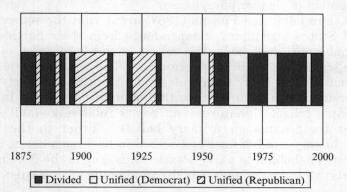

FIG. 5.1. *Divided government in the United States, 1875–2000*
(*Source*: Elaborated from data available for the Office of the Clerk,
United States House of Representatives
[http://clerk.house.gov/histHigh/Congressional_History/partyDiv.php].)

are witnessing fights about how to fix corrupting influences of campaign finance and issues of executive privilege. Overall, however, the United States is recognized for its relatively clean government (see, for example, Kaufmann, Kraay and Zoido-Lobaton 2002), and the United States Congress' role in oversight of the executive is unsurpassed.

Corruption Reform 1: Electoral Reforms

As noted above, machine politics were an important source of corruption in the United States government. Not unrelated to the dirty electoral processes, the ties between the legislators, the bosses, and the executive limited the development of technocratic oversight mechanisms. It is no coincidence that the first United States advocate for the Australian ballot—a single ballot printed by the government and listing all candidates—was a member of the Civil Service Reform Association (Evans 1917: 18). Thus, by itself the legislators' winning of their independence from their parties aided later attempts at developing oversight. The legislators' independence has meant that at least some elements of the executive's party will join the opposition in support of reforms. It is therefore important to consider the electoral reforms as a contributor to both the cleaning of government and the development of future oversight mechanisms. The electoral reforms were largely accomplished at the state level, and thus their source falls somewhat outside of our general theory. Still, the process shows how two of our variables, time and the courts, were important to the development of cleaner government.

Cain, Ferejohn, and Fiorina (1987) argue that the source of the United States legislators' independence from their parties, their 'personal vote,' has been the single member district electoral system, combined with presidentialism. The legislators, however, have not always been such independent operators. Part of this independence has been owed to the nominating system, in which candidates collect signatures and pay a relatively small sum to register their name on primary ballots. Earlier in the United States, history candidates were named in backroom deals, leaving candidates beholden to party bosses. Thus, key to the development of legislative independence was the weakening of boss rule.

To put the situation briefly: In place of the people controlling their service organization—the government—we have had 'boss rule'. Utilizing the lack of popular appreciation of the essential features of an effective mechanism of popular control and taking advantage of the absence of responsible leadership, the designing few, who look upon government as an institution for the grinding of their own grist, have so operated the electoral system that there should be no course open to electors except to elect men picked out for them by the 'boss'... The power of the boss has been developed through his ability to build and operate a machine that converts the political campaign and the election into a marionette show. (Cleveland 1919: 248–9)

Thus, the reforms that ensured fair elections and an end of negotiated outcomes or imposed candidates were not only a direct step towards cleaning up government, they had an indirect effect by counteracting political machines. Further, since politicians unaffiliated with the machines could now participate, there was a growing chance that anti-machine politicians could ride a reformist platform to victory.

The reformers pushing the electoral reforms had two primary goals, only the first of which was arguably accomplished (and only some credit is owed to this change). The successful goal was to diminish political machines' control over candidates and thereby legislatures. Among the tools available that aided the machines in controlling elections were the caucus (as opposed to an open primary) and the less-than-secret ballot. Before the Australian ballot was adopted it was common for parties to print their own ballots, often on brightly colored paper, so as to distinguish themselves from other parties. This, however, compromised the secrecy of the vote (see Evans 1917). By simply imposing white paper ballots, reformers hindered ward leaders' ability to verify who voters were choosing.[6] By itself this did not end the continual vote buying or other abuses such as the falsification of ballots or the rolling together of numerous ballots, thus leading Harris (1934) to conclude that elections were simply shows without public accountability. It was, however, a first important step towards a clean electoral process.

Perhaps the machines were more severely wounded by the cleaning up of the primary system, which greatly limited their ability to name candidates. Prior to the reforms, the primary elections had not been governed under the same laws as general elections.

[6] Opponents, alternatively, argued that bosses would then have to pay off only the few ballot judges instead of multiple voters—thus secrecy would be an impediment to an end of corruption. Their argument is summarized by a quote in a parliamentary debate record: 'Nothing was supposed to prevent misconduct and robbery at night so effectually as gas lamps' (Lord Claud Hamilton, in Hansard Parliamentary Debates CXCIV, 1505, cited in Evans 1917: 21–2 n. 4).

Bribery of voters in an elections, although subject to severe penalties under the law, did not constitute an offense in a primary or caucus and was not punishable. Voters might be bought and sold with no pretense of concealment, for there was no remedy or penalty at law. Another device was the manipulation of the count of the votes. Where the issue was determined by a mass meeting of voters, an autocratic chairman might easily decide the controversy, and from his ruling there was no opportunity for appeal. There was no guaranty that a vote by ballot would be permitted; or if sufficient progress had been made to provide for a written or printed ballot, then the temptation to trickery and fraud was found irresistible. The ballot-box might be stuffed, the count of the ballots might be falsified, and any one of a hundred ingenious devices might be employed to insure the result desired. (Merriam and Overacker 1928: 6)

In response to these problems, almost every state enacted primary legislation by 1917, though many states did not mandate primaries for all elections (Merriam and Overacker: 61). This struck directly at the local bosses, since they could no longer monopolize the nominating process. After the change, potential candidates did not have to rely on backroom dealings to win a spot on the ballot; they merely had to collect signatures and pay a small registration fee.[7]

The second goal for the reformers, about which it would be hard to credit them with much success, was to reduce the influence of money in elections. The idea here was that by transferring the cost of printing ballots from the candidates to the states, the reform was expected to reduce the cost of campaigns and, as a result, the level of corruption. This reduced cost was also supposed to help outsider candidates, which would further dilute the machines' power. The reforms may have eliminated the printing costs, but ambitious politicians—and donors seeking influence—have continued to find new needs for money.

The success of these reforms shows the importance of time and the courts, since the movement took about 40 years to accomplish the electoral reforms and required the courts to uphold the new laws. In the United States, the Australian ballot was first proposed in the early 1880s in a series of pamphlets and magazine articles.[8] The first votes on the reform were defeated (in 1885

[7] See Merriam and Overacker (1928: 77) about the fees.

[8] Harris (1934) and Evans (1917) both discuss how Australian ballot was adopted in Australia, United Kingdom, and then the United States (mostly between 1887 and 1900) after long debates and many political obstacles. It was first advocated in Australia in 1851. Its advocate became a member of the South Australia government in 1857 and the proposal was adapted there and later in other provinces.

and 1887 in Michigan), but by the late 1880s, reformist leagues pushed several states to adopt it. By 1900 most states had passed similar legislation, though it was not universal until much later.[9] It took another 20 years, however, for most states to regulate primaries, and even then many states did not mandate primaries for all elections (Merriam and Overacker 1928: 61).

The reforms were difficult to implement and sustain since they sought to beat back entrenched and strong political interests. A *New York Times* editorial noted that: 'the opposition of the Democratic members of the legislature to the Saxton bill [which introduced the Australian Ballot in New York]... were for the most part small city politicians who owe their chances in politics to the methods which that bill was intended to destroy' (cited in Evans 1917: 20 n.4). The conflict over the primary legislation manifested itself in violent factional struggles in California. In New Jersey, the Democrats opposed reform but the Republicans were so divided that it was loudly debated at the state convention in 1927. In other states several reform attempts failed before winning approval, and in many states politicians fought for long periods to circumvent or reverse the laws (see Albright 1942; Meriam and Overacker 1928: 100–103). The new system was also challenged in court, with opponents contending that the Australian ballot 'embarrassed, hindered, and impeded the electors in exercising their constitutional right of suffrage, that it established physical and educational qualifications for voting in violation of the Constitution, and prescribed restrictions upon the eligibility to office' (Evans 1917: 57).[10] The courts, however, upheld the constitutionality of this reform.

In short, a lengthy period was required to counteract entrenched and corrupt interests, and it was necessary that the courts sided with the reformers. Once implemented, the newly independent legislators, many who had won election on platforms of cleaning up government, had greater interests in overseeing the executive. Their independence probably also increased their motivation in building legislative careers. These factors, then, contributed to the professionalization of the legislature, and its development of oversight institutions.

---

[9] Some states, such as North and South Carolina, however, did not implement the Australian ballot until much later.

[10] Evans extracted this specific criticism from the veto message of the governor of New York.

Corruption Reform II: Civil Service

While the fights over electoral reforms largely took place in the states, at the federal level corruption was fought by the implementation of a meritocratic civil service. This policy resulted from divided government (or the threat of electoral losses) and a public outcry for reform that was spurred by a tragic event. The reformers, again, required a significant period of time to see the realization of their ideas. This conjunction of events, partisan divisions, and continual democratic rule has not been fulfilled in much of Latin America and as a result, few Latin American countries have completed civil service reforms (Geddes 1991).

In the United States, presidents and others who were involved in the process recognized that the 'virus of the spoils system' (Perry Powers 1888: 278) contaminated all aspects of the federal (and local) government. Most directly, the spoils system prevented the professionalization of the bureaucracy, since experience was not rewarded and qualifications were secondary to cronyism for awarding jobs. The system also helped breed irresponsible government and widespread corruption associated with machine politics. Wheeler, for example, citing another book on the spoils system, linked the terribly corrupt Indiana hospitals to the 'incompetence of the political hacks that were put in charge of them' (Wheeler 1919: 486). This problem did not go unrecognized. Several high-level reports in the 1820s through the 1840s severely criticized the system (Perry Powers 1888: 247) and helped generate support for change,[11] but reform attempts failed.

Many analyses of the progressive period suggest that the public outcry about corruption finally led to policy changes. Geddes (1991), however, argues that political competition is also necessary for reform, since those who benefit from the spoils system—the current incumbents—will be predisposed against change. For her, incumbents will only vote for reform if the opposition can capitalize on a reform agenda and the change will not mean unilateral disarming of electoral resources. Thus, they only vote for a meritocratic system if: (a) reform is an important campaign issue; and (b) access to patronage is split relatively evenly between the incumbents and the challengers, so that incumbents and challengers are equally affected. Thus where there has been little competition, as

---

[11] Specifically the reports criticized a 1820s law that mandated four year terms for bureaucrats, ostensibly to allow rotation of office. The reports called for the repeal of that law.

in Argentina during much of the 20th century, we would not expect reform. Geddes, however, does not address this question but focuses on the cases which have had extended periods of democratic government since 1930. She finds that Uruguay, Venezuela, and Colombia approved reform of the civil service at times when the opposition had an important claim to power (such as control of the legislature) and a good chance of winning the presidency. In contrast she finds that legislators in Brazil and Chile had few incentives to vote for reform, and as a result, reform efforts floundered.[12]

This theory is also consistent with the United States experience. The spoils system had been attacked since the 1830s, but between the 1820s and 1840s the incumbent party was reasonably secure, as the Democrats held control of both houses and the presidency for that whole score of years, except 1826–28.[13] After the Civil War the 'exploitation of the spoils of office... became more and more blatant' (Van Riper 1958: 67) and there were more demands for change. Even these increased concerns were insufficient to generate reform, until President Grant (1869–77) began to introduce reform projects in the 1870s. His first efforts failed, in large part because important parts of his own party, which controlled both houses of Congress until 1875, opposed the reforms.[14] But the Republicans lost 96 of their 203 seats in the 1874 election. Only thereafter, as a 'sop to reform' (Van Riper 1958: 75) did the Congress approve a bill making it an 'indictable offence to demand, pay or receive assessments from office-holders "for political purposes"' (Wheeler 1919: 488).[15]

The next major reform, the Pendleton Act, also followed a large change in the composition of the Congress, and again initiated a

[12] In discussing the case of Chile, Geddes adds an additional variable to the analysis: the open list system. In these systems, she argues, legislators are more concerned with battling co-partisans than cross-party rivals. For this reason minority parties cannot band together to pass reforms that would work against the executive.

[13] Until 1824 the Democrats were known as the Democratic Republicans. The Democrats were then formed in 1828. The president's supporters were labeled simply 'administration' for 1824 and 1826 (Stanley and Niemi 1995).

[14] Van Riper notes that Grant was dependent on the 'patronage minded conservatives' of the Republican party, and did not have the full support of the liberals either (1958: 69). Therefore in spite of formally calling for reform and creating a civil service commission, Grant dropped the issue.

[15] In 1871 the congress did pass a bill authorizing President Grant to reform the system, but they failed to authorize any funds to set up the necessary commission (Wheeler 1919: 488).

period of divided government. By the 1880 election, the Republicans had built back their legislative majority, and the party also held the presidency in the name of James Garfield. But, in spite of increasing the size of the House by 32 seats in 1882, the Republicans lost 33 seats in the election, giving the Democrats a solid 200–119 advantage. Garfield was murdered shortly thereafter by a spurned spoils-seeker, and only six months later a colorful commentary in the *New York Times* noted in the Republicans the 'active zeal of these converts preaching the blessed truth that those who are in ought not to be put out' (12/14/1882; cited in Van Riper 1958: 94). The Congress then quickly approved the Pendleton Act—which had been proposed but shelved before the election—thereby inaugurating our merit based bureaucracy.

Finally, it is again important to note the lengthy period that was required to fully implement the civil service policies. Though the Pendleton Act is cited as a path-breaking reform, Perry Powers (1888) argued that it did not cover enough workers to end the spoils system. Further, later reforms did not always advance the effort. Writing at the time of Woodrow Wilson's presidency, Wheeler (1919) gave great credit to Theodore Roosevelt for advancing civil service reforms, but chided Wilson for using riders to approve exemptions to the laws. Geddes (1991) offers the more general finding that there was retrenchment during periods of unified party rule, and notes that when the Republicans gained political dominance after 1896, President McKinley began to disassemble the system. She adds that if it were not for McKinley's assassination, the United States system might today look much more like those found in Latin America. In short, full implementation of the civil service reforms required many decades, as reformers continually faced politicians with interests in reversing the reforms.

Reforming Oversight of the Executive

One of the most important moves towards facilitating legislative oversight of the executive was the approval of the Budget Act of 1921. This reform required the legislators' independence of the executive and a good dose of legislators' interest in developing the technocratic capacity of their institution, the latter of which came with the combined increases in the time that legislators began spending in their posts and the complexity of the legislative process. Polsby (1968) and Marx (1945) suggest that the improving professionalization of the legislature was a reaction to the government's increased reach and budget that came with WWI. The other—arguably related—change at the time was the increasing propensity of legislators to seek long legislative careers. The legislators were thus motivated to develop technocratic oversight institutions by (a) their independence from the executive, (b) their desire for a professional workplace, and (c) the growing complexity of the legislative task.

Until the 1920s the budget had been dealt with through a very decentralized system. Each executive agency was greatly independent as the executive lacked a central office to collect budget requests and synthesize them with expected revenue. It was not the president, however, that took the lead in creating the centralized budget agency. Led by Iowan Representative James Good, the Congress moved to counteract 'extravagance, inefficiency, and duplication of service... [for which] no one is made responsible' (Marx 1945: 657, citing the Congressional Record). The new Bureau of the Budget (renamed Office of Management and Budget in 1970), therefore, helped identify a responsible agent and create the transparency necessary for congressional oversight. Thus, while an important part of the legislative debate over the reform turned on whether the centralization would give too much power to the executive, Rep. Good successfully argued that the reform actually enhanced Congress' power by assuring them more information and a method for acting more efficiently (Stewart 1989: 202). Further, the agency was required to assist legislative committees and turn over any information the Congress requested (Marx 1945: 669).

In addition to facilitating the congressional oversight, the congressional reformers saw the new executive budget agency as a tool for facilitating the executive's ability to check on his own team members. Some of the most corrupt administrations were not headed by corrupt presidents. Ulysses Grant, for example, was known as incorruptible and other presidents apparently were unaware of their appointees' shady dealings. Thus the new bureau, which could demand to see any documents from any bureaucratic agency, was meant to allow the president the information necessary to control the multi-tentacled administration (Marx 1945: 662, 669).

Reforming the executive branch, however, was insufficient, as the legislators were also interested in advancing their own ability to watch the federal purse. The Budget Act thus also created the Government Accounting Office (GAO) which was under legislative control. Though its role has changed over time, in its early years the main role of the GAO was to audit government spending (Pet-rei 1998). In a further effort to gain control over the budget pro-cess, the legislators centralized their own approval structure for government expenditures within the Appropriations Committee (Marx 1945: 659).

The origins of the budget reforms can be traced to divided gov-ernment, or at least a clear separation of powers, and William Howard Taft's administration (1909–13). Taft argued for the need for presidential control over the budget in order to make the gov-ernment 'more responsive to public opinion and responsible for its act[ions]' (cited in Stewart 1989: 184). The Congress, where the President's Republicans only controlled the Senate, was wary of strengthening the presidency and would not even fully support a commission that Taft set up to develop and promote the idea of reform (Stewart 1989: 185–186). Taft and the Democratic Congress continued to spar over the reforms. When Taft issued an executive order demanding that all bureaucratic agencies pass budget requests to him, the Congress passed a bill abrogating this order (Stewart 1989: 187). The president's budget that year (1912) was not even considered by the Congress—and only the Republican Senate, not the Democrat-controlled House printed Taft's budget requests (Stewart 1989: 188).

The unified government and focus on the war that came with Wilson's election in 1912 delayed the reforms. The Democrats' loss of control of the Congress in 1919 is often credited with stifling the development of the League of Nations, in spite of Wilson's well-known plea: 'Dare we reject it and break the heart of the world?'[16] The divided government, however, did result in congressional ap-proval of the Budget and Accounting Act. Wilson vetoed the bill during his last year in office (1919) due to what he perceived as too much legislative control. His particular objection was to the pro-vision that allowed the Congress, by a joint resolution, to remove the comptroller-general. He argued that he supported the object of the bill (concentrating the budgeting authority for the execu-tive) but that the president, not the Congress, should have the power to remove the head of the GAO (Stewart 1989: 208). The Congress was unable to revise the bill before the end of the term, but then brought the same bill back up after the 1920 election, and President Harding signed it into law. Harding did not face a divided government and the bill was passed with little dissent (see

---

[16] Cited in the White House webpage, www.whitehouse.gov/WH/glimpse/presidents/html/ww28.html

Morstein 1945). This thus shows that in addition to partisanship, interests in professionalization and the independence of the branches were important ingredients to the reform.

In sum, the reform of the budget process shows the Congress reasserting its authority, which had been waning since the accession of Theodore Roosevelt (and later Wilson). The near unanimous vote on the Budget and Accounting Act helped later presidents consolidate power, but the act also created a more transparent system and allowed the Congress more access to information. Armed with their new internal organization, as well as their own auditing agency, the legislature laid a foundation for effective control of their political counterweight.

Developing Oversight in Argentina

In this section we provide a historical narrative with a focus on the weaknesses of the institutions entrusted with oversight, as well as the array of incentives and penalties used by the Argentine executive to deter effective control since the 19th century. As we shall see in a moment, the legislators and the courts have been too cowed or disinterested to allow any true scrutiny into its actions. As a result, the type of congressional oversight developed in the United States failed to materialize in Argentina. Civil service recruitment was too often tied to political allegiance, rather than merit. The courts, after enjoying some prestige at the beginning of the 20th century, progressively retreated into a subsidiary role as the fear of retaliation from civilian and military leaders alike made job security everything but safe. Public disgust with government, legislative, and judicial corruption could not find any institutional outlet, thus producing a widespread sense of cynicism among Argentines with regard to accountability issues. Not surprisingly, some strata of society came to support military coups hoping that at least the armed forces could clean up what was perceived as being rampant corruption plaguing civilian administrations, regardless of the party that controlled them (O'Donnell 1988).

Low Motivation, Limited Time, and Weak Courts

First, in spite of a constitution that is relatively similar to that of the United States, the Argentine legislature has generally failed to develop an independence from the executive. Argentine democracy was inaugurated in the early part of the 20th century, but power was solidly held by the Radicals between 1916 and 1930. At times they did not hold a full majority in the Congress, but no other party approached the size of Radicals. Since that time, control of the legislatures that have met has seldom been in the hands of partisans standing in opposition to the executive.[17]

In addition to the lack of inter-branch partisan rivalries, the electoral system does not motivate legislators to act independently of their leaders (who for many is the president). The Argentines moved in the early part of the 1900s to impose a secret ballot,[18] but because they have almost always used a closed list system of proportional representation,[19] legislators have been dependent on the party leaders who draw up the list. The Argentine legislators have thus lacked the motivation and autonomy that led the United States legislators to develop oversight institutions and generally professionalize their institution.

Perhaps even more important than the institutional hindrances to oversight, the legislature has been frequently closed by military governments. These authoritarian interludes have had several negative impacts on oversight. First, these governments turned decree legislation into the norm, and probably heightened the legislature's cautionary approach to overseeing executive actions. Second, they have slowed or curtailed the development of legislative institutions. Reform efforts required constant tinkering in the United States, as early attempts left important loopholes. Thus, the democratic interruptions alone may have been enough to explain the Argentine legislators' failure (even if they had wanted to pursue reform) to build the necessary institutions to counteract the constantly increasing executive complexity or abuse of power.

A final piece of the institutional puzzle regards the judiciary, which has consistently supported executive dominance in Argentina. This stands in contrast to the experience in the United States, where the courts played a crucial role in upholding legislation that, for example, broke the party bosses' power or in later years has forced various presidents to turn over private records.

---

[17] The exceptions are Frondizi (1958–62) who only had majority control of the House, Illia (1963–66) who never had majority support, and Alfonsin, who controlled the House between January 1983 and September 1987, but never had control of the senate.

[18] The Sáenz Peña law of 1912 guaranteed a secret and obligatory vote.

[19] The Argentines did use single member district elections for a brief time in the 1950s.

In Argentina, prior to the 1930 coup, the Supreme Court was generally regarded as a rather professional and independent institution. Indeed, according to Miller (1997: 232), between 1860 and 1929 the Court acted as a 'stabilizing political influence and a soother of political passions in a way that even the U.S. Supreme Court probably did not.' Yet, the 1930 Argentine Supreme Court's decision to treat the authoritarian government created that year as one whose credentials could not be judicially questioned began to erode its prestige, as well as showing that the court was unwilling to counter executive abuse.

Even if the court had been willing to challenge the executive, constitutional limitations would likely have prevented it from playing a serious mediating role. Similar to the United States Constitution, the Argentine Constitution of 1853 does not explicitly state that the Supreme Court can exercise judicial review. The Argentine Supreme Court tried to emulate its United States equivalent by establishing a tradition in this sense but for several reasons it has had much less success. Unlike many European countries where specific constitutional courts exist, any federal Argentine judge can perform judicial review.[20] But, the Argentine judiciary is severely limited in this power, since the applicability of a ruling remains confined to the plaintiff and the defendant, instead of constituting a precedent. Previous decisions from the Supreme Court and the Courts of Appeal can be used to adjudicate a similar case debated later in lower courts, but there is no obligation to abide by them. As a result, the Supreme Court and Appeal Courts' clout in developing binding jurisprudence in Argentina is far more limited than in the United States and imposes smaller restrictions on the executive and the legislative branches.

While these institutional factors have greatly aided the presidents in subordinating the legislatures, the Argentine legislature has not always failed to assert itself. Indeed, below we discuss several examples in which the legislature has been influential in the policy process. Our basic conclusion, however, is that the institutional framework, the fragility of democracy, and the political and economic crises have generally left the Argentine Congress as considerably less than a co-equal branch of government.

---

[20] As in the United States, a federal judge cannot issue opinions of constitutional significance unless a case exists.

Early Attempts at Administrative Reform

Early attempts at reform substantiate the importance of the role of the opposition in instigating reform. They also show however, that the opposition's willingness to use non-democratic means to address short-term demands (at least until the 1980s) has curtailed the development of effective oversight institutions.

Detailed reports of widespread government corruption date back to the colonial period (Rock 1985). The anarchy that followed the independence from Spain added to the abuses of power and cronyism by local strongmen. Starting in the 1880s, the oligarchic governments that ruled Argentina until 1916 made an effort to create a professional civil service mixing elements of the French (line ministries) and British (Central Bank) models. Nonetheless, the executive retained ample freedom to interfere in recruiting standards to ensure the political allegiance of the public administration.

After the extension of suffrage in 1912 that inaugurated formal Argentine democracy, the *Unión Cívica Radical* (UCR) took control of both the presidency and the legislature and during their 15 years in office (1916–30) the Radicals continued their predecessors' practice of using government jobs and contracts as a way to reward their supporters. To discipline the resistance of recalcitrant governors of conservative leanings, President Hipolito Hyrigoyen (1916–22; 1928–30) often used the right of intervention by the federal government in local affairs in ways that outraged the conservatives in the Congress. Since their minority position kept them from blocking the president's initiatives, the conservative bloc supported the 1930 military coup arguing that it would put an end to the rampant corruption and executive abuses. Once the conservatives gained power, however, they not only did much of the same, they also overtly practised electoral fraud as a way to keep the hated Radicals out of power.[21]

This problem of legislative minorities turning to the military has continued. During his first two terms in office Juan Perón (1946–55) escalated even further the politicization of the civil service. Scores of bureaucrats, as well as university professors who had enjoyed a fairly independent status up until then, were purged or forced to resign. Claiming that they were responding to the arbitrary political power and corruption, the military took over in 1955. Again, military-sponsored authoritarian governments were

---

[21] The military withdrew from active participation after 1932 and did not play an active political role until the 1943 coup.

even more inclined to abuses since they appointed to the highest ranks of the public administration 'technocrats' responsive only to them. The military also closed the Congress, and used censorship to mute any opposition outside institutional settings. These experiences all point to the importance of competitive branches of government, which Argentina has usually lacked in times of democracy, and always lacked during authoritarian interludes.

Reforms of the budget and accounting procedures offer an example of the failed efforts. Argentina developed a series of laws, starting with the Accounting Act of 1870 (Law 428), to establish clear procedures regulating the budget process. However, it was not until 1956 that an external oversight agency was created in the *Tribunal de Cuentas de la Nación* (National Accounting Tribunal; TCN). Noticeably, the government that created it resulted from a military coup, albeit one that was reacting to Perón's heavy-handed rule. The TCN was entrusted with the authority to review the legality of the executive's legislative and administrative initiatives using an ex-ante approach at the time typical of similar institutions in Europe. The TCN, therefore, was supposed to exercise preventive controls over executive decrees and pursued account judgments and accountability proceedings all of which were reported to the Congress. Yet this practice was inconsistently applied during civilian governments and ignored under authoritarian ones, clearly showing the importance of an active and opposition legislature in ensuring effective oversight.

Another related reform also seems to indicate the importance of the legislature's lack of professionalization. In 1963, during one of the brief periods when the president (Arturo Illia) lacked majority support in the legislature, the Argentines created the *Oficina Nacional de Presupuesto* (National Budget Office; ONP). Like the United States Bureau of the Budget discussed above, the ONP was supposed to help the executive rationalize the budget process. But unlike the United States Congress, the Argentine legislature failed to concomitantly develop their own controls, and the new office proved to lack any real control over governmental decisions. In point of fact, the budget process was so distorted and out of control that no budget was signed into law by the legislature from 1954 until 1990.

Congressional Oversight Under Alfonsín (1983–89)

The first two post-dictatorship presidencies exhibited distinct patterns in terms of oversight of executive powers. Consistent with what we argued earlier, the administration of Raúl Alfonsín of the UCR (1983–89) faced a situation of divided government that allowed both the congress and the courts to exercise a considerable role in restraining what were believed to be questionable initiatives by the executive. Conversely, President Carlos Menem could count for most of his two terms in office (1989–95 and 1995–99) with both a working majority in the Congress and a docile Supreme Court, which in turn allowed him to undercut most checks and balances. As a result of this different inter-branch balance, as well as the apparent difference in the two presidents' respect for democratic institutions, congressional oversight was relatively important during Alfonsín's period but its development stagnated (or reversed course) during Menem's two terms.

The inauguration of President Alfonsín in December 1983 put an end to the most violent military dictatorship in Argentine contemporary history that lasted between 1976 and 1983. It also ushered in an era of unprecedented political freedom in the country. The widespread human rights violations and catastrophic economic policies inherited from the military regime created a new political climate. Among the important thrusts of Alfonsín's effort was to create public confidence in the three branches of government by abiding by the basic principles of democracy and having the judiciary prosecute human rights violations.

This system did not always work to Alfonsín's advantage. At the beginning of his administration, Alfonsín sent a bill to the Congress that would set the tone of his presidency. It consisted of a new labor code aimed at enervating the labor unions that had traditionally been the backbone of the *Partido Justicialista* (Peronists; PJ). In 1984, the Radicals had an absolute majority in the Chamber of Deputies but not in the Senate where a group of small parties from the interior of the country held the balance. The Radicals were unwilling to compromise with these small parties, thus derailing this important piece of Alfonsín's program. Especially after the Radicals lost their house majority in 1987, the opposition in the Congress further asserted its prerogatives, for example by effectively using its veto powers on controversial government plans (Torre 1993).

Alfonsín also met with considerable scrutiny from the courts. Upon being elected, the Radical president persuaded the Supreme Court justices who had served under the military to resign. He then appointed a court made up by five new justices whose members, in general, enjoyed good standing within the legal profession (of these, two were openly Radical, one was Socialist, one Peronist, and the last one independent). The result was a court that acted rather independently from the government wishes (Verbitsky 1993: 21). For example, in 1987, much to the president's dismay, the Supreme Court refused to take over all the pending judgments concerning military officers in order to avoid a lengthy and politically dangerous trial process in federal courts, which had triggered an army uprising (Acuña and Smulovitz 1995; Verbitsky 1987). The court reasoned that doing so was tantamount to undercutting the jurisdiction of the federal courts. This, and concern with military uprisings, prompted the administration to send to the Congress and push his party (and the PJ) to support a very unpopular Due Obedience Law, which voided most cases but tarnished the Radical's commitment to prosecute human right abuses.[22] As Alfonsín became a lame duck president after the 1987 electoral debacle, the Supreme Court showed an even greater willingness to strike down governmental decisions in the last two years of his mandate (Helmke 1999).

Though these factors could have been a positive step in the direction of effective checks and balances, Alfonsín and later Menem worked to undermine the inter-branch controls. Partially in response to his lack of a legislative majority, together with the majority's opposition to the Radical administration's economic policies, Alfonsín wavered from his support of the democratic process and began to resort to decrees of 'necessity and urgency' (*decretos de necesidad y urgencia* or DNUs). Previous presidents had very rarely used this type of decree power (which was not specified in the constitution)[23] and so when Alfonsín opened this Pandora's door by issuing ten of them,[24] he inadvertently legitimated the process for his successor.

Congressional Oversight Under Menem (1989–99)

President Carlos Menem (1989–99), apparently unburdened with appearances of democratic structures, acted quickly to either eliminate or make ineffectual any type of oversight, and due to his

[22] Passage was aided by the UCR's majority in the House and the support of small parties in the Senate. Further, some members of the PJ were close to the military and the party did not actively oppose the bill in the Congress.

[23] Between 1853 and 1983 presidents had used about 20 DNUs, and then only under circumstances of political and economic emergencies that could potentially endanger the very existence of the nation (Ferreira Rubio and Goretti 1998).

[24] The most important of which created a new currency, the Austral, in mid-1986, which was eventually ratified into law by the Congress a year later.

almost unhesitating reliance on decree powers, he is often cited as the archetypal dominant executive. He succeeded in doing so primarily for four reasons. First, owing to the depth of the economic crisis, the general public was more interested in economic progress than democratic ideals, and the congressional opposition wilted. Second, Menem could count either on a working Peronist majority in Congress supported by small parties (1989–91) or an absolute majority (1991–97). He gained further advantages by skillfully dispensing incentives and punishments to exploit the Congress' traditional weaknesses. Third, through the packing of the Supreme Court with sympathetic justices, Menem assured the support of this key institution against challenges from lower courts and the opposition in Congress to his policies. Finally, he successfully purged the oversight institutions within the public administration of those officials who raised questions about the legality of the executive's reforms.

In spite of these advantages and Menem's general success in circumventing democratic controls, there is another side of the story. As we explain below, Congress' oversight role, while clearly weak, has varied over time as a function of changing socioeconomic situations, the saliency of specific bills, and the partisan composition of the legislature. Further, in the post-Menem years, though excesses have not disappeared, there are signs of the legislature's growing oversight capacity and general policy influence.

Menem was first elected when Alfonsín failed to overcome Argentina's hyperinflation. To prevent the country from collapsing into total chaos, Alfonsín offered to step down six months ahead of schedule.[25] But, in accepting the deal, Menem forced the Radicals to make major concessions, including a pledge to withdraw a sufficient number of their 113 members in the Chamber of Deputies when crucial legislation was introduced. In so doing, the 97 Peronist representatives became de facto the largest bloc in the legislature and could pass the president's emergency measures (Vidal 1995: 53).

The Radicals also agreed not to oppose two laws that granted Menem broad emergency powers, which helped him create the cornerstone of his market reforms. The first one was the State Reform Law, which gave the executive the authority to privatize 32 state owned enterprises immediately and put them in charge of trustees accountable only to the president for a once-renewable period of

---

[25] The election was held in May 1989, but the inauguration had been expected in December.

180 days. The second piece of legislation was the Economic Emergency Law. This law gave the president the authority to change the budget, eliminate subsidies for industrial promotion, modify tax collection, end any legal discrimination against foreign investors, alter the payment system of federal bonds, and reorganize the social security agency. In short, through these laws the legislature delegated to the presidency discretionary powers to legislate via decree on a wide range of matters that, according to the Constitution, were solely ascribed to the Congress for a set amount of time (Ferreira Rubio and Goretti 1998). Eventually, the Congress expanded the extension to three years in the case of the State Reform Law. In short, the combination of economic crisis and electoral losses led Radical legislators to grant Menem sweeping powers.

In delegating such broad authority, the Congress opened the door to Menem's usurpation of even greater powers. As Ferreira Rubio and Goretti (1998: 34) explain, Menem indiscriminately used DNUs 'as a policy-making device, whereby the executive present [ed] legislative faits accomplis that circumvent[ed] the principles of checks and balances, [replacing] the rule of law with presidential fiat.' The number and scope of DNUs he issued was unprecedented. Prior to Menem the Argentine executives had generally abided by the rule that DNUs were to be limited to situations when the Congress was not in session or the regular legislative process could not be used due to an impending national crisis that demanded a quick response. Regardless, DNUs by law had to be submitted for legislative approval at a later date in order to retain their effectiveness. Menem regarded all these requirements as mere formalities—and the legislature appeared powerless to react. Indeed, in 51 per cent of the DNUs issued, the government itself did not identify them as such but nonetheless they were used to repeal or enforce laws without any clear legal ground or congressional delegation. The executive failed to inform the Congress as mandated by the Constitution on another 25 per cent of the DNUs issued in the 1989–92 period (Verbitsky 1993: 169). This high frequency of decrees also allowed Menem to make credible threats. He therefore could intimidate the Congress into approving legislation by threatening to decree objectionable laws.

Menem's strong partisan support, and the economic crisis go far in explaining why the Congress put up little resistance to the president's steam-rolling legislative initiative, especially during Menem's first term (1989–95). The hyperinflation crisis of mid-1989 and early 1990 put the Radicals on the defensive, and public opinion polls showed strong support for decisive government action to fight inflation and promote structural reforms (Mora y Araujo 1991, Palermo and Novaro 1996). Menem skilfully exploited this popular malaise. Any time the Radicals tried to mount some opposition, the president used an effective media campaign charging them with stalling his effort to remedy the chaos that Alfonsín had left behind. This blunted opposition from the Radicals. Without the high level of party unity and the majority status of his party, however, it seems unlikely that Menem could have gained so much power.

Support for these suppositions comes from the changes during Menem's presidency. First, as the economic crisis was brought under control, the legislature, in spite of its image as a supine onlooker to the governmental process, began to experience some success in overturning vetoes and resisting some executive initiatives, particularly after 1994. The constitutional reform passed that year aimed at limiting executive discretionary powers in several important ways. Not all the stipulations were implemented and Menem did continue to bend the rules, but the constitutional changes (or at least the debate that led to them) did lead Menem to issue fewer decrees in the second half of his reign (Ferreira Rubio and Goretti 1998).[26] The Congress also successfully repelled some of Menem's policy initiatives and forced important compromises on issues, such as the privatization of the oil, gas, and electricity companies, a bill dealing with labor issues, and the patent law. In addition, Eaton (2002) stresses the legislature's role in shaping the tax reform in the early 1990s. A final indicator of the legislature's power, was the resignation in mid-1995 of the powerful minister of the economy, Domingo Cavallo, who left office citing his inability to force legislation through the Congress as a primary cause of his decision .

Interviews with members of the Ministry of the Economy and Public Works first under Minister Domingo Cavallo (1991–95) and then under Minister Roque Fernández (1995–99) also support our view about the importance of partisan competition between the branches. Ministry's staffers complained that though the Congress was usually cooperative until 1994, it became more and more self assertive, particularly after the Fall of 1997 when the Peronists lost their majority in the Chamber of Deputies. To stylize the facts, it seems that the Congress was keenly aware of its weakness in

---

[26] Importantly, the Congress even failed to appoint the commission called for in the constitution that was to oversee the DNUs.

dealing with the executive during Menem's first term. Accordingly, legislators avoided challenging Menem on matters dealing with market reforms that were top priority to his administration and chose to hold their ground mostly on bread-and-butter issues where there was greater room for compromise. Conversely, the interviewees indicated that after the PJ lost its congressional majority in 1997, Menem's ability to bypass the Congress diminished appreciably.

Supreme Court

The Supreme Court's inability or unwillingness to address executive abuse is a final factor contributing to the weakness of legislative oversight. This inability or unwillingness, in turn, has resulted from Menem's anti-democratic strategies and the weakness of the Congress in upholding democratic procedures.

Aware of Alfonsín's problems in having the Supreme Court assent to controversial presidential initiatives, Menem proceeded from the start to make sure that the high court would be squarely in his camp. In doing so, Menem resumed Alfonsín's original idea of enlarging the Supreme Court. The attack on the Court's independence started a few weeks after Menem took office. The strategy behind it was exposed by Minister of Justice Jorge Maiorano who candidly stated later on that by electing Menem the people had voted for a new project to transform Argentina. This meant that it was 'absolutely necessary that there be a court that understands the [administration's] policy and be addicted to the program that the [Argentine] society had voted' (*Ambito Financiero*, 11 November 1992). Four out of the five members of the court denounced Menem's packing attempt. But on 5 April 1990, the Chamber of Deputies voted in favour of increasing the number of justices to nine. The Radicals charged that, as happened later in the privatization bill of Gas del Estado, impostors cast the decisive votes (Verbitsky 1993: 49). When they requested a recount, the Peronist president of the Chamber overruled their request. One of the five justices, Jorge Bacqué, quit in protest before the measure became effective, giving Menem the opportunity to nominate not four but five new justices. Three weeks later the Judiciary committee in the Senate approved in only seven minutes the new justices proposed by the executive. The remaining four justices, likely concerned with Menem's threat of impeachment proceedings that could surely be approved in a Peronist-dominated Senate, reversed their initial hostility and decided to lend their support for the controversial government initiatives. In the end, the full Senate put the final seal on the matter as representatives of small provincial parties joined the Peronists by granting the two-thirds majority needed to ratify the candidates.

The packing of the Supreme Court played a pivotal role on the one hand in giving the executive a legal justification for its dubious reforms and, on the other, in thwarting any challenges coming from the Congress, lower courts, and civil society. Within this context, three decisions were key in helping Menem overcoming legal opposition to his authoritarian decision-making style.

The first of such decisions was the *Peralta* decision issued on 27 December 1990. This ruling is fundamental since it legitimized the executive's authority to legislate without congressional approval. Further, it established that the executive could legislate through DNUs and restrict constitutional rights as long as the causes that created the crisis continued. Of course, the Supreme Court left to the executive the determination of whether or not the country is in an emergency situation. As a result, even the lack of enough televised soccer games became the subject of 'emergency' decrees. In short, this decision allowed Menem to justify his continual rule by emergency powers.

The Court justified its decision by stating that situations of 'high social risk', required the application of 'swift measures whose efficacy were not conceivable through other means'. The ruling thus justified the executive's usurpation of legislative powers. It went still further, adding that although the Constitution established the division of power among the three branches of government, this should not be interpreted in a way to allow the 'dismemberment of the State so that each of its parts acts in isolation to the detriment of national unity'. Ironically, this implies that under emergency situations (which the executive could define) not only the Congress, but also the Court should subordinate itself to the executive.

One other point was key in this decision. The only condition the court imposed on the executive's use of decrees was that the executive inform the Congress and that the Congress not express its disapproval. But, to explicitly express its disapproval of a DNU, the court forced the Congress to pass legislation revoking a decree. These bills, however, would be subjected to an executive veto.

The delegation of powers doctrine was reconfirmed in a later case, known as the *Cocchia* case in which the Court reiterated the importance of delegation. A third case took a different tack in affirming Menem's power.

In *Fontela versus the State* the court deprived legislators of the use of the court system in their attempts to hold the Menem administration accountable for its policies. In July 1990, Congressman Fontela filed an injunction before federal judge Oscar Garzón Funes to stop the sale of the national airlines (Aerolíneas Argentinas) until an investigation could ascertain the legality of the transaction. Garzón Funes, who was known as an independent-minded judge, accepted the case and ordered Minister of Public Works, Roberto Dromi, who was in charge of the privatization programme, to restructure Aerolíneas according to Law 19.550. In response, Dromi pleaded for the Supreme Court to take up the case. The Court accepted the minister's request less than an hour after Garzón Funes had issued his order. This move was in open violation of Art. 257 of the Civil and Commercial Procedural Code which allowed appeals to be filed only to the tribunal that had issued the sentence regarding the case. Using an obscure legal procedure called *per saltum*, the Supreme Court claimed the case for itself due to the 'institutional gravity' of the matter without actually specifying what was so critical about selling a state-owned enterprise from a constitutional standpoint. However, Menem needed this ruling badly. Aerolíneas was his first privatization. Had it failed, the whole privatization process could have collapsed. It took only a few minutes for the Supreme Court to rule void Garzón Funes' injunction, paving the way for the airline transfer a few days later. The court justified the *per saltum procedure* by explaining that the United States Supreme Court had ruled on cases without previous sentences. Thus, Menem obtained what he wanted. The message behind the sentence was clear: the Supreme Court was squarely behind the president and could not be counted on to challenge his initiatives (Verbistky 1993: 140).

Conclusion

To summarize, this paper was motivated by the diverging paths taken in the fights against corruption and the development of oversight institutions in the United States and Argentina. Though the two countries shared similar problems with corruption in the 19th century, the United States Congress eventually developed laws and institutions that have helped the legislature serve its Madisonian roles, while the Argentine Congress has generally failed to do so. We have argued that the divergent tracks taken by these two countries is largely the result of the difference in the legislatures' motives and the courts' willingness to check and counter executive action. We have further argued that the divergent motives explain the differing development of legislative capacity, but that the long continuous period of democratic rule has also been necessary to the development of institutions and the attack on corrupt practices. The uninterrupted democracy has given the U.S. legislature time to experiment with new laws and practices to help fill the ever-appearing loopholes. Further, by continually strengthening their oversight capabilities, the legislature has helped build respect for the rule of law. This contrasts with Argentina's turbulent experience with democracy, which has limited the development of a professional legislature able to hold the line on executive abuses and address issues of corruption.

While Argentina's progress towards institutional development has taken different and often erratic turns, there are some propitious signs that suggest that even in spite of its current crisis, the road to reform is pointing in a positive direction. First, a free press has helped create a public disgust with executive abuses. While Menem was admired for his economic achievements, his abuse of power has become widely known and resented. Second, since the end of the dictatorship in 1983, Argentina has now held four presidential elections, three of which have resulted in a change of power among parties. Third and relatedly, the military has ceased to be a central political force, and even during the crisis of December 2001 when President de la Rúa resigned amidst an economic collapse and its resulting social chaos, disgruntled Argentines did not look to the military for answers as has been the case in their history (or in Venezuela in April 2002). This positive step, along with the now 20 years of the continual operation of the legislature (even if it has been chastened at times), has contributed to a growing role and professionalization of that body.

This change is evident in the development of institutions that may well begin to rein in the corruption and executive abuses. A primary example regards the budget which we noted had not, until 1990, even passed through the legislature for over 30 years. The budget process has now become much more regularized, and though this has not always meant careful scrutiny of the president's proposals, the legislature is clearly more involved than in previous years. A second example regards the development of the Anti-Corruption Office (ACO) in December 1999. The ill-fated de la Rúa continued his predecessor's practice of circumventing the legislature by issuing numerous DNUs, but in response to the perceived corruption during the Menem presidency, de la Rúa also took some important steps in creating independent institutions to promote greater oversight. The ACO has been praised both at home and abroad as one of the most significant innovations pursued in the developing world. Staffed by independent judges and technocrats, the ACO has rapidly gained respect for its active role by bringing more than 500 cases to the courts. The fact that President Eduardo Duhalde (who, by means of a legislative vote, succeeded de la Rúa, albeit after the legislature had first installed several caretakers who lasted just a few days each) has decided to retain such an institution, is a positive sign.

We began this chapter on a somewhat hopeful note, explaining that although it took a significant period of time, the United States has experienced tremendous improvement in spite what at one time seemed a hopeless level of government corruption and lack of accountability. While the changes in Argentina do not provide clear signs of a linear movement towards the development of clean government and functioning checks and balances, they show important parallels with the institutional development in the United States. If Argentina's democratic institutions can continue to survive the tremendous challenges that it has faced in recent times, the United States experience suggests that their institutions will incrementally take hold and overcome the many hindrances to their effective functioning.

This conclusion can be extended to other countries in Latin America, most of which have also suffered from a lack of democratic time, low professionalization, and strong ties between the president and the congress. Some legislatures must also overcome constitutions that limit their influence. For example, the constitutions of Brazil, Chile, Uruguay, and others prohibit the legislature from increasing expenditures from the executive budget 'request'. Other constitutions allow the legislatures only a very short time to debate the budget bill, or allow the executive to veto line items, adjust the legislative agenda, and issue decrees. These powers unbalance the inter-branch relations, thus hampering the legislature's efforts.

In spite of these hindrances, many countries in Latin America, like Argentina, appear to be on the road to reform. Though the events in Venezuela remind us that the military can still kick over the democratic playing field, the militaries appear much less willing to do so than in previous times, and the legislatures thus have a chance to develop their technical capacities. Further, though often scorned for the brakes it puts on government policy, the now common situation of presidents facing legislatures where they lack a majority may well encourage the development of legislature-controlled oversight systems. Further, parties in many countries are now experimenting with internal democracy, which will help the legislators develop independence from their parties. Especially if this happens to lead to higher re-election rates (which, in Argentina are just 20 percent and across Latin America they are very low in comparison with the United States) the legislatures may well begin to professionalize. Indeed, we have seen great leaps in the last decade, with the formation of professional staffs, the computerization of legislative operations, and the development of other legislative resources such as libraries and data banks. These new resources will limit the legislatures' previous reliance on the executive branch for the information necessary to perform oversight functions or analyse policy options.

As a result of these changes legislatures have begun to take a much more active role in policy and oversight. In addition to their central role in the process in which Argentine President de la Rúa resigned and was replaced, in the 1990s three Latin American presidents were removed by the legislature, two for alleged corruption and a third for 'mental incapacity'. Further, the presidents that have stayed in their posts, including those traditionally seen dominant, have had to offer important policy concessions to the legislatures. In Brazil, for example, Ames (2002) explains that not a single executive initiative went through the Brazilian Congress without modification. Since 1997 in Mexico, when the PRI lost control of the Chamber of Deputies, the legislature has fought with the president over budget outlays, the bank bailout, the pension scheme, and the peace arrangements with the Zapatistas.

These examples suggest that the legislatures have become more independent of the executive. Assuming they are allowed to continue exercising their constitutional duties, the independence should breed an interest in expanded capacities. While these expanded capacities will undoubtedly lead to inter-branch conflict, it is precisely that conflict that can ultimately motivate the development of effective oversight institutions.

References

Acuña, Carlos and Catalina Smulovitz. 1995. 'How to Guard the Guardians: Feasibility, Risks, and Benefits of Judicial Punishment of Past Human Rights Violations in New Democracies (some lessons from the Argentine experience)'. In A. James McAdams, ed., *Transitional Justice* and the Rule of Law in New Democracies. Notre Dame, IN: University of Notre Dame Press.

Albright, Spencer D. 1942. *The American Ballot*. Washington, DC: American Council on Public Affairs.

Ames, Barry. 2002. 'Party Discipline in the Brazilian Legislature'. In Scott Morgenstren and Benito Nacif, eds., *Legislative Politics in Latin America*. Cambridge: Cambridge University Press.

Benson, George C.S. 1978. *Political Corruption in America*. Lexington, MA: Lexington Books

Brooks, Robert C. 1909. 'The Nature of Political Corruption'. *Political Science Quarterly* 24, 1: 1–22.

Cain, Bruce, John Ferejohn, and Morris Fiorina. 1987. *The Personal Vote: Constituency Service and Electoral Independence*. Cambridge, MA: Harvard University Press.

Cleveland, Frederick A. 1919. 'Popular Control of Government'. *Political Science Quarterly* 34, 2 (June): 237–61.

Cox, Gary W. and Scott Morgenstern. 2001. 'Latin America's Reactive Assemblies and Proactive Presidents'. *Comparative Politics* 33, 2: 171–89.

Eaton, Kent. 2002. 'Fiscal Policy Making in the Argentine Legislature'. In Scott Morgenstern and Benito Nacif, eds., *Legislative Politics in Latin America*. Cambridge: Cambridge University Press.

Evans, Eldon Cobb. 1917. *A History of the Australian Ballot System in the United States. A Dissertation*. Chicago, IL: University of Chicago Press.

Ferreira Rubio, Delia, and Matteo Goretti. 1998. 'When the President Governs Alone: The Decretazo in Argentina, 1989–93'. In John Carey and Matthew Shugart, eds., *Executive Decree Authority*. New York, NY: Cambridge University Press.

Fiorina, Morris. 1977, 1989. *Congress, Keystone of the Washington Establishment*. New Haven, CT: Yale University Press.

Geddes, Barbara. 1991. 'A Game Theoretic Model of Reform in Latin American Democracies'. *American Political Science Review* 85, 2: 371–92.

Gómez, Pablo. 1996. *Los Gastos Secretos del Presidente: Caja Negra del Presupuesto Nacional*. Mexico City: Grijalbo.

Harris, Joseph P. 1934. *Election Administration in the United States*. Washington: Brookings Institution.

Heidenheimer, Arnold J. 1997. 'Problems of Comparing American Political Corruption'. In Arnold J Heidenheimer, Michael Johnston, and Victor T. LeVine, eds., *Political Corruption: A Handook*, pp. 573–86. New Brunswick, NJ: Transaction Books.

Helmke, Gretchen. 1999. 'Ruling Against the Rulers: Insecure Tenure and Judicial Independence in Argentina, 1976–1995'. Department of Political Science, University of Chicago. Working paper.

Hofstadter, Richard. 1955. *The Age of Reform*. New York, NY: Vintage Books.

168   *Scott Morgenstern and Luigi Manzetti*

Howard, George Elliott. 1899. 'British Imperialism and the Reform of the Civil Service'. *Political Science Quarterly* 14, 2 (June): 240–50.

Kaufmann, Daniel, Aart Kraay and Pablo Zoido-Lobaton. 2002. 'Governance Matters II: Updated Indicators for 2000/01'. World Bank Policy Research Department Working Paper.

Marx, Fritz Morsetin. 1945. 'The Bureau of the Budget: Its Evolution and Present Role, I'. *American Political Science Review* 39, 4: 653–84.

Matus, Alejandra. 1999. *El Libro Negro de la Justicia Chilena*. Santiago, Chile: Planeta.

Mayhew, David. 1974. *Congress: The Electoral Connection*. New Haven, CT: Yale University Press.

Merriam, Charles E., and Louise Overacker. 1928. *Primary Elections*. Chicago, IL: University of Chicago Press.

Miller, Jonathan. 1997. 'Judicial Review and Constitutional Stability: A Sociology of the US Model and its Collapse in Argentina'. *Hasting International and Comparative Law Journal* 77.

Mora y Araujo, Manuel. 1991. *Ensayo y error*. Buenos Aires: Planeta.

Morgenstern, Scott, and Benito Nacif, eds. 2002. *Legislative Politics in Latin America*. Cambridge: Cambridge University Press.

North, Douglas. 1990. *Institutions, Institutional Change, and Economic Performance*. New York, NY: Cambridge University Press.

O'Donnell, Guillermo. 1988. *Bureaucratic-Authoritarianism: Argentina in Comparative perspective 1966–1973*. Berkeley, CA: University of California Press.

——. 1994. 'Delegative Democracy'. *Journal of Democracy* 5, 1.

Palermo, Vincente and Marcos Novaro. 1996. *Política y poder en el gobierno de Menem*. Buenos Aires: Grupo Editorial Norma.

Perry Powers, Fred. 1888. 'The Reform of the Federal Service'. *Political Science Quarterly* 3, 2: 247–81.

Petrei, Humberto. 1998. *Budget and Control: Reforming the Public Sector in Latin America*. Washington, D.C.: Inter-American Development Bank, distributed by The Johns Hopkins University Press.

Polsby, Nelson W. 1968. 'The Institutionalization of the U.S. House of Representatives'. *American Political Science Review* 62, 2: 144–68.

Rock, David. 1985. *Argentina 1516–1982: From Spanish Colonization to the Falklands War*. Berkeley, CA: University of California Press.

Stanley, Harold W. and Richard G. Niemi. 1995. *Vital Statistics on American Politics*. Washington, DC: CQ Press.

Stewart, Charles H. III. 1989. *Budget Reform Politics: The Design of the Appropriations Process in the House of Representatives, 1865–1921*. Cambridge: Cambridge University Press.

Torre, Juan Carlos. 1993. 'Governing the Economic Emergency: The Alfonsín Years'. In Colin M. Lewis and Nissa Torrents, eds., *Argentina in the Crisis Years*. London: Institute of Latin American Studies.

Van Riper, Paul P. 1958. *History of the United States Civil Service*. Evanston, IL: Row, Peterson & Co.

Verbitsky, Horacio. 1987. *Civiles y militares, memoria secreta de la transición*. Buenos Aires: Contrapunto.

——. 1991. *Robo para la corona*. Buenos Aires: Planeta.

——. 1993. *Hacer la Corte: La construcción de un poder absoluto sin justicia ni control*. Buenos Aires: Planeta.

Vidal, Armando. 1995. *El Congreso en la Trampa: Entretelones y Escándalos de la Vida Parlamentarias*. Buenos Aires: Planeta.

Wheeler, Everett P. 1919. 'The Rise and Progress of the Merit System'. *Political Science Quarterly* 34, 3: 486–92.

6

The Role of Congress as an Agency of Horizontal Accountability: Lessons from the Brazilian Experience

*Argelina Cheibub Figueiredo**

Analysts of Latin American politics have reached a consensus on the shortcomings of accountability mechanisms in the region's presidential systems. There is, however, considerable dissent with respect to the explanations for the faulty oversight of government by legislatures, courts, and other newly designed agencies of accountability. Other chapters in this volume consider the various institutional and partisan variables which, together or separately, affect accountability.

Presidential systems supposedly have a built in mechanism to ensure horizontal accountability. The independent origin and survival of the executive and the legislature are expected to produce countervailing ambitions that motivate mutual checks and minimize the risks of tyranny of the majority. This seemed to be Madison's intent when he designed a system of government with multiple entry points that both offset the power that any branch of the government might otherwise acquire over another, and assure that if a majority of citizens share a 'common impulse of passion, or of interest,' it should be rendered unable to carry it into effect (Cain and Jones 1989: 27).

Yet presidential systems evolved counter to their original designers' goals. Today the basic conditions for the proper functioning of a system of checks and balances are lacking in many countries. First, Madison's fear of 'stable divisions of political con-

* I would like to thank José A. Cheibub, Simone Diniz, Marcus Figueiredo, Fernando Limongi, Scott Mainwaring, Adam Przeworski, and an anonymous referee for their comments on an earlier version. I am also very grateful to Simone Diniz and Paula Sterzi for research assistance.

flict' has proved justified (Cain and Jones 1989: 20). Political parties have become the main basis of government and, in the 20th century, representative government assumed the form of 'party democracy.'[1] Second, constitutional designs of existing presidential systems have changed drastically.[2] Concentration of legislative power in the executive branch has become a common trait in presidential regimes. In this regard, Madison's fears have not been realized; concentration of power has occurred not in the legislative branch, but rather in the executive.[3]

In this chapter, I want to analyze the effect of an institutionally strong executive and a centralized decision-making process on the role of Congress as an agency of horizontal accountability. My objective is, first, to discuss how institutional and political variables interact to cause Congress members to activate existing oversight mechanisms and, second, the conditions under which their actions may succeed. Success is defined here as (1) the imposition of sanctions in cases of executive omission, improper behavior and corruption, and/or (2) changes in the implementation of public policies. I argue that the macro institutional structure as well as specific micro institutional devices help to prevent effective oversight in a country where we would expect to find a more active legislature if we consider the constitutional separation of power, the federal organization, and the electoral and party systems.

In Brazil, the constitution grants the executive strong legislative agenda-setting powers and congressional rules give party leaders extensive power to control the legislative process. In a multiparty system, where the formation of coalition governments is the dominant pattern,[4] these powers facilitate coordination among coalition members and increase cooperation with the executive.[5] They reduce the influence of individual members of Congress and prevent institutional conflicts arising from differences in constituencies under a system of separation of powers. The power to set the

---

[1] See Chapter 6 'Metamorphoses of representative government' for a characterization of this form of representative government (Manin 1997).

[2] Przeworski, Stokes and Manin (1999: 19) mention the role of party in promoting collusion and the need to take this into account when demonstrating the effects of specific institutional design.

[3] On the risks of concentration of power in the 'legislative department of the government,' see *Federalist Paper* no. 48 (Hamilton et al. 1961: 308–13).

[4] See Amorim Neto (1995, 1998) and Table A6.1 in the Appendix.

[5] Shugart and Carey (1992) and Carey and Shugart (1998), on the contrary, argue that a conflictual relationship is likely to occur between a strong executive and the legislature.

agenda and to control the legislative process makes concerted action by the executive and the leaders of its supporting coalition both possible and effective. Government works as if there existed fusion of executive and legislative powers.[6]

These institutional mechanisms increase the president's capacity to enforce cohesion in the governing coalition and thereby to overcome dissent deriving from ideological differences and policy disagreements among coalition parties. As a consequence, they help increasing presidential success and policy dominance and weaken the role of Congress as a countervailing power to the presidency. Congressional autonomy in policy outcomes is reduced and restricted to specific policy areas.[7]

This institutional framework influences Congress's role as an agency of horizontal accountability in the same way that it affects its role as an autonomous policy making body. As the capacity of the executive to control the government coalition increases, congressional ability to oversee executive action decreases. Agenda-setting powers and the control over the legislative process affect the incentives of members of Congress to initiate oversight activities as well as their chances of success. They also reduce, although they do not entirely eliminate, the role played by the opposition and by the existing legal apparatus, information system, and organizational structure to support Congress's oversight activities. In this institutional context, the effectiveness of Congress as an agency for horizontal accountability depends greatly on external factors such as the mobilization of public opinion by the press and organized groups.

The chapter's empirical focus is Brazil, but the concentration of institutional power and centralization of the decision-making process is not peculiar to that country or to presidential systems. Other new democracies in Latin America, as well as in Southern and Eastern Europe, have similar institutional designs. Similar trends in the direction of centralization, usually referred to as 'rationalization of parliaments,' can also be identified in the post-Second World War European parliamentary democracies.[8]

---

[6] See Figueiredo and Limongi (2000) for the argument that centralization of the decision-making process impacts the functioning of the presidential systems in the same way as it does in parliamentary systems.

[7] Figueiredo (2000) compares the role of Congress in legislative outcomes in these two periods.

[8] Lauvaux (1988) studies this type of phenomenon in various countries and Huber (1996) provides an analysis of France.

I believe, therefore, that the analysis undertaken here applies to a wider range of cases than Brazil alone.

The first part of the paper focuses on the parliamentary investigation committees (*Comissões Parlamentares de Inquérito* – CPIs) formed in the Brazilian lower house during two democratic periods: 1946–64 and 1988–99. I first present the main institutional differences, and then compare the incidence and the success rates of the investigations in the Chamber of Deputies during these two periods. The analysis aims to show how the centralized decision-making structure, in conjunction with specific regulations regarding the formation of CPIs, have an impact on both the strategies and the results obtained by members of Congress with respect to investigations.

The second part of the paper focuses on the current democratic period and considers the various forms of routine oversight existing in the 1988 constitution. I compare the legally enabled oversight mechanisms with Congress's actual capacity to exert effective oversight over government actions. This section demonstrates that the 1988 constitution provides an extensive array of oversight mechanisms and an adequate legal apparatus to sanction the government. It also illustrates the growth of a significant organizational structure which enlarged independent staffs and strengthened agencies supporting congressional activities. These favorable institutional conditions, however, are not sufficient for effective oversight. Congress's legal ability to take on oversight initiatives is much greater than its capacity to achieve actual results.

In the conclusion, I summarize the main findings and briefly discuss their implications for overall government accountability. I argue that although Congress's direct oversight role is diminished, its indirect role is critical. The information it provides through its oversight mechanisms is essential for groups in society to activate other accountability mechanisms. This, of course, also strengthens the mechanisms of vertical accountability that are established between voters and the government.

Institutional Differences Between the 1946 and the 1988 Presidential Regimes

The rules regulating the distribution of power between the executive and the legislative branches of the government differ drastically in the 1946 and 1988 constitutions. The later constitution grants the executive a rather extensive array of institutional agenda-setting powers. The president has the exclusive initiative in the introduction of administrative, budget and fiscal legislation and can request urgency for the bills he introduces, thereby giving them priority in the legislative schedule. The executive has also delegated decree authority, and most important of all, the power to enact decrees with immediate force of law.[9] Under the 1946 constitution, on the contrary, the president held only one of these prerogatives: the one that refers to exclusive initiative to introduce legislation related to administrative matters.[10]

Executive decree is the most powerful instrument for changing results that could be predicted by the distribution of seats in parliament. It endows the president with the unilateral power to alter the status quo and consequently to change the structure of choices available to the legislature. That is, the legislature must take into consideration the changes already produced by the enactment of the decree. This means that an approved decree could have been rejected if introduced as an ordinary bill.

It is perhaps for this reason that the use of decree is usually interpreted as usurpation of the legislature's power and associated with minority governments. However, decree power can also play a crucial role in the hands of an executive holding majority or near majority support, especially in coalition government. The role of decree in majority government is usually neglected by the comparative literature. But executive decree power can also be seen as a useful instrument for solving problems of 'horizontal bargaining' between the government and its supporting majority, rather than 'vertical conflict' between the government and the legislature (Huber 1996). This institutional mechanism, rather than bypassing the majority's will or subjugating the legislature, can be a powerful device to protect government majorities in coalition government. It can be used to protect the government majority from unpopular measures or bills affecting particular constituencies and to preserve policy agreements between the government and its supporting majority in the legislature.[11]

Parallel to the Executive's extensive legislative power, the organization of the Brazilian Congress today is highly centralized. The distribution of parliamentary rights and resources are ex-

[9] These prerogatives correspond only partially to the 'proactive powers' as defined by Mainwaring and Shugart (1997: 49)

[10] For a detailed comparison of the institutional framework in these two periods see Figueiredo (2000).

[11] The whole argument and the comparison of the characteristic of the legislation and the role of Congress in these two periods is in Figueiredo (2000).

tremely favorable to party leaders. The speaker and party leaders exercise tight control over the legislative agenda. They are responsible for the setting of the legislative calendar. Moreover, party leaders have procedural rights that allow them to represent backbenchers (*bancadas*) and thereby control the floor. In this way congressional party leaders in practice make the decisions concerning roll calls, amendments, voting schedules and legislative calendar. Internal rules favor party leaders, especially leaders of the larger parties.

These constitutional rules and legislative procedures provide the executive and party leaders in the governing coalition with the means to promote cooperation from the legislature and to neutralize legislators' individualistic behavior. In a fragmented party system, members of Congress may have electoral incentives to pursue particularistic objectives but they do not have the capacity to achieve them. Institutional arrangements conspire against their capacity to succeed either in legislation or oversight.

Parliamentary Investigation Committees (CPIs) in Different Institutional Contexts

The *Comissões Parlamentares de Inquérito* are temporary committees formed at the request of individual members of Congress to investigate specific allegations of wrongdoing, administrative failures, corruption, etc. The 1988 constitution did not change the rules established by the 1946 constitution, but it reinforced Congress's capacity to initiate investigations. It endowed CPIs with powers of investigation equivalent to those of the judicial authorities and mandated that CPI reports be forwarded to the *Ministério Público*[12] for further investigation and eventual application of criminal or civil sanctions.

Parliamentary investigation committees can be formed in each one of the legislative houses or by both houses jointly. Their formation requires the support of one third of the legislative house in which they were initiated. Today, internal regulations of the lower house imposes limits on the number of CPIs: only five can function simultaneously. For this reason, there is a list of approved CPIs waiting to be able to start their investigations. The formation of a

---

[12] The *Ministério Público* is the institution responsible for the defense of the juridical order having as its main function the promotion of public penal actions. See the chapter by Sadek and Cavalcanti (this volume).

sixth CPI is possible but requires a majority vote of both houses. The establishment of this ceiling reflects the fear of the house leadership that too many investigations could paralyze the legislature.[13]

The approval and formation of a CPI does not imply that the investigation will be completed. In fact, most CPIs never complete their work. Some of them are not even installed, that is, the committee members are not appointed. Often, CPI proponents may not even intend to undertake an investigation. A CPI may be used as currency for political exchange and, thus, its approval alone may be sufficient to produce the intended political consequences. A CPI may also be proposed as part of an individual politician's strategy to establish a record on a particular issue for an upcoming election. With a ceiling on the number of CPIs functioning simultaneously, a CPI can also be proposed in order to prevent the formation of another one. For instance, if the members of the government coalition anticipate that the opposition is likely to gather support for a CPI they find undesirable, they can form another one first, just to beat out the opposition.

Finally, a CPI proposed by a member of the opposition may be approved but prevented from forming by government parties if they do not appoint members to it. Constitutionally, the composition of a CPI must be proportional to the share of seats held by each party in the house and, according to internal rules, party leaders are responsible for the appointment of its members. This means that to come into being a CPI is dependent on party leaders, especially those belonging to the larger parties, and the governing majority can prevent undesirable investigations by simply not taking action.

In sum, the whole process of formation and operation of CPIs is pervaded by political conflict and strategic maneuvering by both individual members of Congress and party leaders. Various institutional and political factors account for the initiation and eventual success or failure of different investigations. In the analysis that follows, I will use the conclusion of an investigation as an indicator of its success. The conclusion of a CPI implies the approval by the committee of a report with recommendations of the actions to follow. The 1988 constitution mandates that a committee's final report be forwarded to the *Ministério Público* for further

[13] The concern with the 'slow pace' and other 'deficiencies' of the legislative work dominated the debates (published in the *Diário do Congresso Nacional*) that preceded the approval of the standing orders in 1989.

investigation and application of civil or criminal sanctions if necessary. The imposition of sanctions, however, depends on the decision of the legislature and/or other agencies of the government. For instance, the report of the joint CPI that investigated corruption during President Collor's administration (1990–92) concluded that the president's behavior was 'incompatible with the dignity, the honor and the decorum of the position of chief of state' (Rodrigues 1999: 228). This conclusion gave support to the lower house's decision to initiate the impeachment of the president. The sanctions that came later depended on the decisions of the Senate and the Judiciary. Changes in public policy originating from investigations follow a similar process. A recent example was a CPI's impact on the Ministry of Health's policy concerning the production of generic drugs. In sum, the conclusion of an investigation is an appropriate indicator of success since it is the necessary first step to the imposition of sanctions or corrections in public policy. The distribution of CPIs proposed and concluded by administration is shown in Table 6.1.

Although the two periods present similar rates of proposition, on average 0.77 and 0.66 CPIs per month, they differ greatly in two respects. First, proposal rates vary from one administration to another, much more in the first period than in the second. This fact, I believe, is probably due to circumstantial factors that led to the intensification of political conflict and social mobilization. Second, CPIs were considerably more effective in the first period than in the second: 57 per cent of the CPIs in the former against only 17 per cent in the latter.

In the two democratic periods, the Brazilian political system has possessed the same basic institutional features: a presidential form of government, open-list proportional representation, and federalism. This institutional framework provides multiple entries into the political system and the appropriate incentives to motivate mutual checks. In both periods, most governments have been multiparty coalitions, as the table with the composition of the coalitions in the period show (see pp. 193–4). Only the first two democratic governments formed two-party coalitions. Dutra's administration (1946–50) was the only one in either period in which the president's party (PSD) held the majority of the seats. In 1988, Sarney's party, the PMDB (*Partido do Movimento Democrático Brasileiro*), held the second largest share of seats. In both periods, the share of seats held by the allied parties in the lower chamber (i.e., coalition parties that support the government) tended to be

TABLE 6.1. *CPIs by Government and Period—1946–64 and 1988–99 Democracies*

Government	Government (months)	Proposed (number)	Concluded (number)	Proposed (monthly average)	Concluded (monthly average)	Concluded (% of total proposed)
		1964 Republic				
Dutra Feb. 1946–Jan. 51	60	16	9	0.26	0.15	56
Vargas Feb. 1951–Aug. 54	42	29	14	0.69	0.33	48
Café Filho Sep. 1954–Nov. 55	15	19	8	1.26	0.53	42
Ramos Dec. 1955–Jan. 56	3	1	—	0.33	—	—
Kubistcheck Feb. 1956–Jan. 61	60	54	31	0.90	0.52	57
Quadros Feb. 1961–Aug. 61	7	12	8	1.71	1.14	67
Goulart Sep. 1961–Mar. 64	31	38	26	1.22	0.83	68
Sub total	218	169	96	0.77	0.44	57
		1988 Republic				
Sarney Oct. 1988–Mar. 90	17	10	—	0.58	—	—
Collor Mar. 1990–Sep. 92	30.5	34	7	1.11	0.22	21
Franco Oct. 1992–Dec. 94	27	13	3	0.48	0.11	23
Cardoso[a] Jan. 1995–Dec. 99	60[b]	32	5	0.53	0.08	16
Sub total	134.5	89	15	0.66	0.11	17
Total	352.5	258	111	1.02	0.31	43

[a] Includes 1999, the first year of Cardoso's second term.
[b] Includes five CPIs in progress in December 1999.

Source: Banco de Dados Legislativos, Cebrap.

greater than the president's party. There is variation within each period, but on average the allied parties held similar shares of seats (48.5 and 47.5 per cent, respectively). The average representation of the president's party in Congress was larger in the first period (27.3 per cent) than in the second (11.7 per cent). Consequently, coalitions supporting the president in Congress were larger in the first period with an average of 75 per cent of the seats compared to 59 per cent in the second.

During these two periods the governing coalitions were both made up of parties with ideological differences. The main governing and electoral alliances were composed of parties with different constituencies: rural and urban-based parties, such as the PSD (*Partido Social Democrático*) and the PTB (*Partido Trabalhista Brasileiro*) in the first democratic period, and the PFL (*Partido da Frente Liberal*) and the PSDB (*Partido da Social Democracia Brasileira*) today. These two democratic periods, however, differ radically with respect to the legislative powers of the executive and the power of congressional party leaders. These institutional mechanisms reduce the effects of the system of government, the form of state organization (federalism), and electoral and party legislation on the functioning of the political system. They endow governments with greater capacity to increase cohesion in their supporting coalitions and to undertake concerted action. A coalition government possessing institutional mechanisms to overcome internal dissent from members of the coalition has greater capacity to avoid or to control congressional oversight actions, especially investigative activities.

In sum, the two democratic regimes analyzed here had the same electoral and party system but differed greatly as regards the decision-making process. If we consider only political variables, such as the distribution of seats and the ideological correspondence between the executive and the legislature, we would expect, first, that the parties outside the government would be the most motivated to request investigations and, second, that within the government coalition, the members of the president's party would be the least motivated to do so. The behavior of the members of the governing coalition would also depend on the ideological distance among the parties in the coalition and/or their policy disagreements. The greater the ideological distance among the parties in the governing coalition, the more difficult it would be to maintain its cohesion. We would also expect the size of the coalition to be important, depending partly on policy and ideological differences. The cost of managing a large coalition composed of heterogeneous parties is greater than a smaller, more homogeneous one.

However, institutional variables can reinforce or counteract the effects of the distribution of preferences in the legislature. In order to verify the role of partisan and institutional variables in determining who proposed and who succeeded in concluding investigations in these two periods, I examine now the rates of proposition and conclusion weighed by the number of party seats in the lower chamber. I classified the parties of the CPI proponents according to their relationship with the government. The proponents were grouped in the following three categories: (1) those who belonged to the president's party; (2) those who held cabinet positions; and (3) the opposition parties, i.e. those who do not participate in the government. Table 6.2 summarizes this information.

The table shows considerable differences both in terms of the number of CPIs proposed by deputy and their rates of success. The number of CPIs per deputy proposed during the 1946–64 democracy is much higher than today, regardless of party affiliation. This difference is greatest with respect to the allied parties: in 1946–64 their members requested six times more CPIs than they did in the 1989–99 period. It is worth noting that in the latter period, the president's party initiated very few investigations and did not conclude any.

In the first period the rates of conclusion per deputy are again much higher than the post-1988 period. The opposition parties had the highest rates of conclusion and the members of the president's party concluded no investigation. In addition to the figures in the table above, it is worth noting that 70 per cent of the CPIs proposed were not even installed in contrast with the lower than 10 per cent rate in the first period. This denotes the lower ability of individual deputies to implement their proposals in the current system. It also indicates the successful use by the government supporters of the strategy of proposing or installing CPIs to prevent others from functioning. In 1999, four CPIs proposed years before were installed and, with all action tabled, the dates for their conclusion were put off in order to prevent the creation of two other CPIs that were next on the waiting list. Representatives of the left opposition perceived this maneuver as a demonstration of the government's excessive power in Congress.[14]

There is also an important difference between the subject matter of the CPIs that were not installed or remained unconcluded and the ones that finished their investigations. As Table 6.3 shows, members of the non-governing parties have been the most suc-

---

[14] See *Folha de São Paulo*, March 22, 2000, *Caderno Especial*, p. A-13.

TABLE 6.2. *Rates of Conclusion and Distribution of CPIs Proposed and Concluded in the Lower House According to the Proponent's Party Affiliation*

Governments	CPIs proposed Per Deputy[a]			CPIs concluded Per deputy[a]			% CPIs concluded		
	Pres. Party	Allied Parties	Oppos. Parties	Pres. Party	Allied Parties	Oppos. Parties	Pres. Party	Allied Parties	Oppos. Parties
1946–1964									
Dutra 1946–51	0.03	0.06	0.09	0.03	0.03	0.02	100	50	29
Getúlio Vargas 1951–54	0.05	0.10	0.08	0.02	0.04	0.05	33	45	67
Café Filho 1954–55	0.13	0.06	—	0.08	0.02	—	67	33	—
Nereu Ramos[a] 1955–56	0.008	—	—	—	—	—	—	—	—
Kubischeck 1956–61	0.13	0.18	0.14	0.09	0.08	0.08	67	45	59
Jânio Quadros 1961–61	—	0.04	—	—	0.03	—	—	73	—
João Goulart 1961–64	0.05	0.07	0.18	0.03	0.05	0.12	87	67	68
Total	0.39	0.49	0.62	0.25	0.24	0.36	73	50	59
1988–99									
José Sarney 1988–90	0.001	0.03	0.02	—	—	0.02	—	—	12
F. Collor 1990–92	—	0.01	0.12	—	—	0.03	—	—	23
Itamar Franco 1992–94	—	0.01	0.04	—	0.003	0.007	—	25	50
F. H. Cardoso 1995–99[b]	0.10	0.03	0.09	—	0.007	0.01	—	33	20
Total	0.13	0.08	0.28	—	0.01	0.05	—	18	21

[a] Number of CPIs proposed and concluded by the number of members of the president's party, the allied and the opposition parties.

[b] 1999 is the first year of Cardoso's second term.

Source: Banco de Dados Legislativos, Cebrap.

cessful in concluding their investigations since 1988. The left wing parties initiated 43 per cent of the 14 CPIs concluded since 1989. However, only one of them directly affected an important area of administration, namely the concession of social security benefits, and it was limited to the state of Rio de Janeiro. The other ones concerned issues whose investigation government parties had no reason to oppose since they did not directly involve specific government agencies, such as: the causes of hunger; the killing of street children; violence in rural areas; criminality in the midwest of the country; etc. On the other hand, CPIs investigating important issues involving government agencies such as the management of large federal funds such as PIS-PASEP and FGTS (retirement and job security funds for workers and public servants); the FNDE (fund for the development of education); the concession of public radio and TV licenses; public sector wage policy; the transfer of federal resources for health care to the states; the action of public banks, such as the Central Bank, the *Caixa Econômica Federal* and the *Banco do Brasil*, and of federal agencies such as IBAMA (the Institute for Environment Protection), and SEAC (the office linked to the presidency which was responsible for social assistance programs) remained unconcluded or were not even installed. The situation was different in the 1946–64 period when there was only a minor substantive difference between the concluded and the unconcluded investigations. Many of the CPIs that were concluded involved investigations of government agencies and programs such as: the *Banco do Brasil*; SUMOC (the ministry of foreign trade); the IAA (the Institute of Sugar and Alcohol Policy); the IBC (the Institute for Coffee Policy); DNOC (the national department to combat and remedy drought); COFAP (agency for price control); and pensions and social security institutes. The differences in the subject matter of investigations in the two periods indicate that the government in the post-1988 period has greater ability to influence the results of parliamentary investigations by preventing the installation and/or the conclusion of investigations affecting the government more directly.

We can see, therefore, that the distribution of seats and the parties' relationships to the government in these two periods are very similar while the results of the CPI's are very different. Thus, these political variables are not sufficient to explain these differences. The greater concentration of power in the presidency and the centralization of the decision-making process in Congress increase the capacity of the government to control its supporting coalition and to preempt action by the opposition.[15]

Routine Oversight Mechanisms Under the 1988 Constitution: Legal and Organizational Empowerment and Actual Capacity

In this section, I focus on the 'police-patrol' type of oversight, that is, centralized, active, and direct oversight that Congress undertakes on its own initiative (McCubbins and Schwartz 1987: 427).[16] Basically, routine congressional oversight in the Brazilian Congress is undertaken by two types of agents with different organizational structures. The first is a central bureau endowed with exclusively supervisory functions, the *Tribunal de Contas da União* or the TCU (Federal Accounting Tribunal) is one example. The second is the congressional committee system that combines legislative and oversight functions. The 1988 constitution, as well as regulations later approved by Congress, improved oversight mechanisms established before the 1964 coup, corrected the restrictions on oversight mechanisms imposed by the military, and extended the range and the scope of congressional oversight action. Brazilian legislation also provides adequate support for imposing sanctions on public authorities in cases of misbehavior and unlawful activity. As a consequence, the Brazilian Congress holds a rather extensive array of formal mechanisms to exercise its constitutionally prescribed oversight function.[17]

In addition, the Brazilian Congress has built an impressive organizational and informational structure to support its legislative

[15] On the relationship between the president and the allied parties as well as the opposition to obtaining political support for legislation in the 1946–64 period see Amorim Neto and Santos (1997) and Santos (1997). For the current period see Figueiredo and Limongi (1999, 2000).

[16] Fire-alarm oversight is, on the other hand, a less centralized and direct intervention than police-patrol oversight. 'Congress establishes a system of rules, procedures, and informal practices that enable individual citizens and organized interest groups to examine administrative decisions (sometimes in prospect), to charge executive agencies with violating congressional goals, and to seek remedies from agencies, courts and Congress itself' (McCubbins and Schwartz 1987: 427).

[17] This is in contrast to other countries, such as Chile, for instance, where legal restrictions imposed by the military were not eliminated (Siavelis, 1999; and Alcalá) (1997).

and oversight roles. The information system serving Congress was created during the military regime, and can be seen as a positive, although unintended, consequence of the bureaucratization and modernization of military rule in Brazil. This system has been continually improved and today it carries out thorough coverage of congressional activities. The improvements in the organizational structure include the growth in the number and specialization of the personnel hired for technical support in the consulting bureaus of both legislative houses. Besides that, today, the organizational support provided in both houses is predominantly connected to the work of committees contrary to the previous emphasis on assistance to individual members of Congress.[18]

However, I will show that despite the legal, informational, and organizational apparatus available, direct and routine oversight is not carried out by Congress. The success rate of oversight initiatives is much lower than the rate at which they are initiated.

Central Control of Government Accounts

The *Tribunal de Contas da União* (TCU) is responsible for routine oversight of government accounts. This bureau has nine ministers and is staffed by public career personnel. Although formally belonging to the legislative branch, this agency has from the outset been strongly associated with the president, who, according to previous regulation, nominated all its members.[19] Senate approval of presidential nominations to the TCU was required even though there has never been a case of rejection. The 1988 constitution diminished the TCU's dependency on the executive. Today Congress has the prerogative of nominating two thirds of the TCU's ministers. On the other hand, the new constitution mandated increased technical capability (expertise in finance, accounting, economics, and public administration) and proven experience (over 10 years of professional activity in those areas) in candidates for a ministerial post at the TCU. Two of the ministers nominated by the president must be chosen from the office's career personnel, a condition that has restricted the president's choice even more. Further legislation and internal regulations corrected previous operational deficiencies and strengthened the TCU's links to Congress, and especially to its committees.

[18] See Diniz (1993) for a study of the *Assessoria Legislativa*.

[19] The following paragraphs on the TCU rely heavily on Pessanha (1998). Besides an account of the institutional changes in the TCU, Pessanha provides a detailed analysis of its composition, showing its increasing independence from the executive.

The constitution also increased considerably the TCU's oversight capacities, as well as the scope of its action. This bureau became responsible not only for the accounting and financial supervision of the government but also for examining the legal and economic aspects of revenue application. This expansion of the TCU's function, as Pessanha (1998: 21) points out, allows it to overcome the strict accounting conception of oversight and to move in the direction of more effective control over the development of governmental projects.

As far as sanctions were concerned, the constitution was also innovative in conferring on the TCU the ability to determine fines proportional to the amount of the damage caused to public funds. The TCU's decisions regarding these fines can be immediately enforced. Finally, the constitution institutionalized broader participation in oversight by ruling that 'any citizen, political party, association or union may legitimately put forward denunciations of unlawful or undue action before the TCU' (article 74, 2). This measure is obviously not self-enforced since it depends on various factors external to the agency, but the TCU has taken some initiative to make it easier for individuals or groups to file complaints.

Notwithstanding these favorable institutional regulations, effective change in the supervision of federal accounts has been slow. Reports on government accounts are in general favorable with specific criticism. The TCU's reports are presented on time, but congressional approval sometimes occurs long after the report has been publicized, and always by unanimous vote. Approval of the government's accounting after the end of the president's term has not been unusual (Pessanha 1998). A positive change is the fact that the TCU's activities seem indeed to be more integrated with the work of the standing committees, as indicated, for instance, by the increase in committees' requests for consultation. However, the improvements in the TCU's technical expertise and capacity for auditing government accounts have outpaced its capacity to impose policy changes and sanctions against the misuse of public resources. The recommendations contained in the reports prepared by the TCU's technical personnel are usually not followed by its board of ministers for political reasons. One example is a recent scandal related to the construction of a building for the Labor Courts in São Paulo, which was disclosed by a CPI formed by the Senate. The chief justice of the tribunal was proved to have embezzled more than 200 million *Reais* (over US$50 million) from the construction of the building. Irregularities in the expenditures for the construction had been detected and the TCU was notified in 1992, but only in 1998 did the TCU's board of ministers decide to include that construction in a list of illicit public works. In the course of the CPI, a PMDB senator was also proved to be involved with the construction of the building and, as a result of public outrage, he was the first senator in history to lose his mandate.

Committee Oversight

Committee oversight takes place under different institutional formats. The supervision of budget implementation is carried out by a large and centralized congressional committee, the *Comissão Mista de Orçamento* (CMO), composed of members of both houses. The standing committee system carries out other kinds of oversight activities, as well as legislative activities.

The Comissão Mista de Orçamento (CMO) and Budget Oversight   Control over budget execution is crucial because budget appropriations approved by Congress are not mandatory and regulations for the execution of the budget allow the government plenty of leeway in reallocating approved budget items. Congress can also pass legislation that modifies the approved budget bill through extraordinary transfers of resources from one budget item to another. Consequently, the CMO must function continuously. This committee has its own support staff. Moreover, the Senate and the Chamber of Deputies have separate consulting offices, with technically trained personnel who are responsible for monitoring the release of resources by the executive. Budget monitoring by the CMO relies on a data base kept by PRODASEN (Centro de Informática e Processamento de Dadas do Sevado Federal), the Senate data processing system. Its data base contains complete information about each one of the thousands of budget items. In addition to information about the nature of each program, activity, place of application, function, and ministerial jurisdiction, it also contains the specific amounts that were in the original executive proposal, the amendments introduced by members of Congress, the amounts approved, the reallocations mandated by further budgetary laws, and the monthly disbursement for each item.[20]

The CMO does not undertake routine budget supervision. Monitoring of the budget implementation is undertaken by the consult-

[20] This information is available on the World Wide Web for budgets from 1995 to the present.

ing offices, i.e., the technical staff belonging to the organizational structure of each legislative house. Their work, however, is directed primarily to aiding individual members of Congress. The opposition, especially the left-wing parties, has had an important role in supervising the implementation of the budget and bringing it before the public for discussion. In addition, as the PRODASEN system can be accessed on the Internet, associations, unions, interest groups and NGOs have increasingly participated in budget oversight.

Standing Committee Oversight Activities The standing committees undertake oversight activities through the following instruments: public hearings (*Audiências Públicas*—AP); proposals for oversight and control (*Proposta de Fiscalização e Controle*—PFC); convocation of ministers to provide information regarding policies in committee meetings (*Convocação de Ministros*—CM), which can take the form of a written requirement or an informal request; and requests for information from ministries and state agencies (*Requerimento de Informação*—RI). These oversight mechanisms, previously regulated by the houses' standing rules, acquired constitutional status in 1988. An individual member of Congress may request any of these oversight instruments but initiatives have to be approved by the appropriate committee.

Table 6.3 shows the number of these oversight activities on an annual basis from 1989–99. There is one common feature in the distribution of all these oversight instruments: the usage increases considerably in the first year of each legislative session in the period—1991, 1995, and 1999. This same pattern occurs with respect to the rate at which legislation is proposed by members of Congress. And as we will see below, just as legislation proposed by members of Congress (rather than the executive) is not likely to pass quickly, the success rate of oversight activities by Congress is much lower than the rate at which they are initiated.[21]

Public hearings (*Audiências Públicas*) combine oversight and legislative functions. They are special committee meetings in which experts or persons with connections to the issue under discussion speak about the subject matter. These meetings can occur either during the formulation of new policy or the review of existing policy. The same meeting may serve both legislative and oversight purposes. Since the records do not break down the nature of the hearings, it is not possible to estimate the amount of time

---

[21] On the legislation see Figueiredo and Limongi (2000).

TABLE 6.3. *Committee's Oversight Activities—1989–99*

Year	Public hearings (PA)	Request for information (RI)	Convocation of ministers (CM)	Proposal for oversight and control (PFC)
1989	124	328	9	—
1990	15	285	8	—
1991	164	1108	20	37
1992	84	889	3	35
1993	105	868	4	19
1994	47	525	3	11
1995	205	1319	21	40
1996	96	864	6	17
1997	144	953	10	30
1998	58	945	8	13
1999	279	1495	14[a]	19
Total	1321	9579	106	221

[a] Thirteen are still in progress.

Source: Banco de Dados Legislativos, Cebrap.

dedicated to either one of these activities. However, unlike the other instruments of oversight, we can presume that the sheer occurrence of these hearings be taken as an indicator of their success.[22]

The standing committees have approved a great number of requests for information from ministries, but it is difficult to assess the consequences. In general, whenever Congress initiates a request for information, it gets some response, either formal or informal. But when too many requests are referred to the same ministry they are usually ignored (Soares 1999). This happens despite the formal requirement that the information be provided within 30 days; if not, criminal charges can be brought against the Minister responsible. There is, however, no reported case of charges as a result of non-compliance. Most demands for information from the ministries and state agencies come from members of

[22] The data available does not allow a distinction between the two. For this distinction in the United State see Aberbach (1990: 132–40).

the left wing parties; they initiated 48 per cent of the RIs approved. The remainder were requested in similar proportions by the members of the center and right wing parties (Almeida 1999: 26). Most requests for information had to do with the management of state agencies (54 per cent); 30 per cent concerned information on social policies, and 16 per cent on the infra-structure (Almeida 1999: 26).

Table 6.3 shows that 106 convocations of ministers were requested in the lower house. However, only four were approved by the committees and actually took place. The great majority (70 per cent) have not even been considered by the committees. On the other hand, informal requests for information were more frequent.[23] This form of communication is in fact a means of preempting formal convocation and is preceded by an agreement between party leaders, usually of the parties that support the government, and the minister. Formal convocation of ministries is basically a strategy of the left wing parties. Although they have never held more than 20 per cent of the legislative seats, they are responsible for more than 50 per cent of the requests. This is particularly true of the Worker's Party (PT), which has been responsible for 30 per cent of all convocations. The members of the president's party rarely use this strategy. Since, throughout the 1988–99 period a coalition of right or center right parties have dominated the government, it is not surprising that communication between Congress and the cabinet has been more informal.

Proposals for oversight and control (PFC) have had an even lower rate of approval and execution than the other instruments of oversight: only five out of 221 proposals have been approved and carried out. This is not a low cost initiative, since the PFC must include a justification, a plan of execution, and a methodology for evaluation. Proposals for oversight and control have also been predominantly used by left wing parties which have been responsible for 52 per cent of the total requests.

Instruments for Punishing Executive Authorities and Suspending Legislative Acts of the Executive

The main punishment Congress can impose on authorities in the executive branch of the government is their removal from office. Constitutionally the lower chamber is responsible for authorizing criminal proceedings against the president, the vice-president and

---

[23] Although I do not have precise figures, information in the press suggests that this often happens.

ministers, for crimes of responsibility; the Senate prosecutes and judges them for these crimes. The process can result in the impeachment of these authorities, but even when the whole legal process is not completed the political removal of ministers is possible as a result of congressional action.

In 1992, President Collor was impeached in a process growing out of a CPI. Formal removal of a minister has not yet happened as a direct result of one of these oversight activities, but political removal has occurred as the result of the withdrawal of legislative support. In some cases, public testimony before congressional committees have played an important role in making it clear that a minister lacked legislative support. One example is the dismissal of the Minister of Communications, Luiz Carlos Mendonça de Barros, in 1998 after his testimony before a Senate committee regarding his conduct during the privatization of the federal telecommunications agency.

Besides the removal of public officers, the 1988 constitution allows Congress to suspend legislative acts of the executive that exceed its power of regulation or the limits of legislative delegation. It also allows judicial review of both congressional and presidential legislative acts through an 'action of direct unconstitutionality' (ADIN) that, according to legislative rules, can be initiated by the speaker, the committees or by individual members of Congress.

Congress has never used its power to suspend legislative acts of the executive. Most ADINs that argue the unconstitutionality of the executive's legislative acts have been initiated by left-wing parties; they account for 93 per cent of the 141 ADINs proposed by political parties.[24] The success of these actions depends on the decisions of the *Supremo Tribunal Federal* (STF, Federal Supreme Court), responsible for judging them. Until 1998, only seven ADINs proposed by the leftist parties had been accepted for consideration by the court.

Concluding remarks

The 1988 constitution empowered the legislative branch with greater oversight ability than it had had before. However, there is a difference between the number of oversight actions proposed and their rates of conclusion. The comparison of investigations in the

---

[24] Of the 336 ADINs proposed by political parties from 1988 to 1998, 141 referred to the federal executive. Vianna et al. (1999: 98–9).

1946 democracy and the post-1988 period demonstrates that partisan control and variation in government support do not account for differences in the effectiveness of congressional action.[25] The multiple entries assured by the political system, a common feature of both democratic periods, provide the motive for launching oversight actions, but today's institutional structure is not conducive to their success. Legislators can be motivated to oversight but they do not control the means to exert effective checks on the executive.[26]

The analysis presented here calls attention to institutional variables usually neglected by studies in comparative politics. A centralized decision-making process based on the institutional prerogatives of the president and party leadership reduces the role of Congress as an agency of horizontal accountability.[27] The Brazilian case shows that the effect of this variable is not reduced by the nature of the electoral and party systems. It suggests that the lack of competition between agenda setters inside the decision-making system can offset competition deriving from the electoral arena and party fragmentation.

Following the prevailing view in comparative politics, Moreno, Crisp, and Shugart sustain, in this volume, that the proper functioning of horizontal accountability depends on 'getting vertical accountability right.' The conditions that produce or enhance vertical accountability in turn depend on the electoral and party systems.[28] I would like to suggest that congressional failure to countervail executive action might also affect vertical accountability. Since mechanisms of horizontal accountability compel the executive to justify and defend its actions before other government branches, they also serve to inform citizens (Przeworski 1996: 32). Concentration of institutional authority reduces the visibility of public decisions and deprives citizens of the opportunity to obtain information about policies, thereby reducing their capacity to control government actions.

[25] In this volume, Manzetti and Morgenstern emphasize the role of partisan differences between the executive and the legislature.

[26] Ferejohn (1999) proposes a model in which authority increases with greater accountability, but he is concerned with the agents' interest in making themselves accountable in order to get the principal to trust them with more resources.

[27] In his analysis of congressional oversight in the United States, Aberbach (1990: 53–73) relates increase in oversight to decentralization of legislative organization.

[28] The authors criticize the use of the concept of horizontal accountability to refer to non-hierarchical relations between agencies. For this reason they adopt the term 'horizontal exchange,' but this is defined quite similarly to O'Donnell's definition of horizontal accountability, (1997).

This, however, does not imply that the oversight activity of Congress, which is guaranteed in the system of representation set up by the constitution, is devoid of meaning or useless. On the contrary, much of this activity both demonstrates the responsiveness of Congress to 'fire alarms' (McCubbins and Schwartz 1987) and allows the flow of information to groups and individual citizens, who then activate other mechanisms of accountability. Thus, the organizational and informational support structures established in Congress can enhance the indirect role of Congress in fostering government accountability.

Congress can also play a role in establishing the conditions for the triggering of 'fire alarms' in a wider network of institutions.[29] One final case in point is the establishment by Congress of a system of rules and procedures regulating public civil action by the *Ministério Público* in the enforcement of collective and diffuse rights. In combination with environmental protection laws and consumer and citizenship rights, also established by Congress, it allows decentralized oversight of government action by social movements and citizens.[30] The fact that Congress does not undertake direct oversight actions does not lessen the role it can play in increasing the overall level of accountability in the political system.

[29] As suggested by O'Donnell (2000).
[30] For this legislation and the practice of the *Ministério Público* that it enabled, see Arantes (1999).

TABLE A6.1. *Presidents, coalitions, and parties' seats in the Lower House*

President	President's party	Parties in government coalition	President's party % seats	Allied parties % seats	Opposition parties % seats
		1946 Republic			
Eurico Dutra I Feb. 1946–Oct. 46	PSD	PSD–PTB	52.8	7.7	39.5
Eurico Dutra II Nov. 1946–May 50	PSD	PSD–UDN–PR	52.8	29.4	17.8
Eurico Dutra III May 1959–Jan. 51	PSD	PSD–UDN	52.8	26.9	20.3
Getúlio Vargas I Feb. 1951–May 53	PTB	PSD–UDN–PTB–PSP	16.8	71.4	11.8
Getúlio Vargas II Jun. 1953–Aug. 54	PTB	PSD–UDN–PTB–PSP	16.8	71.4	11.8
Café Filho Sep. 1954–Nov. 55	PSP	PSD–UDN–PTB–PR	7.9	76.0	16.1
Nereu Ramos Dec. 1955–Jan. 56	PSD	PSD–PTB–PSP–PR	33.9	31.8	34.2
Juscelino Kubischeck Feb. 1956–Jan. 61	PSD	PSD–PTB–PSP–PR	33.9	31.8	34.2
Jânio Quadros Feb. 1961–Aug. 61	PDC	PSD–UDN–PTB–PSP–PR–PSB	2.0	90.5	7.4
João Goulart I Sep. 1961–Jun. 62	PTB	PSD–UDN–PTB–PR–PDC	20.2	64.1	15.6
João Goulart II Jul. 1962–Aug. 62	PTB	PSD–UDN–PTB–PSB	20.2	59.5	20.2
João Goulart III Sep. 1962–Dec. 62	PTB	PSD–PTB–PSB	20.2	38.0	41.7
João Goulart IV Jan. 1963–May 63	PTB	PSD–PTB–PSP–PSB	28.4	40.1	31.5

TABLE A6.1. (*cont'd*)

President	President's party	Parties in government coalition	President's party % seats	Allied parties % seats	Opposition parties % seats
João Goulart V Jun. 1963–Mar. 64	PTB	PSD–PTB–PDC–PSB	28.4	39.9	31.8
Total			27.3	48.5	24.2
		1988 Republic			
José Sarney II Oct. 88–Mar. 90	PMDB	PMDB–PFL	36.8	19.9	43.3
Fernando Collor I Mar. 1990–Apr. 92	PRN	PDS–PFL–PTB (BLOCK)	—	47.9	52.1
Fernando Collor II Apr. 1992–Sep. 92		PDS–PFL–PTB (BLOCK)	8.0	44.7	47.3
Franco I Oct. 1992–Aug. 93	No Party	PFL–PTB–PMDB–PSDB–PSB	—	52.9	47.1
Itamar Franco II Sep. 1993–Dec. 94		PFL–PTB–PMDB–PSDB–PP	—	60.2	39.8
F. H. Cardoso I Jan.1995–Apr. 96	PSDB	PFL–PTB–PMDB–PSDB	12.1	44.2	43.7
F. H. Cardoso II May 1996–Dec. 98		PFL–PTB–PMDB–PSDB–PPB	18.1	56.1	25.7
F. H. Cardoso III [a] Jan. 1999–Dec. 99	PSDB	PFL–PTB–PMDB–PSDB–PPB	18.5	53.6	27.9
Total			11.7	47.5	40.8

[a] First year of the second term.

Sources: Amorim Neto (1995); Hippolito (1985); Santos (1990); Nicolau (1998); Banco de Dados Legislativos, Cebrap.

References

Aberbach, Joel. 1990. *Keeping a Watchful Eye: The Politics of Congressional Oversight*. Washington, DC: The Brookings Institution.

Alcalá, Humberto N. 1997. 'El control parlamentario en Chile'. *Contribuiciones* No. 4. Santiago: Fundación Konrad Adenauer/CIEDLA.

Almeida, Francisco Inácio. 1999. *Idéias para o desenvolvimento do mandato parlamentar*. Brasília, DF: Instituto de Estudos Socioeconômicos (INESC).

Amorim Neto, Octávio. 1995. 'Cabinet Formation and Party Politics in Brazil'. Paper delivered at the meeting of the Latin American Studies Association, Atlanta, GA.

——. 1998. 'Of Presidents, Parties, and Ministers'. Ph.D. Dissertation, University of California, San Diego.

Amorim Neto, Octávio and Fabiano Santos. 1997. 'The Executive Connection: Explaining the Puzzles of Party Cohesion in Brazil'. Paper presented at the XX Congress of the Latin American Studies Association, Guadalajara.

Arantes, Rogério. 1999. 'Direito e Política: o Ministério Público e a defesa dos direitos coletivos'. *Revista Brasileira de Ciências Sociais* 14, 39.

Cain, Bruce and W. T. Jones. 1989. 'Madison's Theory of Representation'. In Bernard Grofman and Donald Wittman, eds., *The Federalist Papers and the New Institutionalism*. New York, NY: Agathon Press.

Carey, John M. and Matthew S. Shugart. 1998. 'Executive Decree Authority: Calling Out the Tanks, or Just Filling Out the Forms?' In John Carey and Matthew S. Shugart, eds., *Executive Decree Authority: Calling out the Tanks or Just Filling Out the Forms?* Cambridge: Cambridge University Press.

Diniz, Simone. 1993. 'A Assessoria Legislativa na Câmara dos Deputados'. São Paulo: Documento de Trabalho, Projeto: Terra Incognita: funcionamento e perspectivas do Congresso Nacional, Cebrap.

Ferejohn, John. 1999. 'Accountability and Authority: Toward a Theory of Political Accountability'. In Adam Przeworski, Susan Stokes and Bernard Manin, eds., *Democracy, Accountability, and Representation*. Cambridge: Cambridge University Press.

Figueiredo, Argelina C. 2000. 'Government Performance in a Multiparty Presidential System: The Experiences of Brazil'. Paper prepared for the XVIII World Congress of Political Science, IPSA, Québec, 1–5 August.

Figueiredo, Argelina C. and Fernando Limongi. 1999. *Executivo e Legislativo na nova ordem constitucional*. Rio de Janeiro: Fundação Getúlio Vargas.

——. 2000. 'Presidential Power, Legislative Organization, and Party Behavior in Brazil.' *Comparative Politics* 32, 2: 151–70.

Hamilton, Alexander, James Madison, and John Jay. 1961. *The Federalist Papers*. New York, NY: New American Library.

Hippolito, Lucia. 1985. *De raposas e reformistas: o PSD e a experiência democrática brasileira (1945–1964).* Rio de Janeiro: Paz e Terra.

Huber, John D. 1996. *Rationalizing Parliament.* Cambridge: Cambridge University Press.

Lauvaux, Philippe. 1988. *Parlementarisme rationalisé et stabilité du pouvoir executif quelques aspects de la réforme de l'État confrontés aux expérience étrangères.* Brussels: L'Université Libre de Bruxelles.

Mainwaring, Scott and Matthew S. Shugart, eds. 1997. *Presidentialism and Democracy in Latin America.* Cambridge: Cambridge University Press.

Manin, Bernard. 1997. *The Principles of Representative Government.* Cambridge: Cambridge University Press.

McCubbins, Mathew and Thomas Schwartz. 1987. 'Congressional Oversight Overlooked: Police Patrol versus Fire Alarms'. In Mathew McCubbins and Terry Sullivan, eds., *Congress: Structure and Policy.* Cambridge: Cambridge University Press.

Nicolau, Jairo. 1998. *Dados eleitorais do Brasil (1982–1996).* Rio de Janeiro: Revan/IUPERJ-UCM.

O'Donnell, Guillermo. 1997. 'Horizontal Accountability and New Polyarchies'. Paper prepared for the conference Institutionalizing Horizontal Accountability. Institute for Advanced Studies of Vienna and Forum for Democratic Studies, Vienna.

———. 2000. 'Further thoughts on horizontal accountability'. Paper prepared for the workshop Institutions, Accountability, and Democratic Governance in Latin America. Kellogg Institute for International Studies, University of Notre Dame, May 8–9.

Pessanha, Charles. 1998. 'O controle externo do Legislativo sobre o Executivo no Brasil: 1946–1998.' Paper presented at the Annual meeting of ANPOCS, Caxambu.

Przeworski, Adam, Susan Stokes, and Bernard Manin, eds. 1999. 'Introduction' in *Democracy, Accountability and Representation.* Cambridge: Cambridge University Press.

Przeworski, Adam. 1996. 'A Reforma do Estado. Responsabilidade Politica e Intervencão Economica.' *Revista Brasileira de Ciencias Sociais* Ano 11, No. 32: 18–40.

Rodrigues, Alberto Tosi. 1999. *A Democracia que nos coube: mobilização social e regime político no Brasil (1989–1994).* Ph.D. dissertation, Ciências Sociais, Unicamp.

Santos, Fabiano. 1997. 'Patronagem e Poder de Agenda na Política Brasileira'. *Dados – Revista de Ciências Sociais* Vol. 40.

Santos, Wanderley G., ed. 1990. *Que Brasil é este? Manual de Indicadores Políticos e Sociais.* Rio de Janeiro: Vértice.

Shugart, Matthew and John M. Carey. 1992. *Presidents and Assemblies: Constitutional Design and Electoral Dynamics.* Cambridge: Cambridge University Press.

Siavelis, Peter. 1999. 'Disconnected Fire-Alarms and Ineffective Police-Patrols: Legislative Oversight in Post-Authoritarian Chile'. *Journal of International Studies and World Affairs* 42, 1: 71–9.

Soares, Rosinethe Monteiro. 1999. 'Instrumentos reguladores da ação fiscalizadora do Congresso Nacional e do Tribunal de Contas da União. Unpublished paper.

Vianna, Luiz Werneck, M. A. Carvalho, M. P. Melo, and M. B. Burgos. 1999. *A judicialização da política e das relações sociais no Brasil*. Rio de Janeiro: Revan.

PART III

The Judiciary, the Public
Prosecution Office, and Rule of Law

The New Brazilian Public Prosecution: An Agent of Accountability

Maria Tereza Sadek
Rosângela Batista Cavalcanti

Political science scholarship and popular anecdotes are replete with affirmations that emphasize the distance between law and social reality in Brazil. In fact, the widespread belief in the difference between the two in Brazil has, since the time of independence, justified arguments in favour of institutional reform and further generated a debate over the potential causes and solutions capable of overcoming this distance. Setting aside this debate, which ranges from the most authoritarian to the most liberal interpretations, the contrast between the universe of legality and that of political, economic, and social institutions is irrefutable.

'Legal' Brazil, even during the period of authoritarian rule has approximated the legal framework of mature democracies in developed countries. From a legal perspective, Brazil values equality, respects individual and collective rights, and limits public power. In short, it is a nation that seeks a just order and attempts to guarantee it through democratic means and the State of Law. The 'real' Brazil, however, is a country that evidences inequality, injustice, and disrespect for legal precepts and the most basic principles of civility.

The distance between legality and reality in Brazil is well encapsulated by popular expressions that reveal the role of law in day to day life: 'the law, what law?'; 'for my friends everything, for my enemies the law'; 'go looking for your rights'; etc. The weak relationship between laws and reality has not been restricted to relationships within civil society, but also extends to the political arena and relationships of power. For example, despite the fact that every republican Brazilian constitution has adopted a system of checks and balances and separation of powers, in practice the executive branch has had few checks upon its power and very little oversight from the legislative and judicial branches. Furthermore, it goes without saying that flagrant disrespect for legality extends from the electoral process to the formulation of public policy.

Our repeated use of the past tense, however, does not imply that we advocate an excessively optimistic assessment of democratic advances achieved in Brazil in the past decade, or that the divide between legality and reality in Brazil no longer exists. Our central argument is that possible advances stemming from the Federal Constitution of 1988 cannot be fully appreciated from an exclusively juridical perspective focusing on formal institutional change. An analysis of formal and written legality must be complemented with its practical, and real-world, consequences. In this vein, the object of this paper is to discuss the extent to which the new Constitution represents an advance over past practices and enables the implementation of a fundamental attribute of democracy—effective mechanisms of accountability. We first examine the formal legal parameters under which institutions of checks and balances, as well as their respective instruments, operate. Second, we focus on the performance of a specific institution: the Public Prosecution (*Ministério Público*). One of the primary functions of this institution is to exert oversight and control over the public administration. Finally, we take into consideration all of the evidence presented in order to discern the Public Prosecution's impact on Brazilian democracy.

The 1988 Constitution

The 1988 Constitution that resulted from the 1987–88 Constituent Assembly had two objectives: (1) to implement a social, economic, and political order that stood in contrast to the previous authoritarian regime and (2) to accommodate all demands pertinent to something called the 'democratic spirit'. Consequently, the final text was long, detailed, and programmatic. In fact, it became one of the most detailed constitutions in the Western Hemisphere, and one that regulates practically all aspects of collective life. It would be hard to find a single issue not open to constitutional purview.

Individual, social, and collective rights were all regulated, thus justifying dubbing the 1988 Constitution the 'Citizen Constitution'. The text developed an extensive list of first-, second-, and third-generation rights, and was innovative with regard to diffuse and collective rights. Juridical equality, ignored in previous Brazilian constitutions, received unprecedented treatment, including clauses demanding direct action.

From an institutional engineering point of view, the Constitution implemented a presidential system with a specific division of powers model. While the Constitution strengthened the Legislature's law-making and oversight capabilities, it did not remove the ability of the Executive to legislate through executive decrees (*medidas provisórias*). At the same time, the judicial branch was given greater independence and was conferred the prerogative of determining the constitutionality of legislative and executive acts.

In effect, there was a tremendous expansion of the possible arenas open to the justice system's[1] purview. This not only derives from the Judiciary's prerogative to act as an arbitrator over executive and legislative conflicts, but from the principle that judicial constitutionality has been privileged over the principle of majority rule.[2] In this manner, the institutions that comprise the justice system have begun to occupy a central position in the political arena. Not only have their newly granted prerogatives enabled them to intervene in decisions enacted by the executive and legislative branches, they have been able to influence how public policy is implemented. Within the set of institutions that comprise the justice system, the Public Prosecution has played a particularly active and important role.

The New Brazilian Public Prosecution

The 1988 Brazilian Constitution assigns to the Public Prosecution two principal responsibilities: to defend the constitutional interests of citizens and society at large and to ensure that the public administration, and all its respective parts, complies with its constitutional responsibilities. The Public Prosecution's responsibilities are best highlighted by citing the constitutional text in question:

The Public Prosecution is a permanent institution, essential to the jurisdictional function of the State, and it is its duty to defend the juridical

[1] By justice system we mean the Judiciary, the Public Prosecution, the Bar Association, the Attorney General of the Union, and public defenders.
[2] For an argument that demonstrates how the principle of judicial constitutionality has taken precedence over the democratic principle subsequent to 1988 in Brazil, see Vieira (1994).

order, the democratic regime and inalienable social and individual interests. (Federal Constitution of Brazil, Art. 127)

As the above citation demonstrates, the constitutional attributes of the Public Prosecution are quite extensive and ambiguous. By virtue of being assigned the role of becoming a defender of the 'juridical order' and 'democratic regime', the 1988 Constitution effectively allows the Public Prosecution to intervene within a wide array of issues, and public policy arenas. Such a degree of discretion is further made evident through listing a few of its institutional responsibilities, which are also detailed in the Constitution:

- to ensure effective respect by the Public Authorities and by the services of public relevance for the rights guaranteed in this Constitution, taking the action required to guarantee such rights;
- to institute civil investigation and public civil suit to protect public and social property, the environment and other diffuse and collective interests;
- to institute action of unconstitutionality or representation for purposes of intervention by the Union or by the states, in the cases established in this Constitution;
- to issue notifications in administrative procedures within its competence, requesting information and documents to support them, under the terms of the respective supplementary law (Federal Constitution of Brazil, Art. 129, Items II, III, IV, and VI).

Such responsibilities stand in sharp contrast to the Public Prosecution that existed prior to the 1988 Constitution. Previous to 1988, the Public Prosecution was almost exclusively confined to criminal law, yet subsequent to 1934 it did come to assume an auditing or oversight role that went beyond merely criminal matters (*custus legis*). It became its duty to see that the laws were faithfully executed and enforced. Its intervention in the judicial process aimed to protect what were considered indispensable values and social interests, such as legal disputes concerning family, marriage, birth and marriage certificates, and the defense of the helpless. These responsibilities defined the Public Prosecutor almost as a judicial expert rendering opinions on legal issues.

During the period of military rule (1964–85) the Public Prosecution was still not autonomous, but became dependent on the Executive rather than subordinated to the Judiciary. During the entire period prior to 1988, members of the Public Prosecution were held in lesser regard and prestige in comparison to fellow members in the judicial branch, despite the fact that both worked together to enforce law and justice.

Most academic papers and press releases published prior to 1988 associated the Public Prosecution only with questions of criminal law. The members of the Public Prosecution were seen only as figures responsible for filing criminal charges.

In addition to its traditional role within the criminal sphere—to investigate penal infractions and ascertain the nature of the offence and the offenders—previous constitutions defined the Public Prosecution as the institution chosen to legally defend the interests of the State and its respective officeholders. Today the Public Prosecution's role has changed radically. For starters, the Public Prosecution has achieved independence from other branches of government—it is not subordinate to either the Executive or the Judiciary. Such an institutional transformation, which culminated in the 1988 Federal Constitution, was accompanied by a large increase in the Public Prosecution's jurisdiction. In addition to maintaining its ability to prosecute in the criminal arena, the institution was granted the responsibility of defending collective and diffuse rights (e.g., those of the environment, the consumer, and properties of artistic, aesthetic, historical, touristic, and scenic value) and protecting minority rights (e.g., those of children and adolescents, the disabled, the elderly).

Due to this tremendous increase in jurisdiction, the Public Prosecution has the ability, for example, to file lawsuits demanding that the State provide education, health services, or shelter for homeless children. In the role of overseeing the public administration, it can file lawsuits of unconstitutionality against existing laws or against normative acts promulgated at the federal, state, or municipal level.

The Public Prosecution wields a powerful juridical instrument to guarantee diffuse and collective rights:[3] the *Ação Civil Pública*, or class action suit, created by Law 7,347 in 1985, constitutes the primary instrument used by the Public Prosecution to defend such rights.[4] Despite the fact other public institutions and civil

---

[3] As formulated in the 1988 Constitution, however, diffuse and collective rights are vague enough to encompass almost any collective or group interest.

[4] The class action suit is a juridic instrument which allows groups within civil society, or the very Public Prosecution, to defend their collective rights, which encompass rights established in civil law. According to the Class Action Suit Law

associations can also make use of this legal instrument, the Public Prosecutor is the institution that has made most use of it.[5]

The Constitution stipulated the Public Prosecution's unity and indivisibility in addition to guaranteeing it administrative and functional autonomy. It granted the Public Prosecution the same prerogatives granted to the Judiciary: lifelong tenure for its members, a guarantee prosecutors won't be transferred to other jurisdictions against their will, and a constitutional guarantee of due benefits.

All of these powers potentially enable the Public Prosecution to defend the so-called 'Social Right',[6] be it through controlling abuses of power within the public or private sphere, or through defending social rights. In other words, these new institutional powers transform the Public Prosecution into a mechanism that can potentially ensure what Guillermo O'Donnell calls 'horizontal accountability', —'the existence of state agencies who have the right, legal power, and disposition to use their attributes, which range from routine supervision to legal sanctions and impeachment, against acts or omissions of other state agencies who can be characterized as delinquent' (O'Donnell 1998b: 40).

(*Lei da Ação Civil Pública*) the Public Prosecution was given the right not only to be a part of the suit, but also to act as a *custos legis*, which means it is responsible for an initial evaluation over its legal consistency. As a result, it has become active in defending any collective or diffuse rights which might have been infringed. In addition to this ample attribute, the Public Prosecution also possesses the responsibility of conducting the preparatory investigative work necessary for a class action suit. Such investigative work is referred to as a civil investigation, which is analogous to a police investigation, but contains characteristics specific not only to its administrative procedures, but also to its investigative work, which seeks to collect sufficient evidence to justify the suit in question.

[5] According to Macedo, 'the Public Prosecutor is today responsible for 96 per cent of all environmental class action suits in the country's courts. Despite the lack of data in other issue areas, one can presume that such a de facto monopoly (since the Public Prosecutor doesn't have a juridical monopoly over the filing of such suits) also extends to civil actions in defense of collective and diffuse rights' (Macedo 1996: 42).

[6] According to Macedo, 'Contemporary Law, a characteristic of the Welfare State and also known as Social Right, is structured according to a new type of juridical rationality. The Social Right increasingly takes into account group interests and social inequalities in order to seek, through distributive justice, a more just and egalitarian social order. Such a logic stands in contrast to a more liberal juridical order. A juridical order based on the Social Right therefore provides protection to specific groups (and, therefore breaks with the liberal paradigm of equality under the same juridical order) such as, for example, consumers, the elderly, minors, the physically deficient...' (Macedo 1996: 46).

From an institutional point of view, changes in the powers and role of the Public Prosecution constitute the most significant reform embodied in the Federal Constitution of 1988. No other institution underwent such a profound reform or expansion of responsibilities. The Public Prosecution was no longer known for its classic *parquet*, or oversight role, and even less for being an advocate or defender of the Executive's interests. Since 1988, the institution has been known primarily as a defender of society's interests. Hugo Mazzilli (1993), among many others, came to the conclusion that the Constituent Assembly effectively transformed the Public Prosecution into a 'fourth power' autonomous from the Legislature, the Executive, and the Judiciary.[7] These types of analysis have also provided fodder to arguments that oppose the new-found role, and power, exerted by the Public Prosecution. Despite such arguments, it is clear that today the Public Prosecution has become a primary actor in Brazilian politics and, according to the Constitution, is entitled to defend the democratic regime, the juridical order, and the interests of society.

The Public Prosecution operates at both the federal and state levels. The Public Prosecution of the Union, which presides at the federal level, is in turn subdivided between the Federal Public Prosecution, Military Public Prosecution, Labor Public Prosecution, and the Public Prosecution of the Federal District and its Territories. Their respective jurisdictions are bound by the facets of law they are dedicated toward: Federal Justice, Federal Military Justice, Labor Justice, and Justice of the Federal District and its Territories. The Federal Public Prosecution, however, is the only division that can litigate in the Superior Justice Tribunal (STJ), which levies verdicts on infra-constitutional law, and in the Supreme Federal Tribunal (STF)—the highest law court in the country—which is the last resort for interpretation of constitutional questions. The distinction between the various subdivisions within the Public Prosecution refers only to differences of

[7] Other notable legal scholars, such as Manoel Martins da Costa Cruz, draw similar conclusions. Cruz (in Mazzilli 1993) states, 'the Public Prosecution presents itself as a veritable State Power. If Montesquieu had written *Spirit of Law* today, the division of powers would be characterized not by three, but four divisions.' While this is not the place to have a discussion over what constitutes a separate power within the State, nor over the relevance of the traditional separation of powers theory, we are merely drawing attention to the considerable consequences associated with constitutional reforms enacted over the Public Prosecution.

jurisdiction, not types of juridical instruments at its disposal, guarantees, or operating principles.

From Potential to Practice

The noteworthy judicial reforms enacted by the 1988 Constitution and the set of laws deriving from them have created a propitious environment to generate a more effective system of justice. Due to the 1988 Constitution, Brazil's justice system has increased its ability to oversee public and private institutions and protect individual and social rights. As we have already noted, however, the constitutional attributes delegated to the Public Prosecution presume the existence of an institution with a high capacity for intervention, whether it be to control abuses of power in the public and private spheres or to defend social rights. In order to help guarantee that such responsibilities are carried out, the Constitution further provided for functional and administrative autonomy of the Public Prosecution.

The re-definition of the Public Prosecution's institutional profile and the expansion of its powers, has brought about a reconstructing of its identity. Legal texts, which include both the Constitution and infra-constitutional legislation, provide the broad parameters and potential for such a reconstruction. The speed and sense of that reconstruction, however, fundamentally depend on its own members. Individual members of the Public Prosecution are particularly important, given the institution's structure, where each member has the ability to act with a high degree of autonomy, without having to strictly adhere to precedents or directives established by the institution's leadership. In other words, there is no strict organizational hierarchy.

The potentially active role played by the Public Prosecution is enhanced by its organizational design and lack of institutionalization. It is decentralized, lacking a functional hierarchy and therefore giving substantial autonomy to each prosecutor. Within any given Public Prosecution individual prosecutors vary considerably, from those who take a very conservative approach to those who espouse the most liberal interpretation of the institution's responsibilities. This lack of institutionalization allows the Public Prosecution's identity to be shaped by the individual characteristics of its members.

The combination of constitutional attributes and guarantees, organizational structure, and paradoxically, its low level of institutionalization, all give the Public Prosecution a great deal of potential and capacity to promote citizen rights. The new legal parameters and 'political will' embodied in the Constitution have, in fact, translated into effective action. The Public Prosecution's performance subsequent to the 1988 Constitution stands in stark contrast to its previous record. Both the Public Prosecution of the Union and the Public Prosecution of the states have adopted their newly granted oversight and control responsibilities. Members of the institution have been utilizing legal instruments at their disposal to intervene in the most diverse spheres within public administration and collective life. The Public Prosecution in Brazil consists of 10,000 members—of which 9,662 are public prosecutors (state level) and 338 are prosecutors of the Republic (federal level)—and rarely a day passes in which the media does not report an action taken by prosecutors to uphold citizen rights.

At the federal level, the members of the Public Prosecution have transformed their institution into a veritable political force. Federal prosecutors have actively participated in political disputes with the Executive, Legislature, or groups in civil society. Indeed, prosecutors of the Republic have brought legal action against government ministers for the misuse of public funds and/or property,[8] have questioned social and economic policies, and have exposed corruption in the financial system. Not coincidentally, federal prosecutors are viewed with suspicion by members of the Executive, senators, federal deputies, directors of state-owned enterprises, and monetary authorities.

Opposition to the power of the Public Prosecution ranges from specific criticisms to more broad misgivings pertaining to the institution's structure and methods. The reaction of the government and that of its sympathizers to a search conducted by the federal Public Prosecution and the federal police in the home of the ex-president of the Central Bank, Franciso Lopes, is an example of such opposition. The warrant that allowed the Public Prosecution to search the home of the ex-president of the Central Bank was approved by the Judiciary and was intended to find evidence to support allegations that the Central Bank had unduly favoured two private banking institutions—Marka and FonteCindam. On that occasion in April 1999, despite the fact that the majority of

---

[8] Since 1999, for instance, the Federal Public Prosecutor has brought legal action against 12 ministers for using the Brazilian Air Force's (*Força Aéria Brasileira*) planes for private benefit. However, even the Attorney General of the Republic faces similar charges.

legal scholars considered the search legal, President Fernando Henrique Cardoso termed the action an 'invasion' and a 'return to arbitrary rule'. Others claimed the action reflected pure exhibitionism, was based on unfounded accusations, and reflected a lack of responsible authority.

Criticisms such as these, in the majority of cases, are not restricted to critiques over possible excesses committed by a few individual prosecutors. Generally, they are accompanied by vehement calls for a change in the role and jurisdiction of the Public Prosecution as a whole. In fact, a Constitutional Amendment that is part of a larger judicial reform bill is currently being examined in the National Congress and contains a series of proposals that seek to diminish the power of the Public Prosecution, particularly with regard to its capacity to question, accuse, or conduct the prosecution of authorities, and therefore to affect public policy.

Despite such criticisms, it is clear that as a result of the Public Prosecution's actions, Brazilian society is gaining a sense that crimes committed by the 'powerful' will not be ignored. This is clearly reflected in this editorial, appearing in the newspaper *Folha de S. Paulo*:

In the past, the flagrant disobedience of the law only occasionally brought consequences. Corruption and crime won't and will never end because of action taken by prosecutors. Nevertheless, a certain sense of impunity has been broken. The imprisonment of a banker and the stripping of a rich and powerful senator's legislative mandate has acted as an Olympic benchmark. They serve to establish a new parameter of morality in which society, little by little, begins to think it possible to attain. (*Folha de S. Paulo*, 9 July 2000)

Despite recent successes, members of the Federal Public Prosecution face a number of obstacles. One problem is insufficient staff—as mentioned earlier, there are only 338 federal prosecutors, and since 1996 the institution has been awaiting approval of legislation that would create 304 new positions. The Public Prosecution also suffers from a lack of technical support. Prosecutors must depend on police investigations to obtain evidence and, according to 93 per cent of federal prosecutors, one of the primary obstacles to attaining justice is a lack of police resources. According to 85 per cent of federal prosecutors, police investigations yield insufficient results (Castilho and Sadek 1998).[9] In addition, the federal

[9] These figures were obtained from a 1997 survey sent to all members of the Federal Public Prosecution. More than half of the federal public prosecutors responded (244 of 516).

Public Prosecution can only have access to private banking or tax records through authorization from the Judiciary, which has given its approval to only 60 per cent of such petitions (CONAMP, July 2000).

Despite the obstacles, according to a prosecutor of the Republic, 'we are convinced we are extending the law to areas that were previously untouched, punishing privileged groups, and increasing the access to justice of excluded groups' (*Folha de S. Paulo*, 28 July 2000). Along similar lines, a federal prosecutor in Rio de Janeiro, Raquel Branquinho Nascimento, who had participated in the investigation of possible irregularities committed by the Central Bank in the selling of dollars below market rate to the Marka and FonteCindam banks, stated in an interview, 'criticism constitutes a right of defense, but they come from a privileged segment of society—politically, economically, and socially—which is not used to receiving the same treatment as others. Our fight is for all to be treated in an equal manner within constitutional principles' (*Folha de S. Paulo*, 26 April 1999).

The institutional performance of the Public Prosecution of individual states varies greatly from state to state. As Ada Grinover observes, 'the Public Prosecution's model employed in the state of São Paulo or Paraná, for example, is not a reality throughout the entire country. ... Not all Public Prosecutions are as independent or autonomous as they could be' (Sadek 1997). Such variation across states is well illustrated by contrasting the cases of Paraíba and Bahia. In Paraíba, for example, the Public Prosecution focuses on administrative improprieties, and has created a 'Permanent Commission in the Combat Against Administrative Impropriety' whose main function is to receive and evaluate accusations of administrative irregularities practiced by mayors or ex-mayors, brought forth by any citizen, the Tribunal de Contas,[10] or by the County Legislature. In contrast, the Public Prosecution in the state of Bahia has demonstrated a clear preference to shy away from activities which have the potential to run against local political interests. In Bahia the Public Prosecution has focused its efforts on monitoring the police departments and responding to grievances pertaining to family disputes like alimony payments and paternity tests. While the oversight of the police department can be considered 'political', such an effort does not come close to the political repercussions associated with judicial action which can eventually lead to the

---

[10] The Tribunal de Contas is responsible for auditing public budgets and it is an institution subordinated to the Legislature.

impeachment of a given mayor. The fact that the Public Prosecution in Bahia rarely investigates the activities of local elected officials is probably a function of the fact that state and local politics have been dominated by a single political faction, headed by the ex-senator and governor Antônio Carlos Magalhães. In other words, when political power is concentrated in a given state, the Public Prosecution does not have the de facto liberty to contradict local political interests.

Even though it might be difficult to provide a single explanation for this variation, a plausible hypothesis, as yet untested, points to the degree of political pluralism present within any given state. The probability that prosecutors will be more 'independent' should increase in states that have a more diversified political and electoral base (i.e., more pluralist), or in states where any elite political faction does not hold a quasi-monopoly on political power within the state. It is important to note, however, that such an explanation does not necessarily coincide with the degree of economic development within states. Even though developed states are more likely to contain rival elite factions, many less-developed states in Brazil are characterized by a 'plural' elite. The states of Sergipe and Pernambuco stand out amongst the set of less-developed states that can be characterized by this type of political pluralism. By contrast, the state of Bahia has demonstrated a political hegemony by the same group for many years, despite a well-developed civil society within the state and numerous NGOs and organized social movements. In that state, both the judicial branch and the Public Prosecution exhibit a low degree of autonomy in relation to powerful public and private groups. While very likely, such a hypothesis merits a strong empirical study.

Another set of contrasting cases can be found within the states of Santa Catarina, Rio Grande do Sul, and Paraná, all located in Brazil's southern region. These states contain very similar socio-economic indicators—their respective Human Development Index (IDH) indicators are the highest in Brazil. Nevertheless, the performance of the Judiciary and the Public Prosecution within each state has varied distinctly. While both are quite active in Rio Grande do Sul and Paraná, in Santa Catarina their performance is more subdued. Therefore, one cannot affirm that there is a direct relationship between degree of economic or social development within a state and the extent to which its Judiciary and Public Prosecution behave in an autonomous or active manner, even though we do not deny that such behavior, and political pluralism, is more likely in developed states. The association between insti-

tutional performance and economic development often finds reson-
ance within members of the institution and within the Judiciary.
Prosecutors frequently assert that they find greater difficulties in
performing their constitutional duties in less developed states.

On the other hand, as we have already mentioned, the performance of the Public Prosecution is greatly conditioned by the individual behavior of its members. Why do some states, however,
bring together a higher number of public prosecutors who can be
classified as more 'active' judicially? While there is not an easy or
single answer to that question, our research has found evidence
that indicates that the degree of militancy and commitment to
social causes is related to class origin and age.

In this manner, the opening of any given Public Prosecution to
diversified candidates, or the democratization of its recruitment,
has increased the number of public prosecutors who come from
lower income and less privileged segments of society. In fact, when
the institution was smaller and the majority of its members came
from elite segments of society, the extent of its involvement in
social concerns was far less. With the entry of a significant number
of public prosecutors from less privileged segments of society during
recent years, however, the degree of activism on behalf of causes
associated with implementing citizen rights has substantially increased. Such a tendency demonstrates a clear commitment
toward underprivileged classes of society and a new sense of public
morality.

The same conclusions can be made regarding age—a correlation
appears to exist between activism and age. In other words, younger
public prosecutors are more likely to exhibit activist behaviour and
political will than their elder counterparts. The age profile of both
the federal and state Public Prosecutions has undergone substantial changes. Currently, both are composed primarily of young
prosecutors. At the federal level, prosecutors of the Republic average 36 years of age and at the state level, 33 years (Sadek 1997;
Castilho and Sadek 1998). Despite variation among states, it is
generally held that the Public Prosecution at the state level has
had an impact on administrative crimes. According to a study that
draws on court records across the country, during the past five
years there have been more than 200 convictions of mayors and
ex-mayors charged by members of the Public Prosecution (Arantes
1999). Here are a few examples.

- In Rio Grande do Sul, a special committee was created to
  investigate infractions committed by mayors. Three hundred

mayors have testified to date and 108 of those testifying have been convicted (*Veja*, No. 27, 5 July 2000).
- In the state of Paraíba, there were 18 convictions, and the Public Prosecution was able to induce mayors and ex-mayors to return one million *reais* of illegally appropriated funds to state coffers rather than face charges (*Veja*, No. 27, 5 July 2000).
- In São Paulo, the Public Prosecution has levied 436 accusations against mayors since January 1997, the majority of which were based on Law 201, which refers to crimes of administrative responsibility, and can be enacted in cases of corruption, misuse of public funds, irregular investment of federal and state funds, irregular use of municipal property, and so on. The number of mayors who have been stripped of office in the state has increased from seven in the previous administration (1993–96) to at least 41 in this last administration (1996–2000). Such a rate over the last three and a half years is equivalent to one mayor per month losing his or her political office due to the Public Prosecution's work. Some of these dispossessed mayors, however, were able to re-assume office through countervailing legal action. The primary charges brought against mayors were the misuse of public funds, irregularities in public employee hiring, inflating the costs of public works projects (which means the money could go to undisclosed third parties), and not transferring due revenue to the County Chamber. With the exception of mayors from the cities of Baurú, with more than 300,000 inhabitants, and Guarulhos, with more than one million inhabitants, available data indicates the majority of mayors who were stripped of their mandate governed counties with less than 20,000 inhabitants. Finally, public prosecutors have demonstrated an exemplary performance in the city of São Paulo, the economic centre of the country. A group of public prosecutors created the GAECCO (Special Group to Combat Organized Crime), which has been responsible for the investigation of a political scandal with national repercussions. The scandal came to be known as *máfia dos fiscais*[11] of the city, and led to stripping the mandates of two county legislators and one state deputy and to the temporary, but profoundly emblematic, removal of the mayor of Brazil's largest city.

---

[11] Or, 'Mafia of the Auditors'.

- In the state of Pará, there were four convictions, with the Public Prosecution bringing charges against 125 mayors and ex-mayors, the majority for misuse of public funds (data from the Public Prosecutor and Justice Tribunals published in *Veja*, No. 27, 5 July 2000).
- In the state of Paraná, located in the southern region of the country and containing 399 counties, 141 mayors have had criminal and civil charges levied against them due to irregular practices in their public administrations. In the criminal sphere, there are 250 suits against 101 mayors currently in office. In the civil sphere, there are 110 suits against 40 mayors (Ministério Público do Paraná, as of 30 June 2000).

The Law of Administrative Impropriety (Law 8.429), passed in 1992, proved critical to the Public Prosecution. In the civil sphere, this law draws the greatest fear from mayors, because it enables public prosecutors to levy charges of illicit enrichment, financial losses to the public sphere, and offences against principles of public administration. In the criminal sphere, the most frequent charges consist of appropriating public funds,[12] fraud, and hiring county employees without a public entrance exam.

The state of Rio Grande do Sul deserves special attention. In this state, the Public Prosecution has received the least amount of resistance from the Judiciary, a traditionally conservative institution that shies away from political conflicts. In 1994, the Justice Tribunal in Rio Grande do Sul established a Criminal Court for the sole purpose of judging mayors.[13] This Court has already convicted 100 mayors, with punishments ranging from required community service to prison sentences for crimes like the misuse of public funds or irregular contracting. As of February 2000 there were two mayors in prison in Rio Grande do Sul.

Due to the Public Prosecution's efforts, the majority of mayors and council members in the country face an unparalleled level of oversight. Whereas in the past mayors were accustomed to governing without limits and to using their mandates either for personal enrichment or as a springboard for higher offices at the state or

---

[12] Known as *peculato* in Brazilian legal terminology.

[13] The fourth Câmara (a court within the Justice Tribunal) was created by the Judge Luiz Melíbio Machado in 1994, and became known as the 'mayors' court'. It must be noted that potential punishments to infractions committed by mayors were delimited well before the new Constitution through Law 20 of 1967. This law, however, had no real effective impact.

federal level, today they find themselves in an uncomfortable position at best.[14] County chief executives unanimously recognize that administering cities has become increasingly difficult each passing year. In this statement, one of them encapsulated the general mayoral sentiment, while attempting to minimize the real motives behind the charges being levied against him, 'If the current economic difficulties weren't enough, we still have to put up with envy.... Since now one can't hunt birds and animals, they have declared open hunting season on mayors.'[15]

It should also be noted that the Public Prosecution appears to have a greater ability to oversee the Executive than the Legislature does. According to existing law, the National Congress is empowered to create a Parliamentary Investigative Committee (CPI) only after obtaining the approval of 171 of 513 federal deputies, and 27 of 81 senators. Such a requirement effectively means that in times of high government support in the Congress it becomes nearly impossible to create a CPI. The opposition would have to find support amongst legislators from parties who support the president. Recent experience indicates that not even broad-based popular support is sufficient to bring about a CPI in a Congress that supports the government's interest. According to Datafolha,[16] in 1997, 91 per cent of the population was in favour of creating a CPI to investigate charges that the government had 'bought' votes in the Congress to obtain approval of a Constitutional Amendment to allow the re-election of all executive posts. Despite such popular support, the CPI was never created. In a similar vein, despite 86 per cent popular support to investigate a current political scandal surrounding the construction of the building that would house São Paulo's Labor Tribunal (*Fórum Trabalhista de São Paulo*, or TST), a CPI most likely will not be created. Very similar difficulties are also found at the municipal and state levels.

It can be argued that the confluence of allegations, popular dissatisfaction with politicians, difficulties encountered by the Legislature to effectively monitor the Executive, and severe criticisms

---

[14] The possibility for oversight always existed, whether it be by the Legislature over the Executive or vice-versa, or through the *Tribunal de Contas*, an organ created with the sole function of overseeing public spending. The *Tribunal de Contas* is an auxiliary agency of the Legislature.

[15] The statement was made by a mayor from the interior region of the state of São Paulo and quoted in *O Estado de São Paulo*, 4 January 2000.

[16] Datafolha is a public opinion polling department within the news organization *Folha de São Paulo*.

wagered by the opposition, have all created substantial opportunities for the Public Prosecution. In the majority of cases the Public Prosecution has known how to take advantage of such opportunities, and they have done so through the aid of mass media and the opposition. Such positioning has affected not only the process by which the institution creates its own identity, but also its public image.

Who Guards the Guardians?

While the Constitution undoubtedly delegates to the Public Prosecution responsibility to oversee and control political and juridical institutions (the Executive, Legislature, and Judiciary), it does not define who should oversee the Public Prosecution. Such ambiguity begs the traditional question: 'Who shall guard the guardians?' As a result, there is growing concern over possible 'excesses' in the actions of members of the institution. Some political analysts, for example, have criticized the Public Prosecution for paralyzing public decision-making, and more seriously, they have questioned the very nature of such oversight capabilities (Kerche 1999). Drawing upon certain ominous parallels from the not-so-distant past, analysts have raised concerns about the ability of non-elected officials to intervene in acts legitimated by the popular vote. Nevertheless, the new structure of the Brazilian Public Prosecution—despite representing a novelty from an institutional point of view—is consistent with a larger process of creating a new type of democracy. This 'new' democracy is one where law increasingly inserts itself into politics, and a growing number of oversight agencies exert control over all branches of government. Political analysts are still groping with how to analyse this new dynamic and the internal and/or external logic of these new institutions of control, which do not seem to fit easily within the classic separation of powers model.

These issues require discussion. First, the institution's particularities within the justice system should be observed; second, the Public Prosecution's limitations within the justice system should be examined; and finally, the existence of internal and external controls over the Public Prosecution should be determined.

Recruitment and promotion patterns within the Public Prosecution are key elements with regard to the institution's particularities within the justice system. Much like the Judiciary, entry into the Public Prosecution is not conducted by election, but through civil service examinations. Potential candidates require only a law degree. The Constitution (Art. 129, Par. 3) states: 'Admission into the career shall take place by means of a civil service entrance examination of tests and presentation of academic and professional credentials, ensuring participation by the Brazilian Bar Association in such examination, and observing, for appointment, the order of classification.' Tenure and merit are the two criteria used for promotion.

Entry and promotion in the Public Prosecution are obviously not controlled through a system consistent with a classic conception of vertical accountability. A lack of internal vertical accountability, however, is not necessarily positive or negative. There are strong arguments in favour of entry through a civil service examination. These include accessibility, and also a set of incentives which discourage (but obviously do not eliminate) political influence and/ or nepotism, and promotion of competence. This manner of selection has shown itself to be 'democratic' through being 'open'. Most recent data show there is a high and growing number of select candidates who come from a diverse pool of public and private universities. Studies conducted by IDESP (Sadek 1997; Castilho and Sadek 1998) indicate that recruitment has increasingly been external or, in other words, there has been an increase in the proportion of entrants whose parents do not have an affiliation with the Public Prosecution (62 per cent of entrants to state Public Prosecutions and 78 per cent of entrants to the federal Public Prosecution do not have family ties to the justice system.) Furthermore, a significant segment of those who are appointed to the Public Prosecution have parents with a medium or low level of education, thus indicating that entry is not limited to the social, political, or economic elite.[17]

Promotion patterns, as mentioned earlier, are determined through tenure and merit. These criteria also reflect positively on the Public Prosecution because they reduce political and party interference over the institution's leadership. Promotion based on

---

[17] A study conducted by IDESP in 1997 reveals that a majority of prosecutors from the Public Prosecutor of the Union come from middle class and lower middle class families. Of all interviewees, only 21 per cent had a parent in a white collar profession, while 57 per cent had parents in blue collar professions (Castilho and Sadek 1998). With regard to members of the Public Prosecutor at the state level, data reveal a very similar picture: 67 per cent come from middle class and lower middle class family backgrounds, and only 15 per cent of all prosecutors did not work prior to entering the institution.

tenure rewards career experience or the length of time one holds office, and is an objective criterion that allows ascension to individuals who do not move within the organization's powerful or influential circles. In contrast to tenure, promotion based upon merit can lead to a mechanism of internal control. Members who occupy the highest positions within the institution—the *colegio dos procuradores* (the prosecutor's college)—can exert internal control over their fellow members because they are responsible for designing merit-based promotion evaluations and criteria.

Internal mechanisms of control are exerted by two agents: the *Corregedoria* and the Attorney General, the institution's highest office. The *Corregedoria-Geral* of the Public Prosecution, a high ranking department within the institution, is broadly responsible for personnel orientation and oversight. Its primary formal responsibilities include conducting inspections of prosecutorial departments, keeping track of progress toward goals established by public prosecutors within their respective programmes, and implementation of disciplinary action against members of the institution, through use of the appropriate administrative sanctions (Law No. 8.625, Art. 17, 12 February 1993). The highest office within the Public Prosecution of the Union is held by the Attorney General of the Republic (*Procurador-Geral da República*), and at the state level it is held by the Attorney General of Justice (*Procurador-Geral de Justiça*). According to Article 128 of the 1988 Constitution, the Attorney General of the Republic is 'appointed by the President of the Republic from among career members over 35 years of age, after his name has been approved by the absolute majority of the members of the Federal Senate, for a term of office of two years, reappointment being allowed. The removal of the Attorney General of the Republic, on the initiative of the President of the Republic, shall be subject to prior authorization by the absolute majority of the Federal Senate' (Federal Constitution of Brazil, Art. 128, Par. 1, 2).[18] The Attorney General of Justice is in turn nominated by the state governor from a list of three candidates, whose names are determined by election from among all members of the respective state Public Prosecutions.[19]

[18] According to a study conducted by IDESP, only 5 per cent of Public Prosecutor members agree with the selection rule for the Attorney General of the Republic. The overwhelming majority of members agree the selection should be conducted without political interference (Castilho and Sadek 1998).

[19] Differences in selection rules for the federal and state Attorney General position can act as indicators of the institution's level of real autonomy.

As was mentioned earlier, the first paragraph of Article 127 of the 1988 Constitution stipulates the institutional principles of the Public Prosecution to be unity, indivisibility, and functional independence. Unity refers to the fact that each prosecutor can have only one institutional affiliation, indivisibility means that members are interchangeable, and functional autonomy means independence in the exercise of its functions (Mazzilli 1993).

The large degree of freedom and autonomy given to members of the Public Prosecution, who are not obligated to submit to the guidelines established by the Attorney General, constitutes the most important criticism of the institution. According to legal determinations, each prosecutor has the right to select his or her own cases according to his or her own criteria. Furthermore, very few, if any, mechanisms of popular control over the Public Prosecution exist.

The Constitution granted a number of guarantees to members of the Public Prosecution (such as life tenure and functional autonomy) to assure the institution's independence—principally against Executive intervention. Those same guarantees, however, can contribute to 'excessive' behavior in which the institution begins to operate beyond the limits of its prescribed mission. But, much like the Judiciary, without these constitutional guarantees the institution would be open to pressure from the private and political arena, making it very difficult to carry out its responsibilities.

Concern over potentially excessive behaviour on behalf of the Public Prosecution, however, should be attenuated by the fact that the institution cannot sentence verdicts. Members of the institution have the power to initiate legal action, conduct investigations, and open public inquiries, but ultimately the Judiciary decides whether the accused party is guilty or innocent. In this manner, the Judiciary, while not being able to prevent eventual abuses conducted by the Public Prosecution, certainly has the ability to correct eventual abuses. Furthermore, prosecutors are not above the law and are bound by ordinary legal constraints.

In comparison to other countries where the Public Prosecution is active, Brazilian prosecutors have relatively limited resources at their disposal. As stated earlier, in order to conduct an investigation Brazilian prosecutors not only need support from the police, but also authorization from a judge to obtain access to classified information. According to CONAMP (National Confederation of the Public Prosecution),[20] in 60 per cent of cases the Judiciary has

---

[20] *Confederação Nacional do Ministério Público* is an association of public prosecutors from all states of the country.

ceded to requests made by prosecutors. In Italy, however, prosecutors can issue temporary arrest of suspects, they have access to classified banking and tax records, and they have the right to install telephone wiretaps and confiscate documents associated with their investigation. In Germany, prosecutors can confiscate goods and documents, intercept correspondence and telephone calls, install undercover agents in organized crime organizations, and issue temporary prison sentences. Finally, in the United States, police officers work under the command of prosecutors. While American prosecutors also need a judicial warrant in order to have access to classified information, their requests for warrants are granted in 90 per cent of all petitions.

One can further argue, at least in the Brazilian case, that dangers posed to democracy from possible excesses committed by members of the Public Prosecution are fewer and of lesser degree than the dangers from a lack of transparency in public administration. In other words, the ransacking of public patrimony, impunity, and corruption of all sorts poses a much larger threat to democratic values.[21] As a public prosecutor from the state of Paraná has stated, 'Corruption has always existed, but it hasn't increased. What changed is that now the Public Prosecution and the population possess the means to control such irregularities' (*Folha de S. Paulo*, 9 July 2000).

The media has contributed toward the dissemination of two contradictory images of the Public Prosecution. On the one hand, the public prosecutor is portrayed as the 'people's true defender', while on the other hand the same public prosecutor is portrayed as an 'irresponsible exhibitionist'. The image of the public prosecutor as the 'people's true defender' is already commonplace in the main news media channels. He or she is a prosecutor who fights the abuse of economic power and corruption, defends minority rights, is not intimidated by other authorities, and 'hunts' mayors, council members, deputies, senators, and ministers. In contrast to this positive depiction, the media also portray a Public Prosecution

[21] According to Werneck Vianna (1999), 'there doesn't exist any record of an equivalent to the "judicialization" of politics [*or, stated in other words, of the affirmation of Law, its procedures and institutions*] in a nondemocratic context, despite the somber predictions of some who interpret it as a threat to majority rule and democratic sovereignty.' He further stipulates that judicial institutions 'don't substitute politics [*or its institutions*], but fill a void that, in mass societies with intense social mobilization (like Brazil), could come to substitute democratic essentials with a variant of popular sovereignty which escapes the institution of suffrage.'

that does not respect due process of law, makes bold statements based on weak evidence, treats suspects as already guilty, and does not hesitate to give interviews.

One must, however, attenuate concerns that the Public Prosecution is excessively interfering, or at least has the potential to interfere, in public policy making. According to CONAMP, in a majority of cases the Judiciary has ruled in favour of public administrators. In most cases judges have ruled that lawsuits against public administrators constitute a violation of the public mandate, and that only the executive branch has the right to determine administrative priorities. Statements made by members of the Public Prosecution reveal how the Judiciary has effectively acted to curb potential excesses by the institution. From the point of view of members of the Public Prosecution and their respective sympathizers, the Judiciary is obviously seen as an institution that has hindered the Public Prosecution's oversight responsibilities.

Through the use of jurisprudence, dozens of class action suits against public authorities have been annulled. These are civil actions which attempted to obligate the State to implement public policy that effectively delivered on rights already granted to citizens, like protection of the environment, children and adolescents, and public assets. (Public Prosecutor for the State of São Paulo, XI National Association of the Public Prosecution, interview by R. Cavalcanti, 23–26 September 1996).

Public authorities can be condemned to carry out their responsibilities, whether it be through reparation of effective or potential wrongdoing. Such a ruling can further be made without violating due administrative discretion or budgetary predictability. (Public Prosecutor for the State of Rio Grande do Sul, interview, March 1999).

All of these issues clearly impact upon the classic division of powers model. As O'Donnell points out, a new type of democracy is emerging, which implements additional mechanisms of control and oversight of public authorities: 'These mechanisms include the classic institutions of the Executive, Legislature, and Judiciary, but in modern polyarchies they also include various other agencies which act as "ombudsman" and which are responsible for overseeing and auditing public agencies' (O'Donnell 1998b: 42). He warns, however, that only under rare exceptions can these agencies function properly when acting in isolation. They may be able to mobilize public opinion with their proceedings, but ultimately their effectiveness rests upon decisions made in court. 'Horizontal accountability isn't a product of isolated agencies, but of a network of agencies which has at its head a justice system devoted to this accountability' (O'Donnell 1998b: 43).

Conclusion

The institutions encompassing the system of justice have undergone a process of profound transformation. A quick analysis of Brazilian politics in the past few years demonstrates the extent to which the Judiciary and the Public Prosecution have stepped out of the shadows to become relevant political actors. Both institutions have been present in practically all significant reforms encompassing Brazil's social, economic, and political spheres. Reforms were implemented or attempted in varied arenas: *economic reforms*, consisting of privatizations, the breaking of state monopolies, and economic opening; *social reforms*, consisting of changes in the system of social security and wage policy; and *political reforms*, consisting of permitting the re-election of executive posts. Magistrates and members of the Public Prosecution came to occupy a position in the public spotlight that was previously reserved only for politicians, whether from the government or the opposition, the Executive or the Legislature. Such a situation, which is classified as 'judicial activism' and unprecedented according to traditional standards, challenges conventional notions of majoritarian democracy, divisions of power, and the very identity of judicial institutions. Today, one would be hard pressed to speak of the Judiciary as a silent power, along the lines of Montesquieu, or of the Public Prosecution as an institution primarily responsible for penal law, as was foreseen in Roman law. The Judiciary has been forced to render its opinion over public policy and governmental decisions. The Public Prosecution, in turn, has activated the Judiciary on questions that reach beyond the limits of criminal law to focus its efforts on the defense of diffuse and collective rights. Under this new scenario, it comes as no surprise that the institutional design of judicial institutions is often identified as an additional consociational element in Brazilian politics (see, for instance, Lamounier 1992). The Judiciary and the Public Prosecution are seen as providing additional evidence for claims that Brazil's political system has adopted an institutional design characterized by actors and/or institutions with veto power.

The Public Prosecution may be the Brazilian institution that has changed most from a constitutional perspective, and as a result it is still attempting to define itself internally and externally. As the current Attorney General from the state of São Paulo has stated, its new attributes 'bring to the Public Prosecution a field not yet delimited, a field of work which we are still exploring; a historically recent field' (Sadek 1997).

In the light of these recent developments, analysts should increasingly turn their attention toward the difficult task of how to reconcile institutional independence with both internal and external accountability (Cappelletti 1995). As we have stated, the Public Prosecution already exhibits the necessary conditions to independently exert its functions. Such independence, however, should not be exerted in an irresponsible fashion, without mechanisms that allow the institution to be held accountable. Independence with an effective delivery of justice cannot exist without responsibility vis-à-vis the law and society at large. On the other hand, a call for effective action in addition to responsibility on behalf of its members depends on the existence of clear and predictable laws. Brazil is therefore a considerable distance away from attaining the right balance between independence, efficiency, efficacy, and responsibility.

The current judicial reform proposal in the Brazilian Congress is interpreted by some analysts as a step toward attaining this balance, while others see it as an obstacle to reconciling judicial efficiency with accountability. An important item in the reform proposal 'prohibits members of the Public Prosecution, the Judiciary, and the police to unduly disseminate to the media, or other third parties, information gathered from carrying out their respective responsibilities which violates confidentiality laws to the detriment of personal privacy and the public image of the individual in question.'

According to the reform proposal that intends to impose a gag rule, the National Council of the Public Prosecution is empowered to fire members of the institution who violate the above clause. Known as the 'Muzzle Law', this reform proposal is supported by the federal Executive and practically all mayors, while it is opposed by members of the Public Prosecution and the media.[22] Those in favour of the reform justify it as a necessary means to protect individual rights. Opponents claim that if approved, the reform will effectively give impunity to public administrators involved in charges of corruption, public contracting fraud, misuse of public funds, and illicit personal enrichment. Arguments against such reform are well illustrated by this editorial in one of Brazil's most respected newspapers:

---

[22] Such a proposal is at the least unsettling because the same limitations are not extended to legislators who, through CPIs, have frequently ignored the principle of presumed innocence.

An independent Public Prosecution has been inconvenient to certain political sectors, both within and outside government. The fearless and consistent work carried out by prosecutors, who have brought charges, lawsuits and judicial indictments, is without a doubt responsible for a new sense of hope that we can end public impunity. (*O Estado de S. Paulo*, 21 February 2000)

In addition to the Muzzle Law, there are three other amendments being discussed in the Congress that seek to restrict the Public Prosecution's autonomy. All have generated intense debate within and outside the Congress. The first amendment stipulates that candidates to the Attorney General of the Republic 'can include any person who is not employed by the Public Prosecution of the Union, but who is at least 35 years of age, has considerable juridical knowledge, and an unblemished reputation.' The second amendment gives the president of the Republic direct authority to determine prosecutor promotions. The third proposal seeks to limit the power of prosecutors who preside at the lower echelons of the Public Prosecution's organizational hierarchy through implementing a 'special forum'[23] for mayors. According to this proposal, only the head of the institution, the Attorney General, would have the ability to initiate legal action against mayors.[24]

Leaving the merits of these reform proposals aside, these amendments provide an obvious indicator that legal reforms implemented in the 1988 Constitution have changed Brazil's justice system performance. Simultaneously, however, there has been a (re)discovery of the rule of law by society (Telles 1997). A significant and growing segment of the population is discovering the justice system to be an effective means to oblige government to carry out its responsibilities. Furthermore, recourse to the justice system has a multiplier effect, which extends benefits granted to the underprivileged population.

Work conducted by the Public Prosecution, specifically its oversight and control responsibilities, has generated a significant response from those groups that feel their interests have been endangered. The proposed 'Muzzle Law' is not only a first and tentative reaction by opponents to the Public Prosecution, but an indicator that the 'formal-legal country' has had an impact on the 'real country'. Clearly, we are referring only to the latent potential

[23] Known as the *foro priviligiado*.
[24] The Attorney General is also the only position within the Public Prosecution over which the Executive has any influence in its nomination. As stated earlier, the Attorney General is nominated by the Executive from a list of three candidates drawn up by the Public Prosecution.

that exists within the model that has been adopted. That does not mean the present configuration has already attained all potential virtues possible within the existing institutional set-up. After all, only 12 years have passed since the approval of the most recent constitutional text. Nevertheless, we can say with certainty that this new legal text has resulted in significant consequences.

The quality of Brazilian democracy depends in great measure on public authorities' adequately performing their responsibilities. Not only must they act with the independence necessary to make decisions and implement public policy, they must do so with the appropriate level of responsibility and efficiency. After all, public administrators should be responsible for, and transparent in, their actions—a fundamental requirement for the exercise of power.

The reform of Brazil's justice system stands as an important marker at a time when the strength of democracy is increasingly seen as a function of the law being equally enforced for all citizens and of the extent to which public authorities take responsibility for mutual oversight to put an end to the abuse of public power (O'Donnell 1998b).

References

Arantes, Rogério Bastos. 1999. 'Direito e Política: O Ministério Público e a Defesa dos Direitos Coletivos'. *Revista Brasileira de Ciências Sociais* 4, 39 (February).

Cappelletti, Mauro. 1995. 'O Sistema de Justiça'. *Revista do Ministério Público*.

Castilho, Ela Wiecko and M. Tereza Sadek. 1998. *O Ministério Público Federal e a Administração da Justiça no Brasil*. São Paulo: Editora Sumaré.

Kerche, Fábio. 1999. 'O Ministério Público Brasileiro e Seus Mecanismos de Accountability'. Paper presented at XXIII encontro anual da ANPOCS, Caxambú, Minas Gerais.

Lamounier, Bolivar. 1992. 'Estrutura Institucional e Governabilidade na Década de 1990'. In João Paulo dos Reis Velloso, ed., *O Brasil e as Reformas Políticas*. Rio de Janeiro: José Olympio Ed.

Macedo, Ronaldo Porto, Jr. 1996. 'A Evolução Institucional do Ministério Público Brasileiro'. In Maria Tereza Sadek, ed., *Uma Introdução ao Estudo da Justiça*. São Paulo: IDESP/Ed. Sumaré, Série Justiça.

Mazzilli, Hugo Nigro. 1993. *Regime Jurídico do Ministério Público*. São Paulo: Saraiva.

O'Donnell, Guillermo. 1998b. 'Accountability Horizontal e Novas Poliarquias'. *Revista Lua Nova* 44. São Paulo: CEDEC.

Sadek, Maria Tereza. 1997. *O Ministério Público e a Justiça no Brasil*. São Paulo: Editora Sumaré.

Telles, Vera da Silva. 1997. 'Direitos Sociais: Afinal do que se trata?' In *Direitos Humanos no Limiar do Século XXI*. Unpublished paper.

Vianna, Luiz Werneck, Maria Alice Rezende de Carvalho, Manuel Palacios Cunha Melo, and Marcelo Baumann Burgos. 1999. *A Judicialização da Política e das Relações Sociais no Brasil*. Rio de Janeiro: Editora Revan.

Vieira, Oscar Vilhena. 1994. 'Império da lei ou da corte?' In *Revista USP*, No. 21.

OFFICIAL DOCUMENTS
CONAMP. Documents of *Confederação Nacional do Ministério Público*.

The Federal Constitution of Brazil, published in *Diário Oficial da União*, No. 191-A (5 October 1988).

Ministério Público do Paraná.

MAGAZINES AND NEWSPAPERS
Jornal *Folha de S. Paulo*.
Jornal *O Estado de S. Paulo*.
Revista *Veja*.

Horizontal Accountability and the Rule of Law in Central America

Michael Dodson
Donald W. Jackson

Introduction

This chapter is concerned with the efficacy of legal reforms in creating effective mechanisms of horizontal accountability and also with how such reforms are perceived by citizens in El Salvador and Guatemala, the two countries on which we focus. In assessing the efficacy of reforms, it is important not only that they are effective in practice; reforms also must be seen to be effective so that ordinary citizens will come to trust reformed institutions as venues in which they can seek redress of their grievances. In our research we ask this question: In Central America's current democratic transitions are reforms producing judiciaries and human rights ombudsmen that are strong enough and independent enough to sustain horizontal accountability of the executive and legislative branches? Are judiciaries and ombudsmen helping to eliminate or at least constrain the impunity previously enjoyed by those who misused public authority? Our inquiry is part of the even broader question being posed in the literature: Will these transitions end in the consolidation of effective liberal democracies throughout Latin America? Research on this question provoked a stimulating process of theoretical reflection, a surge in case studies, and a growing backlash of skepticism (Ames 1999; Schedler et al. 1999; Becker 1999; Méndez et al. 1999; Hammergren 2000). Scholars have recognized the many defects that plague third-wave democracies and threaten to hamper the 'quality of democracy' in many countries (Schedler et al. 1999: 2).

Among the most prominent of these defects of third-wave democracies has been the 'grossly dysfunctional character of judicial systems throughout, much of Latin America' (Diamond 1999: 41). Countries may also consolidate 'electoral democracy', but fail to overcome 'reserved domains of power for the military or other actors not accountable to the electorate', or without establishing the rule of law to assure individual freedom and civic pluralism (Diamond 1999: 10). Such awareness explains what Thomas Carothers has called the 'rule of law revival' (1998: 101) and its enthusiastic embrace by donor countries and international financial institutions. It would also help account for why Central American countries presently seem to be unusually dependent on external scrutiny of their justice systems and relatively open to reform efforts, which often are led from abroad. As Carothers has argued in his most recent book (1999: 164), 'the rule of law appeals as a remedy for every major political, economic, and social challenge facing transitional countries.'

Utilizing his influential distinction between 'vertical' and 'horizontal' accountability, Guillermo O'Donnell (1994) has pointed out that the 'electoral dimension of vertical accountability' is relatively strong these days in many Latin American countries. However, courts or human rights ombudsmen, which function to ensure that citizens' rights are not violated by persons holding public authority, and to enforce the legal and moral obligations of those who exercise power, generally are weaker. O'Donnell has suggested that in order to establish a constitutional state in which the rule of law prevails, the three distinct elements of 'polyarchy' must be combined (O'Donnell 1999a: 29–51). These elements include free and fair elections, the protection of individual rights (liberalism), and insistence on the moral and legal obligations of those who govern (republicanism). Recently, O'Donnell has put the point this way. A political democracy must include a legal system that 'enacts and backs' the rights and freedoms that we ordinarily consider to be part of a democratic regime, and such a system also must prevent anyone from being above the law (O'Donnell 2000a: 46). These last two elements are the primary focus of this chapter.

At the same time, O'Donnell recognizes that those who exercise power must have the capacity to govern effectively. The fact that James Madison was willing to tolerate a certain amount of inefficiency in government in order to protect individual rights does not provide much guidance today in finding the right balance, for example, between the oft-competing values of 'crime control' and 'due process'. As this chapter will show, striking the right balance in countries like El Salvador and Guatemala can be agonizingly difficult. With the growth of the modern state, we have seen the emergence of a set of institutions that O'Donnell collectively calls 'institutions of mandated horizontal accountability' (2000b: 11). Lying outside the traditional tripartite system of government, and therefore not part of a Madisonian balance of powers, these institutions include general accounting offices, the office of the human rights ombudsman, special prosecutors and the like (O'Donnell 2000b: 3). Commenting on O'Donnell's work, Richard Sklar (1999) notes that from one state to the next countervailing powers can be constituted of different mixes of public and private organizations. But O'Donnell is concerned that some non-state mechanisms are so far removed as to represent only an oblique form of accountability, or may even represent aspects of vertical accountability (O'Donnell 1999b: 68–74). Andreas Schedler has helped clarify this approach by dividing accountability into two functional categories: answerability and enforcement. His concept of answerability implies the obligation to respond to probing questions, or conversely, the right to ask such questions, whereas enforcement comes down to rewarding good behavior or punishing bad (Schedler 1999: 14). However difficult it may be to achieve effective horizontal accountability, these concepts at least make clear the implications of the term, and they help guide our thinking in this chapter.

We also acknowledge the merit of Carothers' point that the current transformations associated with democracy's third wave do not normally involve the complete redesign of the state, but rather are institutional reforms within the existing state. Carothers describes what amounts to 'state re-balancing' (1999, see especially Chapter 7) in that it typically entails efforts to strengthen courts and legislatures relative to the executive power. Such reform efforts reflect a neo-Madisonian desire to '...so contriv[e] the interior structure of the government as that its several constituent parts may, by their mutual relations, be the means of keeping each other in their proper places.' With regard to the judiciary in a republican system, Madison himself emphasized two points—that the special function of judges required a de-politicization of their selection, and that permanent tenure guaranteed their independence. As we address this subject, it also is worth remembering Madison's lack of faith in human nature. That lack of faith led him to endorse a 'policy of supplying, by opposite and rival interests, the defect of better motives' in order that ultimately 'the private interest of every individual [officeholder] may be a sentinel over the public rights' (Commager 1949: 85–9). It is well worth asking whether there is any evidence that judicial (and broader justice system) reform has begun to produce this outcome in Central America. Unfortunately, the available evidence will show that, at least in the cases of El Salvador and Guatemala, efforts to render the justice system a more effective instrument of horizontal accountability have yielded disappointing results thus far.

Just as liberal democracy requires more profound achievements than competitive elections and universal suffrage, so does establishing the rule of law require deeper reforms than merely strengthening techniques for administering justice. This deficiency is accentuated when the rule of law is understood only as achieving technical efficiency, rather than as promoting judicial independence and an enhanced role for the judiciary in holding other governmental agencies accountable under the law (Carothers 1999: 164). We understand reforms directed at achieving the rule of law as part of the process of achieving effective horizontal accountability in emerging democratic systems. It is chiefly on that basis that donors have invested heavily in legal reform and judicial strengthening projects in Central America over the past decade, especially in El Salvador and Guatemala.

Conceptualizing Judicial Independence

As we have suggested in a previous article (Dodson and Jackson 1997), modern 'Western' legal systems are thought to rest on a rational–legal model, described long ago by Max Weber and later modified by John Schmidhauser. The important concepts of this rational–legal model envision the judicial role as resting on two key norms: (1) a judge should be independent, fair and impartial, and (2) a judge should be rule-oriented. Judicial independence also involves, to a significant degree, adequate resources and proper institutional relationships (as explained in the discussion below). Being rule-oriented, fair, and impartial are at their core personal qualities that may be sought in a rigorous process of judicial selection, enhanced by proper training and monitored by post-hoc accountability mechanisms (United Nations 1988).

In considering the prospects for genuine judicial independence in Central America, we have followed the approach of Owen Fiss, who divided such independence into three concepts: 'party detachment', 'individual autonomy', and 'partisan (or political) insularity' (Fiss 1993). Party detachment requires judges to be neutral with respect to the litigants who appear before them in court. This is at the core of the judicial role. Thus claims of family, or of personal friendship or the corruption of justice by bribes all violate this principle, but the principle is also violated if a judge's decisions are dictated by the government responsible for a judge's selection. The principle of party detachment is violated whenever a judge favours one party over another without proper consideration of the law and facts of a case.

Individual autonomy involves the power of one or more judges over another or others. Of course, some instances of vertical authority within the judiciary are appropriate, for example, when an appellate court overturns a lower one because of an error revealed in a trial record. But the principle of individual autonomy is violated when one judge, or a group of judges, mandates a judgment that is not strictly required by precedent or by a reasonable interpretation of applicable rules of law. This sort of interference is commonplace in Supreme Court-dominated judicial systems in Latin America. It was especially pronounced during the period of El Salvador's civil war, culminating in the period of Mauricio Gutiérrez Castro's tenure as chief justice (1989–94). Gutiérrez Castro was an openly partisan member of the governing party and controlled the entire judiciary in a personalistic and authoritarian manner, which was carefully documented by the Truth Commission (Comité de Abogados por los Derechos Humanos 1993: 6).

The third element of judicial independence, partisan insularity, involves the relations between the judiciary and other branches of government. Obviously, some forms of attempted influence are appropriate, such as when an attorney from an executive agency makes an argument before a court. But judges are supposed to be free of improper or illegitimate forms of influence, particularly partisan influence. No judicial decision should be dictated strictly by partisanship or by ideology or by any form of coercion aimed at achieving an outcome that is favored by political interests, but not dictated by law.

Given these three concepts, it follows that achieving judicial independence in transitional regimes requires at least the following:

1. Methods of selection that seek to limit, as much as possible, the intrusion of partisanship into judicial appointments. Merit selection based on non-partisan assessment of objective qualifications is probably the best way to achieve this norm.
2. Provisions for tenure of office should establish relatively long or lifetime terms of office, should provide for adequate remuneration, and should be protected by legal safeguards against retaliatory removal for unpopular decisions.

3. Removal for official misconduct (bribery, extremes of professional incompetence or personal disability) should be grounded in clearly articulated standards and in procedures that guarantee due process.

4. Courts must have adequate resources in the form of professional staff support, facilities and finances to accomplish their duties.

5. A legal and political culture that is supportive of the rule of law is, in the end, essential. All the previous elements may be inadequate if there is no broad cultural agreement that everyone is subject to the rule of law, even in the most difficult circumstances.

These are the goals usually sought by those who seek effective judicial reform (United Nations 1988, American Bar Association 1997). While these goals are easy enough to clarify, achieving them is quite another matter.

El Salvador: Showcase of Reform?

A recent issue of *IDB America*, the magazine of the Inter-American Development Bank, heralded El Salvador's 'pioneering efforts' to reform its justice system. Displaying a photograph of prominent Salvadorean jurist and reform advocate, Supreme Court justice René Hernández Valiente, the journal contends that El Salvador 'has embarked on one of the region's most radical efforts to make justice work' (*IDB América* 1999: 9). While conceding that the country's judicial system was weak and dysfunctional prior to the Peace Accords, the report praises the dramatic:

... shift in the way justice is understood and administered in El Salvador. The means of access to the courts, the role of judges and other judicial officials, the definition of crimes, and the way trials are conducted have all been radically transformed in recent years. The financial resources of the institutions that make up the judicial system, as well as the training and compensation of those who work in them, have also been dramatically upgraded. (*IDB América* 1999: 10)

To take the last two points first, it is true that the provision of adequate resources was one of the earliest achievements of the Peace Accords, which called for a constitutional reform mandating that 6 per cent of the national budget go to the judiciary. This allocation made higher judicial salaries possible and has helped fund new training programmes. The other 'achievements' cited above are more problematic. Reform advocates in the peace negotiations clearly wanted far-reaching change in the judicial system. Further, the Truth Commission's scathing indictment of the judiciary's failure to uphold the rule of law during the war weakened resistance to reform. These facts notwithstanding, however, among Salvadorean political actors (including the judiciary itself) attitudes ranged from grudging acceptance of the need for reform to blatant and determined hostility toward change and toward perceived outside interference. As a result, even where important reforms were proposed and put in place there may have been considerable slippage between the letter of reform and implementation by Salvadorean authorities.[1] It will be worth reviewing some of the themes highlighted in the IDB report, including the process of selecting Supreme Court justices, attempts to strengthen the National Council of the Judiciary (CNJ), revision of 'archaic' legal codes, and various reforms of the criminal justice system.

The Salvadorean Judicial System Prior to and After Reform

Prior to the early 1990s Peace Accords the Salvadorean judicial system systematically violated all of the standards of independence outlined above. For instance, before the constitutional reforms of 1991 the judiciary was dependent on the other branches of government in two critical respects. First, the selection of Supreme Court magistrates was based strictly on party loyalty and was guided by the preferences of the chief executive. Second, the Finance Ministry controlled funding for the courts, which meant that the funding was chronically inadequate and subject to executive control. These factors assured the politicization of the administration of justice and violated the principle of 'partisan insularity'. Provisions for the judiciary also concentrated the power to administer the courts in the hands of the President of the Supreme Court of Justice, who, by virtue of selection procedures, was typically a partisan of the governing party. This factor allowed the Chief Justice to personalize the exercise of judicial authority and thus violated the principle of 'individual autonomy'. The judicial system structured in this manner did little to protect the

---

[1] To their credit, the authors of the IDB report concede the point we make here. The full text of their article provides a more nuanced analysis than the passage we have quoted. See, for example, their discussion of 'reparto' (IDB 1999: 13) and the president of the CNJ's comments that Salvadoreans evince a profound lack of trust in the judiciary 'even to this day' (12).

rights of ordinary citizens, while government officials and the social elite usually enjoyed impunity from punishment for crimes or the abuse of power. It is hardly surprising, therefore, that shortly after the signing of the Peace Accords, the Director of the Human Rights Division of the United Nations Observer Mission in El Salvador (ONUSAL) was urging that the justice system 'be completely overhauled' (Holiday and Stanley 1993: 418).

The first objective of judicial reform was to reconstitute the Supreme Court of Justice and the method of electing justices. Reforms enacted in December 1991 provided for the election of Supreme Court justices for a term of nine years by a two-thirds majority of the National Assembly. The Assembly was required to elect candidates from a list prepared by the CNJ, and one-half of the candidates were to be nominated by Bar Associations. The two-thirds majority required for election was intended to make the justices less beholden to the majority party and less vulnerable to political manipulation by the Chief Executive. Some observers have argued that the election of an entirely new Supreme Court in July 1994 resolved the most serious defect of the extant justice system. Even critics of the Salvadorean judiciary agreed that the reformed Supreme Court was a great improvement over the old Court in terms of the justices' qualifications.

There is reason, however, to doubt that 'partisan insularity' has been solidified in El Salvador. Moreover, the structural conditions for a re-imposition of centralized or even authoritarian administration of the courts remain in place. These two points can be illustrated briefly. First, when it came time to renew one-third of the seats on the Supreme Court in 1997 the old traditions of partisanship, or '*reparto*', surged to the fore. Political parties in the Assembly placed less emphasis on judicial qualifications and sought to elect justices based on party affiliation. This same phenomenon revealed itself even more forcefully in the election of the Procurator for Human Rights and in the election of a new Attorney General in 1998. Long delays, intense partisan 'horse-trading', and a clear intention to be guided by political reliability rather than the professional qualifications of candidates marked the actions of the Legislative Assembly (Dodson, forthcoming). This politicization of the election of important agents of horizontal accountability reached its zenith in the 1998 election of Eduardo Peñate Polanco as Human Rights Procurator. In its zeal to limit the activism of the PDDH the Assembly elected a man who, within a year's time, it was forced to remove from office for breaches of legal and ethical norms (Dodson, Jackson and O'Shaughnessy

2001: 66–71). During Peñate's brief tenure the prestige of the Procurator's office was severely undermined and its contact with the
public declined sharply. This result may have embarrassed governing party legislators but it did not seem to disappoint them.
Second, the Assembly has consistently thwarted the reformers'
efforts to alter the highly vertical concentration of administrative
authority in the Supreme Court. Despite the fact that the Truth
Commission emphasized the need to decentralize the exceptional
concentration of functions in the CSJ, and particularly in the hands
of its president, the Assembly has repeatedly failed to pass reform
legislation to achieve this goal. A structural feature of the 1983
constitution, which requires that measures be passed by two con-
secutively elected assemblies in order to become part of the constitutional order, has worked in favor of the opponents of reform
(Popkin 2000: 203–6).

The second key element in the reform of the justice system was
the strengthening of the CNJ. The CNJ was first established in
the constitution of 1983 but Popkin argues that it remained dor-
mant until enabling legislation was passed in 1989, which 'ensured
that the Supreme Court would have absolute control over the
Judiciary Council' (Popkin 2000: 206). The Council's make-up was
revised in December 1992, providing for a Council of eleven
members. The breakdown was to be two lawyers (not justices) proposed by the Supreme Court, one appellate (second instance)
judge, one trial (first instance) judge, three practising attorneys,
one law professor from the University of El Salvador, two law
professors from private universities, and one member from the
Public Ministry. The Council members were to be elected by a two-
thirds vote of the National Assembly from a list of three nominees
for each position. The Supreme Court retained a strong hand in
shaping the Judiciary Council after these reforms because, among
other things, it controlled the Council's budget and provided to the
legislature the lists of nominees from which to select members of
the CNJ based on seniority. The Council was charged to evaluate
the performance of judges and magistrates and to manage the
ongoing training of a range of professionals within the justice
system, including judges. However, the Supreme Court still controlled promotions and disciplinary actions. Not until 1999 did the
Assembly reform the CNJ law to give the Council real independence of the Supreme Court by excluding representatives of the
judiciary from its membership (Popkin 2000: 210).

Reform has placed the Judicial Training School under the authority of the Council, and the school has been working to raise

the level of technical competence within the judiciary. The Council is also charged with the responsibility for identifying those judges who ought to be purged on grounds of incompetence or corruption. In an October 1994 report, the Human Rights Division of ONU-SAL presented a list of 52 judges against whom serious complaints of incompetence or corruption had been made. According to a January 1997 account, in the three years that followed the ONU-SAL report the Salvadorean Supreme Court had sanctioned 57 judges (29 removals, 12 suspensions, four censures and 12 transfers).[2] However, our subsequent interviews revealed that none of the 57 cases involved proven corruption. Instead, most of the cases had come to the Supreme Court from the CNJ, and all of them involved some form of incapacity or incompetence.[3] This seems astonishing given ONUSAL's previous accusations of judicial corruption. Nor does it match public perceptions. In a national public opinion survey carried out in mid-1996, 47 per cent of respondents described the Salvadorean judicial system as corrupt (Jackson, Dodson and O'Shaughnessy 1999: 414; Tojeira 2000: 1124).

At the time of the Peace Accords El Salvador's basic criminal code still dated from the 1860s. Reformers viewed its features as paternalistic and authoritarian, and set their sights on creating new family and juvenile courts and thoroughly modernizing the criminal law (Hammergren 1998: 217–218). Indeed, the breadth of reform efforts in El Salvador may be unique for Central America. At the urging of civil society organizations and with the help of USAID and the United Nations, in 1994 the Assembly passed a Family Code, which afforded women legal protection for the first time. The Assembly followed a year later with the Juvenile Offenders Law, which provided for separate courts in which to try young offenders, alternative sentencing options, and rehabilitation programmes. Reformers focused on passing this law, as well as the new Family Code, in part because resistance to the proposed new Criminal Procedures law was stronger (Popkin 2000: 200, 241). The success of these reforms is mixed, however. On the positive side of the ledger, putting the Juvenile Offenders Law into effect has helped educate Salvadoreans, including members of the legal community, to the importance of due process guarantees. On the other hand, these reforms also generated skepticism about the

---

[2] These data were provided to the authors by Dr. Mario Antonio Solano, Magistrate of the Constitutional Chamber of the CSJ, January 1997.

[3] The process of *depuración* (or purging) began in mid-1994, following election of the first post-Peace Accords Supreme Court.

wisdom of building strong guarantees of due process into the criminal code. The new Juvenile Offenders Law drew attention to the notorious practice of pre-trial detention, which had placed most persons arrested by police in jail or in prison, where they were likely to remain for very long periods without trial. The new law sharply limited pre-trial detention and other, similar authoritarian practices. In the face of sharply escalating crime in the postwar period, such features of the new laws became lightening rods for citizen discontent and political demagoguery (Popkin 2000: 224). In March 1996 the Assembly passed emergency anti-crime legislation that restored the use of preventive detention for youthful offenders between the ages of 14 and 18. This erosion of due process was a setback for reformers and, as Popkin points out, 'threatened to derail the effort to pass the new Criminal Procedure and Penal Codes, since the emergency law gave police a freer hand in law enforcement and limited suspects' rights' (Popkin 2000: 224). Although these laws were subsequently passed and went into effect in early 1998, the head of the National Civilian Police, the Minister of Public Security, and private sector groups worried about crime criticized them frequently in media interviews.

External donor agencies, such as the World Bank, the Inter-American Development Bank, and USAID have made strong commitments to justice reform in Latin America. They have been particularly generous in funding such reforms in El Salvador and Guatemala, providing tens of millions of dollars in recent years. The recipient countries typically want the funding, but do not necessarily share the donors' agendas. Thus, the success of reform programmes comes to depend on the ability of the donors to find common cause with domestic 'stakeholders' and the political elite as to the nature and scope of reform. Alternatively, the money may be spent on programmes that are technical in nature and do not threaten vested political interests.

A recent report prepared for the United Nations Development Program (UNDP) by the Salvadorean Foundation for the Study of Applied Law (FESPAD n.d.) confirms the magnitude of external donor funding to El Salvador in recent years.[4] The report demonstrates that 70 per cent of total funding was provided by three donors—the United States, World Bank, and IDB. Other prominent donors included the European Union, United Nations, and the

---

[4] The unpublished report, entitled 'Evaluación de la Cooperación Internacional para El Salvador en Materia de Administración de Justicia', was provided to the authors by FESPAD.

Low Countries. What is particularly interesting is to note the areas targeted for reform and the priorities of the Salvadorean government. Reform projects targeted five distinct areas: administration of justice, public security, promoting human rights education and awareness, support to vulnerable groups, and support to peace and democracy processes. Of the total funding, 92.6 per cent was dedicated to the first two of the targeted areas, administration of justice (61.5 per cent) and public security (31.1 per cent). Furthermore, of the funds dedicated to justice administration, 73 per cent were specified for institutional strengthening, while nearly 100 per cent of funds going to public security reform went to institutional strengthening projects. FESPAD notes that civil society organizations received only 5.81 per cent of the funding and that almost no funding has been dedicated to joint government/NGO projects. The Salvadorean government has provided 9 per cent of the funding allocated for reform, virtually all of it for institutional strengthening. Finally, of all the funds invested in the justice sector, 57 per cent went to the judiciary and 25 per cent to public security. Only 3 per cent of funding went to the development of the Procurator for the Defense of Human Rights and 2 per cent went to strengthen vulnerable groups, such as women's organizations.

These data reveal clear priorities. The primary emphasis has been to make the courts more competent and efficient, and to target corruption through increased professionalism. An example of success in this regard is the Salvadorean Judicial Training School (heavily supported by USAID funding), which, according to FESPAD, has grown 'impressively' in its ability to train judges, procurators, public defenders, and police. The FESPAD report also praises the overall performance of the CNJ in its role as gatekeeper for entry into the judicial profession. Finally, the report emphasizes the importance of the Peace Accords in fostering the creation of two new institutions, the Inspector General of the Police and the Procurator for the Defence of Human Rights (PDDH), which, together with the CNJ, are potentially critical mechanisms of horizontal accountability.[5]

In spite of these achievements, the FESPAD report identifies a broad range of factors that can negatively affect justice reform in

[5] From the standpoint of the rule of law, or horizontal accountability, all facets of reform in El Salvador flow from the Chapultepec Accords, which were signed in December 1992. Even though in Guatemala formal democratization preceded the signing of the peace accords by a decade, in that country, too, serious reform of the justice system only began as part of the peace process.

El Salvador. In part, FESPAD criticisms concern the substantive issues addressed in reform projects. For example, reform of justice administration has not substantially reduced the concentration of power in the hands of the Supreme Court, nor has it satisfactorily achieved the separation of administrative functions from judicial ones. As a result, Supreme Court magistrates devote much of their time to purely administrative functions. Of course, one major danger is that reform efforts unreasonably raise expectations, which may quickly be frustrated in practice.

What is most striking about the concerns expressed in the FES-PAD report is the degree to which they point to political will and domestic political priorities as the underlying factors contributing to the failures of reform. External donors can commit impressive amounts of money to reform projects, but in the end Salvadoreans must embrace and carry out those projects. With regard to judicial reform, there clearly are leaders within the judiciary who strongly support reform—even if there may be an uncertain number of judges[6] who would prefer to continue in the old ways. But this zeal for reform does not seem to be shared across the spectrum of Salvadorean political leadership or among all the branches of government. FESPAD notes that 'the Legislative Assembly has not facilitated the legal and administrative changes that are demanded in order to modernize the administration of justice. Certain political currents exist that...reject efforts toward modernization' (45). Again, in spite of the broad agreement that an honest, though still partisan, Supreme Court was elected in 1994 (Hammergren 1998: 216), FESPAD repeats the point we made earlier. They contend that political party interests still 'contaminate' the election of Supreme Court justices, members of the CNJ and Procurators in the Public Ministry, not to mention the PDDH. When UNDP and the Low Countries undertook funding of the initial development of the PDDH, it was with the understanding that the Salvadorean government would take over the responsibilities once the institution was set up. 'That did not occur and the budget allocation for the PDDH was not increased to sustain the new structures, which put at risk the achievements of those earlier projects' (70). As we have already pointed out, the Salvadorean Legislative Assembly not only under-funds the PDDH, but has also shown itself willing to engage in *reparto* and political manipulation in electing the nation's ombudsman. FESPAD, con-

---

[6] Based upon our interviews with reform-oriented judges.

cludes its report by noting that there is still little coordination among the various sectors of the justice system, and worrying that there is a potential for strong political backlash toward reform efforts (see also Tojeira, 2000: 1126).

Perceptions of Justice Reform and the Rule of Law in El Salvador

The chief difficulty in assessing the efficacy of the reforms discussed above is that there are no obvious variables that will demonstrate their success or failure. Efficiency, often measured by disposition rates, is no certain indicator of the quality of justice, and it is not sufficient merely to recite the reforms that have been put in place. While the optimistic IDB report and the relatively pessimistic FESPAD report offer contrasting conclusions, there is no objective basis for determining which is the more accurate. As we said at the beginning of this chapter, not only must justice be done, it must be seen to be done, at least by attentive members of the public, if citizens will come to trust in a country's courts. So, we sought to examine how the Salvadorean public perceives efforts to reform the judiciary. We expected that such perceptions in mass publics would be impressionistic and have largely symbolic value, but for reasons explained below there is a substantial theoretical foundation for holding that trust and diffuse[7] support in mass publics are important. To that end we participated in a commissioned survey in El Salvador (Jackson et al. 1999).[8] Of those surveyed only 11.6 per cent thought 'honest' was the best word to describe the judicial system, while 47.1 per cent chose the word 'corrupt' (1999, 414). Across a set of four items measuring diffuse support of the Supreme Court, only 10.8 per cent of those surveyed expressed strong support (411). When we assessed reported confidence in institutions on a 4-point scale, with 0 representing 'none' to 3 representing 'much' confidence, the mean level of confidence for the Supreme Court was 1.156 (413).[9] Not surprisingly, many of

[7] Diffuse support, as contrasted with specific support, involves support for an institution regardless of outcomes in specific cases. Specific support, on the other hand, is outcome specific. Obviously, diffuse support is important in the long run for the legitimacy of an institution.

[8] The survey was conducted by the Public Opinion Institute of the Central American University, San Salvador, in August 1996. The research protocol was designed to be accurate +/−4 per cent.

[9] The middle values were: 1 = little and 2 = some. The lowest reported confidence was 0.917 for the Legislative Assembly. The highest was 1.717 for the Human Rights Ombudsman.

our respondents had low levels of information and declined to answer, so next we sought to enhance our findings by seeking the views of more 'attentive publics', that is, members of relatively elite groups directly involved or more closely concerned with judicial reform than average citizens.

In September 1999, we commissioned focus groups, selecting local magistrates, municipal leaders, civic leaders and the owners of small and medium-size businesses as participants (Sorok 1999). Broadly speaking, we were interested in their perceptions relative to two interrelated questions. First, have efforts to reform and strengthen state institutions (especially in the justice sector) borne fruit in supporting the rule of law? Second, have reforms been effective in addressing the problems of corruption and impunity that plagued the Salvadorean state prior to the Peace Accords? Note that we present our findings from focus groups not for their intrinsic truth or accuracy, but, as we shall see, to illustrate how difficult it is for reforms to affect the perceptions even of community leaders, who are no doubt better informed than are average citizens.

Participants in all four groups gave strong support to the goals of the Peace Accords, and each group pointed to some positive achievements of reforms. Magistrates especially applauded the efforts to provide judicial training and to raise the standards for judicial selection. Business leaders applauded the appearance of new faces in the judiciary and noted that Salvadorean citizens were becoming more aware of their civil rights. But across all four groups favorable comments were overshadowed by expressions of deep concern and even of outright cynicism concerning the efficacy of reforms.

In assessing the comments from our focus groups, keep in mind the three elements from Fiss's analysis of judicial independence: 'party detachment', 'individual autonomy', and 'partisan (or political) insularity' (Fiss 1993). All four groups expressed doubts about the independence of Salvadorean judges, consistent with long standing doubts in the country. Partisan political interests were seen still as threatening judicial independence. Magistrates especially felt that there was little respect for judges and little institutional support for their independence. Referring to the Supreme Court, one magistrate observed: 'The Court is still an institution that depends on politicians and in this there is no consolidation of democracy because its decisions are more political decisions than judicial decisions....' Commenting on judicial appointments, another magistrate argued that in El Salvador '[judges] are always going to be elected by politicians, that is where the bargaining begins...capability and honesty aren't taken into account. What is of interest at the time of making a choice is whether the political party's interests are being served. . . .' Yet another judge asserted that 'here we have the fact that independence is not permitted. Everything has to be done through a political party. . . .' Among this sampling of magistrates, at any rate, there is strong skepticism about how fully partisan insularity has been achieved through judicial reform.

This same skepticism is also evident among magistrates when they evaluate the principles of party detachment and individual autonomy. To take the principle of party detachment, consider the issue of the Emergency Laws, which we discussed earlier. Commenting on that legislation, one magistrate stated: '. . . if they [the Legislative Assembly] have passed an unjust law, like those that were passed—the emergency law—the judges have to apply it. . . . What happens if a judge says no, I won't apply it, and I'm going to base this on a constitutional principle? If there were true independence, that's fine, it could happen. But [in El Salvador] immediately a dossier would be opened. So where is the independence?' A second judge illustrated the problem with the following example. 'If you ask all the judges, all of them say that they feel like they have no support, nobody supports a judge. To face the economic power of this country is difficult; it weighs heavily. All the complaints that I have are from people with money, who see their interests being affected by my decision and I go to the [Supreme] Court and they see that they have no legal basis, but they say that they are going to open an investigation.' A third magistrate concluded, '. . . nobody respects the judge, not even the police.'

Business and civic leaders felt that reforms made little difference unless there was a real will for change among political leaders. 'The judicial reforms are okay but it makes no difference if we make laws as long as there is no political will . . . if there is no political will on the part of the heads of government, of the institutions, it is like throwing salt into the sea. . . .' One business leader noted that '. . . the image of the Court has changed a bit but it is difficult for them to change [the Court] if it is composed of different people from the different political parties and those people are always looking for ways to bring water to their own mills.' He spoke directly to the issue of partisan insularity, saying '. . . the parties get together, everyone names a candidate and nobody thinks about capability. The basic problem is that we are a totally politicized country and the civil society doesn't fit in any decision.'

On the crucial question of impunity, on rendering government officials answerable and subject to punishment for breaking the law (the functional aspects of accountability as defined by Schedler above), our focus group participants were disturbingly pessimistic. 'There really isn't anything institutionalized in this country,' said one civic leader. 'There is no respect for the rights of anyone.... No government official has been warned, sanctioned, charged, put in jail or whatever for illegality, for not obeying the rule of law. I know of no case.' Another put his concerns this way: 'I am very worried. Someone said that we have more freedom of speech, but what good is that when there is a conspiracy among the institutions in this country? Let them [civic organizations] talk because they have no power anyway. Let them talk about their rights. Let them accuse the president of being a thief. Nothing is going to happen to us. Let's not worry, sirs, because in our club (called the government) we do what we please.' The magistrates evinced particularly strong concerns about the failure of the Supreme Court to root out corruption in the judiciary. 'There are good and bad people left over from before. What hasn't been done yet is to separate the bad people from the institution with firmness. That is part of the low credibility we have.' Another magistrate echoed those sentiments, saying '... we can't clean up the honor of the judicial branch when we don't go ahead and remove all those judges and magistrates who, with cause, have been pointed out. It is public knowledge who they are and the Supreme Court justices know who they are. Nevertheless, they don't remove them.' These sorts of comments strongly suggest that, even if free elections are now institutionalized in El Salvador, the nation's professional classes entertain serious doubts that the other two aspects of democracy—liberalism and republicanism—are even remotely institutionalized. In their eyes, reform efforts have not yet achieved either the answerability or enforcement dimensions of accountability. Such perceptions reflect a deep alienation with respect to both the political and legal systems. Such alienation derives in no small measure from the perception that power remains extremely concentrated in El Salvador and that measures for horizontal accountability have not been firmly established or have been successfully thwarted. We assess the implications of these findings below.

Justice Reform and the Peace Accords in Guatemala

On the surface Guatemala would seem to resemble her southern neighbor in that long periods of authoritarian rule, exacerbated by guerrilla war, were finally brought to a close in the 1990s through an internationally mediated peace process. Some important differences should be noted, however. First of all, in Guatemala the transition to peace and democracy was controlled by the armed forces, who, unlike their Salvadorean counterparts, had effectively achieved a military defeat of the United Revolutionary Front of Guatemala (URNG). In the Guatemalan context civilian control of the State was more tenuous due to the 'parallel power exercised by the military and private sector elite vis-á-vis civilian government authorities' (Stanley and Holiday 2002: 437). Second, the major participants in the peace negotiations, the governing National Action Party (PAN) and the URNG, did not represent broad or powerful sectors of Guatemalan society. Indeed, the PAN is a new party with weak links to society and the URNG has very little demonstrated electoral strength. Whereas, it is roughly accurate to say that El Salvador was a polarized society prior to the peace accords, one could say that Guatemala was a deeply fragmented society. For this reason it could be much harder to mobilize support for implementation of the peace accords in that country than it was in El Salvador, where the two principal political forces in the country both endorsed the accords. This underlying political reality has significant implications for justice reform. Where will consistent pressure come from within Guatemalan society and institutions to sustain the reform process? The factor that may offset these concerns somewhat is the relatively greater mobilization and direct involvement of civil society groups in the peace process in Guatemala as compared to El Salvador (Jonas 2000: 3–9, 158–61).

In Guatemala, as in El Salvador, the justice system was profoundly compromised by authoritarianism. Fiss's three elements of judicial independence were, at best, the utopian hopes of those who waited long for reform (Dodson and Jackson 2001: 263–4). The depth of the Guatemalan justice system's subordination to military power was demonstrated in the report of the Commission for Historical Clarification (CEH), which was essentially a truth commission authorized by the parties in the Oslo Accords.[10] The

---

[10] To facilitate peace and reconciliation in Guatemala, the CEH was charged with reviewing human rights violations committed during the conflict and recommending measures to preserve the memory of the victims. This was to include recommendations concerning reparations to be paid to the victims' families. The CEH convened a National Forum on Recommendations in May 1998, which included participation by a broad cross-section of civil society groups. The CEH recommendations were given added weight by the publication of the Catholic Church's report, entitled 'Recuperation of the Historic Memory (REMHI), which was based on thousands of interviews.

report's authors noted that throughout the long decades of Guatemala's armed conflict, the judicial system '...failed to guarantee the application of the law, tolerating, and even facilitating, violence...Impunity permeated the country to such an extent that it took control of the very structure of the State, and became both a means and an end.' The report concluded that '...by tolerating or participating directly in impunity...the judiciary became functionally inoperative with respect to its role of protecting the individual from the State, and lost all credibility as guarantor of an effective legal system.'[11] The judiciary's corruption and subjection to political authority persisted through the early years of the democratic transition, as was illustrated by the judiciary's role in the so-called 'Serranazo', or *auto-golpe* that briefly interrupted Guatemala's transition in 1993. At that point, eight years after the return to civilian government, the Supreme Court continued to behave in an openly partisan manner, much as had the Supreme Court in El Salvador under the leadership of Mauricio Gutiérrez Castro. Indeed, far from becoming an agent of horizontal accountability, Guatemala's Court was still engaging in extra-constitutional maneuvers that demonstrated its deep politicization.

The president of the Supreme Court compromised the independence and integrity of the judicial system by using his position to make political deals with legislators. The executive engaged in clientelism and entered into the deal making prevalent in Congress and the Supreme Court. In short, instead of an established separation of powers between the three branches of government, there was blatant disregard for institutional procedures and the rule of law, open deal making within and among the three branches, and officials' unwillingness to reform. (McCleary 1997: 134)

The Guatemalan peace accords acknowledged that the administration of justice was 'one of the major structural weaknesses of the Guatemalan State'.[12] That view is shared by donor agencies that are funding justice reform throughout Central and South America. A recent report prepared by the Washington Office on Latin America (WOLA) pointed out that international donors had approximately $116 million in funds committed or pending for justice sector reform in Guatemala in 1997. That figure would compare favorably to the heavy investments being made in El Salvador

---

[11] See conclusion number 10 and number 56 of the CEH report.

[12] 'Agreement on Strengthening of Civilian Power and on the Role of the Armed Forces in a Democratic Society', [Government Document online], accessed 3 July 1997. Available from: http://www.un.org/Depts/minugua/paz9.htm.

(Holder 1998: 70). The WOLA report made clear why such extensive projects were needed: 'the judicial system has developed in a distorted manner, generating low motivation, bad practices and corruption.... As a result, the administration of justice is typified by its extreme torpor and fallibility' (Holder 1998: 9). More than a decade after the return to democracy, 50 per cent of Guatemalans had no access to judicial remedies, 74 per cent of the prison population had not been sentenced, and the country had no judicial career law.[13]

In the face of such challenges, the Peace Accords mandated a phased increase of 50 per cent in the judiciary's budget, which had been implemented by fall 1999. In late 1998 a new Supreme Court took office pledging its commitment to reform. Hopes for reform were rising and news of ostensible successes began to surface. For example, the Guatemalan Embassy in the United States reported that in 1998 the Public Defender's Service 'achieved autonomy' within the Public Ministry, and a purging of incompetent or corrupt judicial employees was underway.[14] There are obvious problems with such reports, however. Take the issue of partisan insularity. Reformers have strongly urged longer tenure on the bench in order to shield judges and Supreme Court justices from political manipulation through the appointment process. Guatemalan justices are elected for relatively brief (five-year) terms of office, although they may be re-elected. In the election of the new Supreme Court in late 1998 not a single magistrate of the Court was re-elected. According to the United Nations Special Rapporteur (2000: 16), this reflected the absence of any 'objective criteria... for selection' of the magistrates, which would seem to encourage reliance on partisan criteria. The Supreme Court moved quickly to name a large number of new trial judges, but it bypassed the School of Judicial Training. In other words, the Court chose appointees who had not been screened or trained by the Judicial Training School, as is called for in the reformed judicial procedures. The Special Rapporteur went on to note that lawyers, procurators and judges handling cases concerning contro-

---

[13] The Legislative Assembly passed a judicial Career law on 27 October 1999, apparently with strong lobbying from the judiciary. This information is available at the MINUGUA website: http://www.minugua.guate.net/comunicados/Carrera%20Judicial1.htm.

[14] See: 'Avances en el sistema de administración de justicia', Embassy of Guatemala in the United States, p. 3. Available at: http://www.guatemala-embassy.org/orgjud.htm.

versial human rights violations are 'subjected to threats, intimidation and harassment' (2000: 9). With respect to judges, the policy of the Supreme Court is to transfer those who complain rather than open investigations into the complaints, which is a rather striking example of failure to achieve the answerability and enforcement aspects of accountability. Although the CSJ is obligated by law to offer protection to such judges, it is unable or unwilling to do so. Indeed, the position of judges is so precarious that insurance companies in Guatemala refuse to cover them, either individually or collectively (2000: 11).[15] Moreover, 'the Supreme Court has never made a public statement decrying the threats, harassment and intimidation' (2000: 30). In this respect the Court seems to have been severely marginalized by Guatemala's climate of violence and impunity. The net effect of the armed conflict on the justice sector was to deepen incompetence and corruption. Its legacy was judges and lawyers who are 'very insular' and who reveal little appreciation for 'constitutional values, the principles of judicial independence and due process generally' (2000: 33). Finally, the Rapporteur cited a comment of the head of the Judicial Training School that the applicants who apply for judgeships 'hardly knew what due process was all about' (2000: 32). This last comment—one in a litany of weaknesses and failures—was consistent with the Rapporteur's dismal assessment of the quality of legal education in Guatemala. In Guatemala, as in El Salvador, those who teach law have not become stakeholders in the reform process. Thus, the six existing law faculties prescribe their own curricula and there are no state regulations governing legal education. The quality of the education they offer is uneven, most schools pay little attention to human rights or constitutional law, and graduation alone ensures admission to the bar, without any sort of professional examination.

The Peace Accords stimulated the formation of two entities in Guatemala designed to promote and assist in reform of the justice sector. The Accords established a Commission to Strengthen the Justice System and, with international assistance, the Supreme Court set up a Commission to Modernize the Judiciary. The former body constitutes a stakeholder group (with membership in civil society and within the justice system) that has encouraged consti-

---

[15] This problem has been evident no matter how high-profile the case. Investigation into the murder of Archbishop Gerardi, who was assassinated shortly after issuing the REHMI report (see note 10) was initially stonewalled by the presiding judge and the prosecutor. When their successors tried to pursue a serious investigation they received repeated death threats and both of them fled the country.

tutional reforms to permit the modernization of the judiciary. Its initial report, 'Una Nueva Justicia para la Paz', pointed to one of the great difficulties facing reformers in Guatemala. Acknowledging that a culture of intimidation has enveloped the judicial system, the authors note that '... the tradition has been that the apparatus of public power itself has been the source of this intimidation. The existence of these threats, and the certainty that they may be carried out, constitutes one of the elements that conspire against the consolidation of a judicial career that will be attractive to the best lawyers in the country' (1998: 30). In the mid-1990s several high profile assassinations served to drive this point home most powerfully. In April 1994 assailants assassinated the president of the Constitutional Court, a man who had resisted the Serranazo by declaring the suspension of Congress and the Supreme Court unconstitutional. At the time of his murder, Justice Epaminondas González Dubón was about to rule on whether high-ranking army officers could be prosecuted for the murder of anthropologist, Myna Mack. Later that year the police commissioner who was investigating the murder of newspaper editor Jorge Carpio Nicolle, was also assassinated as he was preparing to make arrests in the case. Two years later the prosecutor in the Carpio case was forced into exile by death threats to himself and his family (Reding 1997). These crimes suggest that no officials in the judicial system are safe from the threats and intimidation to which the Commission to Strengthen the Justice System referred. The fact that these crimes go unsolved only reinforces the sense of impunity enjoyed by those who violate human rights.

The Commission to Modernize the Judiciary has issued a lengthy study that highlights the challenge to reform in Guatemala from another vantage point. Apart from the issues of corruption or marginalization discussed already, there is the simple question of capacity to perform the judicial function. The Commission's report, entitled 'Plan de Modernización del Organismo Judicial 1997–2002', reveals the degree to which Guatemalan judges are poorly prepared in their understanding of the law and judicial process. Despite the fact that a great deal of money has already been spent on training courses, judges reveal far too little professionalism in their handling of cases. The report summarizes a study carried out by MINUGUA through the Judicial Training School, which focused on such issues as how judges handled evidence, how they apply legal norms, and the reasoning used to reach their decision. In reviewing approximately 500 verdicts, the researchers found 'relatively severe deficiencies' in a large number of verdicts. The most serious problems were found in the handling of evidence and the legal reasoning used to reach a decision (Commission to Modernize the Judiciary) 1997: 81–83).

While the limited effects of reforms are indeed discouraging, to make this sad picture worse, in the popular referendum held in May 1999, Guatemalans failed to ratify the constitutional amendments that would have enabled several justice system reforms to go into effect.[16] Despite the deep discontent with the justice system reflected in the comments discussed below, 80 per cent of Guatemalan voters stood aloof from the popular referendum.[17]

1997 and 2001 Gallup CID Surveys

In October 1997 we contracted with Gallup CID to include a small series of questions in their regular survey of public opinion in Guatemala.[18] Even worse than in El Salvador (in which 47.1 per cent chose the word corrupt and 11.5 per cent chose the word honest), of the Guatemalan respondents 58.7 per cent chose the word 'corrupt' to describe the judicial system, while only 7.5 per cent chose the word 'honest'. When asked, 'In general how satisfied would you say that you are with the judicial reforms undertaken in Guatemala?,' 3 per cent were very satisfied, 25 per cent were somewhat satisfied, while 34 per cent either were dissatisfied or very dissatisfied. However, the largest respondent group (37 per cent) did not respond or had no opinion.

In August 2001 we again contracted with Gallup CID as part of their regularly conducted survey.[19] This time we asked respondents about their confidence in institutions, using a 4-point scale with 0 representing no confidence, up to 4, representing 'a great deal' of confidence. The mean confidence level for the judicial system as a whole was 0.817 and for the Supreme Court, 0.932.

[16] 'United Nations Verification Mission in Guatemala: Report of the Secretary General', A/54/526 (11 November 1999), p. 20.

[17] Jonas (2000: 195–213) has offered an interesting analysis of why Guatemalans displayed such apathy toward the referendum.

[18] Gallup Consultoría Interdisiplinaria en Desarrollo, S.A. 1997. The survey was of 1,214 Guatemalans with a margin of error (determined by Gallup CID) of +/– 2.8 per cent. Twenty-nine per cent of the respondents spoke an indigenous language. The survey was representative of the country except for the departments of Petén and Alta Verapaz.

[19] This survey was of 1,220 Guatemalans, again with a reported margin of error of +/– 2.8 per cent. Respondents included 25 per cent speakers of indigenous languages and were representative of the country except for the departments of Petén and Alta Verapaz.

The highest confidence level was for television news (1.286) and the lowest was for the national Congress (0.806).

'Elite' Perceptions of Justice Reform in Guatemala

With the same objective as in our Salvadorean research: to see whether attentive publics perceived that reforms had indeed made a difference, we conducted two sets of focus groups in Guatemala. The first set, conducted in Guatemala City, was with trial judges and with mid-sized business owners. The second set of focus groups was held in Quetzaltenango and Totonicapán, in the predominantly Mayan Western highlands. These were with indigenous community leaders and members of municipal governments, including auxiliary mayors (Palma 1999). As was true in El Salvador, our Guatemalan focus group participants viewed the peace agreements as a positive stimulus to institutional reform. They singled out a number of areas. For example, they praised efforts to expand the number of courts and judges. They noted that the incorporation of oral procedures held the promise of speeding judicial proceedings and they praised the commitment to incorporate indigenous languages. Again, however, such positive comments were strongly overshadowed by concerns and anxieties about the depth of reform and the capacity of reform to bring real change to Guatemala.

However, Guatemalan respondents seemed less willing to view the Peace Accords as a definitive point of departure toward reform and democratization. Their views consistently emphasized the legacy of the long armed conflict. They said that the war contaminated the popular view of the basic civil rights that are essential to liberal democracy. Furthermore, civil society organizations have been left extremely weak and fragmented by the war and were thought to have little capacity to promote justice reform.

Against this backdrop, respondents focused a lot of attention on the underlying causes of public insecurity in Guatemala, which they viewed as little affected by institutional reform to date. Guatemalans seem to consider that both ordinary criminals and those more powerful individuals associated with organized crime are equally able to pervert the justice system. Ordinary citizens are reluctant to use the justice system, participants said, because they perceive that criminals will use bribes or threats of reprisal to intimidate justice officials. Persons involved in organized crime are perceived to be completely immune from prosecution. The public sees organized crime to be the work of ex-military personnel, the police, or ex-guerrillas, all of whom are thought to possess ample resources to guarantee their own impunity in the face of a weak and corruptible judicial system.

Our focus group participants were extremely critical of the Guatemalan judicial system. They faulted the government for not providing adequate budgets, personnel and facilities to support a judicial presence, especially in rural areas. The comments of the Mayan participants were especially illuminating. Auxiliary mayors pointed out that their own credibility as local officials depended on an ability to utilize the judicial system in behalf of their communities. That credibility was undermined when factors such as the distant location of a court, bureaucratic obstacles thrown up along the way and lawyers' fees quickly exhaust local resources. Such factors tend to discourage use of the justice system altogether. This situation is compounded by the threats and intimidation that may accompany sensitive cases, which are rarely investigated by authorities, especially when powerful sectors are involved (Palma 1999: 14).

What all of our respondents described as being institutionalized in Guatemala was the lack of citizen protections that are guaranteed in the constitution. In their view, one's capacity to influence the justice system favorably is a function of social class and status. In Guatemala one sees a 'trinity of impunity, institutional weakness, and failure to protect citizens that prevents the building of the rule of law and weakens civil society' (Palma 1999: 18)

Focus group participants described the judicial system of Guatemala as not only deficient in its own right but as lacking support from, and integration with, other key actors and institutions in the justice system. Judicial support personnel are seen as poorly trained and highly susceptible to corruption, or else vulnerable to intimidation. In short, the Guatemalans who took part in our focus groups contend that the 'values and practices of tolerance, trust, participation and accommodation', which are thought to be crucial to liberal democracy (Diamond 1999: 20), are sorely lacking in their country.

The above picture might look less bleak if our participants thought that government officials and political leaders were seriously committed to reform. However, they emphasized that the practices and attitudes of the authoritarian era still prevail. Judicial independence is undermined, they said, by '... the idea that the executive power of the government can exercise direct pressure over judges and magistrates, or indirect pressure through the Public Ministry and the National Civil Police' (Palma 1999: 26).

The comments of our focus group participants mirror Thomas Carothers' opinion (1999: 174) that the politicians in their country have little interest in supporting judicial reform or making the rule of law a high priority because these are long-term tasks with a 'distant political payoff'.

Trust, Confidence and Their Theoretical Importance

In a recent article and subsequent book, Alec Stone Sweet (1999, 2000) has used a simple triad to describe the phenomenon of 'judging'. Of course, his is only the most recent effort to apply such a concept; the antecedents can be traced at least back to the functional frameworks proposed by social scientists in the 1950s. His triad involves two disputants and a 'dispute resolver'. Compulsory triadic dispute resolution involves processes that are 'triggered' by one party to a dispute against the will of the other party. Once triggered, triadic dispute resolution serves to regulate disputes about what is proper behavior. It does so through a normative structure that specifies the rules of the process, and one aspect of the rules specifies the normative expectations for the 'dispute resolver' (i.e., judge). Many of the normative expectations for judges involve being a fair and impartial resolver of disputes. This is a useful approach, but readers may have noticed that the normative structure that is involved is, in effect, a different formulation of Fiss's tripartite definition of judicial independence. The most important thing is that judges can work effectively only when we trust that they will behave as judges are supposed to behave: they are truly independent dispute resolvers. The reforms we have reviewed in this chapter are directed toward that end, which, as we have seen, is simple to conceptualize, but difficult to achieve. And the key point is that judges in particular, and the justice system in general, can serve the function of horizontal accountability only when: (1) trust in them is *actually justified* by their conduct and/or (2) they are *perceived to be trustworthy*. Note the possible relationships between these two: (1) Trust may be justified by conduct, but judges still may be perceived *not* to be trustworthy; (2) Trust may *not* be justified, but judges may be perceived to be trustworthy; (3) Trust may be justified *and* judges may be perceived to be trustworthy as well; and (4) Trust may not be justified *and* judges may be perceived to be untrustworthy. Is it not clear that only the third outcome is acceptable? The first is unacceptable because unless there is trust, the triadic relationship will not work effectively. The second involves a myth or an illusion.

The fourth is the worst outcome, and it is the one that seems to fit the judicial systems in El Salvador and Guatemala, especially as they functioned prior to the peace accords. Creating trustworthy institutions *and* communicating their trustworthiness to mass publics are both important objectives, but overcoming distrust and cynicism seems especially daunting in Central America.

Are Distrust and Cynicism Obstacles to Effective Reforms and to Effective Horizontal Accountability in El Salvador and Guatemala?

Opinion surveys and our focus group research in El Salvador and Guatemala indicate that citizens in both countries support reforms aimed at strengthening the justice system and enhancing the rule of law. That research also indicates that citizens are deeply skeptical about the efficacy of the reforms that have been attempted to date, and that they are openly cynical about the willingness of political leaders and the 'power elite' to submit to the rule of law. Other recent research has also focused on 'low trust' countries (Camp 2001).[20] Whether we specify interpersonal trust or confidence in institutions, our previous surveys and the elite focus group results reviewed above disclose that citizens in both El Salvador and Guatemala are distrustful and have low levels of confidence for most governmental institutions. Indeed, there seem to be so few persons in either country who believe that you can trust most other people that distrust approaches consensus.

When we encountered the especially low levels of interpersonal trust reported in our 1996 Salvadorean survey (6 per cent trusting)[21] and later in 2001 (3.2 per cent trusting),[22] we were struck by the stark view of the world that the data seemed to reflect. We wondered whether the low level of interpersonal trust, as well as relatively low levels of confidence in traditional government institutions, were the consequences of eleven years of civil war, and/or an even much longer period of repressive government. These possibilities were heightened by the likelihood that the very institutions and officials whose duty it was to uphold the rule of law

[20] See especially chapter three, 'Does Trust Matter', by Timothy J. Power and Mary A. Clark.

[21] This result reported in Jackson, Dodson, and O'Shaughnessy (1999). The article reports data from the Salvadorean survey only.

[22] Gallup CID, Public Opinion in El Salvador, May 2001.

committed most of the rights violations. Was distrust therefore simply a rational response to the political reality that confronted most people? Another possibility was that low levels of trust reflected an even broader and longer-range characteristic of Salvadorean, or possibly even of Latin American, culture. In the latter regard, our Guatemalan survey results (12 per cent interpersonal trust in 1997[23] and 8 per cent in 2001[24]) certainly confirmed that distrust and low confidence was not limited to El Salvador. Of course, the two countries both reflect a history of armed internal conflict and lawlessness.

Some additional light was shed by items from Marta Lagos' 1996 *Latinobarómetro* surveys. Her published results for eleven Latin American countries (none in Central America) reveal that, possibly excepting Uruguay (33 per cent trusting), the levels of interpersonal trust were quite low in all those countries (Lagos 1997: Table 1). In the 2000 Latinobarómetro, for the Latin American region as a whole, those who said that 'you can trust most people' (rather than that 'you can never be too careful when dealing with others' fell from 20 per cent in 1996 to 16 per cent in 2000 (Lagos 2001: 143).

In contrast, the average level of interpersonal trust for the United States in the General Social Surveys conducted between 1972 and 1994 was 41.2 per cent of the respondents 'trusting'. In 1959 it was 58 per cent, while for 1996 it was 36 per cent (Newton 1999: 176). This decline has been a hot topic among social scientists in the United States (Putnam 2000: 17). For contrast, the percentage of trusting people in South Africa in 1990 was 28 per cent (Newton 1999: 176), a remarkable figure for its time, given apartheid, but especially as contrasted with our results from El Salvador and Guatemala.

Marta Lagos concludes from the *Latinobarómetro* data that there is a 'common regional heritage of distrust' in Latin America and that the 'lack of interpersonal trust is at the core of the problem of very low confidence in institutions' (Lagos 1997: 129; 2001: 143–4). If she is correct, pointing to a 'heritage of distrust' simply raises another question: What have been the causes of this heritage? Is a 'heritage of distrust' a contributing cause, or, to the contrary, one of the consequences of the difficulties of creating stable, consolidated liberal democracies in Latin America?

There are competing answers to these questions. Unfortunately, research efforts often have not been as cumulative as they could or

[23] See note 18.   [24] See note 19.

should be. For example, while Thomas Carothers' excellent theoretical work (1999) refers to Robert Putnam's path breaking work on social capital (1993), the role of political culture as an element in democratic transitions is largely absent from his otherwise outstanding book. Similarly, Larry Diamond (1999: 207) cites Marta Lagos's work for the view that interpersonal distrust is an 'archetypical feature of [Latin American] political culture, underlying low levels of trust in institutions'. Diamond goes on to suggest that 'trust in people' may merit more sustained investigation, then he cites an important article that does just that (Muller and Seligson 1994), but without noting their caution regarding Lagos's conclusions.

Muller and Seligson's conclusion, that interpersonal trust is an effect rather than a contributing cause of democracy, is an important contribution to our understanding. Their article raises a serious question about the conventional wisdom represented by Lagos' conclusion. They suggest that interpersonal trust is a consequence of a stable democracy, rather than a cause. Their conclusion is that:

Interpersonal trust is not unrelated to democracy, however. A country's long-term experience of democracy (as measured by its years of continuous democracy since 1900) is estimated to have a positive effect of moderate magnitude on the percentage of the general public with a high level of interpersonal trust. (Muller and Seligson 1994: 647)

A recent paper by Kenneth Newton and Pippa Norris (1999) reviews the theoretical foundations of trust and confidence variables. Their findings were that their data did not support psychological or social/cultural explanations. The stronger associations are at the national level. Thus, nations with high levels of social trust also had high levels of trust in public institutions. But why do they? Newton and Norris offer no solid explanation, but they suggest that social trust and confidence in institutions may both be based on rational appraisals of the performance of one's fellow citizens and the public institutions of a country.

Margaret Levi has noted that, 'Distrust, when it reflects the failure of a state to meet the requisites of trustworthiness, is more salutary than harmful to democracies' (Levi 1998: 85):

The main sources of distrust in government are promise breaking, incompetence, and the antagonism of government actors toward those they are supposed to serve. Citizens are likely to trust government only to the extent that they believe that it will act in their interests, that its procedures are fair, and that their trust of the state and others is reciprocated.

Yet on the positive side of trust, it is important to note that Putnam reports that interpersonal trust has a high correlation with a social capital index that includes 'measures of community organizational life, of engagement in public affairs, of community volunteerism and of informal sociability' (Putnam 2000: 291).

The latest words on this subject are perhaps the most useful, though they are largely consistent with the views expressed by Muller and Seligson, and by Levi. Examining the 1998 Hewlett dataset, Timothy Power and Mary Clark focus on the example of Costa Rica, which they cite as the 'most consolidated democracy in Latin America' (Power and Clark 2001: 57)). However, interpersonal trust was reported at only 24.2 per cent in Costa Rica, while it was almost 45 per cent in Mexico (58).[25] When we administered our own version of this question in Costa Rica in July 2001,[26] excluding those who could not or would not answer, only 5.7 per cent of our respondents were trusting. This puts Costa Rica in the close company of El Salvdaor and Guatemala. In both the Hewlett dataset and in our own results from Costa Rica, higher levels of education were associated with trust. In Costa Rica 10.5 per cent of those answering the 2001 Gallup CID question who had post-secondary education were trusting. Even so that is not a high level of trust, and there were no important differences by education in either Guatemala or El Salvador. In any event, the results from Costa Rica are troubling. Shouldn't we expect a 'consolidated democracy' to have higher levels of interpersonal trust?

The Hewlett dataset reveals that 84 per cent of Costa Ricans were supportive of democracy, compared to 51 per cent of Mexicans (Power and Clark 2001: 63). Despite this difference, Power and Clark conclude that the usual socio-demographic variables fail to account for individual differences in support for democracy. A much stronger explanation can be found—and this is the most interesting point—in country dummy variables, which explain more of the variance than do socio-demographics. Being a Costa Rican or a Mexican citizen makes a difference! The negative

[25] The question was asked in a slightly different form. Respondents were asked whether generally speaking people are trustworthy or not trustworthy, with two responses to choose: (1) Yes, people are trustworthy or (2) No, people are not trustworthy.

[26] Administered by contract with Gallup CID: 'Some say you can normally trust other people. Others say that you have to be wary when dealing with other people. What do you think?' 'Trusting or Wary?'

finding is that interpersonal trust is not a good predictor for support for democracy. Indeed, what Power and Clark describe as *civismo*[27] and spent a good deal of effort analysing, is a somewhat better predictor of support for democracy than is interpersonal trust.

Mitchell Seligson's contribution to the Camp book agrees that the results from the Hewlett survey, 'cast strong doubt on the importance of personal trust for democracy' (2001: 98). Instead, he concludes that Costa Rica has a democratic political culture ('a national myth') that makes Costa Ricans proud of their democratic institutions (2001: 106). Unfortunately, such myths are not written overnight, but are products of experience and socialization.

Of course, it is possible that interpersonal trust is associated with one's willingness to submit one's personal issues or grievances to a stranger, a judge who is supposed to be a fair and impartial decision-maker, even if it is not strongly related to support for democracy. It is not easy to test that proposition when there are so few trusting persons in our sample. For example, in the instance of our 2001 Gallup CID Guatemalan interpersonal trust question, there were only 84 trusting respondents out of a sample of 1,220.

Even so, it seems reasonable to hypothesize that low levels of confidence in public institutions, such as we found in both El Salvador and Guatemala, may represent, in part, a fair and accurate appraisal by citizens of the conduct of fellow citizens and those public institutions. Thus low institutional confidence in most of Latin America may be due to the historical fact of being poorly and harshly governed, with countries such as Costa Rica and Uruguay being the occasional possible exceptions. The solution to low confidence may simply be to create (and sustain over a long-term) institutions that are worthy of confidence. To be sure the short-term experiences of post-Peace Accords El Salvador and Guatemala reveal that this is no easy task. However, the premise that improvement is possible is energizing, while the opposite is a ticket for despair. We should note, however, that demonstrations of trustworthiness require both tangible positive outcomes and powerful

---

[27] *Civismo*, or its opposite, *incivismo*, is represented by one's belief that people in general think that those who do the following are 'very stupid' or 'very smart' (with the appropriate intervening values) when: (a) Cutting in line; (b) Not saying anything if they get extra change; (c) Not paying the subway or bus fare; (d) Run a traffic light at midnight when there is no traffic; (e) Making up a false excuse.

symbolic messages of those outcomes, especially in societies where the citizenry long has had reason to be skeptical.

What Can be Done Actually to Enhance the Trustworthiness of Institutions?

As we have seen, Carothers answers the above question by pointing out that the easiest part of reform consists of rewriting constitutions and laws. Institutional restructuring and retraining personnel are relatively easy things to do. But he concludes that:

> The primary obstacles to such reform are not technical or financial but political and human. Rule-of-law reform will succeed only if it gets at the fundamental problem of leaders who refuse to be ruled by the law.... Western nations and private donors have poured millions of dollars into rule-of-law reform, but outside aid is no substitute for the will to reform, which must come from within. (Carothers 1998: 96)

Carothers refers to the 'rationalization and democratization of main state institutions' as part of a top-down approach to reform in which a common error is that remedies are too often prescribed for visible shortcomings without asking '*why* the judiciary is in a lamentable state'. Reforms are offered in 'pseudoscientific manner as a clinical process' to be implemented through manuals, remedial seminars and the like, this process resting on the assumption that local actors will embrace reforms because they are 'inherently desirable' (Carothers 1999: 101–2). The alternative, a bottom-up approach to reform, is achieved by providing support to NGOs that may become the agents for change from within the society. This alternative also is fraught with difficulties, perhaps the principal one being whether the NGOs are indeed advocacy organizations with a strong popular base in civil society, or merely the willing but isolated (and sometimes elitist) recipients of donor aid (Carothers 1999: 211–19).

On the whole Carothers is skeptical but optimistic that real progress has been made in the 1990s, Guatemala being one of the exemplars (his assessment is more positive than our own). He finds that aid providers now appreciate that the will to reform must exist if outside help is to work and that they are seeking measurable and sustainable results, albeit not necessarily ones that can be measured with calculators. Whether aid providers are in for the long haul—for the duration of time that serious change will require—remains to be seen.

Another perspective is offered by Linn Hammergren's (2000) compelling appraisal of the last 15 years of judicial reform in Latin America, which contains two key suggestions. The first is that most of us have assumed that judicial independence is an objectively desirable goal without taking into account the uses to which independence may be put. She suggests that sometimes independence has 'out-paced reform, giving certain judiciaries more freedom to exercise their traditional vices—misuse of resources, politically motivated decisions, and in some instances partisan conflicts or alliances with other branches of government'. The second key point is that of 'dealing with political will'. Thus, 'It is commonly insisted that reforms can only be undertaken with sufficient political will—that is, with the commitment of a highly placed political and organizational elite. It is equally common to find that what will existed at the outset was less than had been imagined, or was insufficient to meet the increasing demands placed on it.' And the issue, she suggests, 'is how to identify an adequate principal to lead reform' (Hammergren 2000:18–20). Hammergren and Carothers make much the same point: constitutional revisions and a shopping list of structural reforms may be necessary, but not sufficient in themselves.

Conclusion—Some Thoughts on the Efficacy of Reforms

We recall Madison's thesis that if judges have a strong sense of interest imbedded in their office and function, they will fight to preserve their independence and serve as 'sentinels' of the public interest in the process. Based on our own interviews and on the research reported by others, there is little solid evidence from either El Salvador or Guatemala to support the conclusion that reforms have instilled these motives and interests broadly in judges, prosecutors and police. We have found support in our interviews and focus groups for the conclusion that most pressures seem to move in the opposite direction. Further, there is little evidence that political party leaders have a strong commitment to carrying through with Peace Accord mandated reform of the justice system or to strengthen watchdog agencies like the human rights ombudsman. We have found that both the broad public and members of civic and professional elites possess an abiding skepticism concerning the effect of reform in promoting horizontal accountability, yet justice reform does seem to have had positive effects in some areas. The role played by El Salvador's judicial training school, at least in the purging of incompetent judges, is but one example. A major goal of reform has been the promotion of judicial independence. The strengthening of the CNJ and dramatic increases in the judicial budget have contributed to achieving that goal. Nevertheless, our research suggests that these changes have not persuaded rank and file judges that they are autonomous in their own courtrooms. Some judges feel extremely vulnerable to political pressure and view their own Supreme Court as being deeply politicized by the appointment process and ongoing political party interference. Furthermore, our own prior research has shown that after six years of reform (as of the end of 1998) the judiciary had still not found the will to remove anyone from its own ranks on the stated grounds of corruption. Yet all agree that corruption is a profound problem.

Juan E. Méndez has argued that, 'prosecutions and trials, as long as they are held under strict fair trial guarantees, are a necessary and even desirable ingredient in any serious effort at accountability' (Méndez 1997: 255). But we, along with Méndez and many others, have recognized the difficulties that lurk in reforming a country's judicial system to make it an effective arena for accountability, much less one that proceeds under 'strict fair trial guarantees'. Tantamount to achieving effectiveness is the necessity of reforming a judicial system so that it is *perceived* by citizens as a *possible* venue for dispute resolution. That is why symbolic victories may be as important as tangible ones in the short run. The subtext of our chapter has been the resilience of distrust and low levels of confidence, both among mass publics and elites in El Salvador and Guatemala, especially regarding the judicial systems through which accountability might be achieved.

Based on existing research, we are reluctant to accept the view that there are deep-seated cultural obstacles to achieving effective judicial systems either in El Salvador or Guatemala. It remains to be seen whether demonstrated improvements, wherever they may occur, eventually will produce heightened levels of confidence in reformed institutions. But that will take time, and demonstrating such improvements will not come easily.

References

American Bar Association. 1997. *An Independent Judiciary: Report of the ABA Commission on Separation of Powers and Judicial Independence.* Chicago, IL: American Bar Association.

Ames, Barry. 1999. 'Approaches to the Study of Institutions in Latin American Politics'. *Latin American Research Review* 34, 1: 221–36.

Becker, David G. 1999. 'Latin America: Beyond Democratic Consolidation'. *Journal of Democracy* 10 (April): 138–51.

Camp, Roderick Ai. 2001. *Citizen Views of Democracy in Latin America*. Pittsburgh, PA: University of Pittsburgh Press.

Carothers, Thomas. 1998. 'The Rule of Law Revival'. *Foreign Affairs* 77 (March/April): 95–106.

Carothers, Thomas. 1999. *Aiding Democracy Abroad: The Learning Curve*. Washington, DC: Carnegie Endowment for International Peace.

Commager, Henry Steele, ed. 1949. *Selections from the Federalist*. New York: Appleton-Century-Crofts.

Comisión de Fortalecimiento de la Justicia una Nueva Justicia para la Pazi: Resumen Ejecutivo del Informe Final de la Comisión de Fortuleci- miento de la Justicia (Guatemala: April 1998)

Commission to Modernize the Judiciary. 1997. 'Plan de Modernización del Organismo Judicial'. Guatemala City: Commission to Modernize the Judiciary.

Comité de Abogados por los Derechos Humanos. 1993. 'La revolución negociada de el Salvador: perspectivas de la reforma judicial'. New York, NY: Comité de Abogados por los Derechos Humanos.

Diamond, Larry. 1999. *Developing Democracy: Toward Consolidation*. Baltimore, MD: The Johns Hopkins University Press.

Dodson, Michael. Forthcoming. 'Legal Systems of the World: El Salvador'. In Herbert M. Kritzer, ed., *Legal Systems of the World: A Political, Social, and Cultural Encyclopedia*. Santa Barbara: ABC-CLIO.

Dodson, J. Michael, and Donald W. Jackson. 1997. 'Re-inventing the Rule of Law: Human Rights in El Salvador'. *Democratization* 4 (Winter): 110–34.

Dodson, J. Michael and Donald W. Jackson. 2001. 'Judicial Independence in Central America'. In Peter H. Russell and David M. O'Brien, eds., *Judicial Independence in the Age of Democracy: Critical Perspectives from around the World*. Charlottesville, VA: University Press of Virginia.

Dodson, Michael, Donald W. Jackson, and Laura Nuzzi O'Shaughnessy. 2001. 'Political Will and Public Trust: El Salvador's Procurator for the Defense of Human Rights'. *Human Rights Review* 2, 3 (April–June): 51–75.

FESPAD. n.d. 'Evaluación de la Cooperación Internacional para El Salvador en Materia de Administración de Justicia'. Unpublished report.

Fiss, Owen M. 1993. 'The Right Degree of Independence'. In Irwin P. Stotzky, ed., *Transition to Democracy in Latin America: The Role of the Judiciary*. Boulder, CO: Westview Press.

Hammergren, Linn A. 1998. *The Politics of Justice and Justice Reform in Latin America: The Peruvian Case in Comparative Perspective*. Boulder, CO: Westview Press.

——. 2000. 'Fifteen Years of Judicial Reform in Latin America: Where We Are and Why We Haven't Made More Progress'. USAID Global Center for Democracy and Governance. (accessed 1/21/2000: http://darkwing. uoregon.edu/~caguirre/hammergren.htm).

Holder, Rachel. 1998. 'La reforma judicial en Guatemala, 1997–1998: Una guía básica sobre los problemas, procesoso y actores'. Washington, DC: Washington Office on Latin America.

Holiday, David and William Stanley. 1993. 'Building the Peace: Preliminary Lessons from El Salvador'. *Journal of International Affairs* 46: 416–17.

IDB América. 1999. 26 (November–December): 9–20.

Jackson, D. W., J. M. Dodson, and L. Nuzzi O'Shaughnessy. 1999. 'Protecting Human Rights: The Legitimacy of Judicial System Reforms in El Salvador'. *Bulletin of Latin American Research* 18, 4: 403–21.

Jonas, Susanne. 2000. *Of Centaurs and Doves: Guatemala's Peace Process.* Boulder, CO: Westview Press.

Lagos, Marta. 1997. 'Latin America's Smiling Mask'. *Journal of Democracy* 8 (July): 125–38.

——. 2001, 'Between Stability and Crisis in Latin America'. *Journal of Democracy* 12 (January): 136–45.

Levi, Margaret. 1998. 'A State of Trust'. In Valerie Braithwaite and Margaret Levi, eds., *Trust and Governance.* New York, NY : Russell Sage Foundation.

McCleary, Rachel M. 1997. 'Guatemala's Postwar Prospects'. *Journal of Democracy* 8 (April): 134–43.

Méndez, Juan E. 1997. 'Accountability for Past Abuses'. *Human Rights Quarterly* 19: 255–82.

Méndez, Juan E., Guillermo O'Donnell, and Sérgio Pinheiro, eds. 1999. *The (Un)Rule of Law and The Underprivileged in Latin America.* Notre Dame, IN: The University of Notre Dame Press.

Muller, Edward N., and Mitchell A. Seligson. 1994. 'Civic Culture and Democracy: The Quest for Causal Relationships'. *American Political Science Review* 88 (September): 635–52.

Newton, Kenneth. 1999. 'Social and Political Trust in Established Democracies'. In Pippa Norris, ed., *Critical Citizens: Global Support for Democratic Governance.* New York: Oxford University Press.

Newton, Kenneth and Pippa Norris. 1999. 'Confidence in Public Institutions: Faith, Culture or Performance?' Paper presented at the annual meeting of the American Political Science Association.

O'Donnell, Guillermo. 1994. 'Delegative Democracy'. *Journal of Democracy* 5 (January): 55–69.

——. 1999a. 'Horizontal Accountability in New Democracies'. In Andreas Schedler, Larry Diamond and Marc Plattner, eds., *The Self-Restraining State: Power and Accountability in New Democracies.* Boulder, CO: Lynne Rienner Publishers.

——. 1999b. 'A Response to My Commentators'. In Andreas Schedler, Larry Diamond and Marc Plattner, eds., *The Self-Restraining State:*

Power and Accountability in New Democracies. Boulder, CO: Lynne Rienner Publishers.

———. 2000a. 'Democracy, Law and Comparative Politics'. Kellogg Institute Working Paper No. 274.

O'Donnell, Guillermo. 2000b. 'Further Thoughts on Horizontal Accountability'. Paper presented at workshop on 'Political Institutions, Accountability and Democratic Governance in Latin America', University of Notre Dame.

Offe, Clause. 1997. 'How Can We Trust Our Fellow Citizens?' Paper presented at the XVII World Congress of the International Political Science Association.

Palma, Silvia Irene. 1999. 'Percepción de las reformas institucionales de estado posteriores a los acuerdos de paz in El Salvador y Guatemala: el caso de Guatemala. (Report of a focus group study commissioned by Texas Christian University and conducted through the Facultad de Ciencias Sociales of the Universidad Rafael Landívar in Guatemala.)

Popkin, Margaret. 2000. *Peace Without Justice: Obstacles to Building the Rule of Law in El Salvador.* University Park, PA: Penn State University Press.

Power, Timothy J. and Mary A. Clark. 2001. 'Does Trust Matter? Interpersonal Trust and Democratic Values in Chile, Costa Rica and Mexico'. In Roderic Ai Camp, ed., *Citizen Views of Democracy in Latin America.* Pittsburgh, PA: University of Pittsburgh Press.

Putnam, Robert. 1993. *Making Democracy Work: Civic Traditions in Modern Italy.* Princeton, NJ: Princeton University Press.

Putnam, Robert. 2000. *Bowling Alone: The Collapse and Revival of American Community.* New York, NY: Simon & Schuster.

Reding, Andrew. 1997. *Democracy and Human Rights in Guatemala.* Washington, DC: World Policy Institute.

Schedler, Andreas. 1999. 'Conceptualizing Accountability'. In Andreas Schedler, Larry Diamond and Marc Plattner, eds., *The Self-Restraining State: Power and Accountability in New Democracies.* Boulder, CO: Lynne Rienner Publishers.

Schedler, Andreas, Larry Diamond and Marc Plattner, eds. 1999. *The Self-Restraining State: Power and Accountability in New Democracies.* Boulder, CO: Lynne Rienner Publishers.

Seligson, Mitchell. 2001. 'Costa Rica Exceptionalism: Why the Ticos Are Different'. In Roderic Ai Camp, ed., *Citizen Views of Democracy in Latin America.* Pittsburgh, PA: University of Pittsburgh Press.

Sklar, Richard L. 1999. 'Democracy and Constitutionalism'. In Andreas Schedler, Larry Diamond and Marc Plattner, eds., *The Self-Restraining State: Power and Accountability in New Democracies.* Boulder, CO: Lynne Rienner Publishers.

Sorok, Margarita, trans. 1999. *The Peace Process in El Salvador: Views of Judges, Civic Leaders, Businesspeople, Municipal Leaders* (Report of a focus group study commissioned by Texas Christian University and conducted by the Institute of Public Opinion, University of Central America, San Salvador).

Stanley, William and David Holiday. 2002, 'Broad Participation, Diffuse Responsibility in Guatemala'. In Stephen John Stedman, Donald Rothchild, and Elizabeth M. Cousans, eds. Ending Civil Wars: The implementation of Peace agreements. Boulder. CO: Lynne Rienner Publications.

Stone Sweet, Alec. 1999. 'Judicialization and the Construction of Governance'. *Comparative Judicial Studies* 32 (April): 147–84.

Stone Sweet, Alec. 2000. *Governing with Judges: Constitutional Politics in Europe*. Oxford: Oxford University Press.

Tojeira, S. J. and José M. 2000. 'El sistema judicial in El Salvador'. *Estudios Centroamericanos* 625–626 (Noviembre–Diciembre): 1119–1127.

United Nations. 1988. *Basic Principles on the Independence of the Judiciary*. New York: United Nations.

United Nations Special Rapporteur's Report. 2000. 'Judicial Independence in Guatemala'. E/CN.4/2000/61/add. 1 (6 January): 16.

....
Chapter 9
....

Authoritarianism, Democracy and the Supreme Court: Horizontal Exchange and the Rule of Law in Mexico

*Beatriz Magaloni**

Introduction

This chapter focuses on the relationship between democracy, judicial independence, and the rule of law in Mexico. Democracy seems to be a necessary, though not sufficient condition, to institutionalize the rule of law. The mechanisms that relate the rule of law with regime type are not that clear, however. Why are authoritarian regimes less constrained by laws? Why does limited government more often accompany democracy? Under what conditions can democracies exist without effective rule of law? These are central questions that I seek to address in the context of Mexico.

The paper explores, in particular, the relationship between authoritarianism, democracy and the emergence of Supreme Court independence in Mexico. I argue that authoritarianism in Mexico was incompatible with the rule of law and judicial independence for three reasons: (1) The constitution was extremely *flexible* in practice. The president, through his party, possessed the ability to shape and re-shape the fundamental rules of the game. Since the president could set the rules that were supposed to constrain him,

* I am grateful for comments by the participants in the conference 'Institutions, Accountability and Democratic Governance in Latin America', Kellogg Institute for International Studies, University of Notre Dame, 8–9 May 2000. I also wish to thank Scott Mainwaring for his careful reading of the article and useful suggestions, and an anonymous review. Part of the analysis contained in this chapter comes from previous work by the author on the rule of law in Mexico carried out while being a researcher at CIDAC. The author wishes to thank Alberto Diaz, Luis Rubio, Guillermo Zepeda, Edna Jaime, Jacqueline Martinez, Pilar Campos, Roberto Blum, Hector Fix-Fierro and Ana Laura Magaloni for continuous discussions on the problems of the rule of law in Mexico over the years.

there were no binding constitutional limits. (2) Authoritarianism jeopardized Supreme Court independence, as the president exercised a strong control over nominations and dismissals. (3) Politicians opted not to delegate enough constitutional powers to the Supreme Court, excluding from judicial review virtually all cases with so-called 'political' content (see below).

Authoritarianism meant unconstrained rule by the hegemonic party and *presidencialismo*, which in the Mexican literature refers to a powerful presidency that rules above the constitution and overarches the other branches of government (Weldon 1997). The Mexican authoritarian regime placed a lot of emphasis on rules: laws were drafted paying close attention to formal procedures and presidents ruled without recurring to the use of executive decrees. However, these rules were not binding: in the absence of effective veto players, politicians could easily reverse them.

Democratization changed the equilibrium. First, multipartism brought veto players into the policy-making arena and the constitution became binding for the first time. The long lasting ruling party, Partido Revolucionario Institucional (PRI), lost the necessary majority in the Lower Chamber of Deputies in 1988 to unilaterally modify the constitution. All constitutional reforms taking place after 1988 have been negotiated among politicians belonging to different parties. Veto players imply, on the one hand, that constitutional reforms are harder to accomplish, and on the other, that any change to the *status quo* must now benefit all actors whose vote is needed to modify the constitution. Thus, no party can unilaterally impose the fundamental set of rules, as it happened during the era of party hegemony. A second fundamental change is that through the 1994 constitutional reform, President Zedillo (1994–2000) opted to delegate more constitutional powers to the Supreme Court. Through the constitutional controversies (*controversias constitucionales*), the Court can now serve as arbiter of federalism in conflicts arising among different levels of government inhabited by politicians from different partisan affiliations. The Supreme Court can also interpret the constitution with general effects through a form of judicial review known as constitutional actions (*acciones de inconstitucionalidad*). These new constitutional powers have placed the Supreme Court at the center stage of Mexico's system of checks and balances.

Why did politicians in Mexico decide to tie their hands, opting to delegate constitutional powers to the Supreme Court? I argue in this paper that multipartism created the incentives for President Zedillo to delegate. The prevailing equilibrium of *hegemonic presidencialismo*, where the president served as the ultimate, autocratic arbiter of political conflicts ruling above the constitution, began to unravel with multiparty politics. In the era of *hegemonic presidencialismo*, the president employed partisan institutions, and in particular the threat to expel rebellious politicians from the party, to induce compliance among the politicians. As politicians of multiple partisan affiliations began to occupy the multiplicity of elective offices, the president's leadership was challenged, first by members of different parties and soon by his own co-partisans. The president thus delegated to the Supreme Court the power to rule on constitutional issues as a means to solve this dilemma.

Democracy in Mexico has thus enhanced 'horizontal accountability'. My assessment differs from O'Donnell (1994), who is very pessimistic about the quality of horizontal accountability in most of Latin America. The divergence between my assessment and his stems partly from the fact that horizontal accountability is here narrowly defined as checks and balances—what Shugart in this volume calls 'horizontal exchange' and I hereafter do likewise—whereas O'Donnell includes effective rule of law as one dimension of horizontal accountability.

Horizontal exchange contributes to the consolidation of the rule of law inasmuch as checks and balances serve to institutionalize a *limited government*. In the classic Madisonian formulation, checks and balances make it harder for existing power-holders to employ laws that systematically violate minority rights. Checks and balances also make it harder for powerful players to draft laws that systematically favour them as changes to the *status quo* must satisfy the interests of *all* veto players (Tsebelis 1995).

Power-holders are not the only potential threat against individual rights, however (Przeworski and Limongi 1993). Other fellow citizens can also encroach upon individual rights, and here lies a dilemma facing many newly democratized counties such as Mexico: although the state seems to be more capable of refraining from oppressing its citizenry, it is increasingly incapable of defending its citizens against violations by fellow citizens. Democratization in the region has created new, mounting demands for security, as it has generally been accompanied by increasing crime rates, violence and the absence of an effective rule of law.

This chapter unfolds as follows. In the first section, I discuss the relationship between democracy, horizontal exchange, and the rule of law, placing Mexico in comparative perspective. The following sections analyse the relationship between authoritarianism, democracy and the Supreme Court, distinguishing two distinctive eras of Presidential–Supreme Court relationships in Mexico's modern history: (a) The period 1934–94, when the Court had no significant constitutional powers and was extremely subservient to the president. (b) After the 1994 constitutional reform, which empowered the Court with judicial review and the power to solve constitutional controversies. I end up with a discussion of the pending challenges in the consolidation of the rule of law in Mexico.

The Rule of Law, Horizontal Exchange, and Democracy

The rule of law is the institutionalization of individual rights. The rule of law solves two types of dilemmas: Madisonian-like dilemmas or the establishment of limits to the state's ability to predate upon citizens' rights, and Hobbesian-like dilemmas or protection of individuals' rights against encroachments by other private agents. Without a third-party enforcer of rights, citizens would be condemned to live in a prisoner's dilemma-type setting, where a combination of decentralized enforcement mechanisms and brute force are employed to enforce rights.

To solve this Hobbesian dilemma, a state is created, originating a second, liberal dilemma: a state that is strong enough to enforce rights, can also expropriate them (North and Weingast 1989; Weingast 1997; Przeworski and Limongi 1993). Paradoxically, most of the recent literature on the rule of law focuses on the liberal dilemma and fails to systematically explore how a peaceful political order is created (but see, instead, Huntington 1968, Olson 1993, Bates 2001).

Thus there are two dimensions in the rule of law, what I call the *liberty dimension*, where rights must be protected against encroachments by the state; and a second, *security dimension*, where rights must be protected against encroachments by other private agents. In this second dimension, the state must serve as a third-party impartial enforcer of contracts and rights.

To protect liberty, one of the key innovations of the rule of law is that majority decisions can be annulled. Existing legislation can no longer be employed as justification for encroaching rights. The power of the sovereign (e.g., the King or the parliament) is limited. The innovation is particularly important for making democracies less capricious, given that even the majority finds a limit in some fundamental rights. In this sense, the main goal of the liberty dimension of the rule of law is to control *legislative* decisions and it does so mainly through judicial review. Failure to consolidate the rule of law on this dimension leads to tyranny.

To enhance security, the state must protect individual rights against possible encroachments by other private actors. It does so through what Max Weber called the 'legitimate monopoly of violence'. Only law enforcement institutions, such as the police and the courts, can employ violence. Individuals cannot 'take justice in their own hands' to protect their rights. These law enforcement institutions should act as third-party *impartial* enforcers. They must enforce rights, acting within previously specified limits and without systematically favouring any of the parts.

The 'principle of legality' is then a central aspect of the rule of law in this second dimension: the government cannot affect citizens' rights unless it follows laws that were in force beforehand. The main goal of the security dimension of the rule of law is thus to *enforce* pre-existing laws, regardless of their substantive content.

The main source of threat to individual rights on this second security dimension comes from other private agents. However, law enforcement institutions can also encroach upon citizens' rights by not enforcing laws impartially, namely violating the principle of legality. Thus, in protecting the liberty of its citizenry, the state also faces a problem of implementation: agents of law enforcement such as the judges and the police might act above the law to encroach liberty. In this sense, there is also an important aspect of control of state authorities on this second dimension of the rule of law. The control is not over the creation of legislative decisions. Rather it is over law enforcement itself. Below I explore the relationship between both of these dimensions of the rule of law, democratization and horizontal exchange.

The Liberty Dimension of the Rule of Law: Limited Government and the Judiciary as a Source of Horizontal Exchange The literature on limited government is closely associated with that of property rights and is hence motivated by the following question: how can credible limits on the state be established such that investors have some form of guarantee that their investments would not be expropriated? Without this type of limit, growth cannot come about. 'The more likely it is that the sovereign will alter property rights for his or her own benefit, the lower the expected returns from investment and the lower in turn the incentive to invest. For economic growth to occur the sovereign or government must not merely establish the relevant set of rules, but make a credible commitment to them' (North and Weingast 1989: 803).

Most authors agree that limited government was achieved by a combination of popular democracy and constitutionalism. Popular democracy served to align the interests of political actors with those of the enfranchised. Moreover, frequent elections provided a credible threat against government opportunism—voters could now get rid of arbitrary rulers. As Elster (1993: 21) puts it 'the promises of an executive are much more credible if there is a well-established procedure for throwing the executive out of office for failing to keep those promises.'[1]

But elections are not enough to establish a credible political commitment for the protection of rights for two reasons. The first reason, which has been thoroughly analysed by the social choice literature, is that democracy might be unstable and unpredictable over time. Without institutional constraints, direct majority voting can virtually lead to any outcome, making any policy choice subject to reversal at some point in the future by a new majority. Secondly, a majority may be tempted to expropriate minority rights. The fear of 'majority tyranny', as the Federalists put it, inspired the United States founders to draft a constitution where they established the institutions of limited government: a system of checks and balances for dividing power among different branches of government.

Checks and balances serve two goals: 'they protect individual rights, and they form an obstacle to certain political changes which would have been carried out had the majority had its way' (Elster 1993: 3). The first goal, protecting individual rights, is usually the task of courts. Courts can impose *substantive* limits on legislative decisions by, for example, declaring certain changes unconstitutional or interpreting statutes in light of the constitutional rights of citizens (Elster 1993). Judicial review exists in the United States as a result of the famous *Marbury* v. *Madison* decision, where Justice Marshall argued that in the presence of a written constitution and an independent judiciary, the Supreme Court has

---

[1] The extent to which voters actually carry out the threat of punishing an incumbent that fails to keep its promises varies from country to country. For example, if we take economic growth as a measure of 'keeping the promises', there is a great variance in the incidence of economic voting both in Europe (Powell and Whitten 1993) and Latin America (Remmer 1991; Stokes 1996). Przeworski and Cheibub (1999) have even questioned that the mechanism for enforcing accountability is through elections since they find no systematic relationship between economic performance and likelihood of an incumbent been re-elected.

to apply the higher law when ordinary legislation was not in accordance with the Constitution. The United States possesses a decentralized system of judicial review where courts are bound to apply the Constitution over ordinary legislation. Most democratizing countries in Latin America, Mexico now included, follow a different principle: as in Germany, Spain, Italy, Portugal and Belgium, a special tribunal (the Supreme Court or Constitutional Court) interprets the constitution. Ordinary courts may not decide constitutionality questions themselves, although they can submit questions of constitutionality to the Supreme Court.

Centralized systems of judicial review might present some problems. As it will be made explicit in the case of Mexico, the Constitutional Tribunal might be too removed from the citizenry. The Mexican Supreme Court was converted into a Constitutional Court in 1994, but only elected politicians can employ the two new mechanisms of control of constitutionality. Citizens, instead, must employ the *amparo* procedure (see below) to defend their rights; most cases where constitutional issues over fundamental rights are raised never reach the Supreme Court. This means that the new Court is establishing constitutional doctrine only on broader constitutional issues (mostly related to division of powers and federalism) and not on fundamental rights.

The second goal of a Constitution, making it hard for the majority to unilaterally change the status quo, is mainly served by various *procedural* rules that limit majority choices by dividing power among different branches of government (Elster 1993). As said above, checks and balances introduce veto players, which are meant to limit the power of any single political actor. Institutions such as division of powers, bicameralism, federalism, and also Central Banks and Constitutional Tribunals are all meant to limit majority power.

One of the difficulties with checks and balances as a way to enforce limited governments is that they are not always effective. A crucial dilemma, as it will become apparent below when discussing the Mexican case, is that institutions do not divide power where power is not divided. Checks and balances are effective when there is a de facto division of forces in society, such that the interests of the majority in the legislature are not perfectly aligned with the president's. For example, if the same party controls the presidency and the majority in the legislature, and moreover, representatives tend to vote along partisan lines, division of powers is not effective as a source of power checking (Mainwaring and Shugart 1997).

Henisz (2000) constructed a database that quantifies the number of *effective* checks and balances in a large number of political systems. The work on political constraints by Henisz (herein the WH project) quantifies the number of *independent* veto points over policy outcomes, which results from a combination of formal rules and the distribution of political preferences of the actors that inhabit the institutions. In the WH project, a *de jure* veto point is counted as independent when the majority in, let us say, the legislature (L) does not correspond to the same party of the president (E). The measure is then weighted by the Rae measure of fractionalization, a proxy for the difficulty of forming coalitions. Thus, if for example the executive faces a legislature of its own party, executive power increases as the level of fractionalization decreases. The WH project includes courts for a subset of countries in this measure. Court 'independence' is derived from a simple measure of stability of tenure for justices of the highest tribunal.

Table 9.1 shows measures of effective checks and balances (veto players) for Latin American countries from 1960 until 1994 according to the WH project. In 1994, more constrained executives from highest to lowest, were ordered as follows: Brazil, Venezuela, Chile, Uruguay, Argentina, Colombia, Mexico, Bolivia and Peru. After the 1997 elections in Mexico, the relevant measure significantly increased, reflecting the PRI's loss of the majority in the Lower Chambers plus a series of losses in gubernatorial elections and the establishment of a Constitutional Court.

The measure of effective veto players or executive constraints is generally correlated, though not perfectly, with democratization. Thus, for example, the indexes for Chile and Uruguay collapse with the military coups of 1973 and 1974, respectively, and experience sharp increases with the transition to democracy. Similarly, the index of executive constraint starts increasing for Argentina after the transition to democracy. In Venezuela and Colombia, two countries that were democracies between 1960 and 1994, the index of executive constraints does not vary much. Peru is a case where both democratization and effective constraints on the executive experienced reversals in the 1990s. Mexico's gradual and protracted democratization process is correlated with similarly gradual introduction of constraints on the executive. The only exception to this pattern seems to be Brazil, where the transition

TABLE 9.1. *Constraints on the executive (WH project on effective veto players)*

	(1) 1960–64	(2) 1965–69	(3) 1970–74	(4) 1975–79	(5) 1980–84	(6) 1985–89	(7) 1990–94	(8) 1995–98	Change (8)–(1)	Correlation with Polity 98 Democracy Index
Mexico	0.0376	0.0966	0.1128	0.1294	0.1814	0.1902	0.2862	0.4741	0.4365	**0.9104**
Colombia	0.4010	0.4125	0.3026	0.4322	0.3998	0.4274	0.4388	0.4584	0.0574	**0.2288**
Venezuela	0.7395	0.7992	0.7171	0.7876	0.7523	0.7757	0.7701	0.7108	−0.0287	−0.0513
Ecuador	0.0000	0.0000	0.0000	0.1340	0.7243	0.7151	0.6973	0.6921	0.6921	**0.9268**
Peru	0.2278	0.1131	0.0000	0.0000	0.0000	0.3045	0.1170	0.0000	−0.2278	**0.5417**
Brazil	0.7943	0.6667	0.6667	0.6667	0.7282	0.8607	0.7955	0.6948	−0.0995	**0.6512**
Bolivia	0.0940	0.0000	0.0000	0.0000	0.0966	0.4918	0.2751	0.5594	0.4654	**0.8297**
Paraguay	0.0000	0.0000	0.0000	0.0000	0.0000	0.0000	0.2903	0.7217	0.7217	**0.9360**
Chile	0.6982	0.7917	0.4497	0.0000	0.0000	0.0000	0.7880	0.8300	0.1317	**0.9695**
Argentina	0.0000	0.0000	0.0000	0.0000	0.0725	0.3769	0.7131	0.7974	0.7974	**0.7761**
Uruguay	0.4602	0.4131	0.1979	0.0000	0.0000	0.4239	0.5277	0.5639	0.1037	**0.9287**

Source: Calculated from the Polecon Index Database by Henisz (2000).

to democracy did not produce significant changes on executive constraints, at least on the basis of this measure.

The last column of the table presents the correlation between the level of democracy in each country, as measure by the POLITY index, and the degree to which the executive constrained. There is a clear positive correlation between both measures for the overwhelming majority of cases, supporting the hypothesis that democratization is systematically accompanied by an increase in horizontal exchange.

Beyond formal institutions and the effective partisan balance of forces in society, culture and values appear to shape the likelihood of institutionalizing a limited government. Weingast (1997) has argued that enforcing a limited government requires some form of social consensus on the appropriate limits of the state. Consensus is necessary for individuals to coordinate opposing encroachments by the state. Without this form of coordination, the state might be tempted to encroach upon one group of citizens, taking advantage of a divide-and-rule strategy to remain in power. An implication of this argument is that the rule of law is harder to accomplish in highly polarized social settings, where coordination among the citizens against an arbitrary state is more difficult.

In Weingast (1997), the state is conceived as a unitary actor. In newly democratizing settings, most of the violations to fundamental rights now take place in a decentralized fashion, under the hands of lower level bureaucrats, courts and the police and coordinating against so many potential sources appears to be much harder. As I emphasize below, one of the crucial dilemmas with the rule of law in newly democratizing settings comes from an agency problem: the state fails to control the behaviour of its agents of law enforcement. Liberty is threatened not so much because the state legislates encroaching individual's rights, but because there is not effective and impartial enforcement of laws.

The Security Dimension of the Rule of Law: The Police and the Judiciary as Third-party 'Impartial' Enforcers   The literature on property rights emphasizes the state as the main source of encroachments to individual rights and argues that a limited government is central for growth to come about. Legal protection of individual rights against the state is not all that matters for development, however. 'No society can work satisfactorily if it does not have a peaceful order' (Olson 1993: 567). Underdevelopment, as the new development economics submits, is not only caused by lack of capital accumulation. It also results from pervasive market failures, lack of complete markets and problems with moral hazard and asymmetric information.[2]

The literature on industrial organization makes clear some of the implications of a lack of effective legal institutions for market exchange. In a nutshell, the argument is that individuals will fail to capture the full gains from trade where there is a high *ex ante* probability that their agreements and contracts will not be fulfilled. Where some citizens believe that they cannot enforce their contracts against opportunistic behaviour by their contractual partners, they will possess incentives to perform transactions outside of the market, that is, only in their extended families, their clans, their firms, or economic groups (Coase 1937; Williamson 1985; Eggertsson 1990).[3]

In the absence of a legal framework that can universally enforce rights, violence increases. This is because individuals will opt for private and personal enforcement of their rights. The issue has become pervasive in Latin America, where an explosion of crime rates in the 1980s and 1990s, coupled with inefficient and corrupt law enforcement institutions, was accompanied by an explosion of 'private-order' enforcement solutions ranging from guarded neighbourhoods, and armoured cars, to mutual protection associations and paramilitary groups. The problem is particularly acute in Colombia, Brazil and Mexico (Ayres 1998).

Democratization is often linked to an increase in crime rates. Russia is a clear case in mind. But criminal behaviour is becoming a major concern in many democratizing Latin American countries. The Latin American region not only presents the highest international homicide rates but, together with Sub-Saharan Africa, has shown the highest increase in criminal behaviour during the last decade. Table 9.2 shows homicide rates per 100,000 inhabitants in selected countries of Latin America and how they changed during the last decades. The data show that except for

[2] Economists have long noted that poor countries allocate resources inefficiently and keep many economic transactions outside of the market. The poor also tend to engage in seemingly sub-optimal contractual arrangements chosen not out of irrationality, but as 'second-best' solutions due to market failures. The persistence of these inefficient contractual arrangements responds to lack of markets for land, credit, and insurance, among others, and the protection of investment per se can do nothing to solve these kinds of problems. See, for example, Stiglitz (1974).

[3] These types of 'private governance structures' employ alternative enforcing mechanisms of contracts, such as reputations mechanism and internal sanctioning devices. However, since internal institutions are, by their own definition, only effective within the governance structure, dealings and exchange across different private governance structures are costly.

TABLE 9.2. *Homicide Rates per 100,000 inhabitants*

Country	Late 70s/Early 80s	Late 80s/Early 90s
Colombia	20.5	89.5
Brazil	11.5	19.7
Mexico	17.7	18.2*
Venezuela	11.7	15.2
Trinidad y Tobago	2.1	12.6
Peru	2.4	11.5
Panama	2.1	10.9
Ecuador	6.4	10.3
United States	10.7	10.1
Argentina	3.9	4.2*
Costa Rica	5.7	4.1
Uruguay	2.6	4.4
Paraguay	5.1	4.0
Chile	2.6	3.0

* Is from Lederman (1999).
Source: Ayres (1998).

Costa Rica, the United States and Paraguay, violent crime increased in all of these countries. In Panama, Colombia, Peru, and Brazil the rate of increase in violent crime was dramatic. The increase in homicide rates in Mexico is more significant in the largest metropolitan cities. Homicides per 100,000 inhabitants in Mexico City went from 9.3 in 1989 to 14.2 in 1995. Among the Latin American countries, Colombia, Brazil and Mexico rank as the three most dangerous places to live as measured by intentional homicide rates (Fajnzylber et al. 1998; Ayres 1998).

Part of the dilemma in building the rule of law in newly democratizing countries comes from the fact that law enforcement institutions, such as lower level courts and the police, fail as third-party enforcing devices. They fail partly because the demand for law enforcement is simply too high, as is reflected in the spur in crime rates and the public discontent with public insecurity that is reflected in survey after survey. But they fail also because these institutions, accustomed to enforcing the laws in authoritarian settings, cannot meet their obligations under more open, fair conditions. They either violate individual rights when enforcing the laws, or let crime go unpunished.

Society's control over the agents of law enforcement is simply too imperfect. Not all authoritarian institutions disappear with democratization. By their own institutional design, the judicial power and the police can serve as ideal authoritarian enclaves. Politicians possess imperfect control over the judicial power partly due to institutions that seek to insulate judges from politics. Thus, for example, politicians normally do not control promotions and dismissals, and these rules are binding because they are written in constitutions. But even if politicians could unanimously agree to replace these rules, it would be simply impossible to replace the entire judicial power—there are simply not enough available qualified people. A similar dilemma is related to the police. Politicians cannot simply replace the police from scratch.

To summarize, in many Latin American countries, there seem to be improvements in the liberty dimension of the rule of law, as reflected in better functioning systems of checks and balances that are there to limit the power of majorities—to solve, that is, the classic Madisonian dilemma of 'majority tyranny'. These improvements, however, are not matched with improvements on the security dimension of the rule of law. There is more insecurity and most encroachments of individual rights by the state take place in a decentralized fashion, not by the main political players such as the head of the Executive or the majority in Congress, but under the hands of lower level bureaucrats, judges and the police.

The argument can be graphically summarized in Figure 9.1. The vertical axis represents the liberty dimension of the rule of law and the horizontal axis is the security dimension. There can be more liberty, at the expense of security and legality, as in some democratization processes. Conversely, there can be more security at the expense of liberty, as was the case during the breakdown of democracy in the Southern Cone, for example. The optimal equilibrium is where the state is both strong enough to enforce rights, but sufficiently limited so as not to prey on its citizens.

The worse possible scenario is the lower-left quadrant where there is neither liberty nor security. Here the state preys upon the citizenry *and* citizens encroach upon each other's rights. Olson (1993) provides an example of this type of equilibrium, namely a state composed of roving bandits who live on the basis of stealing from the citizens, who in turn arm themselves to protect their rights.

	Security (Principal source of threat to rights comes from private agents, although institutions for law enforcement can encroach by not enforcing the laws)	
	No	Yes
Liberty (Principal source of threat to rights is the state) Institutions for Limited Government exist; Legislative decisions are controlled; likelihood of 'unjust laws' minized through checks and balances and judicial review.	**Yes** — Limited government, powerless state	Rule of Law
	No — Anarchy with 'Roving Bandits'	Autocratic Social Order

FIG. 9.1. *The dual dimension of the Rule of Law*

The authoritarian state can prey upon citizens' rights, although it normally can enforce the laws and generate order. Many strong authoritarian systems do not face acute agency problems, and the autocrat can control its agents of law enforcement to apply the laws, unjust as they might be. In these systems there is law and order at the expense of liberty. This is the lower-right quadrant, where laws are enforced, there is little crime, but there are not effective limits on the state. Cases such as Chile under Pinochet and Spain under Franco fit this characterization. As the autocrat weakens, facing agency problems in the enforcement of laws or competition from other violent holders, the system moves toward the lower-left quadrant.

The ideal is the upper-right quadrant where a fairly limited government exists such that checks and balances minimize the likelihood of majority tyranny, and the existing institutions for law enforcement enforce the laws in an impartial manner, respecting fundamental rights and successfully apprehending and punishing criminals.

In the upper-left quadrant a fairly limited government exists in the sense that there are sufficient veto players to inhibit majority tyranny, but where the state fails enforcing the laws. As said above, it can fail because there is simply too much crime or because of an agency problem that allows arbitrary law enforcement. Here private agents *and* lower level bureaucrats, courts and the police, rather than legislative decisions, encroach rights. In this type of system there is a fairly functioning system of horizontal exchange (checks and balances), but no effective rule of law. As the following sections try to show, Mexico should be currently located in this upper-left quadrant.

Horizontal Exchange, the Supreme Court and Party Hegemony

Until very recently, checks and balances did not work in Mexico and the president, if he so desired, could always use his power arbitrarily. The Mexican political system was characterized by a strong *presidencialismo*, a strong dominance of the president over other branches of government deriving from sources beyond the constitution (Weldon 1997; Casar 1999; 2002).

Formally and compared to other presidential systems, the Mexican president is not a very powerful player. In fact, the Mexican presidency ranks among the weakest of the Americas in its legislative and budgetary authorities (Mainwaring and Shugart 1997; Diaz-Cayeros and Magaloni 1998). Nonetheless, in practice the president dominated the other branches of government because separation of powers was not effective. The president dominated Congress for three reasons beyond the constitution succinctly stated in Weldon (1997) and Casar (1999, 2002): (1) The president was the leader of the hegemonic party; (2) The hegemonic party controlled the majority of seats in the Lower Chamber and the Senate—the PRI did not lose the majority in the Lower Chamber until 1997 and the majority of the Senate until 2000, when it also lost the presidency; (3) Control of nominations and lack of political competition made the party extremely disciplined.

The conditions driving *presidencialismo*, in particular the executive's domination over Congress and the states, are well understood. An often-overlooked aspect of presidential power has been the lack of judicial checks on the executive. Three conditions explained presidential domination over the Supreme Court and the federal judicial power:

1. The constitution was *flexible* in practice. The president, through his party, possessed the ability to shape and reshape the fundamental rules of the game. Since the president could set the rules that were supposed to constrain him, there were no binding constitutional limits.
2. The president exercised a strong control over nominations and dismissals despite formal rules or so-called 'judicial guarantees'. As I demonstrate below, notwithstanding life-appointments, justices' tenures were extremely short and every single president from 1934 to 1994 was able to shape the composition of his 'own' Court.
3. Constitutional rules did not grant sufficient power to the Supreme Court. Politicians did not delegate enough power to interpret the constitution to the Supreme Court, excluding from judicial review virtually all cases with so-called 'political' content (cases related to elections and constitutional controversies among different branches and levels of government).

Lack of judicial checks on the executive enabled the arbitrary exercise of political power in Mexico. The president was above the constitution, which meant that there did not exist effective *substantive* limits to his power. Below, I explore each of these sources of presidential domination over the Supreme Court.

Party Hegemony and a Flexible Constitution

A constitutional tribunal is the guardian of the constitution, reviewing politicians' actions in light of some fundamental principles and rules. In particular, through judicial review, a constitutional tribunal can control legislative decisions, forcing the majority to legislate according to constitutional principles. The Court makes sure that a constitution binds shifting majorities across time, making some fundamental principles last for several generations and adapting such principles to changing societal circumstances.

As argued by Lijphart (1999), judicial review can only work effectively if it is backed by constitutional *rigidity*. A *flexible* constitution implies that the majority can always respond to an adverse judicial interpretation by changing the constitution. Thus, judicial review and constitutional rigidity require each other and are both necessary for making a constitution binding (Lijphart 1999: 29).

In Mexico, the constitution is formally rigid, requiring the approval of two-thirds of both federal assemblies plus the majority of state's legislatures. During the years of party hegemony, however, the constitution was in practice *flexible* and endogenous to the president's will. Until the national elections of 1988, the PRI enjoyed the necessary super-majorities to unilaterally amend the constitution. The PRI recovered the necessary majority to amend the constitution unilaterally in 1991–94, but President Carlos Salinas (1988–1994) followed the practice to include the PAN in all major constitutional changes taking place in that period so as to legitimize them.

Between 1917, when it was originally drafted, and 1988, the constitution was unilaterally amended by the PRI more than 400 times. Presidents tended to imprint their policy agendas in the constitution, starting their terms with a long list of constitutional amendments. Thus, all major policy shifts such as the nationalization of the oil industry, electricity and the banks were included in the constitution. As with the nationalization of the banks in 1982, Mexican politicians often implemented policies of questionable constitutional validity and ex post 'legalized' these policies by reforming the constitution. Since PRI politicians could set the rules that were supposed to constrain them, there were no binding constitutional limits for courts to interpret and enforce.

Mexican Presidents also employed their power over the constitution to increasingly restrict the powers of the Supreme Court. Through the years, presidents added in the constitution a long list of substantive issue-areas that could not be reviewed through the *amparo procedure* such as conflicts over property rights arising from the agrarian reform; electoral issues, which included not only conflicts over the constitutionality of electoral laws, but in addition, all conflicts surrounding the organization, monitoring and sanctioning of elections, among others.

Equally significant, presidents employed their power over the constitution to jeopardize the Supreme Court by continuously modifying the rules for appointing and dismissing Justices. Table 9.3 presents an overview of the constitutional changes dealing with the federal judicial power since 1917 until the present. These changes reflect a court that until 1994 became increasingly weaker over the years. Below I review the constitutional changes regarding the size of the Court and appointments and dismissals.

TABLE 9.3. *Change of constitutional rules regarding size, appointments, terms and dismissal of the Supreme Court*

	No. Justices	Subunits?	Appointments Justices	Terms Justices	Dismissal Justices	Appointments Magistrates and Judges (Federal Judicial Power)	Terms Magistrates and Judges (Federal Judicial Power)
1917	11	None	States with a 2/3 vote of Chamber of Deputies and Senate	Life (from 1923)	Impeachment	Supreme Court	4 yrs (law establishes life tenures for appointments after 1923, not constitution)
1928	16	3	President with approval by majority in Senate	Life	Impeachment 'or' misconduct	Supreme Court	Life (law establishes, however, life tenures only for appointments after 1928)
1934	21	4	President with approval by majority in Senate	Six years	Impeachment 'or' misconduct	Supreme Court	6 yrs
1944	26	4	President with approval by majority in Senate	Life	Impeachment 'or' misconduct	Supreme Court	Life

TABLE 9.3. *contd.*

	No. Justices	Subunits?	Appointments Justices	Terms Justices	Dismissal Justices	Appointments Magistrates and Judges (Federal Judicial Power)	Terms Magistrates and Judges (Federal Judicial Power)
1951	26	5	President with approval by majority in Senate	Life	Misconduct with prior impeachment	Supreme Court	4 yrs and after tenure revision, life
1967	26	5	President with approval by majority in Senate	Life	Impeachment 'or' misconduct	Supreme Court	4 yrs and after tenure revision, life
1982	26	5	President with approval by majority in Senate	Life	Impeachment, according to Título IV of Constitution	Supreme Court	4 yrs and after tenure revision, life
1987	26	5	President with approval by majority in Senate	Life	Impeachment, according to Título IV of Constitution	Supreme Court	6 yrs and after tenure revision, life
1994	11	2	President with approval by 2/3 vote of Senate	15 years	Impeachment, according to Título IV of Constitution	Federal Judicial Board	6 yrs and after tenure revision, life

Size of the Court   Between 1917 and 1994, the Court increased from 11 justices to 26 and back to 11. A larger Court means a weaker body. The Court became larger because it gradually became the last court of appeals in the country (*tribunal de casación*), rather than a tribunal devoted to constitutional interpretation. As a last instance, the Supreme Court reviewed *all* the trials taking place in the country, both in federal and state courts.[4]

The 1994 reform established a Court of 11 justices, reducing also the workload of the Court, since it reviews *amparo* sentences that explicitly raise constitutional issues and retains the right of *certiorary*. As I discuss below, the 1994 reform created two new mechanisms for the control of constitutionality. Today the Supreme Court is hence a true Constitutional Tribunal.

Nomination Procedures   Originally, state legislatures proposed the nominees, who had to be approved by a two-thirds vote in both chambers. In 1928 nominations were given to the president, who required a simple majority in the Senate for approval. Thus, presidents could very easily nominate justices without having to negotiate, since the PRI always had much more than majority control of the Senate. With the 1994 reform, the president keeps the right to nominate but he has to obtain the approval of a supermajority of two-thirds. As I discuss below, this rule was not binding when the new Court was created in 1994 because the PRI controlled the super-majority in the Senate. However, President Zedillo opted to negotiate with the PAN at least 4 of the 11 justices.

Length of Tenures and Dismissal Procedures   To generate a Court's independence, constitutions generally establish particular rules for length of tenures and dismissal (so-called 'judicial guarantees' in legal parlance). The idea is to insulate justices from politicians, restricting the latter's power to promote, demote or fire; cut salaries or give bonuses according to the content of a justice's decision. Constitutions normally establish life-appointments (e.g., the United States or Mexico before 1994). Other constitutions tend to establish tenures lasting for periods longer than normal electoral periods (most countries in Europe or Mexico after 1994). In either

---

[4] This is because of the nature of the *amparo* procedure. *Tribunales Colegiados* review decisions of the district courts and the decisions of the Superior Tribunals of the states. *All* the decisions of the *Tribunales Colegiados* could be appealed to the Supreme Court. Not until 1987 was the Supreme Court given the *right of certiorari*—to decide to hear a case.

case, to enhance a Court's independence, justices should only be dismissed for extraordinary reasons and through special procedures (e.g., impeachment). Politicians should not be able to cut the justices' salaries.

The 1917 constitution established that justices appointed after 1923 had life tenures and could only be dismissed through impeachment. President Lázaro Cárdenas (1934–40) dissolved the Supreme Court and established a brand new one, increasing the size of the Court as a means of filling it with justices of his liking. He also abolished life-appointments, which were reintroduced in 1944[5] and remained untouched until 1994, when 15-year tenures were introduced following similar rules to most constitutions in Europe.

Cárdenas shut down the Court because he was confronted by liberal justices who opposed agrarian reform and the series of legislations he promoted to expand the range of federal government intervention in economic activity. He also disliked the existing Court for being sympathetic to his worse enemy, former president Calles, and then still leader of the party.

The episode had long-lasting consequences for presidential–judicial relations in Mexico. It made it clear that an all-powerful presidency could respond to Supreme Court activism by shutting down the Court. Justices responded strategically by bowing their heads.

Despite life-appointments through much of the period between 1917 and 1994, dismissal procedures were extremely flexible, which in practice jeopardized life-tenures. President Calles (1928–32) introduced an important ambiguity in the constitution that made dismissal procedures very flexible: justices could be removed from their posts through impeachment 'or' due to misconduct (*mala conducta*), which had to be ratified by Congress. Although only three justices were dismissed through misconduct, the very existence of the clause conceivably established a powerful deterrent against Court confrontation with the executive (Domingo 1997: 7). The same rule applied for removing judges and magistrates of the federal judicial power. Misconduct as a means for dismissal was temporarily erased between 1951 and 1967, when misconduct could only be claimed through impeachment. Impeachment became the only legal dismissal procedure from 1982.

Presidents thus exercised as strong control over the Supreme Court by shaping the rules of the game. The constitution was not binding because the power it was meant to constrain could modify

---

[5] Although not reported in the table, judges and magistrates of the federal judicial system are appointed for six years and after that they can get tenure.

it. By directly controlling the PRI, and indirectly the Federal Congress and state legislatures, the president became the de facto legislator in the country. And the Supreme Court could not impose substantive limits to his legislative decisions because the president also determined constitutional rules.

Presidents Jeopardized Supreme Court Independence

The second reason driving the Supreme Court's subordination is that the president controlled nominations and dismissals despite formal rules that established life-appointments. To see why control over nominations and dismissal is central for explaining presidential control over the Court, consider the literature on industrial organization.

When a principal (let us say the president) wants a certain agent (the Supreme Court) to perform certain functions on his behalf (interpret the constitution according to his interests), it has to successfully delegate authority. By definition, if there is unsuccessful delegation, the Supreme Court becomes independent.

Delegation contracts require solutions to two types of problems: problems of *adverse selection*, which result from lack of information of the agent's 'type', and *moral hazard*, resulting from the impossibility of fully monitoring the agent's job. Adverse selection problems can be overcome by screening devices and moral hazard ones by sanctioning (Kiewiet and McCubbins 1991).

In the game between the president and the Supreme Court, what this implies is that the Court should be more subservient to the President (act in his behalf) as he exercises stronger control over the nomination of justices, *and* as he possesses more instruments to sanction them. Control over nominations is weaker as the number of veto points necessary for approving them increases. An increase in veto points is a form of establishing multiple principals, which tends to increase the power of the agent (Kiewiet and McCubbins 1991).

Hegemonic *presidencialismo* implied that presidents could unilaterally choose justices of their liking because they confronted no veto players in the Senate. One could argue that although justices were highly *partisan*, presidents would anyway face constraints by inheriting justices nominated by previous presidents. However, presidents inherited few justices from the past, which implies that each president was able to shape the composition of his 'own' Court.

Table 9.4 presents the number and percentage of justices that each president appointed since 1934 until the present. The

TABLE 9.4. *Number of Justices appointed by President*

President	Number of Justices	% of Court appointed
Lázaro Cardenas (1934–1940)	24	114%
Manuel Avila Camacho (1940–1946)	24	96%
Miguél Alemán (1946–1952)	12	48%
Adolfo Ruiz Cortinez (1952–1958)	18	72%
Adolfo López Mateos (1958–1964)	9	36%
Gustavo Diaz Ordaz (1964–1970)	14	56%
Luis Echeverría Alvarez (1970–1976)	13	52%
José López Portillo (1976–1982)	16	64%
Miguel de la Madrid Hurtado (1982–1988)	20	80%
Carlos Salinas de Gortari (1988–1994)	8	30'%
Ernesto Zedillo (1994–2000)	11	100%

Note: Justices appointed the year when a presidential term starts are counted for the coming president.

Sources: Own calculations come from Magaloni (1996) with data from Camp (1982) and on the basis of *Diccionario Biográfico del Gobierno Mexicano*, years 1984, 1989 and 1992.

overwhelming majority of presidents appointed more than 50 per cent of justices during their terms. These figures are more striking when considering that during most of this period, the constitution established that justices were appointed for life. Lázaro Cárdenas (1934–40), Manuel Avila Camacho (1940–46) and Ernesto Zedillo are the exceptions since in 1934, 1940 and 1994 the Court was temporarily dissolved, only to reinstall a totally new one under a different set of rules.[6] Hence each of these presidents appointed their entire Court.

Table 9.5 presents information on the turnover rates of justices. The average tenure lasted for only 10 years. On average, the appointment age was 56 and the retirement age was 63. This demonstrates that age is actually not driving instability of tenures, since most retirements occurred quite early. What is most striking is that between 1934 and 1994, when appointments were for life,

[6] Recall that in 1934 Cardenas abolishes life-appointments to establish a six-year rule. Avila Camacho re-established life appointments but almost completely renewed the Court. In the last reform only two justices out of 11 were reappointed.

close to 40 per cent of justices lasted less than 5 years, coming and going according to the presidential term.

What stands out more about Tables 9.4 and 9.5 is that during most of the time life-appointments existed. The president could thus somehow create vacancies to be filled by justices he appointed or, put in other terms, he could either dismiss justices or induce early retirements, or both.

A way to empirically test whether justices left due to threats or freely is by looking at what they did after the Court. After all, justices resigned a lifelong appointment and presumably, if they left freely, they should have resigned to achieve a more prestigious or powerful position—an awkward alternative for justices who strictly follow judicial careers.

In Magaloni (1996), I codified judicial careers according to the positions justices occupied before and after leaving the Court. Justices came from a mixture of political and judicial tracks. I found that of the justices who occupied the Court between 1934 and 1994, 38 per cent had had a judicial career; 26 per cent a political career, by which I mean that they at least occupied one elective office before arriving to the Court; and 33 per cent had a career within the federal or state bureaucracies prior to appointment. In Domingo's (1997) data, 29 per cent occupied a position in the judiciary prior to appointment and 47 per cent a political position, which seems to include elected and non-elected positions.

TABLE 9.5. *Turnover rates of Justices of the Supreme Court*

Range of term (years)	Percentage
1–5	39
6–10	27
11–15	25
16–20	7
21–25	2
Average term	10
Average age of incoming justices	56
Average age of outgoing justices	63

Source: Own calculations come from Magaloni (1996) with data from Camp (1982) and on the basis of *Diccionario Biográfico del Gobierno Mexicano*, years 1984, 1989 and 1992.

For the purpose of the argument, the information of what they did after the Court is more important. Of the justices who left the Court between 1934 and 1994, I found that only 23 per cent occupied significant positions *immediately* after leaving the Court (for the rest there is no data to tell where they went). Of those who had an important position after the Court, I find that the largest percentage (38) left the Court to occupy a governorship, followed by a variety of posts in the federal executive (26), a senatorial seat (26) and a seat in the chamber of deputies (5).

These data reveal an important trait of Mexico's political system under the PRI and how this impacted presidential–Supreme Court relationships. As has been noted, most public offices, elective or not, were employed as part of a system of inducements and constraints to coordinate political ambitions within a single-party label (Smith 1979; Camp 1980). Due to the rule of non-consecutive re-election for all elective offices, politicians circulated from one institution to the other—from governorships, to congressional and senatorial seats, to jobs in the bureaucracies and back again. The Supreme Court formed part of this partisan system of elite circulation, where politicians arrived to the Court and left, following their political ambitions. Put succinctly by Domingo (1997), 'the Supreme Court is seen as one more position in a political career which aspires to reach higher levels of office. The dynamic nature of career paths in the Court, despite life tenure is also clearly an indication of the relatively low esteem in which the office of Supreme Court minister in held' (Domingo 1997: 15).

Thus, not all justices who left the Court did so because they were threatened. Some left because they preferred to be governors or high-level bureaucrats. Others left because they were told to do so and were given nothing in exchange. The president, as head of the party that controlled nominations, had a strong say in all of these decisions.

The Supreme Court was thus subservient to the president because most justices tended to follow *partisan* careers before or after leaving the Court, creating strong incentives to please the leader of the party, namely the president, as a means to further their political ambitions.[7]

---

[7] By *partisan* careers I not only mean careers within the party but moving, along the structure of political opportunities in Mexico's one-party dominant system, from the state bureaucracies, to elected positions, to the party and back again or vice versa.

An additional important implication of the merging of *partisan* and judicial carriers was that justices were socialized within the PRI system. Although it would be impossible to determine what a 'PRI judicial philosophy' exactly looked like, no doubt it was anti-pluralistic and deferential toward the presidency, none of which were conducive for constitutional interpretation and Court activism. Constitutional interpretation requires differing points of views regarding a conception of government power and its limits. It is when these issues are contested that constitutional interpretation serves some important function in politics and society.

Politicians Delegated Limited Constitutional Powers to the Supreme Court

Up until 1994, Mexican politicians did not delegate enough power to interpret the constitution to the Supreme Court and the federal judicial power, excluding from judicial review virtually all cases with so-called 'political content': cases related to the organization, monitoring and implementation of elections and electoral laws; and 'constitutional controversies' or conflicts among different branches or levels of government with respect to their constitutionality of their acts. This meant that an impressive variety of cases were out of the reach of the Court. If, for example, the government stole an election from an opposition candidate, he or she could not raise the issue to any tribunal within the judicial power in the country, let alone the Court. If the government issued biased electoral laws, they could not be questioned before the Court. Similarly, the Court could not hear conflicts between the federal government and the states and so issues of fiscal federalism and the distribution of resources across subunits; territorial limits; inter-state commerce; and conflicts among governors and municipalities were resolved informally, through internal party rules, not constitutional rules.

The Federal Judicial Power decided on *amparo* trails. Through the *amparo*, individuals can sue state authorities for violating their rights or issuing and applying laws that go against the constitution. Federal Courts have tended to limit themselves to enforce the 'principle of legality' instead of interpreting laws or government's actions in light of the constitution. The Courts, that is, have tended to serve as agent of the politicians, monitoring how state authorities enforce laws previously approved by Congress and the President, and have seldom questioned the substantive content of those laws. But even when Courts have questioned laws, the *cláusula Otero* implies that decisions on constitutionality do not have 'general effects', but only affect the parts in the specific dispute. In practice this means that politicians validly can enforce laws that the Courts regard as unconstitutional, affecting the rights of all individuals who did not employ an *amparo* trail.

These set of rules that severely limited the role of the Supreme Court derive from the constitutional doctrine dating back from the 19th century. Before the constitutional crisis of 1876, the Supreme Court played an active political role, arbitrating conflicts between the federation and the states and, beyond that, enforcing the federal constitution against local authorities that violated state constitutions or perpetuated themselves in power by stealing the elections. The Court then heard electoral conflicts and often annulled elections.

Problems were encountered when the Court questioned the legitimacy of local authorities; however, when it questioned the legitimacy of the president, a constitutional crisis resulted. President Lerdo de Tejada (1872–76) re-elected himself under very questionable elections. The then president of the Court and vice-president of the country, Jose Maria Iglesias, sought to nullify the elections and call for a new ballot, where his name would not appear. A violent rebellion threw Lerdo de Tejada out of office and in his place the soon to become dictator for close to 30 years, Porfirio Diaz, assumed the presidency.

The new president of the Supreme Court, Ignacio Vallarta, dramatically changed constitutional doctrine on two grounds. First, he argued that the judicial power should not hear electoral conflicts because politics would 'contaminate' the Court. Secondly, he argued for self-restraint on constitutional issues. Constitutional controversies gave a lot of power to the Supreme Court; but according to Vallarta, the Court should employ such power with moderation, restraining itself so as not to invade or overshadow the other branches of government or encroach on state's sovereignty. Vallarta believed that instead of the Court, a political body such as the Senate should arbitrate constitutional controversies.

The Iglesias–Vallarta controversy had an echo in the drafting of the 1917 Constitution. Constitutional delegate Machorro Narváez defended a more activist approach, arguing that the Court should hear constitutional controversies. According to him, conflicts among different branches of government, and in particular, among the powers of a state, all necessarily had constitutional content, notwithstanding that they were actually political in nature. 'Conflicts among different branches of government will all revolve around the application of a law, which each branch will interpret in their favour' (Diario de debates del Congreso Constituyente 1987: 486). Delegate Hilario Medina, instead, argued that the Court should not hear conflicts with 'political content': 'it is dangerous that the Court hears political conflicts; these will jeopardize its prestige, will corrupt it. Political parties, demagogues, the media, will all go to the Court to do politics' (Diario de debates 1987: 486). According to Medina, a political body such as the Senate should arbitrate constitutional controversies.

The debate was not settled and the 1917 Constitution actually reflects both constitutional doctrines. Thus, according to articles 76 and 105, both the Senate and the Court could hear 'constitutional controversies', namely controversies arising among different branches or levels of government about the constitutionality of their acts. In the 1920s and beginning of the 1930s, the Supreme Court heard various types of constitutional controversies (Gonzalez Avelar 1994). Most often these included conflicts between local legislators and governors (e.g., legislators recurred to the Court because they were expelled from the assembly) or between governors and municipalities (e.g., a governor simply decided to disappear a municipality). A procedural problem was that all these conflicts had to be raised through the *amparo* procedure, and the claimant had to argue that his individual rights had been violated.

Some years later, the Senate actually absorbed all constitutional controversies, including the controversial 'dissolution of local powers' of the states. The Court eventually established a doctrine of self-restraint *a la* Vallarta, arguing that constitutional controversies had a strong 'political content' and that the Court should not hear political issues—obviously including electoral disputes.

Once the hegemony of a single-party was established, politicians no longer chose the Court as the appropriate forum. In the 1920s, a multiplicity of parties, many centred on powerful regional bosses, governed in the country. Politicians thus turned to the Court because the PRI did not exist as a coordinating device. After the PRI established its hegemony in government, conflicts among different branches or levels of government, if they existed, were solved internally and the ultimate arbiter was the party's leader, the president.

Thus, party hegemony and the resulting *presidencialismo* not only implied that checks and balances did not work, but compromised the political role of the Supreme Court as arbiter of constitutional conflicts between different branches of government and guardian of federalism. The constitution thus did not serve as coordinating device in Mexico's political system. The president solved all political disputes in the country through his leadership of the hegemonic party, the PRI.

Democratization and Horizontal Exchange: A New Constitutional Role for the Supreme Court

In 1994 President Zedillo obtained approval of a constitutional reform that transformed Mexico's Supreme Court into a constitutional tribunal. As said above, the reform reduced the number of justices from 25 to 11. Life-appointments were changed to 15-year appointments. The president nominates justices, who now have to be approved by a two-thirds vote in the Senate. The reform also established a controversial Judicial Board (*Consejo de la Judicatura*) in charge of administering the federal judicial power and in particular to select judges and determine promotions. The most significant changes were the introduction of two new mechanisms for the control of constitutionality.

In the constitutional controversies (*controversias constitucionles*) the Court can adjudicate controversies among different branches or levels of government with respect to the constitutionality of their acts. Thus, the Court can now hear conflicts among the executive and the legislative branches; the Federal government and the states; and the municipalities and the governorships.

The second mechanism for the control of constitutionality is the so-called constitutional actions (*acciones de inconstitucionalidad*), a form of judicial review. Constitutional actions can be promoted by 33 per cent of the members of the Chamber of Deputies or the Senate against federal laws or international treaties; 33 per cent of the members of the local assemblies against state laws; the Attorney General (Procurador General) against federal and state laws or international treaties; by the leadership of any political party registered before the Federal Electoral Institute against federal electoral laws. Local parties can also promote an action of unconstitutionality against local electoral laws. Judicial review for electoral laws was not part of the original reform; it was added in 1996. The Supreme Court's decisions can have general effects only when eight justices vote in favour, and the decision involves constitutional interpretation.

These reforms are markedly against the Vallarta doctrine that so strongly influenced Mexican constitutional doctrine during the entire century. The crucial question is then why politicians, and in particular the president, decided to create a more powerful and independent Supreme Court. Why did they choose, that is, to endow the Court with the power of judicial review and constitutional controversies?

The answer to these questions is found in the changing nature of the party system that democratization brought about. A distinctive trait of Mexico's democratization process is that democracy was gradually constructed from the localities to the center (Diaz-Cayeros et al. 2000). The equilibrium of hegemonic *presidencialismo*, where the president serves as the ultimate, often arbitrary, arbiter of political conflicts under a not binding set of constitutional rules is no longer stable with multipartism at the local level. PRI politicians possessed incentives to abide the president's decisions because otherwise they faced a credible threat of expulsion from the party. However, when politicians of different partisan affiliations govern at the local level, they no longer possess incentives to abide by the president's decisions.

By the time the 1994 constitutional reform was enacted, Mexico was no longer a one-party dominant system. Elections were highly competitive and politicians of different parties governed at the local level. By 1994, the PRI had already lost three gubernatorial elections, and the opposition governed in more than 20 per cent of the municipalities. There was a tipping point around 1995, when municipalities and states started to defect from the PRI *en masse*. After 1995, the PRI systematically lost both in local and federal races.

Democratization and electoral pluralism drove the president to empower the Supreme Court. Politicians needed to find alternative mechanisms for solving disputes and coordinating political life under a different, multiparty polity. When there was only one party in office, the party provided, through the presidency, such a device. Multipartism implies that the president can no longer serve as the arbiter of political conflicts. As was clear before the introduction of the 1994 constitutional reform to the Supreme Court, elected politicians of different partisan affiliations had either the option to continuously crash onto each other or, instead, search for a coordinating device in the constitution. They eventually turned to the constitution and chose to delegate to the Supreme Court rather than the president the power to interpret it.

The reform appears to anticipate the era of intense electoral pluralism that came after the critical year of 1995. However, the difficulty of making politicians abide by the president's decisions was evident before the tipping point took place. This difficulty is clearly exemplified with the so-called *concertaceciones*, first during the Carlos Salinas presidency and later during Zedillo's. In several instances, the most notorious being the 1989 elections in Guanajuato, Carlos Salinas opted to 'solve' controversies that arose between the PRI and the Partido Acción Nacional (PAN) over contested local electoral results by siding with the PAN and forcing the PRI to step down from office. Salinas sided with the PAN in Guanajuato for three reasons: first, the PAN threatened to paralyze the state and called for a general strike; second, Carlos Salinas needed the PAN's support for the approval of his constitutional reforms and gave in exchange his support in contested local electoral races such as Guanajuato; third, the president anticipated that the local PRI organization and the candidate, Ramón Aguirre, would abide by his decision. Although Carlos Salinas was right in that Ramón Aguirre stepped down from office, the *concertacesiones* created serious bitterness within the PRI.

The PRI would eventually rebel against the president, however. Years later, when Ernesto Zedillo attempted to solve, through a *concertaceción,* a conflict between the Partido de la Revolución Democrática (PRD) and the PRI in the state of Tabasco, the candidate of the PRI, Roberto Madrazo, refused to step down from office. The PRI's rebellion in Tabasco took place one month before Zedillo propose the 1994 constitutional reform where he delegated power to the Court. The president opted to delegate to the Supreme Court the power to rule on constitutional issues as a means to protect his authority and leadership.

The new Supreme Court is really an arbiter of political conflicts, now available for elected politicians of different partisan affiliations. Table 9.6 shows the number of constitutional actions and constitutional controversies that the Court received between 1995 and 1998. Clearly, elected politicians are employing the Court. Most notably, the overwhelming majority of constitutional controversies and constitutional actions involve elected politicians belonging to different partisan affiliations. A thorough study of these decisions is needed to determine whether there are systematic biases in the Court's decisions and the evolution of constitutional doctrine, a task that goes beyond the scope of this paper. There is evidence that seems to indicate that the new Supreme Court is becoming a highly independent and ever more powerful body.

TABLE 9.6. *Number of actions and controversies filed at the Supreme Court*

	Constitutional actions	Constitutional controversies
1995	1	19
1996	10	57
1997	10	36
1998	12	29

Source: Supreme Court, Unidad de Controversias Constitutionales.

Thus, the conditions explaining presidential control over the Court have changed. First, the constitution is not any more endogenous to presidential interests, since the PRI no longer holds the necessary supermajority to amend it. Nomination procedures also changed, since a two-thirds vote in the Senate is required for approval. The president nominated the current justices after negotiations with the PAN. Current justices appear to be less *partisan*[8] than previous and their tenures seem to be more stable, since none of the justices have left the Court prematurely. Finally, the Supreme Court now has the power to interpret the constitution. The Court is thus becoming an important player within the institutions of checks and balances and particularly federalism.

And the Rule of Law?

A more independent and stronger Supreme Court certainly moves in the right direction toward the consolidation of the rule of law. The changes are an improvement along what I have labelled the *liberty* dimension of the rule of law. Despite the reform, more than ever before, there is a strong demand for the 'rule of law' among the population on what I have called the security dimension of the rule of law.

[8] Of the original 11 justices, only two justices were reappointed. There is also some change in the personal profile of justices since the overwhelming majority (64 percent) came from the judicial power or had been public notaries (18 percent). Only two justices (18 percent) had had a carrier in the federal government and none had occupied elected-offices.

In the quarterly surveys collected since March 1998 by *Reforma* newspaper in Mexico City, crime, violence and public insecurity have been continuously mentioned as the main problem facing the City by close to 60 per cent of respondents (see Table 9.7). Most citizens, moreover, believe that these problems are mainly the product of police corruption and the inefficiency of public institutions that prosecute and punish crime. In the same surveys, close to 60 per cent believe that the police are corrupt and 30 per cent believe that the 'overwhelming majority of policemen are committing the crimes'.[9]

The Zedillo administration proposed several policy initiatives to combat crime that seem to have been ineffective. President Zedillo proposed the so-called 'National Program of Public Safety, 1995–2000', which included a variety of measures. In particular, he allocated an emergency fund to the states that must be entirely devoted to 'public safety'. The emergency fund became a permanent federal transfer to states in the 1999 and 2000 budgets. He has also introduced several bills that seek to reform important aspects of Mexico's criminal justice system ranging from an increase in the legal sanctions, to an attempt to directly involve the army in fighting crime. Third, the national programme of public safety included a series of measures aimed at creating better instruments for screening, monitoring, and sanctioning police corruption and the so-called 'infiltration' of criminals into the police.

TABLE 9.7. *In your opinion, which is the principal problem in Mexico City?*

	May 98	June 98	Sep. 98	Dec. 98	May 99
Public safety/crime	63	54	59	59	60
Economic crisis/ unemployment	11	15	12	12	9
Corruption	8	14	8	4	4
Pollution	6	9	3	4	10

Source: *Reforma* newspaper. Columns do not add to 100% because other, less important, problems listed are not shown.

[9] The infamous series of kidnappings in the state of Morelos could be used as supporting evidence. More than 500 people were kidnapped during the last couple of years in that state. Most of them managed to get back to their families alive after paying considerable ransom. It was later discovered that most of the state police were accomplices. After a series of massive demonstrations, the scandal forced PRI governor, Carillo Olea, to resign.

Why do elected politicians, either of the PRI or the opposition, seem so incapable of supplying security to their voters, who are clearly demanding it in survey after survey? One hypothesis is that voters might not vote on the basis of politicians' performance in office or that voters do not know whom to hold accountable, the federal or state governments, for poor law enforcement and crime rates. If this were correct, the answer would be that failures in 'vertical accountability' are to blame: voters do not hold politicians accountable for law enforcement.

Another hypothesis is that the problem is beyond politicians' control. The cross-country study of Fajnzylber, Lederman and Loayza (1998) on crime suggests that this is partly true. They find that 'the rise in the crime rate may be felt long after the initial shock—countries can be engulfed in a crime wave' (1981: 26). One of the implications of their econometric results is that economic shocks and other non-economic shocks such as a sudden rise in drug trafficking can have long-lasting effects. Most transitions to democracy in Latin America and former socialist countries were triggered by poor economic performance—the debt crisis in Latin America and the economic collapse of centrally planned economies in post-communist countries. The economic downturn produced crime shocks, which tend to be perpetuated over time.

Figure 9.2 provides some evidence of the impact of economic performance on the evolution of crime rates in Mexico. It reports the total number of crimes reported per 100,000 inhabitants from 1991 to 2000, and the total number of homicides in Mexico City from 1991 to 1999. There is a sharp jump in crime rates after 1994 that seems to be the product of the Peso Crisis and the resulting economic collapse of 1995–96. Crime rates decreased slightly in 1998, but then began to increase again. Thus, there seems to be some evidence for the Mexican case that crime shocks tend to be perpetuated over time. This argument, however, is not consistent with the evolution of violent crime. Homicide rates in Mexico City did increase significantly in 1995 with the economic recession but began to decrease after 1995.

A third hypothesis is that politicians face an acute agency problem. Politicians have imperfect control over the judicial power partly due to institutions that seek to insulate judges from politics. But even if politicians could unanimously agree to replace these institutions, it would be simply impossible to replace the entire judicial power and the police—there are simply not enough available qualified people.

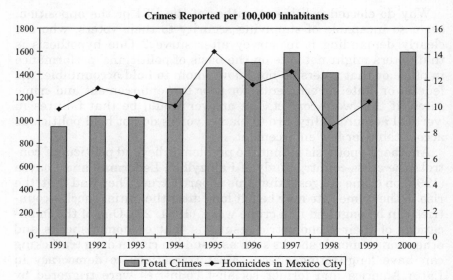

FIG. 9.2. *Crimes reported per 100,000 inhabitants (Source: Zepeda [2002].)*

A reform of the institutions of law enforcement is still pending. Judicial reform that permeates beyond the Supreme Court is essential. This implies not only reforming the federal judicial power—and the highly obsolete *amparo* procedure—but equally significant the judicial power of the states, where most civil and criminal cases are heard.

Police reform must deal with one of the central driving causes of crime rates, utter failure in the investigation and apprehension of criminals. As shown in Magaloni and Zepeda (forthcoming), most crimes go unpunished because the police fail to investigate and apprehend the criminals, not because of leniency in the judiciary. In 1997, the police and agents of the *ministerio público* managed to apprehend and bring before a court of law a suspect in 4 out of 100 crimes reported. Once the suspect reached the courts, the conviction rate by the judiciary was close to 93 percent, however.

Unfortunately, the Supreme Court or the federal judicial power have proven incapable of exerting any form of control over actions of this type on the part of the police and those who investigate and prosecute crimes. Part of the problem lies in the highly obsolete *amparo* procedure (Rubio et al. 1993). Citizens have instead opted to recur to the Human Rights Commissions. In 1998, for example, two-thirds of the cases in the National Human Rights Commission were related to violations perpetuated by the criminal justice system and the prosecutor's offices. The overwhelming majority of the cases dealt with failure to investigate and prosecute a crime.

Another strategy many follow is simply not to report crimes. The recent victimization survey conducted by the Mexican government shows that 90 percent of crimes are not reported. The comparable figures for the United States, Chile and Argentina are 63, 64 and 70 percent respectively (Zepeda 2002). Mexican citizens do not report crimes because they anticipate no reaction from the prosecutor's officials and the police. Indeed, in Magaloni and Zepeda (forthcoming) we show that the overwhelming majority of crimes reported are simply lost in the archives of the *ministerio público*.

Citizens possess no effective legal defense against prosecutors and agents of the *ministerio público*. The Constitution grants them a monopoly over criminal investigation and prosecution, which in practical terms means that no institution can effectively force them to conduct effective investigations. The agency problem in the enforcement of laws seems to stem largely from this institutional structure.

Conclusion

This paper presents a mixed evaluation of democracy, horizontal exchange and the rule of law in Latin America and Mexico. The paper gives, on the one hand, an optimistic evaluation of how democratization has enhanced horizontal exchange, namely checks and balances, and is contributing to protect liberty. It provides a more pessimistic evaluation on the prospects for building the rule of law along what I called the security dimension – enforcement of rights by an *impartial* third-party, the state.

The rule of law is the institutionalization of individual rights. The rule of law, I have argued, solves two types of dilemmas: Madisonian-like dilemmas or the establishment of limits to the state's ability to predate upon citizens' rights by adopting unfair or tyrant majority decisions; and Hobbesian-like dilemmas or protection of individuals' rights against encroachments by other private agents. I labelled these two dimensions of the rule of law as the liberty and security dimensions.

Democratization has brought significant improvements in the first dimension of the rule of law by revitalizing checks and balances and enhancing horizontal exchange. The main source of threat to individual rights no longer appears to be the 'state'— either the majority in the legislature or the president or both—

through legislative decisions. More veto players in the policy-
making arena work at minimizing the risks of excessive concentration of power in the president's hands or unrestrained majority rule
by the legislature.

But rights continued to be threatened. They are threatened both
by organized crime and decentralized encroachments by law enforcement institutions such as bureaucrats, the police and the courts.
The state is thus failing to solve the Hobbesian dilemma: protection of individuals' rights against encroachments by other private
agents by a third-party *impartial* enforcer. The rule of law does
not imply, that is, brute exercise of violence on the part of the state.
It requires the state to enforce rights according to some previously
specified rules and in an impartial manner.

A difficulty that young democracies face is that democratic politicians seem to have too little control over the institutions for law
enforcement. By their own design, the judiciary seems to be insulated from politics and is hence not accountable. Corrupt police
corps are often out of control, and it is simply too hard to replace
them from scratch. Law enforcement institutions appear to be
ideal authoritarian enclaves.

I illustrated these points with an analysis of the Mexican case,
concentrating on the role of the Supreme Court in the institutions
of checks and balances and constitutionalism. I provided three
mechanisms that explain why party hegemony meant unrestrained rule by the president; the strong dominance of the head
of the executive over the Supreme Court; and the absence of a rule
of law. The mechanisms are: a *flexible* constitution that could be
modified by the power it was supposed to restrain; the president's
unilateral control of nominations and dismissals; constitutional
rules that did not delegate enough power to the Supreme Court to
interpret the constitution.

Democratization has changed this equilibrium. The constitution
is no longer endogenous to the president's will since no party
holds the necessary supermajority to amend it. Nomination procedures also changed, since a two-thirds vote in the Senate is
now required for approval and the PRI no longer controls such a
supermajority. Finally, the Supreme Court now has the power to
interpret the constitution. Through the constitutional reform of
1994, the president opted to delegate power to the Supreme
Court to solve 'constitutional controversies' arising among different levels or branches of government about the constitutionality of
their acts. He also granted the Court judicial review through
'constitutional actions'.

The constitutional reform of 1994 produced a profound change in the relationship between the president and the judiciary and a revitalization of the Supreme Court within the system of checks and balances. The significance of these changes should be underscored, particularly considering the prevailing constitutional doctrine, dating back to the turn of the century. The Supreme Court had played no role in interpreting the constitution and controlling legislative decisions. Rather the Court had become an agent of the president and legislators, basically limited to enforcing the 'principle of legality', monitoring how state authorities enforced the laws, regardless of their substantive content. Recent decisions by the Court appear to indicate that this is no longer the case.

My optimism about democracy in Mexico comes from these changes. The pessimism comes from the fact that the revitalization of checks and balances and effective constitutional constraints have not significantly reshaped how lower level state authorities, such as the police and the lower courts, interact with citizens, and law enforcement is dismal. A reform of the institutions of law enforcement is thus still pending.

References

Ayres, Robert L. 1998. 'Crime and Violence as Development Issues in Latin America and the Caribbean'. Washington DC: World Bank.

Bates, Robert. 2001. *Prosperity and Violence*. New York and London: Norton.

Camp, Rodric. 1980. *Mexico's Leaders: Their Education and Recruitment*. Tucson, AZ: The University of Arizona Press.

Camp, Roderic. 1982. *Mexican Political Biographies 1935–1981*. Tucson, AZ: The University of Arizona Press.

Casar, María Amparo. 1999. 'Las Relaciones entre el poder Ejecutivo y el Legislativo: el caso de México' *Política y Gobierno* 1: 83–128.

Casar, María Amparo. 2002. 'Executive-Legislative Relations: the Case of Mexico (1946–1997)'. In Scott Morgenstern and Benito Nacif, eds., *Legislative Politics in Latin America*. Cambridge: Cambridge University Press.

Coase, Ronald C. 1937. 'The Nature of the Firm'. *Economica* 4 (November): 386–405.

Diario de Debates del Congreso Constituyente. 1987 (1917). Querétaro: Gobierno del Estado de Querétaro.

Diaz-Cayeros, Alberto and Beatriz Magaloni. 1998. 'Autoridad Presupuestal del Poder Legislativo en México: una Primera Aproximación'. *Política y Gobierno* 5, 2: 503–28.

Diaz-Cayeros, Alberto, Beatriz Magaloni, and Barry Weingast. 2000. 'Democratization and the Economy in Mexico: Equilibrium (PRI) Hegemony and its Demise'. Stanford, CA: Hoover Institution.

Domingo, Pilar. 1997. 'Judicial Independence: The Politics of Supreme Court Judge in Mexico'. Documento de Trabajo No. 64, División de Estudios Políticos. México DF: Centro de Investigación y Docencia Económicas.

Eggertsson, Thrainn. 1990. *Economic Behavior and Institutions*. Cambridge: Cambridge University Press.

Elster, John. 1993. 'Introduction'. In John Elster and Rune Slagstad, eds., *Constitutionalism and Democracy*. Cambridge: Cambridge University Press

Fajnzylber, Pablo, Daniel Lederman and Norman Loayza. 1998. 'What Causes Violent Crime?' Washington, DC: The World Bank.

Gonzalez Avelar, Miguel. 1994. 'La Suprema corte y la Politica'. Mexico City: Coordinacion dé Humanidades, UNAM.

Henisz, Witold J. 2000. 'The Institutional Environment for Economic Growth'. *Economics and Politics* 12, 1: 1–31.

Huntington, Samuel. 1968. *Political Order in Changing Societies*. New Haven, CT and London: Yale University Press

Kiewiet, Roderick and Mathew McCubbins. 1991. *The Logic of Delegation*. Chicago, IL: The University of Chicago Press.

Lederman, Daniel. 1999. 'Crime in Argentina: A Preliminary Assessment'. Washington, DC: The World Bank Documents.

Lijphart, Arend. 1999. *Patterns of Democracy: Government Forms and Performance in Thirty-Six Countries*. New Haven, CT: Yale University Press.

Magaloni, Beatriz. 1996. 'Ambición Política y Suprema Corte en México'. Centro de Investigación para el Desarrollo (mimeo).

Magaloni, Beatriz and G. Zepeda Lecuona. Forthcoming. 'Local Institutional Performance and Violent Crime in Mexico'. In Kevin Middlebrook, ed., *Dilemmas of Change in Mexican Politics*. San Diego, CA: Center for U.S.–Mexican Studies, University of California, San Diego.

Magaloni, Beatriz and G. Zepeda Lecuona. n.d. 'La Geografía del Crímen y sus Causas'. Unpublished paper.

Mainwaring, Scott and Matthew Soberg Shugart. 1997. 'Presidentialism and Democracy in Latin America: Rethinking the Terms of the Debate'. In Scott Mainwaring and Matthew Soberg Shugart, eds., *Presidentialism and Democracy in Latin America*. Cambridge: Cambridge University Press.

Navarro, J. C and R. Pérez Perdomo. 1991. *Seguridad Personal: Un Asalto al Tema*. Caracas: Ediciones IESA.

North, Douglas and Barry Weingast. 1989. 'Constitutions and Commitment'. *Journal of Economic History* 49, 4: 803–32.

O'Donnell, Guillermo. 1994. *Counterpoints: Selected Essays on Authoritarianism and Democracy*. Notre Dame, IN: University of Notre Dame Press.

—— 1999. *Counterpoints: Selected Essays on Authoritarianism and Democratization*. Notre Dame, IN: University of Notre Dame Press.

Olson, Mancur. 1993. 'Dictatorship, Democracy and Development'. *American Political Science Review* 87, 3: 567–76

Powell, Bingham G. and Guy D. Whitten. 'A Cross-National Analysis of Economic Voting: Taking Account of the Political Context'. *American Journal of Political Science* 37, 2 (May 1993): 391–414.

Przeworski, Adam and Fernando Limongi. 1993. 'Political Regimes and Economic Growth'. *Journal of Economic Perspectives* 7(Summer): 51–69.

Przeworski, Adam and Jose Antonio Cheibub. 1999. 'Democracy, Elections and Accountability for Economic Outcomes'. In Adam Przeworski, Susan Stokes, and Karen Remmer. 1991. 'The Political Impact of Economic Crisis in Latin America in the 1980s'. *American Political Science Review* 85: 777–800.

Rubio, Luis, Edna Jaime, and Beatriz Magaloni. 1993. *A La Puerta de la Ley*. México: Cal y Arena.

Smith, Peter. 1979. *Labyrinths of Power: Political Recruitment in Twentieth-Century Mexico*. Princeton, NJ: Princeton University Press

Stiglitz, Joseph E. 1974. 'Incentives and Risk Sharing in Share Cropping'. *Review of Economic Studies* 41, 2: 219–55.

Stokes, Susan C. 1996. 'Introduction to Public Opinion and Market Reforms: The Limits of Economic Voting'. and 'Economic Reform and Public Opinion in Peru: 1990–1995'. Both in *Comparative Political Studies* 29, 5 (October).

Tsebelis, George. 1995. 'Decision Making in Political Systems: Veto Players in Presidentialism, Parliamentarism, Multicameralism and Multipartyism'. *British Journal of Political Science* 25, 3: 289–325.

Weingast, Barry. 1997. 'The Political Foundations of Democracy and the Rule of Law'. *American Political Science Review* 91, 2 (June): 245–63.

Weldon, Jeffrey. 1997. 'Political Sources of *Presidencialismo* in Mexico'. In Scott Mainwaring and Matthew Soberg Shugart, eds., *Presidentialism and Democracy in Latin America*. Cambridge: Cambridge University Press.

Williamson, Oliver E. 1985. *The Economic Institutions of Capitalism: Firms, Markets, Relational Contracting*. New York, NY: The Free Press

Zepeda, Guillermo. 2002. *El Crímen y la Procuración de Justicia en Mexico*. Doctoral dissertation, Instituto de Investigaciones Jurídicas, UNAM.

Societal Accountability

Part IV

Societal Accountability

10

Societal and Horizontal Controls: Two Cases of a Fruitful Relationship

Catalina Smulovitz
Enrique Peruzzotti

Introduction

Citizens' actions aimed at overseeing political authorities are becoming an established aspect of political life and are rapidly redefining traditional links between the represented and their representatives. The emergence of a politics of rights-oriented discourses, of media scandals exposing governmental wrongdoing and of social movements organized around the demand of due process are only a few examples of the ways in which this politics of accountability is taking place.

In spite of the scope of the phenomenon, recent evaluations of the institutional performance of Latin American democracies have belittled the significance of these societal mechanisms of accountability (Smulovitz and Peruzzotti 2000; Peruzzotti and Smulovitz 2002). Current debates on the nature of these regimes tend to view the weakness or inadequacy of traditional accountability mechanisms as the defining characteristic of these democracies.[1] By focusing on the workings of traditional mechanisms of accountability, such as elections or the division of powers and the existence of an effective system of checks and balances among them, these diagnoses tend to ignore the growth of alternative forms of political control that rely on citizens' actions and organizations.[2] By focusing on traditional mechanisms, the literature is overlooking the fact that societal mechanisms of accountability are not only dis-

[1] O'Donnell (1993b, 1994, 1995, 1998); Schedler, Diamond and Plattner (1999); Shifter (1997); Stokes (1999); Zakaria (1997). For a critical review of some of those arguments, see Peruzzotti (2001a, 2001b).

[2] For this distinction see O'Donnell (1998).

310   *Catalina Smulovitz et al.*

tinctive features of the recent wave of democratization in Latin America, but also that they are critical for the activation of horizontal mechanisms.

In this chapter we analyze the ways in which these different mechanisms of accountability interact. We consider some conceptual aspects of this relationship and analyse its actual operation through two specific cases.

Social Initiatives and Horizontal Mechanisms

Societal accountability involves actions carried out by actors with differing degrees of organization that recognize themselves as legitimate claimants of rights.[3] A wide array of citizen associations, movements, or the media initiates these actions. They aim to expose governmental wrongdoing, bring new issues to the public agenda or influence or reverse policy decisions implemented by public officials. They employ both institutional and non-institutional tools. In the first case, they involve the activation of legal claims in oversight agencies or participation in institutional arenas for monitoring and policy-making. In the second, they encompass social mobilizations and media denunciations. 'Societal accountability' is a non-electoral, yet vertical, mechanism that enlarges the number of actors involved in the exercise of control. In contrast to electoral mechanisms, societal ones can be exercised between elections, do not depend on fixed calendars, and are activated 'on demand'.

In contrast to horizontal mechanisms of accountability, societal ones perform watchdog functions without fulfilling special majority requirements or constitutional entitlements. This allows societal mechanisms to give visibility to and articulate demands of actors that may be disregarded in the representative arena (Cohen and Arato 1992; Diamond 1999: 242; Melucci 1996). Societal mechanisms also differ from horizontal and electoral (vertical) ones in that they do not entail mandatory legal sanctions, but symbolic ones. Since the imposition of costs is linked to the capacity to enforce decisions, and as these forms of control expose wrongdoings but do not have mandatory effects, some authors regard them more as window-dressing activities than as real checks on power. Andreas Schedler, for example, has characterized them as 'weak', 'toothless',

---

[3] For an analysis of the emergence of a politics of rights in Argentina see Peruzzotti (2002).

or 'diminished' forms of control (Schedler 1999: 16). However, even though societal mechanisms rely on soft forms of punishment based mostly on public disapproval, this does not necessarily mean that they lack control capacities or that the controls they exercise are weak or without institutional consequences. It is our contention that although not all societal mechanisms have mandatory effects, they can have 'material consequences'. First, because the disclosure of illegal or corrupt practices can destroy a fundamental resource of electoral politics: the symbolic capital or reputation of a politician or institution. Second, because very often these symbolic sanctions are needed for the activation of the mechanisms that have 'teeth'. That is, societal strategies are able to activate horizontal mechanisms because they can threaten public officials with the imposition of reputational or electoral consequences. Unless societal mechanisms 'turn on the alarm', it is unlikely that vertical electoral and horizontal mechanisms start to work.[4] What, then, do societal mechanisms of accountability do? And how do they affect the workings of horizontal ones?

Societal Mechanisms Expose and Denounce Wrongdoings Censure of specific cases provides vivid illustrations of shortcomings in the performance of horizontal agencies. Exposition and denunciation of wrongdoings allow the identification of real victims and victimizers as well as the identification of the scope of the damages and harms done. Public denunciations signal the existence of issues in ways the citizenry can relate to, and thereby place specific issues in a wider picture. Calling public attention to an issue may produce changes in the social appreciation of a particular phenomenon, transforming it into an issue of a more general and public interest.[5]

Signalling and exposing behaviour may have two different results. It can lead to controlling specific issues or claims or, when transformed into a topic of the public agenda, it can result in the expansion of the number of issues under surveillance. When the signalling of a problem results in the incorporation of a new topic on the public agenda, it increases the number of questions public officials can be held responsible for and can be expected to answer.

---

[4] See McCubbins and Schwartz 1984.
[5] If we were to use Keck and Sikkink's terminology this phenomenon implies 'framing' particular events into a wider cognitive frame capable of linking and organizing specific experiences into a broader interpretative understanding (Keck and Sikkink 1998: 225).

Therefore, societal mechanisms also contribute to the exercise of horizontal ones, insofar as they result in the extension of the scope of conflicts and issues public officials are obliged to answer and inform the public about.[6] The way in which specific claims regarding police violence have been transformed into an issue of citizen insecurity and police abuse illustrates this logic (Smulovitz forthcoming).

Societal Mechanisms Impose Symbolic Sanctions on Public Officials or Institutions In many occasions socially engineered strategies of accountability do not entail mandatory sanctions, but rather, symbolic ones. In democratic contexts, where the political life of elected officials depends on getting the greatest number of votes, the reputational costs that may result from these actions can become a threat to their political survival (Thompson 2002). Public disclosure of wrongdoings or of policy flaws can destroy the symbolic capital (trust and credibility) public officials may have (Thompson 2002). In contexts where political survival rests on the extension of support, public officials cannot disregard reputational threats. It could make a difference in their political survival.

Societal Mechanisms Activate the Operation of Horizontal Ones Activation of horizontal mechanisms may result (1) when a social movement organizes and mobilizes around a particular demand or claim, (2) when the media gives coverage to actions or claims of a particular movement or when it develops its own investigation with regard to an issue, or (3) when individuals or associations activate regular local judicial proceedings, international ones, or oversight agencies (Waisbord 1996, Rey 1998, Muraro 1997). These actions may result in the activation of horizontal mechanisms of accountability because they involve, on the one hand, an increase in the reputational costs confronted by public officials, and on the other, the threat of being taken to court.

Societal mechanisms can activate horizontal ones indirectly when they produce reputational costs, through social mobilization or media denunciation. The efficiency of the societal mechanisms, in this case, is mediated by public officials' evaluation of the anticipated costs of public criticism. Therefore, although these societal mechanisms may be effective, there is no guarantee that public officials will evaluate the risks faced either in a unique fashion, or

---

[6] Schedler has distinguished two main dimensions in the concept of accountability: answerability and enforcement (Schedler 1999: 14).

that they will act accordingly. If public officials become concerned about the reputational costs that social mobilization or criticism from the press may involve, the officials may attempt to minimize them by making or reversing decisions in ways that may appear responsive to the perceived public flaws. Those decisions could entail the activation of judicial procedures, of parliamentary investigative commissions, or of policy changes. Cases such as the 'María Soledad' and the 'Budge' murders analysed in this article, or the constitution of the different Comissoes Parlamentares de Inquerito in Brazil, illustrate the way in which this soft type of societal accountability results in the activation of horizontal mechanisms (Schilling 1999).

The case studies illustrate that this indirect activation of horizontal mechanisms is possible because claimants organize and mobilize, but also because they reach the media or the media reaches them. Regardless of the reasons why the media covers some of these events, one of the consequences of this new role of the media has been its simultaneous conversion into public prosecutor and judge (Camps and Pazos 1999; Waisbord 1996). Thus, once the media is revealed as an effective mechanism for controlling and accelerating public decisions, civil society organizations have used this discovery to get access to an alternative route to justice, to get attention from the public authorities, and to informally judge presumed illegal activities. Examples of this use of the media can be verified in cases such as the process that led to the impeachment of Collor or the legislative discussion about legal limitations to press freedom in Chile brought about by the Matus case. Also, the acknowledgement of this new role of the press has given rise, in some countries, to the emergence of a strong and sometimes threatening investigative journalism.

Social mechanisms directly activate horizontal mechanisms when, for example, individual or social legal mobilization activates judicial proceedings or oversight agencies (Smulovitz 1997, 1998). Since state authorities must respond to legal petitions, successful legal petitions advanced by individuals or associations allow them to use the state coercive powers to pursue their interests. For these reasons, some authors have argued that legal mobilization can be considered the paradigmatic form of democratic participation (Zemans 1983). Insofar as legal demands force the state to publicly and officially reply to the advanced legal petitions, legal mobilization (individually or collectively driven) could lead to the activation of horizontal mechanisms of control.

In recent years, two different developments can be observed in some Latin American countries with regard to the use of legal petitions that activate horizontal ones. On the one hand, in some countries (Argentina and Brazil mainly) the number of judicial claims initiated in regular courts increased (Smulovitz 1995; Vianna et al. 1999; Correa Sutil 1999). On the other hand, a number of NGOs have appeared with the purpose of using the law as an instrument to make public institutions accountable.[7] Although originally the efforts of some these organizations were centred on demands related to the violation of human rights, lately some new ones have emerged and some old ones have expanded the scope of their activities to include additional public interest concerns (Peruzzotti 2002). Their expanded agenda includes the use of the law to demand environmental rights, health rights, indigenous rights, and due process. Their activities result in the societal activation of horizontal mechanisms insofar as their petitions have, in some cases, brought about legal sentences that have forced bureaucratic agencies, the executive, and the legislatures to change policies considered unlawful. Legal mobilization has also been used to activate newly created oversight agencies such as *defensorías* and ombudsman agencies. In many cases petitions made at these oversight agencies led to claims in the judiciary, that have resulted in reversions of policies or in punishment of public officials (Smulovitz 1997; Defensoría del Pueblo de Perú 1999). Among the examples that illustrate this use of legal mobilization are the 195 municipal 'prefectos' and 'ex prefectos' that in the last five years have been sentenced for administrative wrongdoing due to claims filed at the Brazilian Ministerio Público (*Veja,* October 6 1999), or the 'collective amparos' (collective writ) that have been presented regarding discriminatory behaviour of bureaucratic agencies in Argentina (Saba and Bohmer 2000; Saba n.d.).

Societal Mechanisms Establish Parallel 'Societal Watchdog' Organizations That Monitor the Performance of Specific Public Agencies or Offices Experience shows cases in which, after some particular issues have become the object of recurrent public criticism, civic associations have been formed with the goal to continuously over-

[7] As a recently published book shows the use of the public interest law with the purpose of controlling public policy is not constrained to the Latin American experience. Similar examples are registered in Africa and Asia (McClymont and Golub 2000).

see the behaviour of certain public officials in specific policy arenas. The institutionalization of some of these movements into more permanent organizations has resulted, in some cases, in the establishment of a parallel society-based structure of oversight actors (i.e., Ouvidorias Policiales in Sao Paulo; Coordinadora contra la Represión Policial e Institucional and Centro de Estudios Legales y Sociales in Argentina; Alianza Cívica in Mexico; Transparencia in Peru). Thus, societal mechanisms can influence the performance of horizontal ones by adding relatively persistent and newly organized grassroots 'guardians of the guardians'.

In the following section, we will analyse two specific cases that will allow us to confirm some of the propositions advanced regarding the working of societal mechanisms of accountability and to formulate new ones.

The Workings of Societal Accountability: The María Soledad and Ingeniero Budge cases

Ortiz Iramaín,
para la mano dura,
también para los pobres
se acabó la dictadura
(Slogan against one of the justices that was involved in the María Soledad trial and who was suspected of partiality.)

The two cases selected will help us test the advanced propositions and will also allow us to formulate new hypotheses about the operation of societal mechanisms of accountability and their impact on horizontal ones. The cases, extracted from the Argentine scenario, have been selected because the four statements developed in the previous section can be observed. They show how societal mechanisms expose and denounce wrongdoings, how they impose symbolic sanctions, how they activate horizontal mechanisms and finally, in the second case, how societally based watchdog associations are formed. The cases are also relevant for this analysis because the three strategies—legal, mobilizational and mediatic—that can be used in the exercise of societal accountability are present. Lastly, the cases help us test the relevance of societal mechanisms for the exercise of horizontal control insofar as they took place in areas where the operation of horizontal mechanisms was impaired. The first case analysed—the María Soledad case—refers to the demand for justice in the case of a high school student who was found raped and murdered in the province of Catamarca. The second one—the Ingeniero Budge case—involved an episode of police violence that resulted in the death of three youngsters in a neighbourhood of the poor periphery of Greater Buenos Aires. In the two cases, a murder gave rise to a claim for justice and to a social mobilization aimed at guaranteeing that the public authorities did not obstruct the investigation and the judicial process. In both cases, there were trials and the culprits were found guilty. And in both cases, both the press and the population followed the development of the investigation and the judicial process closely.

Both episodes took place in what O'Donnell—in a work that analysed the uneven distribution of the rule of law within a nation-state—designated as 'brown areas', that is, areas where liberal guarantees are absent or are frequently violated by state agencies (O'Donnell 1993a.). Within the jurisdiction of a particular legal-democratic state, he argued, we can find different degrees of stateness. He distinguished three types of situations that might coexist within the same territory: 'blue areas', characterized by a high territorial and functional presence of the state; 'green areas', characterized by a high territorial presence but a low functional one; and 'brown areas', where both dimensions are low or non-existent. While in the latter, vertical electoral mechanisms of accountability may be in place and functioning, horizontal ones might be very weak or absent. In such a situation, the population of those 'brown' areas might find themselves at the mercy of discretionary public agencies and authorities.

For O'Donnell, the distribution of 'brown' spots within a national map can follow a geographical pattern (territories in the periphery that are far from central areas) or a class pattern (poor or marginal populations) (O'Donnell 1993a: 70, 1999). Each of the selected cases corresponds to one of those patterns. The María Soledad case took place in a north-western province that has been traditionally characterized by the overwhelming presence of patrimonialist circuits of power. The Ingeniero Budge case took place in a poor neighborhood of Greater Buenos Aires where discretionary police behaviour is common. In this sense, the cases may serve to show how societal mechanisms of accountability help foster horizontal mechanisms in regions in which the latter are non-existent or weak and consequently almost irrelevant for the enforcement of the rule of law. They might also serve to expose the ties and connections between certain sectors of the 'green' areas with 'brown' ones (see O'Donnell 1993a: 72). We will consider some of the characteristics of each one of them.

The María Soledad Case[8]

The María Soledad case provides a paradigmatic example of societal accountability since it combines all of the main strategies that we have distinguished in our description of societal mechanisms of accountability: social mobilization, judicialization, and mediatization. The case is also relevant due to the broad repercussions it had on Argentine public opinion and for the way it implicated different horizontal agencies, at both the local and central levels.

The case started in September of 1990 after the body of a high school student, María Soledad Morales, was found in the outskirts of the capital city of the province of Catamarca. This north-western province has been the traditional domain of the Saadi family, which dominated local politics since the late 1940s. The patriarch of the family, Vicente Leonides, was governor of the province for two terms and served twice in the Senate as representative for Catamarca. His son Ramón was elected governor in 1983 and re-elected in 1988 (succeeding his father who was governor between 1987 and 1988). Catamarca provides a textbook example of O'Donnell's 'brown' areas. Catamarca was a province crossed by circuits of privatized and sultanistic power where vertical electoral mechanisms— although in place—were permeated by extensive political clientelism, while horizontal mechanisms of accountability were largely absent. The following statement by provincial congressman Angel Luque helps illustrate the level of discretionalism under which this patrimonial system operated. Against the accusations that placed his son Guillermo as the main suspect of the murder of María Soledad, he came to his son's defence by stating if that had really been the case, 'he had enough power to be able to make the corpse "disappear"' (Uribarri n.d.). The fact that this did not happen showed, in his view, that the suspicion that some members of the local political society were indirectly involved was unfounded.

A few days after María Soledad's body was found, social mobilizations in the provincial capital were organized to demand justice. The so-called 'marches of silence' (*marchas de silencio*)—a silent demonstration in the city's main square to press for a speedy investigation and a fair trial—introduced an innovative form of pro-

[8] We would like to thank Daniela Uribarri and Elizabeth Jelin for letting us use the research reports they had written on the María Soledad case. These reports are part of an unpublished study written by Daniela Uribarri 'Informe: El Caso de María Soledad' (Uribarri n.d.) in a project directed by Elizabeth Jelin titled 'Respuestas Sociales a la Violencia Estatal: Hacia una Construcción Social de la Responsabilidad'.

test that contributed to the expansion of the existing repertoire of collective actions of Argentine civil society. This type of mobilization would be later adopted by other movements. The first march took place just a week after the crime and it consisted of a silent walk from the high school to the cathedral in the main square headed by María Soledad's mother and Sister Pelloni, the principal of María Soledad's high school. The mobilizations demanded an active and impartial investigation of the case, since there were rumours that the son of provincial congressman Angel Luque had been involved in the murder. Between 1990 and 1996, there was a total of 82 marches of silence in Catamarca, 107 counting the ones that took place nationwide.[9] The marches drew large numbers, reaching at one point 30,000 people in a province whose total population is 210,000. Eventually, marches of silence were organized in different cities all over the country, particularly after the media 'nationalized' the case.

As in many cases involving human rights violations, the first initiative came from the family and friends of the victim: the Morales family, Sister Pelloni, and María Soledad's classmates. The movement was highly successful in drawing public support and the endorsement of different sectors of Catamarca's civil society. During its different stages, the movement received the support of the local church, student associations, bar association, medical doctors' union, and the independent press. The church and the student movement were among the first groups that mobilized to support the cause. Church support for the movement came not only from the crucial figure of Sister Pelloni, but also from a group of priests that decided to join the fourth march of silence and from the Bishop of Catamarca himself, Elmer Miani, who on several occasions referred to the movement's struggle in public statements to the press. In January 1991, Sister Pelloni and a representative of the bishop met president Menem to request a federal intervention of the provincial judiciary. Students' organizations were another important actor in the mobilizations and represented an important group within the mobilizations. After finding out that María Soledad's classmates were involved in the organization of a march to demand justice, student organizations suspended the traditional celebration of spring day—which coincided with the date set for the first march of silence—and joined the demonstration (Morandini n.d.: 79).

In January 1991 the provincial medical doctors' union went on strike to support eleven colleagues who had been suspended from

---

[9] 'Movilizaciones: Reacción en Cadena' (*Revista Noticias 1996*: 7)

their positions for having attended a march of silence. The local press, particularly *El Ancaster* and *La Union,* were also receptive to the denunciations of the movement. Both newspapers refused to publish a paid ad aimed at discrediting the figure of a congress-man who was highly supportive of the movement. The president of the local bar association joined the Morales' lawyer, Dr. Zafe, in her request for a federal intervention of the provincial judicial power. Lastly, but not least, the mobilizations drew the support of a large number of independent citizens who walked silently in demand for justice.

Along with the marches, which were crucial in drawing media and national attention to the case, a 'Commission for Justice and Truth' was created on 11 November. The idea came from María Soledad's father, Elias Morales. In his view, such a commission was necessary since 'the workings of the legal mechanisms do not seem to be guided by a will to find the truth.'[10] The commission was composed of approximately 40 members: the Morales family, Sister Pelloni, human rights activists, politicians, trade unionists, teachers, neighbours, classmates, and others. By acting as a soci-etal watchdog of the police investigation and judicial proceedings, the commission provided an important complement to the mobili-zational strategy.

Media attention to the case was the third variable that contrib-uted to the success of the cause. The marches of silence served to draw the attention of the national media and public opinion. The latter was crucial for 'nationalizing' the case, turning what could have remained as local news in the police section of provincial newspapers into one of most significant political events of the moment.[11] When the trial finally started, the media—in this case television—also played a crucial and unexpected role as a guaran-tor of due process.

---

[10] Quoted in Uribarri (n.d.). In an open letter, Elias Morales declared that he had initially abstained from participating in the marches of silence on the grounds that he did not want to give the idea that he had no trust on the police department and the judiciary. Due to the lack of results exhibited by both institutions, he decided to join the actions in demand for justice (Uribarri n.d.).

[11] The case was covered practically on a daily basis by most national news-papers. The story echoed in the international press (The *New York Times, Jornal do Brasil, El País*). It was the cover story of best-selling magazines like *Somos, Gente* and *Noticias.* Several books of investigative journalism based on the case were published. A TV series was produced and transmitted by one of the main TV stations in 1993 (*Casi Todo, Casi Nada*) and director Héctor Olivera made a movie based on the story (*El caso María Soledad*). See Ford (1999: 267); 'Golpe editorial' (*Revista Noticias* 1996: 12–13).

The second stage of the María Soledad case began with the broadcast of the trials on national TV. This stage helps illustrate another dimension of the role of the media for the exercise of societal accountability. If in the first stage the media was crucial in giving voice and visibility to the case nationwide, in the second stage the media acted as a guarantor of transparency and due process. The broadcast of the trial started in February 1996 and was closely followed by a massive audience.[12] At a certain point in the trial, a gesture made by one judge to another produced an immediate audience reaction. The gesture showed that two of the judges were in agreement and making procedural decisions that were systematically favouring the indicted. The incident generated public uproar and TV stations were flooded by calls from viewers criticizing the attitude of the magistrates. The lawyer of the Morales family asked for the impeachment and removal of the magistrates. The tribunal decided to suspend the televising of the trial to prevent further incidents, and the Supreme Court of Justice of Catamarca rejected the petition to separate the magistrates from the cause. In the following days, massive demonstrations spread all over the country questioning both decisions and demanding the live broadcast of the trial. A few days later, the magistrates in question stepped down and the trial was suspended. A new trial with new judges was finally held in August 1997 and resulted in the indictment of the accused in February 1998.

The success of the movement activated horizontal mechanisms at both the local and national levels. The fruitful combination of social pressure and mobilization, the existence of a watchdog commission that closely monitored the progress of the case, and extensive media coverage generated diverse reactions within horizontal agencies.

[12] The trial was televised across the country by approximately 40 open TV and cable stations. *Todo Noticias*, a news-cable channel, transmitted live the whole trial without interruptions. On the only occasion they interrupted the broadcast—to show the image of former governor Angeloz in tears during his deposition to the chamber of deputies where he was being questioned on corruption charges—the audience complained and demanded non-interrupted broadcast. From then onwards, the trial was broadcast live and without cuts by the channel. This placed *Todo Noticias* number one in the cable rankings. *Crónica TV*, another nationwide news-cable channel devoted 80 per cent of its air space, that is, an average of 19 hours of transmission. *Red de Noticias* the third nationwide news-cable channel devoted 70 per cent of its air space. The trial also received wide attention on open air TV. According to Sibila Camps and Luis Pazos, the trial took an average of nine hours of programming. The estimated audience was between seven to ten million spectators. See Camps and Pazos (1999: 244); 'Una Pasión de Multitudes' (*Revista Noticias* 1996: 70–2).

On the one hand, the cause drew support from some members of the local political society, mainly from opposition figures. Congressman Marcolli, for example, was a crucial ally of the movement and a member of the 'Commission for Justice and Truth'.

On the other hand, the actions activated the usual 'brown' strategies of local 'horizontal agencies' aimed at 'surviving accountability' (Maravall 1999). Those strategies included: the tampering and hiding of evidence by the local police chief, commissioner Angel Ferreira; exerting political pressure on the successive local judges that were in charge of the case; diversionary tactics aimed at drawing attention away from the main suspects (Angel Luque, the Jallil brothers, Ferreira Jr.), the search for scapegoats (Luis Tula and Ruth Salazar); a smear campaign against Sister Pelloni and Marcolli by congressman Brizuela and other provincial public officials; and the organization of a mobilization (*marcha por la verdad*) by the governor the same day and at the same time as the seventh 'march of silence' was scheduled to take place.[13] As we can see, the main local horizontal agencies were involved in a series of initiatives aimed at avoiding accountability.

Yet, those attempts at diluting the case or blocking the investigation met with a strong and persistent societal resistance. Periodic mobilizations, the establishment of a monitoring commission, and media denunciations were crucial to block the workings of 'brown' mechanisms. The social demand for truth and justice and the imposition of reputational costs, both at local and national level, were able to obstruct the attempts to dilute the inquiry. Actually, those manoeuvres only served to politicize the case since they presented a tragic example of the corrupted nature of the local political landscape and brought to the fore many instances of misuses of power. As María Soledad's father stated: 'It is obvious that the crime did not have a political nature, the covering up activities do.'[14] In this sense, those schemes backfired on the administration: the evidence of repeated cover-up actions became self-incriminating.

The visibility gained by the case nationwide activated national horizontal mechanisms. The National Congress appointed a special commission to analyse the provincial situation and to follow the progress of the case. On 6 February and 21 March 1991 radical legislators presented two demands requesting federal intervention

[13] Seven judges were involved in the cause. Former judge Morcos, for example, acknowledged before the local bar association that he had been pressured by governor Saadi to find a scapegoat for the crime. See 'Un Calvario de Seis Años' (*Revista Noticias* 1996: 11).

[14] Quoted in 'Cuarto Informe Preliminar (September 1992–1993)' (Uribarri, n.d.)

in Catamarca. The projects did not prosper due to lack of quorum on the justicialista's side. President Menem held audiences with Sister Pelloni and Father Carniello (the latter representing the Bishop of Catamarca) on one occasion and with the father of María Soledad in another one. After meeting with Elias Morales in Anillaco, Menem made a public promise that the murderer, 'whoever he was', was going to be found. After the resignation of the third judge in charge of the case, the National Secretary of Justice, César Arias, decided to step in and appointed Judge Ventimiglia. On 4 April the central executive power declared a federal intervention in the province's judiciary, and two weeks later (17 April) Menem announced on national radio and television the federal intervention of Catamarca, which put an end to the government of Ramón Saadi.

The spilling of the case to national horizontal agencies generated many instances of conflict between provincial and central authorities. It was a federal appointee, Judge Ventimiglia, who forced the resignation and prosecution of the governor's right hand, commissioner Ferreira, and of six other police officials that had been involved in the cover-up operations. Ventimiglia also asked for the capture and prosecution of Guillermo Luque. Finally, in light of his statements and participation in diversionary tactics aimed at misleading the prosecutor, Catamarca's Peronist party expelled Angel Luque from its ranks. Federal involvement strained the relations between the governor and Menem. Ramón Saadi energetically rejected the possibility of any form of federal intervention and declared that in Catamarca 'there is an absolute separation of powers'. Menem's decision to intervene unleashed verbal attacks against him and his cabinet from the governor. To guarantee that his appointee, Luis Adolfo Prol, could take office without any obstacles, the federal government sent troops to Catamarca.

The case and its ramifications not only helped expose Catamarca's political structure but also the ties and connections between 'brown' and 'green' areas. After all, Menem and his brother Eduardo, as well as other members of the senate and some high-ranking officials, came from provinces that did not greatly differ from Catamarca. Some of them, including the president, had personal ties with some of the protagonists of the case.[15] Such disclosures called for some 'spin control' to avoid reputational costs.

---

[15] Angel Luque, one of the key characters of the play, bragged of his close friendship with the president and of how Menem never missed attending his birthday celebration. See the interview in *Revista Noticias*, 7 March 1991, reprinted in 'Angel Luque: Voy a Hacer una Fiesta' (*Revista Noticias* 1996: 39).

Lastly, the case had a direct impact on vertical electoral mechanisms: the elections held in October 1991 led, for the first time in the history of Catamarca, to the electoral defeat of the Saadi family. Ramón Saadi, son of Vicente, lost to a coalition of radicals, dissident Peronists and independents. In the following years his attempts to become National Senator found the resistance of the other senators that had to approve his credentials. However, in the 1999 elections he was elected as representative of Catamarca (*La Nación,* 1 September, 6 December, 1999).

The former reconstruction illustrates that, in this case, societal mechanisms of accountability were critical, in at least two different instances. First, they were necessary to activate the operation of the horizontal ones. Secondly, once horizontal mechanisms had been activated, they were decisive in guaranteeing that the operation of the horizontal mechanisms would follow due process; thus, they concentrated their efforts on the surveillance of the police and judicial proceedings. These two instances of control of the societal mechanisms show the shift that took place in the type of demands that dominated the public agenda. While in the first stage, societal mechanisms concentrated on bringing the case to the court of public opinion in order to generate a response from the appropriate horizontal agencies, in the second stage, they were mainly geared toward assuring the transparency of the procedures. It was the reinforcing combination of judicial, mobilizational and media strategies that effected societal mechanisms.

The Ingeniero Budge Case

In May 1987, a police patrol shot three youths who were drinking on a corner in the Ingeniero Budge labour neighborhood.[16] The incident must not be considered an isolated one, but one that represents a widespread practice of the Argentine police in certain 'brown' areas: according to statistics, an average of one hundred young people (under 24) of low socioeconomic strata are killed yearly allegedly in 'confrontations', with police forces.[17] In this case, however, such practice met with a strong and concerted reaction of

[16] For an interesting and in depth analysis of this case see Gingold (1991, 1997). In regard to police violence and citizen insecurity see Smulovitz (1998b); Maier, Abregú and Tiscornia (1996); CELS (1998, 1999).

[17] See Centro de Estudios Legales y Sociales (CELS), *La Construcción Social de Imágenes de Guerra* (October 1990), quoted in Gingold (1997: 13). For updated statistics on Police Violence see CELS (1999) and CORREPI, *Archivo de Casos 1983–1999.*

the community. As in the María Soledad case, the immediate reactions of state agencies were geared toward avoiding accountability by fabricating an armed confrontation that never existed. As in the previous case, those 'brown' strategies backfired. As Laura Gingold argues,

> ... after witnessing how the police murdered those three youngsters and then proceeded to reconstruct a false scenario that simulated a shooting between the victims and their victimizers, the neighbour's indignation turned into an input for organization. The attempt by the police to cover up worsened the situation because it moved the witnesses to action (Gingold 1997: 33. Our translation.)

While the first reaction led to a violent confrontation with the police forces, subsequent actions were geared toward organizing a social protest to criticize ingrained police practices and to demand justice in this particular case. The next day, a neighbourhood commission was established ('Comision de Amigos y Vecinos'), composed of 96 members. Family members and friends of the victims, neighbours, the priest and two nuns from the local parish, and activists from the 'unidades basicas' that operated in the neighbourhood were among the members of the commission. The first action of the association was the establishment of guards on the site of the crime to prevent the police from tampering with the evidence. It also organized a search for potential witnesses to the killings. The reaction of the police was swift: witnesses in the trial and members of the commission were harassed and threatened.[18] To protect themselves from police retaliation, the neighbours established an informal alarm system (*cacerolazos*) to prevent police harassment and an escort service that would accompany the witnesses to the court house.

Social demonstrations and marches to the court of justice, the Governor's Palace, Mayo Square, and petitions to the public authorities and other forms of collective action were successful at getting media attention. The denunciations made it into the main newspapers and television and cable news, giving national visibility to the movement. Since then, other cases of police violence started to be framed as part of the wider problem of citizen insecurity and police abuse. One indicator of the change in the social consideration of the problem is the fact that the topic of police violence (*gatillo fácil*) has left the police column of most news-

---

[18] In June, the car of the lawyer that represented the victims was stolen and burned.

papers to become a topic of the political section. The mobilization and social reaction generated by the case had an important demonstration effect: although police violence in Ingeniero Budge as in many other popular neighbourhoods had always been and is still present, the impact the murders of 'Ingeniero Budge' had on public opinion have led to the organization of other protest movements to respond to new cases of police violence (perhaps the most notorious ones being the Schiavini and the Bulacio cases).

Not only did the Ingeniero Budge case inspire other movements to denounce police violence and demand justice, it also gave rise to the conformation of national organizations such as the *Comision de Familiares de Victimas Inocentes* (COFAVI) and *Coordinadora contra la Violencia Policial e Institucional* (CORREPI), as well as local organizations such as *El Agora* in Córdoba. These new organizations, together with old ones like CELS, have been playing a crucial watchdog role over police forces and have engaged in active campaigns aimed at placing the issue of police reform on the public and political agenda.

The actions of these movements and associations have been decisive in placing illegal behaviour of police officials in the spotlight, in denouncing numerous cases of police misbehaviour and violence, and in demanding justice and institutional reforms. Police violence and 'gatillo facil' have become an issue that no longer goes unnoticed and that hence deserves to be criticized and dealt with. Even though there are still numerous cases of 'gatillo facil' denounced, police misconduct is now being monitored and followed by an array of organizations that have the capacity to grant public visibility to their criticisms. It is now common to observe that many of these cases lead to judicial demands. One of the goals of CORREPI, for example, is to provide legal assistance and representation to the victims and their relatives. The legal actions of these organizations and movements have had different outcomes. In some cases, as in the Ingeniero Budge case, a very long judicial process led to the indictment of the policemen that participated in the killings.[19] In others, like the Bulacio case, the case is still open. According to a CORREPI document, in 1997 the organization intervened in eleven judicial cases (CORREPI, ¿Que Hacemos...n.d.). Of them, five led to prosecutions, four led to criminal trials of policemen, in one there was a mistrial and the case has been appealed, and the remaining case is still in a preliminary stage. CORREPI has also brought a case to the Inter-American

[19] Officer Balmaceda is serving an 11-year sentence.

Commission of Human Rights. In brief, these social movements and civic associations play the role of a citizenship-based monitoring mechanism on police forces that has contributed to increasing the costs of extra-legal police behavior.

Besides being successful at placing the issue of police violence and corruption on the public agenda, these organizations were instrumental in forcing horizontal agencies to review both existing legislation and their position on issues such as the adequacy of the existing institutional structure of police agencies, or the effectiveness of existing mechanisms of political control on the institution. Although it is risky to make predictions on the processes of police reform under way, in several of them a diverse array of citizen associations that deal with those issues were invited to participate in the debates alongside technocrats, public officials and political representatives.[20]

Conclusions

What can be learned about the ways in which societal and horizontal mechanisms of accountability interact? The cases analysed show that the activation of the horizontal mechanisms was possible due to pressures from below. The actions of individuals, associations, and the media were able to transform local and particular cases into issues on the public agenda. It was their ability to transform particular cases into public and wider issues that forced horizontal agencies to acknowledge and give some kind of answer to these demands. Their success in 'constructing' public issues and in expanding the number of actors involved, blocked attempts to convert their claims into 'non-issues'. In addition, the actions of these movements and organizations monitored the operation of horizontal agencies, preventing their attempts to sidetrack the consideration of the claims. In the specific cases analysed in this paper, the constructed public issue became, in turn, a denunciation about the failure of the horizontal mechanisms of accountability and a demand for their proper operation. The deficits of horizontal mechanisms became, then, not only a topic of the public debates but also one of the central axis of the political disputes of the period.

[20] 'Foros Vecinales, Municipales or Departamentales' in the province of Buenos Aires; 'Juntas Barriales de Seguridad Comunitaria' in Santa Fe; neighbourhood-based 'Consejos de Prevención del Delito y la Violencia' in the city of Buenos Aires provide some examples of attempts at incorporating societal voices.

The establishment of societal watchdogs, with continuous or sporadic existence, raised the costs of unlawful behaviour both for public officials and institutions. Increased and credible reputational costs gave political opponents additional weapons and forced reluctant public officers to activate horizontal mechanisms. Therefore, societal mechanisms proved to be not only successful but also a necessary condition for the activation of horizontal ones. Finally, the two analysed cases show that citizen initiatives to control public officials and public policies can also be successful in 'brown' regions characterized by notorious deficits of horizontal accountability.

A final remark on the workings of societal accountability: societal mechanisms tend to be successful in those cases where an interaction between the use of social mobilization, legal actions, and media exposure and denunciations can be found. That is, the politics of societal accountability appears to achieve its goals when citizens not only initiate a legal action but when they also support those actions with some kind of social mobilization and some sort of media exposure. There does not appear to be a sequential relationship among these three strategies. It is, however, their joined activation that determines the ability to bring a problem to attention and to make evident the costs that public authorities should accept or avoid. In contexts in which claims are backed with mobilization and media exposure, the likelihood of postponing or ignoring legal demands is reduced. In those cases, the exercise of societal accountability is likely to be successful because the task of control is distributed among different agencies with autonomous interests, and because the number of 'external eyes' overseeing the problem increases. When the three strategies coexist, each one controls the other and compels its consideration. The media observes and reports on the organization and mobilization of civil society. The organization of the civil society listens and impels the media, and at the same time, activates legal actions. This continuous and reciprocal observation forces state institutions to give preferential treatment to a problem.

The concept of societal accountability expands the classic understanding of the system of checks and balances among state agencies to include a societal arena composed of a multitude of autonomous and heterogeneous associations. In this sense, the concept of societal accountability revives the pluralist argument about the importance of the societal sphere as a counterbalancing power that complements horizontal mechanisms of accountability. Further analyses on the workings of societal mechanisms can therefore

328   *Catalina Smulovitz et al.*

contribute to the enrichment of current debates on accountability by including a series of social initiatives that we believe can play an important role in addressing many of the institutional deficits of horizontal mechanisms.

References

Camps, Sibilia, and Luis Pazos. 1999. *Justicia y Televisión. La Sociedad Dicta Sentencia*. Buenos Aires: Editorial Perfil.

Centro de Estudios Legales y Sociales (CELS). 1998 *Las Reformas Policiales en Argentina* (Mimeo).

Centro de Estudios Legales y Sociales (CELS). 1999. *Derechos Humanos en la Argentina. Informe Anual Enero-Diciembre 1998*. Buenos Aires: Eudeba.

Cohen, Jean, and Andrew Arato. 1992. *Civil Society and Political Theory*. Cambridge: Cambridge University Press.

Correa Sutil, Jorge. 1999. 'Cenicienta se queda en la Fiesta: El Poder Judicial Chileno en la Década de los 90'. In Paul Drake and Iván Jaksic, eds., *El Modelo Chileno: Democracia y Desarrollo en los Noventa*. Santiago de Chile: LOM Ediciones.

CORREPI. n.d. 'Archivo de Casos 1983–1999' (mimeo).

CORREPI. n.d. '¿Que Hacemos en el Ambito Judicial?' (mimeo).

Defensoría del Pueblo de Perú. 1999. *Resumen Ejecutivo del Segundo Informe del Defensor del Pueblo al Congreso de la República*. Lima: Defensoría del Pueblo de Perú.

Diamond, Larry. 1999. *Developing Democracy: Toward Consolidation*. Baltimore, MD: The Johns Hopkins University Press.

Ford, Anibal. 1999. 'La Exasperación del Casa.' In *La Marca de la Bestia. Identificación, Desigualdades e Infroentretenimiento en la Sociedad Contemporánea*. Buenos Aires: Grupo Editorial Norma.

Gingold, Laura. 1991. 'Crónicas de Muertes Anunciadas: El caso de Ingeniero Budge'. *Documento Cedes* No. 65.

Gingold, Laura. 1997. *Memoria, Moral y Derecho. El Caso de Ingeniero Budge (1987–1994)*. Mexico City: Facultad Latinoamericana de Ciencias Sociales.

Keck, Margaret and Kathryn Sikkink. 1998. 'Transnational Advocacy Networks in the Movement Society'. In David Meyer and Sydney Tarrow, eds., *The Social Movement Society. Contentious Politics for a New Century*. Lanham MD: Rowman & Littlefield Publishers.

Maier, Julio, Martín Abregú, and Sofía Tiscornia. 1996. 'El Papel de la Policía en la Argentina y su Situación Actual'. In Peter Waldmann, ed., *Justicia en la Calle. Ensayos sobre la Policía en América Latina*. Medellín, Colombia: CIEDLA.

Maravall, José María. 1999. 'Accountability and Manipulation'. In Adam Przeworski, Susan C. Stokes, and Bernard Manin, eds., *Democracy,*

Accountability and Representation. Cambridge, UK and New York, NY: Cambridge University Press.

McClymont, Mary and Stephen Golub, eds. 2000. *Many Roads to Justice: The Law Related Work of Ford Foundation Grantees Around the Word.* n.p.: Ford Foundation.

McCubbins, Matthew, and Thomas Schwartz. 1984. 'Congressional Oversight Overlooked: Police Patrols versus Fire Alarms'. *American Journal of Political Science* 28, 1.

Melucci, Alberto. 1996. *Challenging Codes. Collective Action in the Information Age.* Cambridge: Cambridge University Press.

Méndez, Juan E., Guillermo O'Donnell, and Paulo Sérgio Pinheiro, eds. 1999. *The (Un)Rule of Law And the Underprivileged in Latin America.* Notre Dame, IN: University of Notre Dame Press.

Meyer, David and Sydney Tarrow, eds. 1998. *The Social Movement Society: Contentious Politics for a New Century.* Lanham, MD: Rowman & Littlefield Publishers.

Morandini, Norma. n.d. *Catamarca.* Buenos Aires: Planeta/Espejo de la Argentina.

Muraro, Heriberto. 1997. *Periódicos, Periodistas y Ciudadanos.* Buenos Aires: Fondo de Cultura Económica.

O'Donnell, Guillermo. 1993a. 'Estado, Democratización y Ciudadanía', *Nueva Sociedad* 128: 62–87.

O'Donnell, Guillermo. 1993b. 'On The State, Democratization And Some Conceptual Problems: A Latin American View With Glances At Some Postcommunist Countries'. *World Development* 21, 8.

O'Donnell, Guillermo. 1994. 'Delegative Democracy'. *Journal of Democracy* 5, 1.

O'Donnell, Guillermo. 1995. 'Citizen Information and Government Accountability: What Must Citizens Know to Control Governments'. Paper Delivered at the *1995 Annual Meeting Of The American Political Science Association*, Chicago. August 1995.

O'Donnell, Guillermo. 1998. 'Accountability Horizontal'. *Agora. Cuaderno de Estudios Políticos* No. 8.

O'Donnell, Guillermo. 1999. 'Polyarchies and the (Un)Rule of Law in Latin America: A Partial Conclusion'. In Juan E. Méndez, Guillermo O'Donnell, and Paulo Sérgi Pinheiro, eds., *The (Un)Rule of Law And the Underprivileged in Latin America.* Notre Dame, IN: University of Notre Dame Press.

Peruzzotti, Enrique. 2001a. 'Cultura Política, Esfera Pública y Aprendizaje Colectivo en la Argentina Post-dictatorial'. In Isidoro Cheresky and Inés Pousadela, eds., *Política e Instituciones en las Nuevas Democracias Latinoamericanas.* Buenos Aires: Paidós Editorial.

Peruzzotti, Enrique. 2001b. 'The Nature of the New Argentine Democracy. The Delegative Democracy Argument Revisited'. *Journal of Latin American Studies* 33.

Peruzzotti, Enrique.2002. 'Towards a New Politics: Citizenship and Rights in Contemporary Argentina'. *Citizenship Studies* 6, 1.

Peruzzotti, Enrique and Catalina Smulovitz, eds. 2002. *Controlando la Política. Ciudadanos y Medios en las Nuevas Democracias.* Buenos Aires: Editorial Temas.

Revista Noticias. 1996. Edición Especial No. 18 (April 2).

Rey, Germán. 1998. *Balsas y Medusas. Visibilidad Comunicativa y Narrativas Políticas.* Bogota: Fescol-Fundación Social-Cerec.

Saba, Roberto. n.d. 'The Human Rights Movement, Citizen Participation Organizations and the Process of Building Civil Society and Rule of Law in Argentina'. Unpublished paper.

Saba, Roberto, and Martín Bohmer. 2000. 'Participación Ciudadana en Argentina: Estrategias para el Efectivo Ejercicio de los Derechos'. In *Rompiendo la Indiferencia. Acciones Ciudadanas en Defensa del Interés Público.* Santiago de Chile: Fundación Ford, Oficina para la Región Andina y el Cono Sur.

Schedler, Andreas. 1999. 'Conceptualizing Accountability'. In Andreas Schedler, Larry Diamond, and Marc Plattner, eds., *The Self Restraining State: Power and Accountability in New Democracies.* Boulder, CO: Lynne Rienner Publishers.

Schedler, Andreas, Larry Diamond, and Marc Plattner, eds. 1999. *The Self Restraining State: Power and Accountability in New Democracies.* Boulder, CO: Lynne Rienner Publishers.

Schilling, Flávia. 1999. 'Corrupcao: Ilegalidade Intoleravel?: Comissoes Parlamentares de Inquérito e a Luta contra a Corrupcao no Brasil (1980–1992)'. Unpublished paper. Instituto Brasileiro de Ciencias Criminais.

Shifter, Michael. 1997. 'Tensions and Trade-Offs in Latin America'. *Journal of Democracy* 8, 2.

Smulovitz, Catalina. n.d. 'Inseguridad Ciudadana y Miedo: Respuestas Públicas y Privadas en el Caso Argentino'. Paper presented at the Wilson Center's Working Group on Citizen Security in Latin América.

Smulovitz, Catalina. 1995. 'Constitución y Poder Judicial en la Nueva Democracia Argentina'. In Carlos Acuña, comp., *La Nueva Matriz Política Argentina.* Buenos Aires: Nueva Visión.

Smulovitz, Catalina. 1997. 'Ciudadanos, Derechos y Política'. In Felipe González Morales, ed., *Las Acciones de Interés Público: Argentina, Chile, Colombia y Perú.* Santiago de Chile: Escuela de Derecho de la Universidad Diego Portales.

Smulovitz, Catalina. 1998. 'Acciones Judiciales y Fiscalización de la Política Pública'. Unpublished paper.

Smulovitz, Catalina. Forthcoming. 'Citizen Insecurity and Fear: Public and Private Responses in the Case of Argentina'. In Hugo Fruhling, Josepth Tulchin and Heather Golding, eds., *Crime and Violence in Latin America: Citizen Security, Democracy and the State.* Baltimore, MD: The Johns Hopkins University Press.

Smulovitz, Catalina and Enrique Peruzzotti. 2000. 'Societal Accountability: The Other Side of Control'. *Journal of Democracy* 11, 4.

Stokes, Susan. 1999. 'What Do Policy Switches Tell Us About Democracy?' In Przeworski, Adam, Susan Stokes, and Bernard Manin, eds., *Democracy, Accountability and Representation*. New York, NY: Cambridge University Press.

Thompson, John, B. 2002. 'Naturaleza y Consecuencias de los Escándalos Políticos'. In Enrique Peruzzotti and Catalina Smulovitz, comps., *Controlando la Política. Ciudadanos y Medios en las Nuevas Democracias* Buenos Aires: Editorial Temas.

Uribarri, Daniela. n.d. 'Informe: El Caso de María Soledad'. Mimeo.

Veja (6 October 1999).

Vianna, Luiz Werneck, Maria Alice Rezende de Carvalho, Manuel Palacios Cunha Melo, and Marcelo Baumann Burgos. 1999. *A Judicializaco da Politica e das Relacoes Sociais no Brasil*. Editora Revan.

Waisbord, Silvio. 1996. 'Investigative Journalism and Political Accountability in South American Democracies'. *Critical Studies in Mass Communication* 13.

Zakaria, Fareed. 1997. 'The Rise of Illiberal Democracy'. *Foreign Affairs* 76, 6.

Zemans, Frances. 1983. 'Legal Mobilization: The Neglected Role of the Law in the Political System'. *American Political Science Review* 77.

Index

Abregú Martín 323 n
Acuña, Carlos 157
accountability
  and answerability 7, 9–10, 13, 18, 312 n
  competing concepts 3, 9–18
  deficiency in Latin America 79–127
  definition 56, 80 n
  and democratic legitimacy 68–74
  enforcement of 312 n
  in hierarchical vs horizonatal relationships 85
  in presidential system 82–91
  principal-agent relationships and 14–16, 18–19
  and responsibility 57
  and sanctioning rights 80
  types of 18–21 see also under specific types, viz democratic accountability, electoral accountability, horizontal accountability, intrastate accountability, non-institutionalized accountability, political accountability, public accountability, reputational accountability see also under country headings
accountability deficiency 22
  in Latin America 3–6, 29, 79–127
  linkages and interactions among 49–51
accountability mechanisms 4–6
Aguirre, Ramón 296
Albright, Spencer D. 145
Alemán, Miguél 288
Alfonsin, Raul 155–8, 161
Almeida, Francisco Inácio 188–9
Altman, David 3 n
Alvarez, Luis Echeverría 288
American Bar Association 233

Ames, Barry 166, 228
Amorim Neto, Octávio 171 n, 183 n, 194 n
answerability
  and accountability 7, 9–10, 13, 18, 57, 63, 312 n
  and horizontal accountability 80
Arato, Andrew 310
Aristotle 41
Ayres, Robert L. 276–7
Argentina 94, 108, 133–4, 136–7, 151, 301
  Accounting Act 155
  administrative reforms 154–5
  Condue Obedience Law 157
  Comision de Familiaries de Victimas Inocentes (COFAVI) 325
  Congress oversight 155–61
  Coordinadora Contra la Violencia Political Inocentes (CORREPI)
  CORREPI see Coordinadora Contra la Violencia Political Inocentes
  developing oversight institutions 151–66
  Economic Emergency Law 159
  homicide rate 277
  Ingeniero Budge case
    societal accoutability effectiveness 313, 315–16, 323–6
  Marío Soledad case
    societal accountability effectiveness 313, 315–26
  National Accouting Tribunal (TCN) 155
  National Budget Office (ONP) 155
  ONP see National Budget Office
  political rights 310 n
  societal accountability effectiveness 315–28

Argentina (*cont.*):
State Reform Law 158
TCN *see National Accounting Tribunal*
under Alfonsin 155–7
under Menem 157–61
Union Civica Radical 154
Athens 38, 50
origin of democracy 38–42
Australia 133, 143–5

Bacqué, Jorge 161
Barker, F. J. 114
Bates, Robert 269
Becker, David G 228
Benson, George C. S. 141
Blum, Roberto 266 n
Bobbio, Norberto 50 n
Bohmer, Martín 314, 330 n
Belgium 272
Brazil 56, 58, 94, 107, 112, 115, 135, 147, 165, 276
"action of direct unconstitutionality" (ADIN) 190
budget oversight 186–7
CMO *see Comissão Mista de Orcamento*
Comissão Mista de Orcamento (CMO) 186–7
Congress
authority to punish executives 189–90
committee system 184
as horizontal accountability agent 170–94
and oversight mechanism 183–92
Parliamentary Investigation Committees (CPI) 173, 175–82, 216–17,
CONMAP *see National Confederation of Public Prosecution*
Constitution(1966) 173–5
Constitution (1988) 171, 173–5, 201–2
justice system reform in the 208, 225
oversight mechanism in the 173, 183–92, 208

and public officers 190
Public Prsecution in the 203, 206, 217–20
Datafolha public opinion polling 216
executive authorities punishment of 189–90
Federal Accounting Tribunal (TCU) 183–6
homicide rate 277
horizontal accountability and Brazilian Congress 170–94
in Human Development Index 212
IDESP study on Public Prosecution 218–20
judicial activism 223
judicial reforms 208, 224–6
Law of Administrative Impropriety 215
"Mafia of the Auditors" 214
"mayors' court" 215
"Muzzle Law" 224–5
National Confederation of the Public Prosecution (CONMAP) 220–2, 224
oversight mechanism 183–92
constitutional provision 173, 183–92, 208
Parliamentary Investigative Committees (CPI) 173, 175–82, 216–17, 224 n
oversight activities of 182
Political parties
Partido Social Democràtico (PSD) 177, 179, 193–4
Partido Social Democràtico Brasiliero(PSDB) 179, 194
Partido Trabalhista Brasiliero (PTB) 179, 193–4
Partido da Frente Liberal (PFL) 179, 194
Partido da Movimento Democrático Brasiliero (PMDB) 177
Worker's Party (PT) 189
Presidents (1946–99) 181, 193–4
PRODASEN 186
public hearings of oversight 187
Public Prosecution (Ministerio Publico)

as agent of
accountability 201–26
Attorney General and 219–20,
223, 225
constitutional provisions
for 206, 217–18, 220
Corregedoria-Geral and 219
IDESP study on 218–20
judiciary and 217, 220, 222–3
overseeing of 217–22
recruitment and
promotion 217–19
Special Group to Control
Organized Crime
(GAECCO) 214–15
standing committees
oversight activities 187–9
STF *see Supreme Federal Tribunal*
STJ *see Superior Justice Tribunal*
TCU *see Federal Accounting
Tribunal*
Superior Justice Tribunal
(STJ) 207
Supreme Federal Tribunal
(STF) 190, 207
British House of Commons 86
Brooks, Robert C. 132
Brown, L. David 8–9, 17
Bucarám Ortiz, Abdalá 56, 67 n
impeachment of 58

Cain, Bruce 142, 170
Caldwell, Michael 86, 90, 93
Calles 286
Camacho, Manuel Aliva 288
Camp, Roderick Ai 254, 288, 290
Campos, Pillar 266 n
Camps, Sibilia 313, 320 n
Cappelletti, Mauro 224
Cárdenas, Lázaro
impeachment of 286, 287–8
Cardoso, Fernando Henrique 178,
181, 193 , 210
Carey, John M. 80, 84, 92–3,
112–14, 171 n, 174 n
Carothers, Thomas 229, 231, 253,
256, 258
Casar, María Amparo 280
Castilho, Ela Wiecko 210, 213
Castro, Maurice, Gutiérrez 232,
246

Cavalcanti, Rosãngela Batista 21,
25, 27–8, 49, 101, 107, 175 n
Cavallo, Domingo 160
Central America *see also under EL
Salvador and Guatemala*
horizontal accountability
in 228–61
rule of law 228–61
Chávez, Hugo 28, 56, 72–4
Cheibub, Jose Antonio1 70, 271
Centro de Estudios Legales y
Sociales 323 n, 325
checks and balances
and horizontal
accountability 16–18, 268
in limited government 271–2
Chile 64, 103, 106–07, 108 n, 115,
135, 147, 165, 279, 301
homicide rate 277
citizen's rights
and rule of law 300–2, 309
Clark, Mary A. 254 n, 257–8
Cleveland, Fredrick A. 141, 143
Clinton, W. J. 56, 101
impeachment of 58
Close, David 55 n
Coase, Ronald C. 276
Cohen, Jean 310
Collor, Fernando 58, 177–8, 181,
193
impeachment of 58, 313
Colombia 56, 58, 94, 97, 101, 107,
108, 112–13, 147, 276
homicide rate 277
as horizontal accountability
agent 170–94
Supreme Court 102
Commager, Henry Steele 230
Commission to Modernize the
Judiciary 249–50
Conaghan, Catherine M. 117
Coppedge, Michael
Correa Sutil, Jorge 103, 314
CORREPI 323, 325
Cortinez, Adolfo Ruiz 284
Cox, Gary W. 93, 136
constitution making
balancing contradiction and
convenience 40
corruption
and oversight institutions 136

Costa Rica 107, 114, 257–8
  homicide rate 277
Cubas 56
  impeachment of 58

Dahl, Robert A. 51, 71
Day, Patricia 5, 8, 12, 17
Defensoría del Pueblo de Perú 314
de la Rúa, Fernando 135, 164–66
de Tejada, Lerdo 292
delegative democracy 24, 26, 55 n
democracy 38, 42, 68–74
  vertical accountability and 69
democratic accountability 3, 29
  definition 8–9
democratic legitimacy
  and accountability 68–74
Deuhalde, Educardo 165
Diamond, Larry 8, 24, 55 n, 229, 252,
  256, 309 n, 310
Diario de Debates del Congress
  Constitayente 293
Diaz, Albert 266 n
Diaz, Porfirio 292
Diaz-Cayeros, Alberto 280, 295
Diniz, Simone 170 n, 184 n
Dodson, J. Michael 22, 24–5, 27,
  231, 235, 237, 241, 245, 254 n
Domingo, Pilar 286, 289
Downs, Anthony 23
Dromi, Roberto 163
Duhalde, Eduardo165
Dunn, Delmer D. 9, 12, 37
Dunn, John 12, 24, 80
Dutra, Eurico 177–8, 181, 193

Eaton, Kent 160
Eggertsson, Thrainn 276
Elster, John 14 n, 17, 38, 57, 83,
  271–2
Ecuador 56, 58, 104 n, 107, 117, 135
  homicide rate 277
  justice system 104 n
  National Judicial
    Commission 104 n
  President Bucarám
    removal of 67 n
  impeachment of 58
  Supreme Court 102, 104 n
elections, fair
  concept of 36 n

electoral accountability 3, 6, 8,
  23–6
  and intrastate
    accountability 21–4
electoral reforms 142–6
  and intrastate accountability 23
  and vertical accountability 108–17
El Salvodor 114, 230–3
  CNJ *see National Council of the
    Judiciary*
  FESPAD *see Salvadorean
    Foundation for the Study of
    Applied Law*
  horizontal accountability in 228–9,
    231, 254–9
  judicial reform 233–41
  human rights 235–6, 239
  National Council of the Judiciary
    (CNJ) 234–7, 239
  ONUSAL *see United Natins
    Observer Mission in EL
    Salvador*
  peace accord 258, 260
  Procurator for the Defence of
    Human Rights (PDDH) 239
  Procurator for Human
    Rights 235–6
  public perception 241–4
  public prosecutors 221
  Salvadorean Foundation for the
    study of Applied Law
    (FESPAD) 238–41
  Salvadorean Judicial Training
    School 239
  Truth Commission 232, 234
  United Natins Observer Mission in
    EL Salvador (ONUSAL) 235,
    237
Epstein, Leon D. 93
Evans, Eldon Cobb 142–5

Fajnzylber, Pablo 277, 299
  Fearon, James D. 14 n, 24
(The) Federalist 40–2, 59–60
  Ferejohn, John 8, 23–4, 142,
    191 n
Fernández, Roque 160
Ferreira Rubio, Delia 157, 159–60
FESPAD 238–41
Figueiredo, Argelina Cheibub 25,
  172 n, 174 n, 183 n, 187 n

Figueiredo, Marcus 170 n
Filho, Café 178, 181, 193
Fiorina, Morris P. 5, 8, 134, 139, 142
Fiss, Owen M. 231, 242
Fix-Fierro, Hector 266 n
Flores Nano, Lourdes. 106 n, 116 n
Ford, Anibal 319 n
Fox, Jonathan A. 8, 9, 17
Franco, Francisco 279
Franko, Itamar 178, 181, 193
Fujimori, Alberto Keinya 27–8, 46,
    56, 64–6, 72–4, 106
Fumes, Oscar Garzón 163

Garfield, James Abram
    assassination of 133, 135, 140,
    148
Garzón Valdes, Ernesto 50 n
Geddes, Barbara 146–7
Gerardi (Archbishop)
    assassination of 248 n
Germany 272
Gingold, Laura 323 n, 324
Golub, Stephen 314 n
Gómez, Pablo1 38
Gonzalez Avelar, Miguel 293
Good, James 149
Goretti, Matteo 157, 159–60
Goulart, João 178, 181, 193
Grant, Ulysses 147
Greece(Ancient) 68
Grinover, Ada 211
Grofman, Bernand N. 83
Guarnieri, Carlo 44 n
Guatemala 107, 108 n
    Commission for Historical
        Clarification (CEH) 245–6
    Commission to Strengthen the
        Justice System 249
    "elite" perception of 251–3
    Gallup-CID survey of public
        opinion 250–1
    horizontal accountability 228–9,
        231, 254–9
    judicial reform 244–51, 254–61
    Judicial Training School 247–9
    legal education 247–9
    National Action Party (NAP) 245
    peace accords 244–51
    public opinion
        Gallup-CID surveys 250–1

    Recuperation of the Historic
        Memory (REMHI) 246 n,
        248 n
    United Revolutionary Front of
        Guatemala (URNG) 245
    Washington Office on Latin
        America (WOLA) 246–7

Haggard, Stephan 89, 92
Hagopian, Frances 34 n
Hamilton, Alexander 40 , 171 n
Hammergren, Linn A. 228, 237, 260
Hansen, M. H. 38
Harding, Warren G. 150
Harris, Joseph P. 143–4
Hartlyn, Jonathan 55 n
Hasgard to Heinsz, W.
Heidenheimer, Arnold J. 140
Henisz, Witold J. 273–4
Hensz's Database *see Polecon Index
    Database*
hierarachical vs transactional
        systems
    judiciary in 89–90
hierarchical vs horizontal
        relationships
    accountability in 85
Hippolito to Hyrigoer
Hippolito, Lucia 194 n
Hirschman, Albert 36
Hofstadter, Richard 134, 135 n
Holder, Rachel 247
Holiday, David 235, 245
Holmes, Stephen 38, 44 n
Howard, George Elliott 132
Huber, John D. 172 n, 174
Huntington, Samuel 269
Hurtado, Miguel 288
Hyrigoyen, Hipolito 154
Hobbesian-like dilemma 37, 269, 301
horizontal accountability *see also
        horizontal exchange* 10–12,
        18–20, 24, 27, 206, 268
    legal institutionalization of 34–52
    definition 13 n, 34, 35 n, 57, 79
    misturst about 34–52
    concepts 56–8
    between agencies and state 60–2
    and sanctions 62–6
    and unlawfullness 66–8
    and checks and balances 16–18

horizontal accountability (*cont.*):
  and answerability 80
  and rule of law
    in Latin America 228–61
  and societal acountability 310–15
horizontal exchange 15–16, 81,
    86–9 *see also horizontal
    accountability*
  definition 35 n
  in presidential system 88
  and superintendance 92, 95–9
  and vertical accountability 91–5
horizontal mechanism
  of accoutnability *see horizontal
    accountability*
horizontal-vertical accountability 48
human rights 235–6, 239, 301,
    325–6
Hurtado, Miguel 288

IDB America 233, 234 n
Iglesias, Jose Maria 292–3
Illia, Arturo 155
Inter-American Commission of
    Human Rights 325–6
intrastate accountability 8, 11–12,
    19, 25–9
  in Brazil 25, 28
  definition 13
  and electoral
    accountability 21–4
  and electoral reforms 23
  in Latin America 24–9
  Ombudsman and 13, 15, 27
  public prosecutors 221
Ippolito-O'Donnell, Gabriela 34 n
Italy 93 n, 272
  public prosecutors 221

Jackson, Donald W. 22, 24–5, 27,
    231, 235, 237, 241, 254 n
Jacobson, Gary 93
Jaime, Edna 266 n
Janes, Susanne 245, 250 n,
Jefferson, Thomas 60
Jelin, Elizabeth 317 n
Johnson, Andrew 134, 140
  impeachment of 134, 140
Jones, W. T. 170
judicial independence
  concepts 231–3

judicial reforms 208, 224–6, 233–41
judiciary
  in hierarachical vs transactional
    systems 89–90

Kada, Naoko 96
Kaufmann, D. 142
Keck, Margaret 311 n
Kenney, Charles D. 3 n, 9–17, 19–20,
    27, 47, 60 n, 80, 96
Keohane, Robert O. 9, 17
Kerche, Fábio 217
Key, Vernon O. 5, 8
Kiewiet, Roderick 83, 287
Klein, Rudolf 5, 8, 12, 17
Klingemann, H. 114
Kraay, Aart 142
Kubischeck, Jascelino 178, 181, 193
Kulisheck, Michael 117

Lagos, Marta 255–6
Lakoff, S. 68 n
Lamounier, Bolivar 223
Latin America
  accountability deficiency
    in 79–127
  electoral-vertical accountability 48
  horizontal accountability 74
  independence of non-elected
    agencies 99–108
  intra state accountability 24–9
  judicial system 232
  Latinobarometro surveys
    of public opnion 255–6
  rule of law 228–61, 301
  societal accountability
    and rule of law 228–61, 301
  Washington Office on Latin
    America (WOLA) 246–7
Lauvaux, Philippe 172 n
Laver, Michael 11, 14 n, 17
Lecuona, G. Zepeda 266 n, 276,
    300–1
Lederman, Daniel 277, 299
legislative oversight 26
  in Argentina 132–66
  in the United States 132–66
legislatures
  and developing oversight
    institutions 137–8
Levi, Margaret 256–7

liberalism 39
  vertical accountability and 69
liberty dimension
  of rule of law 269–75, 298
Lijphart, Arend 40, 89, 282
limited government
  checks and balances in 270–2
Limongi, Fernando 170 n, 172 n,
    183 n, 188 n, 268–9, 271
Loayza, Norman 277, 299

Macedo, Ronaldo Porto, Jr. 206 n
Machado, Luiz Melibio 215 n
McCleary, Rachel M 246
McClymont, Mary 314 n
McCubbins, Mathew D. 83, 86,
    89–90, 183, 191, 287, 311 n
Mack, Myna 249
McKinley
  assassinatin of 148
Maddex, Robert 44 n
Madison, James 40–1, 44, 56, 60,
    80–3, 91, 96, 134, 163, 170–1,
    229–30, 280
Madisonian-like dilemma 260,
    268–9, 278
Madrazo, Roberto 296
Magalhàes, Antôna Carlos 212
Magalhães, Pedro 44 n
Magaloni, Ana Laura 266 n
Magaloni, Beatriz 11, 21–2, 26, 28,
    99, 108, 276, 280, 288–9, 295,
    300–1
Maier, Julio 323 n
Mainwaring, Scott 17, 48 n, 55 n, 81,
    112, 170 n, 174 n, 266 n, 273,
    280
Maiorano, Jorge 161
Manin, Bernard 8, 14, 23–4, 41, 44,
    49, 55 n, 70 n, 171 n
Manzetti, Luigi 3 n, 24–5, 28, 48 n,
    190 n
Maravall, José Mariá 8, 23–4, 321
Marshall (Justice) 271
Marshall, William 92
Martinez, Jacqueline 266 n
Marx, Fritz Morsetin 148–50
Mateos, Adolfo López 288
Matus, Alejandra 135
Mauceri, Philip 55 n
Mayhew, David 92, 134, 139

Mazzilli, Hugo Nigro 207, 220
Medina, Hilario 293
Melucci, Alberto 310
Méndez, Juan E 228
Menem, Carlos Saul 27, 156–64, 318,
    322
Merriam, Charles, E. 144–5
Merritt, Martha 3 n, 6, 9, 17
Mexico 94, 97, 107–8, 115, 116, 257
  authoritarianism
    and the Supreme Court 266–303
  Constitutional Court 272
  democracy
    and horizontal
      exchange 269–80, 294–7
    and rule of law 269–80
  Federal Electoral Institute 294–5
  homicide rates 277
  horizontal accountability 268
  horizontal exchange
    and democratization 294–7
    and party hegemony 280–94
    and rule of law 269–80
    and the Supreme Court 280–94
  judicial review 272
  National Human Rights
    Commission 300
  National Program of Public
    Safety 298
  political parties
    Partido Acción Nacional
      (PAN) 296–7
    Partido de laRevolución
      Democrática (PRD) 296
    Partido Revolucionario
      Institucional (PRI) 267, 280,
      282–3, 287, 290–1, 293–7,
      299
  political party hegemony
    and flexible constitution 281–5
    and horizontal exchange 280–94
    and the Supreme Court 280–94
  rule of law 268, 297–301
    and democracy 269–80
    dual dimension 279
    and horizontal exchange 269–80
  Supreme Court
    appointment and dismissal of
      judges 282–7
    and authoritatianism 266–303
    constitutional powers 291–4

Mexico (*cont.*):
  new constitutional role
    of 294–7
  and horizontal exchange 280–94
  and party hegemony 280–94
  presidential hegemony
    over 287–91
  and rule of law 297–301
  size of 282
Mexico City
  crime and violence 298–300
ministerial accountability 6, 11
Michael, Laver 83
Miller, Jonathan 153
Moe, Terry 83, 86, 93
Moncrieffe, Joy Maria 6 n, 9, 17
Money, Jeannette 86
Montesimos, Vladimiro 64–5
Montesquieu 41, 207 n
Morandini, Norma 318
Mora y Araujo, Manuel 160
Moreno, Erika 6, 9, 11–18, 20–4, 26,
    34, 48, 52, 58–9, 191
Morgenstern, Scott 24–5, 28, 48 n,
    136, 190 n
Muller, Edward N 256
Muraro, Heriberto 312

Narváez, Machorro 292
Nascimento, Raquel
    Branquinho 211
nested hierarchy
  in parliamentary sytem 85–7
Newton, Kenneth 256
Nicolau, Jairo 194 n
Nicolle, Jorge Carpio
  murder of 249
Niemi, Richard G. 147
Noll, G. 86, 89–90
non-elected agencies
  independence of 99–108
non-electoral accountability 3, 5–6, 8
non-institutional accountability 9
Norris, Pippa 256
North, Douglas 133, 269, 271
Novaro, Marcos 160

Oakerson, Ronald J. 9
O'Donnell, Guillermo 3 n, 6, 9–21,
    24–6, 28–30, 34 n, 36 n,
    42–3, 46, 48–9, 50 n, 55–62,

    64–71, 79, 80, 90, 109, 136,
    152, 191 n, 192 n, 206, 222,
    268
Olea, Carillo 298
Olson, Mancur 83, 269, 275, 278
ombudsman
  and intrastate accountability 13,
    15, 27
Ordaz, Gustavo Diaz 288
O'Shaughnessy, Laura Nuzzi 235,
    237, 241, 245, 254 n
Overacker, Louis 144–5
oversight
  concept and theoretical
    frame 136–40
oversight institututions 4, 7, 12, 22
  and corruption 136
  developing in Argentina 151–66
  developing in the USA 140–51
  role of legislators 137–8

Palermo, Vincente 160
Palma, Silvia Irene 251–2
Palmer, Matthew 83, 93
Panama
  homicide rate 277
Paraguay 58
  homicide rate 277
  presidential impeachment 28
  Supreme Court 106
Pásara, Luis 22, 23 n, 25, 27
Pasquino, Pasquale 44 n
Pastor, R. A. 55 n
Paul, Samuel 9
Pazps, Luis 313, 320 n
Pederzoli, Patrizia 44 n
Pérez, Carloso Andres 56
  impeachment of 58
Peron, Juan 154
Perry Powers, Fred. 146–8
Peru 47 n, 56, 65–6, 72, 74, 94, 96–7,
    103, 107, 113, 115,
    135
  homicide rate 277
  Supreme Court 106
Peruzzotti, Enrique 7–8, 16, 21, 25,
    47, 48 n, 61, 309–10, 314
Pessanha, Charles 185–6
Petrei, Humberto 150
Pinochet Ugarte, Augusto 64, 115,
    279

Plattner, Marc F. 55 n, 61, 309 n
Polecon Index Database
  on effectiveness of veto
    players 273–4
politial accountability 5–18
Polity 98 Democracy Index 274–5
Polsby, Nelson W. 148
Polybius 41
Popkin, Margaret 236–8
Powell, Bingham G. 271 n
Power, Timothy J. 254 n, 257–8
Portugal 272
presidential impeachments 28, 58,
    134, 140, 286, 288, 313
presidential system
  accountability in 82–91
  horizontal exchanges in 88
Preuss, Ulrich 43
principal-agents relationships
  and accountability 14–16, 18–19
Pérez-Liñán, Aníbal 28
Przeworski, Adam 5, 8, 14, 23–4,
    49, 55 n, 70 n, 171 n, 191,
    268–9, 271
Putnam, Robert 255–7
public accountability 9
Pulic Prosecution (Minsterio
    Publico) 201–26

Quadros, Jânio 178, 181, 193

Ramos, Nereu1 78, 181, 193
Ramseyer, J. Mark 89
Rawls, John 43
Reding, Andrew 249
Remmar 271
republicanism 38, 68–74
  vertical accountability and 69
reputational accountability 9
responsibility
  and accountability 57
  and answerability 57
Rey, Germán 312
Rock, David 154
Robespierre
  cruelty of
Rodrigues, Alberto Tosi 177
Roosevelt, Theodore 151
Rosenbluth, Frances McCall 89
Rubio, Luis 266 n, 301
rule of law

and citizens' rights 301–2
in Latin America 228–61
liberty dimension 269–75, 298
public perception of 241–4
security dimension 269, 275–80
Russia 276

Saba, Roberto 314
Sadek, Maria Tereza 21, 25, 27–8,
    49, 101, 107, 175 n, 210–11,
    213, 218, 219 n, 224
Salinas, Carlos 282, 288, 296
Samper Pizano, Ernesto 56, 58
sanctioning rights
  and accountability 80 n
sanctions 9, 11, 12–14, 20
Santos, Fabiano 183 n
Santos, Wanderley G. 194 n
Sarney, José 177–8, 181, 194
Sartori, G. 72
Savonarola
  tyranny of
Schedler, Andreas 6, 11, 13, 17,
    55 n, 62–4, 228, 230, 244,
    309 n, 311, 312 n
Schilling, Flávia 313
Schmidhauser, John 231
Schmitter, Phillippe C. 11, 28, 61, 64
Schumpeter, Joseph 23
Schwartz, Thomas 183, 191, 311 n
Scott, John T. 38
Scully, Timothy 114
security dimension
  of rule of law 269, 275–80
Selano, Movio Antonio 237 n
Seligson, Mitchell A. 256, 258
Shapsle, Kenneth A 11, 14 n, 17,
    83, 92
Shifter, Michael 309 n
Shugart, Soberg Matthew 3 n, 17,
    58–9, 80, 84, 92–3, 112–14,
    171 n, 174 n, 191, 258, 273,
    280
Siavelis, Peter 183 n
Sikkink, Kathryn 311 n
Sklar, Richard L. 61, 230
Smith, Peter 290
Smulovitz, Catalina 7–8, 16, 21, 25,
    47, 48 n, 61, 157, 309, 312–14,
    323 n
Soares, Rosinethe Monteiro 188

societal accountability 7–8, 25,
    47–9
  case studies 315–26
  definition 47, 310
  effectiveness of 312–15
  and horizontal
      accountability 310–15
societal mechanism
  of accountability *see societal
      accountability*
societal oversight *see societal
      accoutability*
societal-vertical accoutability 47–9
"Societal Watchdog" 314–15, 327
Socrates 38
Sorok, Margarita 242
South Africa 64
Spain 154, 272
Spiller, Pablo 89
Stalin, Joseph V.
  secret laws of 50 n
Stanley, Harold W. 147
Stanley, William 235, 245
Starr Kenneth 101
Sterzi, Paula 170 n
Stewart, Charles H. III 150
Stiglitz, Joseph E. 276 n
Stokes, Susan C. 5, 8, 14, 23–4, 49,
    55 n, 70 n, 171 n, 271 n, 309 n
Stone Sweet, Alec 44 n, 89, 95, 253
Strøm, Kaare 12, 14 n, 83, 86, 89, 93
Sunstein, Cass R. 38
superintendence agencies
  and horizontal
      accountability 90–1
  and horizontal exchange 91, 95–9
  and vertical accountability 92,
      95–9

Taft, William Howard 150
Tate, C. Neal 44 n
Telles, Vera da Silva 225
Thompson, John B. 312
Tiscornia Sofía 323 n
Tojeira, S. J. 237, 241
Torre, Juan Carlos 156
transactional vs hierarchal systems
  judiciary in 89–90
Trinidad and Tobago
  homicide rate 277
Tsebelis, George 86, 268

UK 144
United Nations 231, 233
United Nations Special Rapporteur's
    Report 247–8
United States 58, 81, 89, 93, 133–7,
    139–42, 144, 146–8, 271–2,
    301
  Budget and Accounting
      Act 150–1
  civil service reforms 146–51
  Congress 84–5
  Constitution 40, 83
  constitution making 40
  corruption eradication 142–51
  developing oversight
      institutions 140–51
  electoral reforms 142–6
  Freedom of Information Act 141
  Government Accounts Office 141,
      149–51
  homicide rate 277
  Office of Independent Council 101
  Pendelton Act 147–8
  presidential impeachment 28
Uruguay 113, 147, 165
  homicide rate 277
Uribarri, Daniela 317 n, 319 n, 321 n

Valenzuela, Arturo 114
Vallarta, Ignacio 292–3, 295
Valloder, Torbjorn 44 n
Van Riper, Paul P. 140, 147–8
Vanberg, Georg 44 n
Vargas, Getúlio 178, 181, 193
Venezuela 56, 58, 72, 74, 94, 107,
    135, 147, 165
  Constitution 83, 102
  presidential impeachment 28
vertical accountability 18–20, 22, 36,
    56
  definition 12
  and democracy 69
  and electoral reforms 108–17
  and horizontal exchange 91–5
  and liberalism 69
  and republicalism 69
  and superintendence
      agencies 91–5
vertical-horizontal accountability 48
vertical-societal
    accountability 47–9

Verbitsky, Horacio 134, 157, 159, 161, 163
Vianna, Luiz Werneck 190 n, 221 n, 314
Vidal, Armando 158
Vieira, Oscar Vilhena 203 n
Vile, M. J. C. 41

Waisbord, Silvo 312–13
Waldron, Jeremy 44 n
Waley, Daniel 38
Walpole, Robert 132–3
Washington Office on Latin America (WOLA) 246–7
Wattenberg, Martin 114
Weber, Max 231, 270
Weingast, Barry R. 86, 89–90, 92, 269, 271, 275
Weldon, Jeffrey 98, 267, 280

Welna, Chris 3 n, 55 n
Wessels, B. 114
Wheeler, Everett P. 147–8
Whitten, Guy D. 271 n
Williams, S. 56–7
Williamson, Oliver E. 276
Wilson, (Thomas) Woodrow 150–1
WOLA *see on Office on Latin America*
Woodhouse, Diana 6, 11–12

Zakaria, Fareed 71, 309 n
Zedillo, Ernesto 267, 285, 294, 296, 298
Zemans, Frances 313
Zinser, Adolfo Aguilar 116
Zoido-Lobaton, Pablo 142
Zuckert, Michael 38